“*Collected American Classics*
Volume 1

Level 1 & 2

Pearson Education Limited
Edinburgh Gate, Harlow,
Essex CM20 2JE, England
and Associated Companies throughout the world.

ISBN 0 582 454387

This collection of classics first published 2001

The Adventures of Tom Sawyer
Copyright © Penguin Books 2000

The Gift of the Magi and Other Stories
Text copyright © Penguin Books 2000
Illustrations copyright © George Sharp (Virgil Pomfret) 2000

The House of the Seven Gables
Text copyright © Penguin Books 2000
Illustrations copyright © Victor Ambrus 2000

Rip Van Winkle and The Legend of Sleepy Hollow
Text copyright © Penguin Books 2000
Illustrations copyright © Ron Tiner 2000

Call of the Wild
Copyright © Penguin Books 2000

The Last of the Mohicans
Text copyright © Penguin Books 2000
Illustrations copyright © David Cuzik (Pennant) 2000

White Fang
Text copyright © Penguin Books 2000
Illustrations copyright © Rob Hefferan (advocate) 2000

Typeset by Pantek Arts Ltd, Maidstone, Kent
Set in 11/14pt Bembo
Printed and bound in Denmark by Norhaven A/S, Viborg

*All rights reserved; no part of this publication may be reproduced, stored
in a retrieval system, or transmitted in any form or by any means,
electronic, mechanical, photocopying, recording or otherwise, without the
prior written permission of the Publishers.*

Published by Pearson Education Limited in association with
Penguin Books Ltd, both companies being subsidiaries of Pearson Plc

Contents

	page
The Adventures of Tom Sawyer	1
The House of the Seven Gables	33
Rip Van Winkle and the Legend of Sleepy Hollow	65
The Gift of the Magi and Other Stories	97
The Call of the Wild	129
The Last of the Mohicans	177
White Fang	225

The Adventures of Tom Sawyer

MARK TWAIN

Level 1

Retold by Jacqueline Kehl
Series Editors: Andy Hopkins and Jocelyn Potter

Introduction

One Saturday afternoon Tom wanted to have an adventure because he didn't want to think about Injun Joe. He went to Huck and said, "I'm going to look for treasure. Do you want to come with me?"

Tom Sawyer loves adventures. He has a lot of adventures at home, at school, and with his friends. He has one adventure in a cave. But why is he there? What does he see in the cave? And why is he afraid?

Mark Twain (1835–1910) is a famous American writer. His name was Samuel Clemens. Young Samuel lived in Hannibal, Missouri, a small town on the Mississippi River. He loved the river and he liked watching the big boats on it.

Samuel loved adventures. He worked on boats on the Mississippi River for two years. Then he went to Nevada. He looked for treasure, but he didn't find it. He worked for a newspaper there. His stories were in the name of Mark Twain, and people loved them.

Later, Samuel lived in New York. His book *The Adventures of Tom Sawyer* (1876) is about a young boy in a small town in the 1800s. Huck Finn is his friend. *The Adventures of Huckleberry Finn* (1884) is about Huck's adventures. These two books are very famous.

Today, many people visit Hannibal because they want to see Mark Twain's home and the Mark Twain Cave, the cave in *The Adventures of Tom Sawyer*.

Chapter 1 The Fence

Tom Sawyer lived with his aunt because his mother and father were dead. Tom didn't like going to school, and he didn't like working. He liked playing and having adventures. One Friday, he didn't go to school—he went to the river.

Aunt Polly was angry. "You're a bad boy!" she said. "Tomorrow you can't play with your friends because you didn't go to school today. Tomorrow you're going to work for me. You can paint the fence."

Saturday morning, Tom was not happy, but he started to paint the fence. His friend Jim was in the street.

Tom asked him, "Do you want to paint?"

Jim said, "No, I can't. I'm going to get water."

Then Ben came to Tom's house. He watched Tom and said, "I'm going to swim today. You can't swim because you're working."

Tom said, "This isn't work. I like painting."

"Can I paint, too?" Ben asked.

"No, you can't," Tom answered. "Aunt Polly asked me because I'm a very good painter."

Ben said, "I'm a good painter, too. Please, can I paint? I have some fruit. Do you want it?"

"OK," Tom said. "Give me the fruit. Then you can paint."

Ben started to paint the fence. Later, many boys came to Tom's house. They watched Ben, and they wanted to paint, too.

Tom said, "Give me some food and you can paint."

Tom stayed in the yard, and the boys painted.

Tom stayed in the yard, and the boys painted. They painted the fence three times. It was beautiful and white.

Tom went into the house. "Aunt Polly, can I play now?" he asked.

Aunt Polly was surprised. "Did you paint the fence?" she asked.

"Yes, I did," Tom answered.

Aunt Polly went to the yard and looked at the fence. She was very surprised and very happy. "It's beautiful!" she said. "Yes, you can play now."

Tom walked to his friend Joe Harper's house and played with his friends there. Then he walked home again. There was a new girl in one yard. She had yellow hair and blue eyes. She was beautiful. Tom wanted to talk to her, but she didn't see him. She went into her house. Tom waited, but she didn't come out again.

Chapter 2 In the Graveyard

One morning before school, Tom's friend Huck Finn waited for him in the street. Huck didn't have a home, and he never went to school. People in the town didn't like him. But Tom liked Huck.

Huck said, "Let's have an adventure."

"What can we do on our adventure?" Tom asked.

"Let's go to the graveyard at night—at twelve o'clock!" Huck answered.

"That's a good adventure," Tom said. "Let's meet at eleven o'clock."

Then Tom went to school, but he was late. The teacher was angry. He asked, "Why are you late again?"

"I'm late because I talked to Huck Finn," Tom said.

Then the teacher was very angry. "Sit with the girls," he said to Tom.

Tom sat near the beautiful new girl. He was happy. He looked at her.

"What's your name?" he asked.

"Becky," she answered.

Tom smiled and said, "My name's Tom."

The teacher was angry again. "Tom Sawyer, stop talking! Go to your place now," he said. Tom went to his place.

At twelve o'clock Tom and Becky didn't go home. They stayed in the school yard and talked. Tom said, "I love you. Do you love me?"

"Yes," Becky answered.

"Good," Tom said. "Then you're going to walk to school with me every day. Amy always walked with me."

"Amy!" Becky said angrily. "Do you love her?"

"No," Tom answered. "I love you now. Do you want to walk with me?"

But Becky was angry with Tom. She walked away and didn't answer. Tom was unhappy. He didn't go to school in the afternoon.

That night Tom went to bed at nine o'clock, but he didn't sleep. At eleven o'clock he went out his bedroom window to the yard. Huck was there. They walked to the graveyard. They stopped behind some big trees and talked quietly.

Suddenly, there was a noise. Three men came into the graveyard—the doctor, Muff Potter, and Injun Joe. Injun Joe and the doctor talked angrily. Then Injun Joe

Then Injun Joe killed the doctor with a knife.

killed the doctor with a knife. Tom and Huck watched. Then they went away quickly because they were afraid.

They went to Tom's yard. Huck said, "We can't talk about this. Injun Joe can find us and kill us, too."

"That's right," Tom said. "We can't talk about it."

Tom went in his bedroom window. He went to bed, but he didn't sleep well. Tom and Huck didn't talk to their friends or Aunt Polly about that night because they were afraid of Injun Joe.

Later, some men went to Muff Potter and said, "You're a bad man. You killed the doctor."

Chapter 3   A Bad Day

Becky was sick and didn't go to school for many days. Tom was very sad. One morning, he said to Aunt Polly, "I'm very sick, and I want to stay home from school."

Aunt Polly said, "Here's some medicine. Take this and you can get well quickly."

But Tom didn't like the medicine. Peter, the cat, came into the room and looked at Tom.

"Peter!" Tom said. "Have some medicine!"

Peter had some medicine. He didn't like it! He went quickly out the open window and into the yard.

Aunt Polly watched Peter. "Why did you do that, Tom?" she asked angrily. "You're a very bad boy! Go to school now."

Tom arrived at school early and he waited for Becky at the school fence. She arrived early, too, but she didn't

Peter had some medicine. He didn't like it!

look at Tom. She went into school. Tom walked away. He didn't want to go to school now. He was very sad.

Joe Harper was near the school. He was sad, too, because his mother was angry with him. The two boys walked and talked.

Tom said, "Let's run away."

"Yes, let's!" Joe said.

The two boys went to the river. Huck Finn was there. Tom and Joe said, "We're going to run away. Do you want to come with us?"

"Yes," Huck answered. "Let's go across the river. We can have a good adventure there."

The boys went home because they wanted to get food for their adventure.

Chapter 4 Across the River

Tom, Joe, and Huck went to the river. There was a small boat there. The boys went across the river in the small boat. They said, "This is a good place because we can play all day. There's no school here."

They played and then went to sleep.

In the morning, the boys were happy again. They said, "Let's stay here for a long time."

In the afternoon, they played near the river again. Suddenly, there was a noise from a big boat on the river. The boys stopped playing and watched the boat.

"Listen," Tom said. "The men on the boat are talking about us."

The boys stopped playing and watched the boat.

The boys listened quietly. A man said, "The boys are in the river. They're dead."

Tom said, "Those men are looking for us in the river. We're here, but they don't know that."

That night, the boys were sad. Huck and Joe went to sleep, but Tom didn't sleep. He went home in the small boat. He quietly went in his bedroom window. Then he went under his bed and stayed there.

Aunt Polly and her friends came into his room. Aunt Polly said to her friends, "Tom was a good boy, and I loved him. Now he's dead, and I'm very sad."

Tom wanted to say, "I'm not dead." But he stayed quiet.

Aunt Polly went to sleep. Tom went out the window very quietly and went back across the river.

In the morning, Joe and Huck said, "We're not happy here now. We want to go home."

Tom said, "Let's go home on Sunday. We can go to church. People are going to be very surprised!"

Sunday morning, many children were at church. They talked about the three boys. They were sad because their friends were dead. Becky was sad, too.

Suddenly, the three boys walked into the church. People were very surprised, but they were very happy, too.

Chapter 5   At School

Monday morning, Tom went to school. The children wanted to hear about his adventure, and Tom liked talking about it. Becky wanted to talk to Tom, but he didn't look at her.

Then Tom talked to Amy. Becky watched him and she was angry. She said to her friends, "I'm going to have an adventure day. You can come on my adventure." But she didn't ask Tom.

Later in the morning, Tom talked to Amy again. Becky talked to her friend Alfred and looked at a picture-book with him. Tom watched them and he was angry with Becky.

In the afternoon, Tom waited for Becky at the school fence. He said, "I'm sorry."

But Becky didn't listen to him. She walked into the school room. The teacher's new book was on his table. This book wasn't for children, but Becky wanted to look at it. She opened the book quietly and looked at the pictures.

Suddenly, Tom came into the room. Becky was surprised. She closed the book quickly, and it tore. Becky was angry with Tom and quickly went out of the room.

Then the children and the teacher came into the room and went to their places. The teacher looked at his book.

"Who did this? Who tore my book?" he asked angrily.

The room was very quiet. The teacher started to ask every child, "Did you do this?"

They answered, "No, I didn't."

Then he looked at Becky. "Becky, did you do this?"

"I did it. I tore your book."

Tom wanted to help her. Suddenly he said, "I did it. I tore your book."

"Tom Sawyer, you're a very bad boy. Stay here after school!" the teacher said angrily.

At five o'clock Tom started to walk home. Becky waited for him at the school fence. "You're a very good friend," she said.

Tom smiled at her and they walked home.

Chapter 6   The Trial

Summer vacation started, and Becky went away with her family. Tom was unhappy.

Then Muff Potter's trial started. Tom and Huck remembered the night in the graveyard. They were afraid of Injun Joe again.

"Did you talk about the night in the graveyard?" Tom asked Huck.

"No, I didn't," Huck answered. "Did you?"

"No," Tom answered. "But I'm sorry about Muff Potter. He's always friendly to us. He didn't kill the doctor. I want to help him."

"Let's take some food to him," Huck said.

The boys visited Muff Potter. "Here's some food," they said.

Muff Potter said, "Thank you. You're good boys."

Tom and Huck went to the trial and listened for two days. Tom didn't sleep well at night because he wanted to help Muff Potter.

On day three of the trial Tom talked.

A man asked him, "Where were you on the night of June 17th?"

"I was in the graveyard," Tom answered.

"Did you see any people there?" the man asked.

"Yes. Injun Joe, the doctor, and Muff Potter were there. They didn't see me because I was behind some big trees."

"What did you see?" the man asked.

"Injun Joe and the doctor talked angrily," Tom answered. "Then Injun Joe killed the doctor with his knife. Muff Potter didn't do it."

The people at the trial were surprised. Injun Joe quickly went out of the building.

Tom and Huck were very afraid. Tom said, "Now Injun Joe knows about us. He can kill *us*, too."

Many people wanted to hear about the boys' adventure in the graveyard. Tom liked talking about it. He was happy, too, because he helped Muff Potter. But he didn't sleep well because he was afraid of Injun Joe.

Chapter 7   Injun Joe's Treasure

One Saturday afternoon, Tom wanted to have an adventure because he didn't want to think about Injun Joe. He went to Huck and said, "I'm going to look for treasure. Do you want to come with me?"

Huck always liked an adventure. "Oh, yes," he said. "Where can we look?"

"Let's start looking in the old house near Mrs. Douglas's house. Old houses are good places for treasure," Tom answered.

The boys went to the old house. They wanted to look at every room. First they went into the kitchen, and then they went into the bedroom.

Suddenly, two men came into the kitchen—Injun Joe and his friend. The boys were afraid and stayed in the bedroom very quietly.

Injun Joe walked across the kitchen. "We can put our money here," he said to his friend.

He started to dig under the floor with his knife.

"What's this?" Injun Joe said. "I'm going to get it out."

There was a big box under the floor. He opened it with his knife. There was a lot of money in the box.

"Look at that money!" his friend said. "Let's go now. We can come back and get it tomorrow."

"No," Injun Joe said. "We're going to take it with us now. We can take it to that place. You know—the place under the cross."

Then the men went out of the house. Injun Joe talked quietly to his friend. The boys listened and were afraid.

Tom said, "Did you hear that? He wants to kill us."

They went out of the house quietly and went home.

The boys were afraid of Injun Joe, but they wanted to find his treasure. They watched his house every night, but they didn't see Injun Joe or his treasure.

There was a lot of money in the box.

Chapter 8 Becky's Adventure Day

In August Becky's family came back from their vacation. Tom was very happy and he didn't think about Injun Joe's treasure.

Becky's adventure day was Saturday. Her mother said, "You can sleep at Susy Harper's house after your adventure."

"Good," Becky said.

Becky and her friends went on the river on a big boat. The boat went down the river and across it. Then it stopped. The children went out of the boat and played games near the river. In the afternoon one boy asked, "Who wants to go to the big cave?"

The children went to the cave. It was dark and cold there, but they played games. In the evening they went back to the boat and went home.

Sunday morning, Becky's mother and Aunt Polly talked to Mrs. Harper at church. Becky's mother asked, "Where's my Becky? Did she sleep at your house?"

"No, she didn't," Mrs. Harper answered. "I didn't see her."

Aunt Polly said, "My Tom didn't come home. Did he stay at your house?"

"No, he didn't," Mrs. Harper answered.

Then Aunt Polly and Becky's mother asked the children, "Did Tom and Becky come home? Did you see them on the boat?"

The children answered, "No, we didn't see them, but it was dark."

Then a boy said, "Maybe they're in the cave!"

Two hundred men looked for Tom and Becky in the cave. They looked for three days, but they didn't find them. People in the town were very sad.

Chapter 9 Huck's Adventure

Huck didn't go on Becky's adventure. He stayed home and watched Injun Joe's house that night. At eleven o'clock Injun Joe and his friend came out and walked down the street. There was a box in his friend's hands.

Huck said quietly, "Maybe that's the treasure box." He went after the two men.

They walked to Mrs. Douglas's house and stopped in her yard. Huck stayed behind some small trees. The men talked, and Huck listened to them.

Injun Joe was angry. "I want to kill her," he said to his friend. "Mr. Douglas was bad to me. He's dead now, but I remember."

"There are a lot of lights in the house. Maybe her friends are visiting," Injun Joe's friend said. "We can come back tomorrow."

"No," Injun Joe said. "Let's wait now."

Huck liked Mrs. Douglas because she was always good to him. He wanted to help her. He quietly walked away and then he started to run to Mr. Jones's house.

Mr. Jones opened the door. "What do you want?" he asked Huck.

"Injun Joe and his friend are in Mrs. Douglas's yard," Huck said. "They want to kill her. Can you go there and help Mrs. Douglas?"

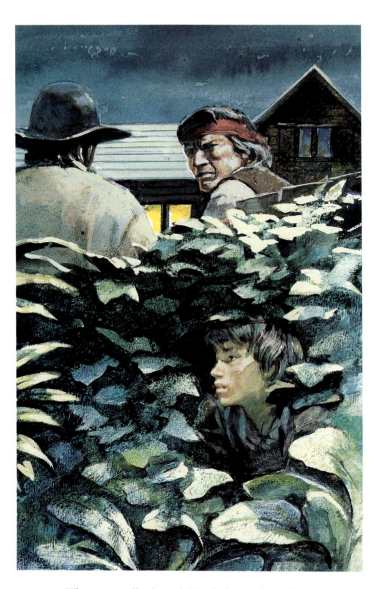

The men talked, and Huck listened to them.

"Yes. My sons and I can go there," Mr. Jones answered. "You can go home."

In the morning, Huck went back to Mr. Jones's house.

"How's Mrs. Douglas?" he asked.

"She's OK," Mr. Jones answered. "The men went away because we arrived."

"Good," Huck said. But he was afraid of Injun Joe. "Please don't say my name to Mrs. Douglas."

Mr. Jones looked at him, and then he said, "You aren't well. Go and sleep in my bedroom."

Later, Mrs. Douglas visited Mr. Jones.

"You helped me yesterday night. Thank you," she said. "You're a good man."

Mr. Jones said, "We didn't know about the men in your yard. A boy was there and he wanted to help you. He came here, but I can't say his name."

Mr. Jones and Mrs. Douglas went to church. People there talked about Tom and Becky. Mr. Jones and his sons went to the cave with the men, but on Monday morning they went home. Huck was in bed and was very sick. The men went back to the cave, but Mrs. Douglas stayed with Huck.

Chapter 10   In the Cave

Saturday, Tom and Becky walked and played in the cave. Then they stopped near some water.

"What time is it?" Becky asked.

"I don't know," Tom said. "Let's go back now."

The two children walked and walked. But they didn't find the door to the cave. Becky was afraid. She wanted to sit down and eat. "Maybe they're looking for us now," she said.

"Here's some food," Tom said. "Eat this and wait here. I'm going to look for the door."

Tom walked and walked. But he didn't find the cave door. Suddenly, there was a man near him. Tom was afraid, but he stayed quiet. He looked at the man. It was Injun Joe!

Tom was very afraid and he made a noise. Injun Joe went away quickly. Tom went back to Becky, but he didn't talk to her about Injun Joe.

They were in the cave for three days. Tuesday, Becky didn't want to walk. Again Tom said, "Stay here. I'm going to look for the door."

This time he went to a new place. There was light there. He went to the light. It came from a small door in the cave.

Tom went out of the cave. Then he went back to Becky. "Come with me," he said. "We can go out of the cave now."

Tom and Becky went out of the cave. They were very happy. They went to the river and waited there. Some men in a small boat came to them.

Tom said, "We want to go home. Can you help us?"

The men answered, "Yes. We can take you home."

Tom and Becky went in the boat with the men. They arrived home very late Tuesday night, and people in the town were very happy. Tom talked all night about their adventure in the cave.

Tom went out of the cave.

Chapter 11 In the Cave Again

Tom and Becky stayed home for many days. Then, two weeks after their adventure, Tom visited Becky and talked to her father.

Mr. Thatcher said, "You're a very good boy, Tom. You helped Becky in the cave. Thank you. People can't go into it now because it has a new big door."

"But Injun Joe's living in the cave!" Tom said.

Some men went down the river to the cave. Tom went with them. They opened the new door. Injun Joe was there, but he was dead.

Tom wanted to talk to Huck. Later in the week he went to Mr. Jones's house. The two boys talked about their adventures.

"The money isn't in Injun Joe's house," Tom said. "It's in the cave! I know, because Injun Joe was there. Let's get it!"

Huck was afraid. "But maybe we can't find it."

"I can find it again," Tom said. "I know about a small door at the back of the cave. Becky and I came out there. We can go in that door, and I can find Injun Joe's treasure."

"OK," Huck said. "Let's go today."

That afternoon the boys went in a small boat to the back of the cave. Tom walked first, and Huck went after him. They walked and walked.

Then Tom said, "This is the right place! Injun Joe was here."

The boys looked for a good place for treasure.

Suddenly, Tom said, "Look! There's a cross! Injun Joe said, 'under the cross.' Let's look there!"

"Look! It's the treasure box!"

The boys went to the place with the cross. Tom said, "I'm going to dig here with my knife ... Look! It's the treasure box! Let's get it out now. The treasure's ours!"

"This box is very heavy," Huck said. "We can't take it with us."

"I have some small bags," Tom said. "We can put the money in them and take it home."

The boys went out of the cave with the money.

Chapter 12   At Mrs. Douglas's House

Tom said, "Let's take the money to the old house near Mrs. Douglas's house. That's a good place for it."

They started to walk to the old house. Mr. Jones was in Mrs. Douglas's yard. He called to the boys.

"A lot of people are waiting for you. Come with me," he said. They went into Mrs. Douglas's house.

"Hello, boys," Mrs. Douglas said. "Come with me."

Tom and Huck went with her to a bedroom. There were new shirts and jeans on the bed.

"Wash your hands and faces and put on these shirts and jeans," Mrs. Douglas said. "Then come to the big room."

The boys went to the room. A lot of people were there.

Mrs. Douglas said, "First I want to say 'thank you' to Mr. Jones and his sons. They helped me. They're very good people."

"Huck helped, too," Mr. Jones said.

"Thank you, too, Huck," Mrs. Douglas said. "You're a good boy, and I like you. I want to give you a home and some money."

"But Huck has a lot of money!" Tom said.

He went to the bedroom and came back with the bags of money. "We have this money from the cave. There's a lot of money in them, and it's ours now."

There was $12,000 in the bags. The people were very surprised. They asked about the boys' adventure.

Chapter 13 Huck's New Home

Huck lived in the big house with Mrs. Douglas. He was a new person. He washed every day, and he went to school and church. But he wasn't happy. He stayed there for three weeks, and then he ran away.

Tom went to Huck. "Why did you run away?"

Huck answered, "Mrs. Douglas is a good woman. I like her, but I can't live with her. I don't like washing every day, and I don't like going to school and church. I don't want to have a lot of money. But I want to be your friend. OK?"

"No," Tom said, "I can't be your friend, because the boys at school don't want to play with you. We're thinking about a lot of new adventures. Please live with Mrs. Douglas and come to school. Then the boys at school can play with you."

"I want to be your friend," Huck said, "and I want to have adventures with you and the boys at school. Maybe I can live with Mrs. Douglas. I don't know, but I'm going to try it again for a month."

"Good," Tom said. "The boys are meeting later, at twelve o'clock at night. You can come, too."

"Good!" Huck said.

ACTIVITIES

Chapters 1–6

Before you read

1 Find the words in *italics* in your dictionary. They are all in the story.

   a Answer the questions.

   What *adventures* are on TV? What *adventures* do you have?

   What are you *afraid* of?

   Do you like *cats*?

   What makes you *sad*?

   When are you *surprised*?

   b Put a word on the left with a word on the right.

   aunt .... dead
   church .... family
   fence   sick
   graveyard   police
   medicine   picture
   paint   yard
   trial   Sunday

   c Put these words in the sentences.

   help   kill   tore (to tear)

   The man is going to ..... the animal with his knife.

   She's unhappy because she ..... her new dress.

   He likes to ..... his mother with her work.

After you read

2 Why

   a is Aunt Polly angry with Tom?

   b do Tom and Joe want to run away?

   c doesn't Becky talk to Tom?

d do Tom and Huck want to help Muff Potter?
   e are Tom and Huck afraid of Injun Joe?

Chapters 7–13

Before you read
3 Are Tom and Huck going to see Injun Joe again?
4 Find the words in *italics* in your dictionary. Answer the questions.
   a What can you buy in a *box*?
   b Is it light or dark in a *cave*?
   c The teacher put a *cross* on your answer. Is the answer right or wrong?
   d What can you *dig* with? A ticket, a book or a knife?
   e What are your *treasures*?

After you read
5 Answer the questions.
   a How many nights are Tom and Becky in the cave?
   b Why is there a new big door on the cave?
   c How is Huck a new person?
6 Where are they?
   a Injun Joe finds the treasure box.
   b Aunt Polly and Becky's mother talk to the children.
   c Tom and Huck find the treasure box.
   d There is a surprise for Huck.

Writing
7 Is Tom a good boy or a bad boy? Why? Write about it.
8 You are Tom or Huck. What are you going to do with your money from the treasure box? Write about it.

The House of the Seven Gables

NATHANIEL HAWTHORNE

Level 1

Retold by Michael Mendenhall
Series Editors: Andy Hopkins and Jocelyn Potter

Introduction

She was at the door of the House of the Seven Gables, but she was not afraid.

Phoebe Pyncheon arrives at her cousin's big old house. Hepzibah is opening a small store, and Phoebe wants to work for her. Then Hepzibah's sick brother arrives. But where did he come from? And why does Judge Pyncheon want to see him?

In this story Nathaniel Hawthorne (1804–64) writes about a New England family. For many years the family is unhappy. Are they unhappy because a dead man cursed them? Hawthorne answers this question, but he gives us a love story too.

Hawthorne loved New England and America, his young country. But this story is not about America. It is about happy times and unhappy times, good people and bad people.

It was a dark old house.

Chapter 1 The Store

Miss Hepzibah Pyncheon lived in the House of the Seven Gables, on Pyncheon Street. It was a dark old house. There was a small room in the front gable and today, for the first time in many years, that room was a store again.

Hepzibah did not want to work in the store. It was very difficult for her. The people in the town did not like her. She was old, and her face was not beautiful. But she needed money. She needed food!

She went into the store and her first customer arrived. It was young Mr. Holgrave! He lived in one of the seven gables. He took pictures, usually of people's faces. Hepzibah started to cry.

"Ah, Mr. Holgrave, I cannot do this. I'm old, and only a woman. My father and mother and sister are dead. I want to go too."

"Oh no!" the young man answered. "This is a good day for the Pyncheons. I can say that because we're friends."

Holgrave wanted some biscuits, but Hepzibah did not take any money from her only friend. Holgrave went away with his biscuits, and Hepzibah started to cry again.

"People here are cold," she thought. "They aren't going to buy from me."

Then the door opened again. It was only a little schoolboy. He asked for a biscuit from the window. Hepzibah did not take any money from her customer.

But then he came back and asked again for a biscuit! This time Hepzibah took his money. She needed it. But that morning Hepzibah did not make a lot of money.

In the afternoon, a man stopped in Pyncheon Street. He looked at the old house, and at the store window. He smiled at Hepzibah. It was her cousin, Judge Pyncheon!

Hepzibah did not love her cousin. He had a cold face, and she did not like his smile. She was afraid of him.

She went into a room at the back of the house and looked at an old picture of Colonel Pyncheon. He had the same cold face! Why did he build the House of the Seven Gables? He took the land for the house from Matthew Maule, the wizard. Then Maule cursed the Colonel and his family. The Colonel finished his house, but he was dead in his chair the same day! Was it the wizard's curse?

There was a customer in the store again. It was an old man with white hair. Mr. Venner did little jobs for people. He was slow, but he was smart about many things.

"You're working, Hepzibah! This is good," Mr. Venner said. "Smile for the customers. It's important!"

But she was an unhappy person, in an unhappy house.

Then Mr. Venner asked her, "When is he coming home?"

"*Who* is coming home?" Hepzibah said, with a white face.

"Ah, you don't want to talk about it. Then, goodbye."

That afternoon Hepzibah had many customers, but she did not make a lot of money. The schoolboy came again and asked for biscuits.

"Take them," she said. Then she closed the store.

Why did he build the House of the Seven Gables?

At the same time, a bus stopped on Pyncheon Street. A young girl said goodbye to the driver and went to the front door of the house. Hepzibah watched her.

"Who is it?" she thought. The girl was young and happy. She was at the door of the House of the Seven Gables, but she was not afraid.

Hepzibah opened the door. It was her little cousin Phoebe, from the country!

"Cousin Phoebe! Come in! What are you doing here?"

"Oh, you didn't get my letter!" Phoebe said. "I want to visit you for a week or two."

"Let's talk about it," Hepzibah said. "This house is cold and dark. You're young. It's not the right place for you."

"Cousin Hepzibah, maybe you're right. But I want to work and do things for you," Phoebe said.

"Yes, you're a good girl," Hepzibah answered. "I'm going to ask the man of the house about this."

"Who is that?" Phoebe asked.

"Did you never hear of Clifford Pyncheon?" Hepzibah asked. "He's my brother!"

"I know the name," Phoebe answered. "But he's dead!"

"Maybe he was," Hepzibah said. "But in this old house dead people can come back again!"

Chapter 2 Phoebe at Home

The morning light came into Phoebe's bedroom. She went to the window and looked down at the garden.

"Those white flowers are very beautiful," she thought. She went down to the garden, and she took some flowers back to her room. "Now this bedroom is mine," she thought.

She opened her door and started to go down again. Hepzibah called to her.

"Phoebe! Come into my room! Look at this."

Phoebe went in and Hepzibah opened her hand. Phoebe looked at a very small picture of a beautiful young man.

"He has a child's face!" Phoebe said.

The old woman started to cry.

"Don't cry, Cousin," Phoebe said. "Come, let's go to the kitchen."

In the kitchen, Hepzibah was quiet. Phoebe worked well.

"I can hear a customer in the store," Hepzibah said.

"Can I go, Cousin, please?" Phoebe asked.

"You, child!" Hepzibah said. "What can a country girl know about work in a store?"

But Hepzibah did not stop Phoebe. She watched her at work with a difficult customer. Phoebe finished and smiled.

"You can stay," Hepzibah said. "You're good in the house and good in the store too!"

"Oh, thank you, Cousin Hepzibah!" Phoebe said.

Phoebe worked all day in the store. Customers came and went. Then they closed the store for the night.

Phoebe said, "Cousin, we need biscuits again, and people are asking for fruit. But look at our money!"

"You did well, Phoebe," Hepzibah said. "You're a good worker. The Pyncheons aren't good workers, because we have this house and land. But is it our land, or not?

"He has a child's face!" Phoebe said.

Colonel Pyncheon had the answer, but he's dead! Come with me, and you can see the Colonel's picture."

Phoebe went with her cousin. In the back room there was a picture of the Colonel, but she did not like his cold face.

Hepzibah talked about their family. One story was about beautiful Alice Pyncheon. Alice loved flowers, and people called the white flowers in the garden "Alice's Flowers." But Alice was sick, and in a short time she was dead. Was it the wizard's curse?

Then Hepzibah talked about Holgrave. "I like him," she said. "But sometimes I'm afraid of him."

"Afraid!" Phoebe said. "Then send him away."

"I can't," Hepzibah answered. "He's my only friend."

Phoebe wanted to go into the garden. She liked it because she was from the country. She looked at the beautiful flowers and trees.

"Who works in this garden?" Phoebe thought. "It isn't old Hepzibah," she said.

"It's me," a man behind her said.

Phoebe looked at the young man. "You?" Phoebe said.

"Yes. My name's Holgrave. I live in one of the seven gables, and I sometimes work in the garden. In my rooms in town I take pictures of people. I like taking pictures of their faces. Some faces are cold, but your face is a flower from this garden. Are you from the Pyncheon family?"

"My name is Phoebe Pyncheon," the girl said.

"What do you think of this picture?" Holgrave asked.

"I know that cold face," she answered.

Phoebe took a picture from his hand and looked at it. "I know that cold face," she answered. "It's Colonel Pyncheon in a new coat, and with no hat."

Holgrave smiled. "Look again," he said. "It's not Colonel Pyncheon. But you're going to meet this man one day."

"He has the same cold face," Phoebe said. "My cousin has a small picture of a beautiful young man. I like *his* face."

"Yes, Miss Hepzibah often talks about that picture," the young man said. "I want to see it too. Did you see his unhappy eyes?"

"Unhappy?" Phoebe said. "He has the face of a child."

"Maybe," Holgrave said. "Maybe a bad child."

"How can you say that?" Phoebe said. "You don't know the picture!"

She started to go. "Wait!" Holgrave said. "There's a lot of work here, in the garden. Let's do it—you and I."

Phoebe worked with Holgrave. They stayed in the garden for a short time. Then it was dark.

"Good night, Miss Phoebe Pyncheon," Holgrave said. "One day, put a flower in your hair and come to my rooms in town. I want to take your picture."

Holgrave went into the house. Phoebe went in too.

"Good night, Cousin," she said to Hepzibah.

"Good night, my child." Hepzibah kissed her.

"My cousin loves me very much," Phoebe thought. She went to bed, but that night she did not sleep well.

Chapter 3 Phoebe's Family

In the morning, Phoebe went down to the kitchen. Hepzibah smiled at her.

Phoebe started to make some coffee and hot food. She worked quickly, and in a short time it was on the table. There were flowers on the table, and three chairs.

"Why does she want three chairs?" Phoebe thought.

Then Hepzibah started to cry.

"Cousin, what's wrong?" Phoebe asked.

Hepzibah took her hand. "Oh Phoebe, he's coming! Stand in front of the door. I'm old, but you're young and happy. Smile for him, Phoebe, smile. Sh–sh–sh! I can hear him. He's coming!"

There was a noise behind the door. Hepzibah opened it, and there was an old man with long hair. Phoebe looked at him. Was this the man in Hepzibah's picture? Was this the man with the face of a child?

"Clifford, this is our Cousin Phoebe," Hepzibah said slowly. "Little Phoebe Pyncheon—Arthur's only child, you know! She's visiting us from the country."

"Phoebe? Phoebe Pyncheon?" Clifford said. "I can't remember."

"Come, brother, sit in this chair," Hepzibah said. "Let's eat!"

Phoebe watched him. He moved very slowly and did not talk. But he liked his food! He smiled at Phoebe. "Yes," Phoebe thought. "It *is* the same man—Hepzibah's brother. But where did he come from?"

"Would you like some coffee?" Hepzibah asked him.

Clifford looked at Hepzibah's face. It was not beautiful.

Was this the man in Hepzibah's picture?

"Are you angry with me, Hepzibah?" he asked.

"Angry!" Hepzibah said. "Clifford, there's only love here. You're at home!"

Clifford smiled, but suddenly the light went from his eyes. Phoebe thought quickly.

"Cousin, here's a flower from your garden," she said.

"Ah, thank you!" Clifford said. "Ah, I remember this flower. Now I'm young again. But what's that noise?"

"Phoebe, please go and see our customer," Hepzibah said. "Clifford, we don't have much money. I opened a little store in the front gable. We need money for food."

"'We don't have much money,'" he said quietly, with a little smile. Then he closed his eyes and went to sleep.

Phoebe went into the store. It was the schoolboy again. This time he wanted one or two things for his mother. The boy went away with his bag. Then the door opened again. A fat man in an expensive black coat came in.

"This is an important man," Phoebe thought.

"Excuse me. I'm looking for Miss Hepzibah Pyncheon," he said. He smiled at Phoebe. "Do you work here?"

"Of course," Phoebe said. "But I'm Miss Hepzibah's cousin. I'm visiting her."

"Her cousin? And from the country? Are you Phoebe Pyncheon, the only child of my cousin Arthur? Do you know me, my child? I'm Judge Pyncheon, your cousin!"

He wanted to kiss Phoebe. He came near, but she moved back. "I don't want to kiss him," she thought. "But why?"

She looked up at his dark face. Suddenly she

"I don't want to kiss him," she thought.

remembered Holgrave's picture. This was the same man—the man with Colonel Pyncheon's face!

"What's wrong?" the Judge asked. "Are you afraid of me?"

"Oh no, Cousin!" Phoebe answered. "But you want to talk to Cousin Hepzibah. I can get her for you."

"No, wait!" the Judge said. "What's wrong? Is there a visitor in this house? Are you afraid of him?"

"Oh no!" Phoebe said. "There are no bad men in our house. There is only Cousin Hepzibah's brother. He isn't very well, but I'm not afraid of him."

"Not afraid?" the Judge said. "Then you don't know his story. He did a very bad thing. But we were friends. Is he here? I'm going to see."

"Wait, Cousin," Phoebe said. "Clifford's sleeping, I think. Let's ask Cousin Hepzibah first."

"No, no, Miss Phoebe!" the Judge said. He was angry. "I know the house well, and Hepzibah, and her brother Clifford. I want to talk to him—it's important. Remember, Phoebe, I'm at home here and you are the visitor. Ah! Here is Hepzibah!"

Hepzibah stopped at the door. She looked at the Judge. Her eyes were very small and cold.

"Hepzibah!" the Judge said, and smiled. "I'm very happy for you, and for us. Clifford is home! Can I see him now?"

"No," Hepzibah answered. "He cannot see visitors!"

"A visitor, Cousin? Do you call me a visitor? Please, come to my house in the country. Clifford can be happy there. Don't think about it—come!"

"Clifford has a home here!" Hepzibah said.

The Judge was angry. "Woman," he said, "why do you want to stay here? Do you have money? No! But why am I talking to you? You're only a woman! I want to see Clifford. Now move!"

Then a cry came from behind the door. "Hepzibah, Hepzibah, go down on the floor! Kiss his feet! I don't want to see him! Please!"

The Judge moved to the door. His face was angry. "Is he going to hit Hepzibah?" Phoebe thought.

Suddenly he stopped, and he smiled.

"Of course," Judge Pyncheon said, "Clifford isn't well. Maybe we can talk later. Goodbye!"

Hepzibah's face was white, and she took Phoebe's hand.

"Oh, Phoebe!" she said. "I can never love that man. When am I going to say it to his face?"

"Is he very bad?" Phoebe asked.

"Go now and talk to Clifford," Hepzibah said. "I'm going to work in the store."

Phoebe went to Clifford. "Is Judge Pyncheon bad?" she thought. "But he's an important man!"

Chapter 4   House and Garden

In the mornings, Clifford liked to sleep. Phoebe worked in the store and Hepzibah stayed with Clifford. In the afternoons, Hepzibah worked in the store and Phoebe stayed with Clifford. Phoebe often took Clifford into the garden. They talked about the flowers and she liked reading to him. He was happy there, with his young cousin.

The three cousins were usually in the garden on Sunday

*"Of course," Judge Pyncheon said, "Clifford isn't well.
Maybe we can talk later. Goodbye!"*

afternoons. Holgrave and Mr. Venner often came too.

One day Mr. Venner said, "Miss Hepzibah, I like meeting you here on Sundays. One day you can come and visit me in my house in the country."

"Mr. Venner is always talking about his 'house in the country,'" Clifford said, "but it's very, very small."

"We would all like a house in the country," Phoebe said.

And Phoebe was right. They loved the garden. It was their place in the sun.

But Phoebe and Clifford did not always go to the garden. Sometimes they went up to a room with a big window. It looked down on the street. They opened the window, and then Clifford watched the street. People came and went. Children played their games, and Clifford was happy. Or a train came, and he was afraid.

One day Clifford said, "I can hear music!" He moved near the window because he wanted to see. In the street, people walked to the music.

"I'm going to walk with them," Clifford thought. His foot was on the open window, and he started to go out. Hepzibah and Phoebe quickly stopped him.

"Clifford! What are you doing?" Hepzibah's face was white. Phoebe started to cry. "What's wrong with you?" Hepzibah asked.

"I don't know," Clifford said. "I wanted to be with people."

Phoebe was friendly with Holgrave. He was interesting, and she often talked with him about her family.

"How is Clifford?" Holgrave asked one day. He did not often see Clifford. "Is he happy?"

"Children are sometimes unhappy," Phoebe said. "Clifford is unhappy too."

"Why?" Holgrave asked.

"I don't know," Phoebe answered. "I don't want to ask him about it. Why are you asking?"

"Because he's interesting," Holgrave answered. "I want to know about the Pyncheons. Do you know the story of the wizard Maule and Colonel Pyncheon?"

"Yes, I do," Phoebe answered. "Cousin Hepzibah talks about it. 'We're an unhappy family because the wizard cursed us,' Hepzibah says. What do you think?"

"Hepzibah is right!" Holgrave said. "And Colonel Pyncheon is with us again! Do you remember my picture? Was it a picture of Colonel Pyncheon or the Judge?"

"What are you saying?" Phoebe asked. "Are you sick?"

"I'm sorry," Holgrave said. His face was red, and he was quiet. Then he said, "I write stories. I have a story about the Pyncheons. Can I read it to you?"

Phoebe smiled at him. "Yes, I would like that."

Phoebe listened to his long story. It was about beautiful Alice Pyncheon, and Maule's curse. Phoebe's eyes were heavy, and they started to close.

Holgrave finished and looked at her. "Miss Phoebe," he said, "are you sleeping?"

"Me—sleeping?" Phoebe answered. "Of course not! I listened to your story. It was good."

"It's a beautiful evening," Holgrave said, "and now I'm happy. Tomorrow's a new day!"

"Yes, it is," Phoebe said. "But I'm not happy. Tomorrow I'm going to my mother's house. But only for a short time. My cousins need me, and this is my home now."

"You're right," Holgrave said. "They need you here."

"Are you afraid?" Phoebe asked. "What are you thinking?"

"I can't say," Holgrave answered. "But come back quickly. Goodbye, my friend!"

Phoebe went to her mother's house, and the House of the Seven Gables was dark again. Hepzibah had a lot of work in the store. But she was unhappy, and her customers started to stay away. Clifford was unhappy because Phoebe was not there. He only wanted to stay in bed. It was a difficult time for them.

One day, Judge Pyncheon came into the store. He smiled.

"How do you do, Cousin Hepzibah?" he said. "And how is Cousin Clifford? What do you need? Ask, and I can get it for you!"

"We don't need you," Hepzibah answered.

"But where is Clifford?" the Judge asked. "When is he going to meet his old friends?"

"You cannot see him," she answered. "He's in bed."

"Is he sick?" the Judge asked. "I'm going to see him. Maybe he's dead!"

"No, he isn't!" she said. "But you would like that!"

"Cousin Hepzibah," said the Judge. "You don't know me! I'm not a bad person. Clifford went to prison, but now he's home! Be happy!"

"Stop!" Hepzibah said. "You never loved my brother, and you don't love him now! Clifford went to prison because you wanted it!"

"Clifford is home again because I wanted it," the

Judge said quietly. "But I'm a judge, and I can put him back in prison! Now, take me to Clifford!"

"Never!" Hepzibah said. "Why are you doing this?"

"Cousin Hepzibah," the Judge said. "Do you remember the question about the Pyncheon land? Is it ours or not? Cousin Clifford has the answer! I want to ask him about it."

"You're wrong!" Hepzibah said.

"Take me to him, or I'm going to put him in prison again!" the Judge said.

Hepzibah looked at him. "The hair on your head is white, and you can only think about money! Maule's curse is working on you! I'm going to get Clifford. You're wrong, but you can hear it from him!"

They went from the store into the house. Hepzibah was afraid for Clifford. "But what can I do?" she thought. She opened the door to his bedroom.

"Clifford!" she called. But there was no answer. "Where is he? I'm going to the police," she thought. "No, first I'm going to find the Judge!" She went back.

Suddenly Clifford was there. His face was very white.

"Hepzibah," he said. "Now we can dance, now we can play! Look!"

Hepzibah went quickly into the room. There was Judge Pyncheon, dead in his chair!

"What are we going to do?" Hepzibah asked. She looked at her brother. He had his coat on.

"Come!" he said. "The Judge can have this old house!"

But Hepzibah was afraid, and did not move.

"Why are you waiting?" Clifford said. "Get your coat! Get your money! Come, Hepzibah!"

There was Judge Pyncheon, dead in his chair!

She started to move. "What am I doing?" she thought.

"Be quick!" Clifford said. "Or the dead can catch us!"

They went into the street. Clifford took his sister's hand, and they walked to the station.

"Get on the train," said Clifford.

"Which stop would you like?" the ticket man asked.

"It's not important," Clifford answered. "We like going on trains!"

The man took his money, and Clifford started to talk to people on the train.

"Clifford! Be quiet!" Hepzibah said.

"No!" Clifford answered. "For the first time in thirty years I can talk. I'm a new man!"

Chapter 5 Goodbye!

In the morning people came to the store, but it was closed. Where was Hepzibah? Then they started to ask about the Judge. Where was he? Phoebe arrived from the country. She tried the door to the store, but it did not open. She went to the front door. The schoolboy watched her from the street.

"Miss Phoebe!" he said. "Don't go in! It's bad!"

"Why is he running away?" Phoebe thought. The front door did not open. She went to the back door. She was afraid, but her hand was on the door. Suddenly it opened!

"It's Hepzibah!" thought Phoebe. She went in and the door closed behind her. It was dark. A hand took hers, and they walked into a big room. "But this isn't Hepzibah's hand!" Phoebe thought.

"Holgrave!" she said. He smiled at her, but his face was white. "Where are Hepzibah and Clifford? Why is the house quiet?" Phoebe asked.

"They aren't here," he answered.

"Where are they?" Phoebe said. "I'm going to find them."

"Wait!" Holgrave said. "Judge Pyncheon is dead. And he's sitting in Colonel Pyncheon's chair! I wanted to find Hepzibah, and there was the Judge, dead in his chair!"

Phoebe was afraid. "Did you call the police?" she asked.

"No," Holgrave said. "Clifford and Hepzibah went away. The police are going to want Clifford."

"Clifford!" Phoebe said.

"You don't know his story!" Holgrave said. "He went to prison for thirty years because Judge Pyncheon wanted him there. Clifford went to prison for the murder of his father's brother. But it wasn't murder! His father's brother had a bad heart, and Judge Pyncheon had a bad heart too. *That's* the curse of the Pyncheon family!"

"Open the doors!" she said. "Then the town can hear."

"You're right," Holgrave said, but he did not move. He talked slowly. "Phoebe, I was here with the Judge. I looked into the dead man's eyes, and I thought about Clifford and his thirty years in prison. Thirty years! Phoebe, I'm not thirty years old! But then you came back. I took your hand, remember? Phoebe, I love you."

"How can you love me?" Phoebe asked. "We're not the same. How can we be happy?"

"I can only be happy with you!" Holgrave said.

"And I'm afraid," Phoebe said. She moved near to him.

"Phoebe, do you love me?" Holgrave asked.

"Ah, the Pyncheon land. Don't think about it, Hepzibah. We don't need it."

Phoebe looked down. "Yes, I do," she said.

They were quiet, and happy. Then Phoebe asked, "What's that noise?"

"Maybe it's the police," Holgrave said.

"Brother, we're home!" It was Hepzibah. "And here is our little Phoebe—and Holgrave too!"

They went to the police, and doctors came to the house.

"Yes, the Judge had a bad heart," they said.

One day, Hepzibah, Clifford, and Phoebe were in the room with Colonel Pyncheon's picture. Holgrave and Mr. Venner were there too.

"Clifford," Hepzibah said, "now the Judge's money and his big country house are ours. But is *this* house and the Pyncheon land ours too? Do you know the answer?"

Clifford smiled. "Ah, the Pyncheon land. Don't think about it, Hepzibah. We don't need it."

"You're right," Holgrave said. "And it isn't your land."

"But how do you know?" Phoebe asked.

Holgrave looked at her. "My family knows," he said. "I'm a Maule—but I'm not a wizard!"

"We're going to move to the Judge's country house," Phoebe said. "Mr. Venner, please come and live with us. We have a big garden there. Would you like that?"

"Yes!" he said.

They closed the House of the Seven Gables and moved to the country. Phoebe took some flowers with her. They were Alice's Flowers.

ACTIVITIES

Chapters 1–2

Before you read

1 Read the Introduction to the book. Is this a happy story?
2 Find the words in *italics* in your dictionary. They are all in the story.

   a Look at the pictures in the book. Find these things:
   flower gable garden

   b Write the right words.

NOW	THEN
curse	cursed
cry	
kiss	
need	
	thought
	took

   c Answer the questions.
   What are you *afraid* of?
   What do you do with a *biscuit*?
   Is a *colonel* usually a man or a woman? And a *judge*?
   Do you have a *cousin*?
   Is a *customer* always right?
   What can you do with *land*?
   Is a *wizard* always bad?

After you read

3 Answer these questions.

   a Look at the picture of the House of the Seven Gables on page 36. What do you see?

63

    b What did the wizard do to Colonel Pyncheon?
    c Which flowers does Phoebe take from the garden?
    d Who is Holgrave?
 4 Work with a friend. Read Phoebe's talk with Holgrave in Chapter 2. Then close the book. Have the talk again.

Chapters 3–5

Before you read

 5 Phoebe sees Hepzibah's picture of a beautiful young man. She talks with Holgrave about it. Who is in the picture? Is he a "bad child"? What do you think?

 6 Answer the questions. Find the words in *italics* in your dictionary.
    a Why is a bad *heart* a problem?
    b Is *murder* always wrong?
    c Why do people go to *prison*?

After you read

 7 Who says:
    a "Are you angry with me?"
    b "Are you afraid of me?"
    c "I can hear music!"
    d "Maybe he's dead!"
    e "I'm a new man!"

 8 Which person in the book do you like? Talk about him/her.

Writing

 9 You are Phoebe. Write a letter to your mother about Holgrave.

10 Write about the Pyncheon family. What do you know about the Colonel, the Judge, Hepzibah, Clifford, and Phoebe?

Rip Van Winkle
and The Legend of Sleepy Hollow

WASHINGTON IRVING

Level 1

Retold by Margaret Murphy
Series Editors: Andy Hopkins and Jocelyn Potter

Introduction

"Let's go to the mountains," Rip said to Wolf. "I don't want to see my wife and I don't want to listen to her."

One day Rip Van Winkle, a farmer, goes to the mountains with his dog, Wolf. There he meets some old men. Who are these strange men? Why are they there? And what are they drinking?

The Legend of Sleepy Hollow is about a teacher, Ichabod Crane. He likes listening to stories about ghosts. But *are* there ghosts in Sleepy Hollow? And is Ichabod going to see a ghost?

The stories in this book are about people—and about ghosts. There are a lot of questions in the stories, but not many answers.

Washington Irving (1783–1859) is a very famous American writer. He lived in New York, but later he worked in Europe for seventeen years. Then he went back to the United States and lived near the Hudson River.

In the years 1770 to 1810, people came to America from Holland and lived in the mountains near the Hudson River. The stories in this book are about these people.

At that time, America was British. The king was King George III. Then, in 1775, Britain and America started a war. The war finished in 1783, and there was a new country—the United States of America.

RIP VAN WINKLE

Chapter 1 Rip's Wife is Angry

There was a small town in America. Near this town were some very beautiful mountains, with many trees on them. The mountains were beautiful—but they were strange, too.

"Maybe ghosts live there," the people in the town said.

They said this because sometimes strange noises came from the mountains.

A man lived in this small town and his name was Rip Van Winkle. The people in the town liked him. He liked talking to people and he liked helping them.

Rip was a farmer, but he didn't like working. He liked going to the bar in the town and talking to the men. They talked often, sometimes every day. The name of the bar was the *King George*. King George was the British king, and America was British then.

Rip had a wife, a daughter, and a son. His wife was always angry because Rip didn't work. She was angry, too, because he talked in the bar all day.

"Rip, stop talking! Go to work!" she said. "You sit all day with your friends at the bar. But we have children, Rip. We have a farm. Come home now and work!"

Rip had one very good friend—his dog, Wolf.

"Let's go to the mountains," Rip said to Wolf. "I don't want to see my wife and I don't want to listen to her."

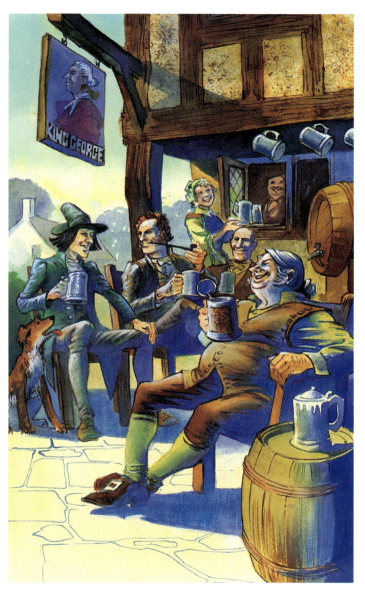

He liked going to the bar in the town and talking to the men.

Chapter 2   Rip Meets a Strange Man

One beautiful day, Rip and his dog walked to the mountains and stayed there all day.

"I love the mountains, and the trees. My wife isn't here and I'm very happy with you, my friend," Rip said to Wolf. "But now it's evening, and my wife's waiting for me at home."

They started to go down the mountain, but suddenly there was a noise:

"Rip Van Winkle! Rip Van Winkle!"

"Who's there?" Rip asked. "Who's calling my name?"

The mountain was quiet. Rip and his dog were afraid.

"What was that noise?" Rip asked Wolf.

Then he looked down the mountain, and there was an old man. He had a lot of white hair and a long beard. The man walked up the mountain. He walked slowly, because he had a big barrel on his back.

"This is strange," Rip said. "People don't usually come up here. And the man has a big barrel with him. What's in it? Maybe he's from my town. Come, Wolf, let's help him."

Rip and his dog walked down the mountain to the man. He wasn't from Rip's town, and Rip didn't know him. Rip looked at him, and the man looked at Rip.

"Hello," Rip said.

The man didn't answer.

"Hello. What's your name?" Rip asked, but the man didn't answer.

"Do you want my help?" Rip asked. "You have a big barrel on your back. Is it heavy? Can I help you with it?"

The man didn't answer, but he looked at Rip.

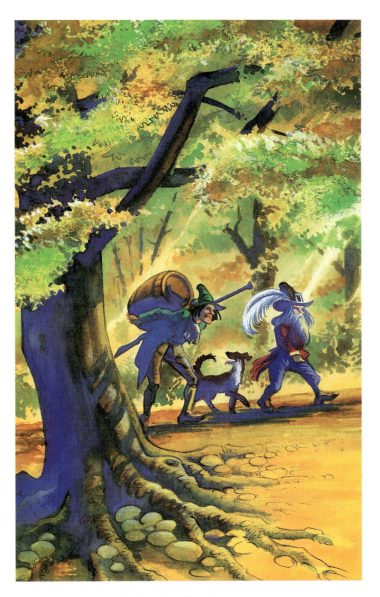

They walked and walked up the mountain.

"Yes, you want my help," Rip said to the man.

Rip went with the man. They walked and walked up the mountain. The barrel was on Rip's back now.

"Where are we going?" Rip asked.

But the old man didn't answer. Strange noises came from the mountain.

"What are those noises?" Rip asked.

Again, the man didn't answer.

Chapter 3   Rip Drinks from the Barrel

The man and Rip came to a big building in the mountains. There were a lot of men there, but Rip didn't know them. They had very long, white beards, and they were old. They played a game, but Rip didn't know it.

The old men looked at Rip and stopped playing their game.

"Hello," Rip said to the men.

The men didn't answer. They looked at Rip, and then looked at the barrel.

"What's in this barrel?" Rip asked.

He looked in the barrel. There was drink in it.

"Do you want some?" Rip asked.

They looked at him, but they didn't answer.

"Yes, you want some," he said.

The old men had a drink from the barrel. Then Rip had a drink from it, too. He liked it and he had a lot of drinks. The men had a lot of drinks too, but they didn't talk. They played their game again.

"This is strange," Rip said. "They're drinking, but they aren't talking."

Rip wasn't afraid. He was happy and he didn't want

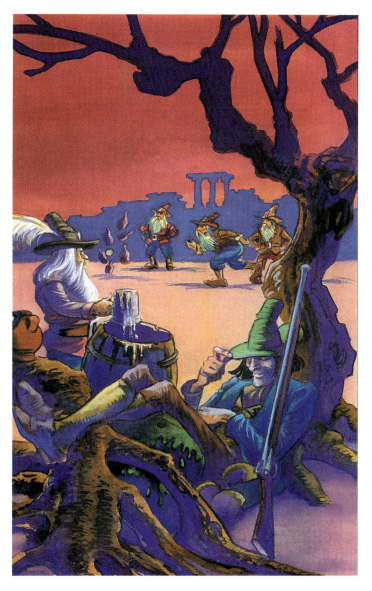

"I want to sleep now," he said, and he closed his eyes.

to go home. It was late in the evening, but Rip stayed with the men for a long time.

"I want to sleep now," he said, and he closed his eyes.

Chapter 4   Rip Goes Home

Rip opened his eyes. He was under a tree, in the mountains. It was morning. He remembered the strange men, and the strange building.

"Oh!" he said. "I'm in the mountains. I didn't go home. I stayed here all night. The men! Where are the men? And where's the building? That drink was bad, very bad. My wife! I know she's angry. And where's Wolf?"

Rip wanted to find his dog. He looked and he looked. He called, but Wolf didn't come.

Slowly, Rip walked down the mountain to his town. He was unhappy, because he didn't have his dog. He was afraid, because he didn't want to see his wife.

He looked at the houses in the town. They were strange. He looked at the people, but he didn't know these people. There were children in the town, but Rip didn't know them. The people weren't the same, and the houses weren't the same.

"Who are these people? Maybe I'm not in my town. Oh, that drink was bad!" he said.

Then Rip walked to his house. It was very old.

"Wife, wife, where are you? Children, where are you? Are you there? Please answer me!" Rip said.

But his wife wasn't there and his children weren't there.

"Wolf, Wolf, you're here!" Rip said. But the dog didn't know Rip.

"Are you my dog?" Rip asked.

He didn't understand. Where was his family? Why was his house old? Why were the people in the town strange? Who were they? He was unhappy. He walked quickly from his house to the bar in the town. He wanted to find his friends.

Chapter 5 "Who am I?"

Rip walked to the bar, but the bar wasn't the same. The name of the bar wasn't the *King George*. It had a new name—*The Union Hotel*. A lot of people were there.

Rip looked for his friends.

"Excuse me. I'm looking for some people. They're my friends. They come here every day," he said to the men in the bar.

"Who are these people?" the men asked, and Rip said their names.

"No, no, no. They don't live here now," the men said.

"They lived here yesterday. Where are they now?" Rip asked.

"Yesterday? No, no, they weren't here yesterday. They're dead," the men said.

"Dead?" Rip said. "How? When?"

"A lot of people are dead. Remember, the war?"

"War? Which war?" Rip asked.

"The war with Britain," the men said.

"I don't remember a war with Britain," Rip said.

"You don't remember? We had a war with Britain. Now we're a new country—the United States of America!" they said.

"What?" Rip said.

"Yes," they said. "But, old man, who are you?"

"Old man? Am I an old man?" Rip asked.

"Yes, you are. You have a long, white beard," they said.

"Oh—I *am* old. My name's Rip Van Winkle," he said.

"Rip Van Winkle! No, you aren't Rip Van Winkle!" said the men. Many people from the town came to the bar. They wanted to listen.

"Yes, yes, I *am* Rip Van Winkle. Please believe me, I'm Rip Van Winkle," Rip said.

"No, no. Rip Van Winkle *was* here in this town—but not now," the people in the town said.

Rip didn't understand. The people didn't believe him. Why?

"People here don't know me. I don't have a home, a family, or a dog," Rip said.

He wasn't happy, and he started to walk slowly away.

Chapter 6   Rip's Daughter

A young woman came to the hotel. She looked at Rip.

"Don't go," she said. "You're unhappy and afraid. I can see that. Stay here with us."

"Do I know you?" he asked.

"No," she answered.

"Young woman, who is your father?" Rip asked.

"Rip Van Winkle," she answered. "But he doesn't live here now. He went to the mountains with his dog, and he didn't come home."

"Where's your mother?" he asked.

"Daughter, I'm your father. I'm Rip Van Winkle!"

"She's dead," the young woman answered. Rip wasn't unhappy about that!

"Daughter, I'm your father. I'm Rip Van Winkle!" he said.

"What?" she said.

People came out of the hotel and listened to them. An old woman looked at Rip.

"Yes, it *is* you, it *is* Rip Van Winkle! I remember you. You're home, Rip!" the old woman said.

Rip was very happy.

"Daughter, you're not a child. You're a young woman," Rip said.

"Yes, father, I'm a young woman, and I have children," she said.

"Daughter, I don't understand. Yesterday, you were a child, and now you're not. Yesterday, I was young, and today I'm old. Yesterday, I had friends at this bar, and today they're not here. They're dead. I don't understand," Rip said.

"Father, it wasn't yesterday. You walked to the mountains with your dog in 1770. Now it's 1790. Twenty years, father, twenty years!" she answered.

"What?" Rip asked.

"Yes," said his daughter. "Twenty years. Where did you go, father?"

Rip said, "Yesterday, I was in the mountains with my dog. There was a strange man there and I walked with him to a strange building. There were a lot of strange men near this building. They played a game, and we had many drinks. It was late, and I closed my eyes. This morning, I opened my eyes and I was under a tree in the mountains. I came home and now I'm here."

"Did you sleep?" his daughter asked.

"Yes, I did," he answered.

The people in the town listened to Rip. A lot of people didn't believe his story.

But one man said, "I believe you. I understand. The mountains are strange. There are strange noises up there. I hear them, too."

"What noises?" people asked.

"I don't know. Maybe they're ghosts. But I believe this man and his story," the man said.

Then the people in the town believed Rip, too.

Chapter 7   Rip is Home Again

Rip lived with his daughter and her family. Rip's son lived with them, but he didn't like working. He didn't work on the farm.

Rip didn't work because he was old. He played with the children and he talked to the men in the hotel. Some men were his old friends. Rip liked the people in the town, and they liked him. He had new friends. They talked to him about the war with Britain, and about their new country, the United States of America.

People often came to Rip and asked, "Are you Rip Van Winkle?"

"I am," he answered.

"Did you sleep for twenty years in the mountains?"

"Yes, I did."

"Can we hear your story?" they asked.

"Yes," he said. And he started his story—the story of Rip Van Winkle.

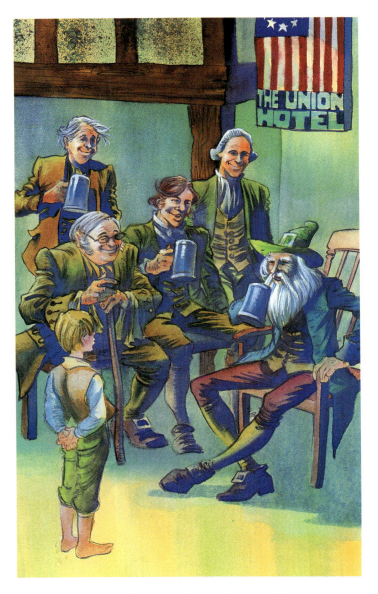

Rip didn't work because he was old.

THE LEGEND OF SLEEPY HOLLOW

Chapter 1   Tarry Town

Tarry Town was a small town near the Hudson River. Sleepy Hollow was a place near the town.

"There are ghosts in Sleepy Hollow," some people said.

Ichabod Crane wasn't from Tarry Town, but he was a teacher there. He was a very good teacher. He played with the big boys after school, and he walked home with the small boys. He liked meeting their mothers and sisters. He liked eating, and they often had food for him.

Ichabod was a tall, thin man. He was very friendly and he had many friends in the town. He stayed with a lot of families because he didn't have a house in Tarry Town. He helped the farmers and played with the children. He liked hearing people's stories.

"Do you know any stories about ghosts?" he often asked.

"Yes," they said. And they talked about the ghosts in the country near the town.

Ichabod went into the country after school. He liked reading there, but he was sometimes afraid. *Were* there ghosts? Did he believe the stories?

Chapter 2   Ichabod and Katrina

There were a lot of young, beautiful girls in Tarry Town. Ichabod liked them, and he liked talking to them. Katrina Van Tassel was eighteen, and very, very beautiful. Her father had a big farm, with many fruit

Ichabod Crane wasn't from Tarry Town, but he was a teacher there.

trees and animals. Ichabod liked Katrina and he wanted her father's farm.

"Maybe I can marry Katrina," Ichabod said. "She's beautiful and her father has a lot of money. Katrina can be my wife, and I can have the farm and the money."

Ichabod was often at Katrina's house. He was a good singer and he was the family's singing teacher.

Katrina's father liked Ichabod and they often talked in the evening. But a lot of men in Tarry Town liked Katrina. They wanted to marry her, too, and they wanted her father's money. Brom Van Brunt was a tall, strong man with short, black hair. He was a very good horse rider, and he liked riding in the country with his friends. He often visited Katrina.

Katrina liked Ichabod *and* Brom. She talked to them and she walked with them in the country. Sometimes, Brom went to the Van Tassels' farm and Ichabod was there. Brom didn't like this, and he stopped visiting Katrina.

Chapter 3   A Letter from Mr. Van Tassel

One beautiful October afternoon, Ichabod was at school with the boys. A man came to the school. He had a letter for Ichabod. It was from Baltus Van Tassel, Katrina's father.

"Please come to my farm this evening, Ichabod," it said. "Many people from the town are coming. We are going to eat and talk. We are going to sing and dance."

Ichabod was very happy.

"Boys," he said, "go home. Go home and play."

"What—now? Go home?" they said.

"Yes. It's a beautiful day. You're good students, and

you work well. You can go home now. This afternoon is a vacation for you and for me," he said.

"Let's go!" they said.

The Van Tassels' house wasn't near the school, and Ichabod wanted to get there quickly. He walked to the house of an old farmer, Hans Van Ripper. This man had a horse.

Ichabod arrived at the man's house.

"Excuse me!" Ichabod said.

"Yes?" Mr. Van Ripper answered.

"I want to go to the Van Tassels' home. Can I have your horse for this evening?"

"Yes, you can have him. But Gunpowder is very old and he only has one eye. He can't run very quickly. Do you want him?" he asked.

"Yes, please," Ichabod said.

"Can you ride?" Mr. Van Ripper asked Ichabod.

"Yes, but I'm not a good rider. Old Gunpowder is good for me," Ichabod answered.

Ichabod started to go to the Van Tassels' farm on the old horse. He went near Sleepy Hollow. Ichabod looked at the beautiful brown and yellow trees, the green country and the mountains. He was very happy.

"Oh, this beautiful country, and my beautiful Katrina!" he said to his horse.

Chapter 4 At the Van Tassels' Farm

Ichabod arrived at the Van Tassels' farm in the evening. There were a lot of people from the town there—young, beautiful girls, old women, young and old men, and a lot of families. Katrina was there, and Brom was there, too.

Ichabod was very happy because there was a lot of food. He talked to people and he danced with Katrina. Brom watched them and he was unhappy.

Some people from Sleepy Hollow were there. They talked about the strange noises and ghosts there. One story was about a woman in Sleepy Hollow.

"She's a white ghost. We can hear her in the winter," they said. They talked about a big tree near a river, too. "We can hear noises near the tree," they said. "There's a ghost in that tree."

One story was very interesting. It was a story about a horse rider. He was a ghost and he *didn't have a head*! He lived in Sleepy Hollow, and the people were afraid of him.

"He's often near the small river in Sleepy Hollow," a woman said. "Remember Mr. Brouwer? He went to Sleepy Hollow one night, and the ghost was there. He threw Mr. Brouwer in the small river."

"Yes, we remember that story," people said.

"I know that ghost," Brom said. "He was in Sleepy Hollow one night, and I was there, too. But I'm a very good horse rider and he didn't catch me." He had a smile on his face.

Some people didn't believe him, but Ichabod believed every story.

Then it was late.

"Let's go home," the farmers said.

Ichabod stayed at the Van Tassels' house because he wanted to talk to Katrina. But Katrina didn't want to talk to him.

"It's late Ichabod. Go home," she said.

"I'm going now," he said.

He was unhappy, but he went.

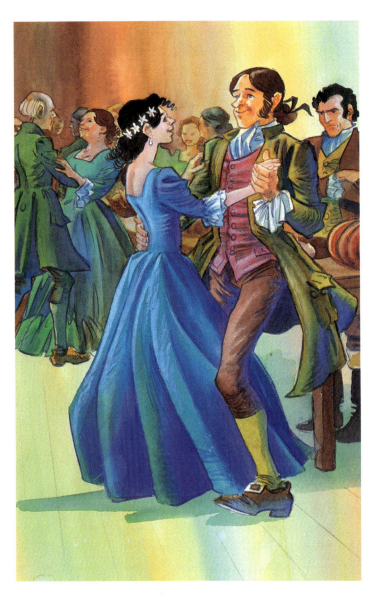

Brom watched them and he was unhappy.

Chapter 5 Ichabod in Sleepy Hollow

Ichabod was on his old horse. It was night, and it was very dark and quiet. In Sleepy Hollow Ichabod remembered the ghost stories and he was afraid.

"Maybe the ghosts are here now," he said.

Ichabod came to a tree. There was a white thing in the tree. Was it the tree with the ghost? There were strange noises. His horse was afraid, too, but it walked slowly.

"Please, horse, walk quickly! I don't want to be here, in Sleepy Hollow. I want to go home quickly!" he said.

Suddenly, his horse stopped near a small river.

"Go, Gunpowder. Go across the river!" Ichabod said.

But the horse didn't move.

Was there a person near Ichabod and his horse? Ichabod looked. It was dark. He looked again, and there was a big, strong man on a black horse on the road.

"Who's there?" Ichabod called.

The strange man didn't answer.

"Who are you? Talk to me! What's your name? Come here. I want to see you," Ichabod said.

Again the man didn't answer. Was he a ghost? Did he have a head? Ichabod's horse was very afraid, and started to run. The strange man's horse started to run, too, near Ichabod's horse. Who was the man?

"Run quickly, Old Gunpowder, run quickly!" Ichabod said to his horse.

The strange man and his horse were there. Ichabod looked at the man. Then the man came near Ichabod. He *didn't have a head*! It was the ghost! Ichabod looked again. The ghost's head *was* there, but it was on the horse's back. Ichabod was very afraid now.

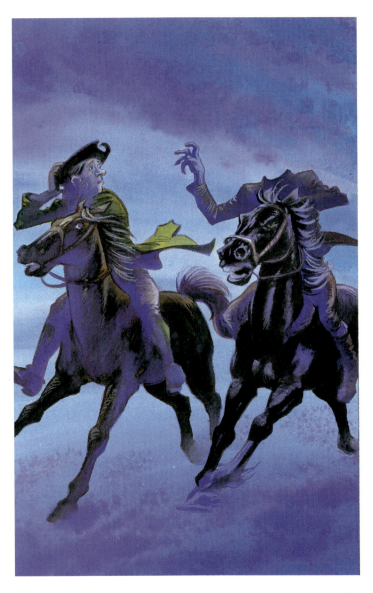

Then the man came near Ichabod. He didn't have a head!

"Run!" Ichabod said to his horse.

But the ghost's horse came after him. The two horses went quickly down the road. The ghost was a very good rider, but Ichabod's horse went in front of the ghost. Ichabod looked behind him. The ghost had his head in his hands. Then the ghost threw his head at Ichabod!

"Ahhhhhhhhhhhhhhhhhhhhhhhhh!" Ichabod said.

Chapter 6 Where is Ichabod Crane?

Ichabod's horse walked home in the night. Hans Van Ripper looked at his horse in the morning.

"*You're* home, Old Gunpowder, but where's Ichabod?" Mr. Van Ripper said.

Ichabod wasn't in the town, and he wasn't at school. The boys waited, but their teacher didn't come. He wasn't at the Van Tassels' house.

"Where is he?" the people in the town asked.

"Maybe he's in Sleepy Hollow," some people said. "He was there, on his horse, after the dance. Maybe he's there now."

Some people went to Sleepy Hollow. They looked for Ichabod.

"Ichabod! Ichabod! Are you here, Ichabod? Where are you?" they asked.

They walked and looked. There was a hat near the river.

"Is this Ichabod's hat?" a man asked.

"Yes it is," a woman answered.

They looked in the river, but Ichabod wasn't there.

"What's this?" a man asked.

There was a pumpkin near Ichabod's hat.

"Why is there a pumpkin here?" the man asked.

"Maybe a person threw this pumpkin at him," the woman said.

"Who?" the man asked.

"Maybe it was the ghost! Maybe the ghost threw it," she answered.

"Is Ichabod dead?" he asked.

"I don't know," she answered. "Let's go back to town. Maybe he's there now."

They walked back to Tarry Town.

People asked, "Was Ichabod in Sleepy Hollow?"

"No, he wasn't," they answered.

"Where is he?" the people asked.

They all talked about Ichabod.

"He's dead," some people said. "Maybe the ghost rider in Sleepy Hollow threw the pumpkin at Ichabod, and now he's dead."

A lot of people in the town believed this, but some people didn't believe it.

Chapter 7   Brom and Katrina

The people in Tarry Town were unhappy. They liked Ichabod. They didn't go to Sleepy Hollow, because they were afraid of the place. They didn't want to see the ghost.

A new teacher came to Tarry Town, and the boys went to school again. Katrina, the beautiful daughter of Mr. Van Tassel, married Brom Van Brunt. People often talked about Ichabod Crane.

A long time after this, an old farmer went to New

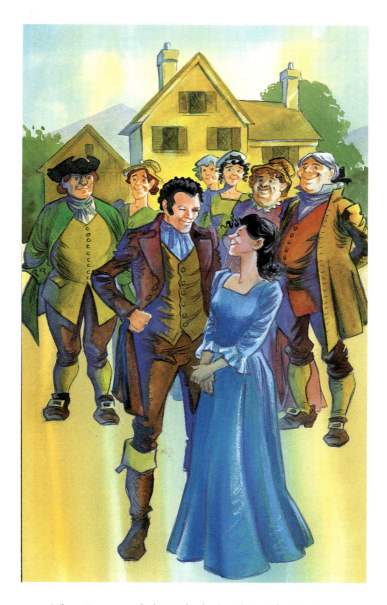

Then Brom smiled. He looked at his wife, Katrina.

York. He came back to Tarry Town and said, "Ichabod Crane isn't dead! He lives in New York."

"Why did he go there?" the people asked him.

"On the night of the dance at the Van Tassels' farm, he went to Sleepy Hollow. He was afraid of the ghosts there, and of the ghost rider in Sleepy Hollow. He went away."

Brom and Katrina were there. They listened to this story of the big, strong ghost rider and Ichabod Crane.

"Do you believe the story about Ichabod and the ghost rider?" Brom asked people.

"Do *you* believe it?" they asked him.

"Maybe. I don't know. It's very strange," he said.

Then Brom smiled. He looked at his wife, Katrina. He had her, and he had her father's farm. Ichabod wasn't there and he was very happy! Brom smiled again.

ACTIVITIES

Rip Van Winkle

Before you read

1. Look at the pictures in this story. Who are the people? What are the stories about?
2. Find the words in *italics* in your dictionary. They are in the story.

   a Which word is it?

   dog   farm   ghost   king   mountain

   a tall place in the country   an animal

   a place with a lot of animals   a dead person

   a very important man

   b Put these words in the sentences.

   afraid   believe   help   strange

   That's heavy. Can I ..... you?

   I don't ..... in ghosts.

   Sometimes I'm ..... at night.

   A ..... man was here yesterday.

   c What's the answer?

   Do you put water or children in a *barrel*?

   Do you have a *beard* on your leg or your face?

   Do two people or two countries have a *war*?

   Is your father's *wife* your mother or your sister?

After you read

3. Answer the questions.

   a Who does Rip see in the mountains?

   b What does Rip do with them?

   c What does Rip do for twenty years?

4 Work with a friend.

Student A: You work for a newspaper. Rip is at home again. Ask him questions.

Student B: You are Rip. Answer the questions.

The Legend of Sleepy Hollow

Before you read

5 Do you believe in ghosts? Do you know any ghost stories?

6 Look at these sentences. What are the words in *italics* in your language? Look in your dictionary.

   a He has a *horse*, and he *rides* it very well.
   b There are *legends* about ghosts in my country, too.
   c I love you, and I want to *marry* you.
   d Americans eat *pumpkins*, and they make faces from them.
   e Can you *sing* for us?
   f Please throw that to me. My son *threw* it in your yard.

After you read

7 Answer these questions.

   a Who loves Katrina?   **d** Who marries Katrina?
   b Does Brom see a ghost?   **e** Where does Ichabod go?
   c Does Ichabod see a ghost?

8 You are visiting a friend in Sleepy Hollow. Ask your friend about the strange noises.

Writing

9 Write the stories of Rip Van Winkle and Ichabod Crane for a newspaper.

The Gift of the Magi
and Other Stories

O. HENRY

Level 1

Retold by Nancy Taylor
Series Editors: Andy Hopkins and Jocelyn Potter

Introduction

"How can I buy a special Christmas gift for Jim with $1.87? What am I going to do?" she thinks.

O. Henry's short stories are often about the difficult times of people in America from 1902 to 1910. In a lot of these stories we visit New York. Other stories take us to Texas and Oklahoma, away from the towns.

Money is a big problem for many people in the stories. They work long days, and they live in cold apartments with only a little food. The people in Texas and Oklahoma have problems with money, too. But in those stories we see people in the fields and on ranches. In some stories, people have money. They don't usually have difficult problems, but they have interesting stories.

O. Henry writes about love problems, too. Is an old man going to find love? Can a young man tell a woman about his love for her? Is a woman going to find the right man?

Many people remember O. Henry's stories because they think, "How is this story going to finish?" You never know. Then you finish the story and you smile.

O. Henry was William Sydney Porter (1862–1910), a famous short-story writer from the United States. His family lived in North Carolina, and they had very little money. In 1882, William went to Texas and started to write for a newspaper. He had problems with money at work, and the police put him in jail for three years. At that time, he started to write short stories.

In 1902 he moved to New York. There he finished ten books of short stories. One famous book is *Cabbages and Kings*. There are movies of three of his stories.

The Gift of the Magi★

The year is 1905. We are on the streets of New York, with its tall buildings, expensive stores, and important people. But what do we know about the little people? Who lives behind that door? Who works in that small, dark office?

Let's open a door and watch two young people on a cold day in December. The apartment is small. It has only two rooms. There are no pictures or photos. We can't see any special things on the table. But it is a happy home.

Mr. and Mrs. James (Jim) Dillingham Young live here. It is their first home—at $8 a week. Jim works six days a week for $20. Every evening he walks slowly home. His days are long and his feet are heavy. But then he opens the door of the apartment.

There is Mrs. Young—his Della! She is the light in his dark days. She has food on the table for him, and she looks at him with her beautiful brown eyes. Jim always smiles. He is a happy man in his apartment with Della, and she is happy, too.

This afternoon we can see Della in the apartment. Jim is at work. Della puts her money on the table. She has $1.87, and tomorrow is Christmas.

"How can I buy a special Christmas gift for Jim with $1.87? What am I going to do?" she thinks. Della walks across her kitchen. "What can I buy for Jim?"

Della looks at the window. She can see her unhappy face in it. She looks at her long, beautiful hair. Jim always says, "I like to see your hair every morning in the sun. At work, I think about your hair."

★ Magi: in the Christmas story, the three Magi (three kings) come to Bethlehem with special gifts for the new child, Jesus.

Mr. and Mrs. James D. Young have two special things: Della's hair and Jim's gold watch. The watch was a gift from Jim's father, and Jim always has it with him.

Sometimes Della says, "Excuse me, Mr. Young. What time is it?" Then Jim smiles, and he takes the gold watch from his coat. He opens the watch and looks at it with love. Then he tells Della the time.

But now Della is thinking about her beautiful hair. Quickly she puts on her thin, black coat and old hat. She goes into the street. She runs to Mrs. Sofronie's store on First Street. The old woman buys hair.

"Can you buy my hair?" Della asks.

Mrs. Sofronie smiles. "I can give you $20 for it."

"OK, but, please, take it quickly," Della says.

Della sits down and Mrs. Sofronie starts to work. Della doesn't look at her hair on the floor. At three o'clock she takes the $20 from Mrs. Sofronie and puts on her hat. She runs quickly to Fourth Street and looks in every store. She finds her gift for Jim: a beautiful gold chain for his watch, for $21.

Della runs home and finishes the Christmas food. She is happy because she has the chain for Jim's watch. Then she sees her hair in the window.

"Is Jim going to love me with short hair?" Della thinks. "But I did it for him. I wanted a gift for him."

At seven o'clock, Della hears Jim at the door. He is never late. Della has her gift for him in her hand. The door opens and Jim walks into the kitchen. He looks thin, and he is cold in his old coat and shoes. Then he sees Della's hair. He isn't angry, but he is quiet.

"Jim, talk to me. I'm going to have long hair again one day. But this evening I have a special gift for you. Let's be happy. It's Christmas tomorrow," Della says.

Della sits down and Mrs. Sofronie starts to work.

"But . . ." Jim says. "Where is your beautiful hair?"

"At Mrs. Sofronie's store. She has my hair now, and I have a gift for you. And, I love you," Della says.

Jim doesn't answer. He looks at Della. Then he says, "Della, I loved you with long hair and I love you with short hair. And, I have a special gift for you, too."

Della opens the gift quickly, and she finds two expensive combs for her long, brown hair. Della knows these combs because she sees them every day in a store window on Fifth Street. She loves them, but now she has no hair for them!

"Jim, they're beautiful, and in six months I can put them in my hair," says Della. "But, wait! I have a gift for you."

Jim opens his gift slowly, and he looks at it.

"Jim, do you like it? I looked in every store. Give me your watch. Let's put it on your watch," says Della.

But Jim doesn't give Della his watch. He sits down and smiles.

"Della, let's put our gifts away for a year," he says. "I don't have my watch. I went to that store near my office. They buy watches there. You can see my watch in their window now, and you have the combs."

What do we have here? The story of two people. They don't have a lot of money, but they have a lot of love. And now they are going to have a happy Christmas because they understand about special gifts.

And now they understand about special gifts.

The Art Game

"Jeff, my friend," Andy Tucker says one day, "we aren't making any money. Let's try a new game."

"Well, Andy," Jeff says, "tell me your plan. But remember this. I don't want to take money from people."

"We aren't going to *take* money from them. They're going to *buy* things from us," Andy says.

"But that's our old game. What's new?" Jeff asks.

"We're playing a child's game here. People buy our things for one dollar. Let's move to Pittsburgh. We can find some millionaires and make a lot of money," Andy says.

"Why do you want to go to Pittsburgh?" Jeff asks.

"The millionaires in Pittsburgh worked for their money. It's new to them. Now they want to buy beautiful, expensive things," Andy says.

"But what are they going to buy from us?" Jeff asks.

"Wait and see," Andy says.

After three days in the bars and restaurants of Pittsburgh, Jeff and Andy meet at their hotel on Thursday evening.

"Let's have a drink, Jeff," Andy says. "I know a Pittsburgh millionaire."

"Where did you meet him?" Jeff asks.

"At a little coffee bar on Twelfth Street. Pittsburgh millionaires don't like expensive restaurants and bars. We talked, and he liked me. His name is Scudder. I went to his house, too. He has $12,000,000 in the bank, but he's a new millionaire. Now he wants to know about good books, the theater, and beautiful art. He wants to be a gentleman," Andy says.

"How is he going to do that?" Jeff asks.

"Let's have a drink, Jeff," Andy says. "I know a Pittsburgh millionaire."

"He has teachers, and he buys expensive books and pictures," Andy says.

"OK, but what is he going to buy from us?" Jeff asks.

"He has a lot of pictures in his house. He has a famous little gold horse, too. It's from Egypt and it's very old. I asked him about it. He said, 'There are two of these gold horses. I want the other horse, but I can't find it.'"

"We don't know about art. Where can we find a gold horse for Scudder?" Jeff asks.

"Wait and see, my friend," Andy says.

On Friday, Andy comes back to the hotel in the afternoon. He has a bag in his hand.

"Look, Jeff. I was in a little store near here. Look at this," Andy says. He opens the bag.

"Andy!" Jeff says. "Is this a gold horse from Egypt?"

"It is. It was under some old things in the back of the store. I said to the old man, 'Can I have that horse for $2?' He said, 'That's a beautiful little thing. Give me $35 and it's yours.'"

"What did you give him?" Jeff asks.

"He was happy with $25, and Scudder is going to be *very* happy. He's going to buy my little horse from you."

"Why from me?" Jeff asks.

"You're going to call him. You are a famous art teacher. You want to buy *his* horse," Andy says.

After Jeff's telephone call, Mr. Scudder arrives at the hotel. He wants to see the art teacher's gold horse.

"It's beautiful!" Mr. Scudder says. "It's the other horse from Egypt."

"Yes, yes, I know about your horse. Now I want to buy it. I want to put the two horses in a special place at my art school. I can give you $2,000 for your horse," the "art teacher" says.

"It's beautiful!" Mr. Scudder says.

"Never! You can't buy my horse. I'm going to buy yours. Here's $2,500," Mr. Scudder says.

"OK. With $2,500 I can buy two or three pictures for my school," the "art teacher" says.

"Now I'm going to have two horses in my bedroom," Mr. Scudder says.

Jeff runs to Andy's room. Andy is looking at his watch. "Did Scudder buy the horse?" he asks.

"Yes. He loved it. The money is in my bag," Jeff says.

"Good, good. Let's go. There's a train to Cincinnati at 10:45," Andy says.

"Why? Let's stay in Pittsburgh for the weekend. Mr. Scudder is happy and we're happy. He has two horses and we have $2,500. No problems," Jeff says.

"You're right and wrong. We have $2,500, but Scudder has only one horse," Andy says.

"Andy, did you take that horse from his house?" Jeff asks.

"Yes. It wasn't difficult," Andy says.

"But why did you tell me that story about the old man and the store near here?" Jeff asks.

"Oh, because you never want to take money from people. Mr. Scudder had a horse for his money," Andy says.

"But . . ."

"Jeff, stop. No questions. Let's go! The train is waiting," Andy says.

The Troubadour

Sam Galloway is a troubadour. He moves across Texas and Oklahoma. He goes from place to place and plays music. He tells stories, too, and he talks to people about their good days and their bad days. The ranchers and their families like listening to him, and Sam gets a bed and food and drink for his work.

On this hot summer day, we are at the Merrydew Ranch in Texas. The Merrydews are good people, and their ranch is big. There are always a lot of people in the house, and there is a lot of noise. After six weeks with the Merrydews, Sam is putting his things on his horse and moving to a new place. He wants to go to a ranch with strong coffee, good food, and some quiet people.

That afternoon, Sam arrives at old man Ellison's sheep ranch. Mr. Ellison and his men are very happy with this new visitor. The men sit at a big table in the evenings. They eat and drink well. Then they listen to Sam's stories and his music. Mr. Ellison always wants to hear Sam's story about an old boat, and Sam tells it every evening.

Mr. Ellison is a good rancher, but he is getting old. Now he has problems with his sheep and with the bank. He doesn't always have money for a lot of food and drink. He can't buy things for his house and his ranch. Every day he thinks about his problems. "What am I going to do?" the old man thinks. But at night he listens to Sam Galloway's music and stories and he smiles. He thinks, "Tomorrow is going to be OK."

But it isn't OK. In the morning, Mr. Ellison gets on his horse and goes to the fields. He wants to look at his sheep. On the road he meets a tall young man on a horse.

"Good morning," Mr. Ellison says.

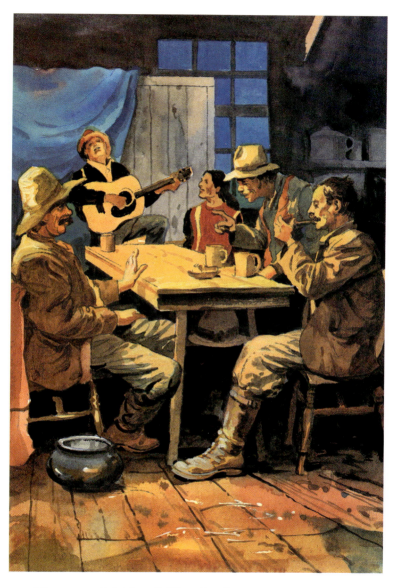

They eat and drink well. Then they listen to Sam's stories and his music.

"Good morning," the young man says. "Are you Peter Ellison?"

"Yes, I am," Mr. Ellison says. "What can I do for you?"

"My name is James King, but people usually call me King James. These are my fields. I don't want your sheep here. Move them or they're going to be dead sheep."

"But, Mr. King, I don't have ...," Mr. Ellison starts to say.

"You have one week, Mr. Ellison. Seven days. Goodbye," James King says.

Mr. Ellison arrives home in the early evening. He is quiet and his eyes are unhappy. After a little food, he sits with Sam Galloway at the table.

"Sam, play some music, please."

"OK, Mr. Ellison, but why are you unhappy this evening? Problems?" Sam asks. A troubadour knows about ranchers' problems.

"Yes, a very big problem. His name is James King."

"Oh, King James. I know about him. People talk about him on every ranch in Texas. He has a lot of animals, and he has money in every bank in the country. He's a difficult man. Don't go near him," Sam says.

"That's the problem," Mr. Ellison says. "My sheep are in James King's fields, and he doesn't want them there. I don't have any good fields for sheep. But, that's not *your* problem. Please, play some music for me."

Sam plays his music, but he watches the old man. King James is going to be a big problem for old Mr. Ellison.

In the morning, Mr. Ellison goes to the store and to the bank. He is looking for an answer to his problems. He talks to some ranchers, but he can't find an answer.

In the afternoon, Mr. Ellison is looking at his sheep. Suddenly King James comes across the field to him. "Good afternoon, Mr. Ellison," the young man says. "I want to talk to you. It's important."

"These are my fields. I don't want your sheep here."

"I'm sorry, Mr. King. I don't have a place for my sheep. I'm looking for a new field for them," Mr. Ellison says.

"I don't want to talk about the sheep. I have some questions for you. First, are you from Jackson, Mississippi?"

"Yes, I lived there for twenty-one years," Mr. Ellison answers.

"Do you know the Reeves family in Jackson?" Mr. King asks.

"Yes, I do. Mrs. Caroline Reeves was my only sister."

"Mr. Ellison, please, listen to my story. I can remember an important day in 1902. It's a cold winter day and I am only fifteen years old. I arrive in Jackson with no family, no food, and no money. Mrs. Caroline Reeves sees me on the street and takes me to her house. She gives me food, a heavy coat, and good shoes. Then she finds a job for me at the Jackson Hotel, and every Sunday for five years I go to her house. She is my friend and my family.

"In 1907, I have some money in the bank. I talk to Mrs. Reeves about my plans. She listens and she gives me some money and a gold watch. I say goodbye and then I go to Texas. I buy my first field and four sheep. Today I have a lot of fields and a lot of sheep because Mrs. Caroline Reeves was good to me one day in 1902.

"I want to be good to you, too. I have a lot of fields. Your sheep can stay here. And, do you have any problems with money?" King James asks.

The old man tells the young man about his problems with the bank and with the ranch.

"You aren't going to have any problems after today. I'm going to put $2,000 in the bank for you tomorrow morning. I'm going to talk to Mr. Brooks at the store. Buy the things for your house and your ranch. I'm going to give Mr. Brooks the money for them. You're Mrs. Caroline Reeves's brother. That's very special to me," King James says.

Mr. Ellison goes back to his ranch with a smile on his face. He wants to hear some music, but Sam Galloway isn't in the house.

In the evening, Mr. Ellison is drinking coffee at the table. The door opens, and Sam walks in.

"Hello, Sam," Mr. Ellison says. "You're very late. Did you go to Frio for the day? Play some music for me, please. I'm a happy man and tomorrow is going to be a new day."

But Sam doesn't play any music that night. He sits at the table and looks at Mr. Ellison. "I went to Frio, and I looked for King James. I had your big knife in my coat. He was in the hotel behind the theater. His hand moved to his knife, but I was quick. You aren't going to have any problems with him tomorrow. He's dead," Sam says.

Mr. Ellison is quiet. Then he looks at Sam and says, "Can you play some music now? I can't understand things this evening. Maybe tomorrow . . ."

Money Talks

Number 24 Park Street is a big, expensive house. Old Mr. Anthony Rockwall lives there. He worked for many years, and now he has a lot of money. He is old and he doesn't work. A man drives his car for him. A woman makes his food. A boy brings the newspaper to him. Mr. Rockwall sits in his big chair and smiles. He is a happy man.

Mr. Rockwall calls his son, "Richard, come here. I want to talk to you."

Mr. Rockwall's son comes in and sits down. He is a quiet young man of twenty-one. "Yes, father?"

"Richard, the men on this street are gentlemen. They come from good families and have a lot of money. We aren't a famous old family, but we have a lot of money. My money makes *you* a gentleman, too. Money can open a lot of doors for you," Mr. Rockwall says with a smile.

"It can open *some* doors, father, but not *every* door," Richard says.

"My son, don't say that. We have no problems. Ask people on the street. Ask your friends. What door doesn't open with money?" Mr. Rockwall asks.

"Money can't buy a place at the table of the right people," Richard says.

"You're wrong, young man," his father says, and he looks into his son's eyes. "Son, the families of these men didn't always have a lot of money. They know about work. You make a lot of money with a lot of work."

Richard is quiet.

"Money can open a lot of doors for you," Mr. Rockwall says
with a smile.

"Son, what's the problem? Are you sick? What's wrong? You can talk to me," Mr. Rockwall says.

"Father, I'm not sick. I have a good home, an interesting job, and a smart old father. But . . ."

"What's her name?" Mr. Rockwall asks.

"Oh, Father. She's beautiful and very special. Her name is Ellen Lantry. She's the only woman for me," Richard says.

"Talk to her. Dance with her. Walk in the rain with her. She's going to love you, too," his father says. "You're a good young man. You're special, too."

"But she's always with people," Richard says. "I never have any time with her. She never has time for me."

"Richard! Take some money, and buy some time with her. Talk to her about your love," the old man says.

"I can't," Richard says. "She's going to Europe by boat tomorrow morning. She's going to stay there for two years. This evening I'm going to take her to the theater, but it's a very short drive. I'm not going to have much time with her, and you can't buy *her* time."

"OK, Richard, now I understand. Your love for her is very strong, but she doesn't know about it. That's your problem," Mr. Rockwall says.

"She can't know because there isn't time," Richard says. He's very unhappy. "Your money can't talk to her."

At eight o'clock in the evening, Richard goes to the beautiful young woman's house.

"Good evening, Richard," Miss Lantry says. "Mother and Father are waiting for us at the theater. I don't want to be late."

"To Wallack's Theater, please," Richard says to the driver. But at Thirty-fourth Street, the car stops.

"What's wrong?" Richard asks.

"I'm sorry, Mr. Rockwall," the driver says. "There are cars to

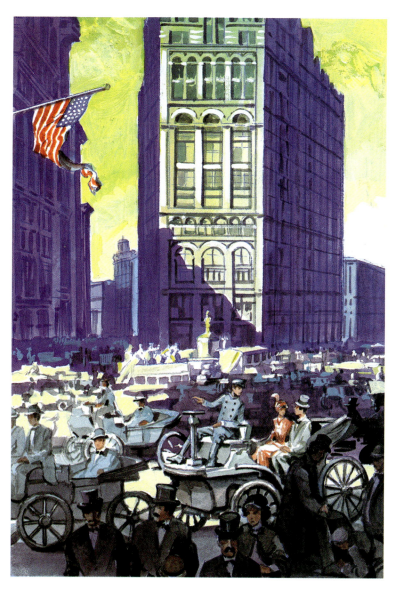

"We can't move. Every car in New York is sitting here."

the left, to the right, and behind us. We can't move. Every car in New York is sitting here."

"Oh, Richard. Are we going to be late?" Miss Lantry asks.

"I'm very sorry, Ellen. No theater for us this evening," Richard says.

"That's OK. I don't like theater very much. I'm happy here in the car with you," Miss Lantry says.

"Are you?" Richard asks with a smile.

Later the same evening, Richard walks into his father's office. The old man is reading his newspaper.

"Father," Richard says, "Miss Lantry and I are in love!"

"Very good, Richard. I'm happy for you," his father says.

"We talked and talked. She loves me! You see! Money can't buy love," Richard says.

Then the happy young man goes to bed. But let's finish his story. At seven o'clock in the morning, Mr. Kelly comes to the door of Mr. Rockwall's house.

"Good morning, Mr. Kelly," Mr. Rockwall says. "You did a good job yesterday evening. Here's your $5,000."

"It was difficult, Mr. Rockwall. The drivers of the cars wanted $10, and the policemen wanted $50. But cars stopped for us on every street. Did it all go well?" Mr. Kelly asks.

"Well? Yes! It was *beautiful*. Let's drink to love and to money!"

Soapy's Winter Home

Soapy lives on the streets of New York. He likes the sun and the trees. He doesn't like buildings or houses or jobs. For nine months of the year, Soapy is a happy man. Then the first week of December comes. At night Soapy puts on his old coat and hat, and he puts three newspapers under him. But he is cold and he can't sleep. He gets up and he walks up and down the streets. He can't live on the streets all winter.

But Soapy has a plan—he has the same plan every December. He is going to do a bad thing. Not a *very* bad thing, but a policeman is going to put him in jail for three months for this thing. Then Soapy is going to have food and a bed for the winter. In March, he is going to finish his time in jail. He is going to be on the streets of New York again for nine beautiful months.

Soapy thinks about his plan. He is going to visit a very smart restaurant. First, he is going to eat some expensive food, and then he is going to sit in the bar with an expensive drink. After his food and drink, Soapy is going to say, "I'm sorry, but I don't have any money." Then the men at the restaurant are going to make a telephone call. A policeman is going to come and put Soapy in jail for three months. No cold streets for the winter.

Soapy smiles and walks into Sanborn's Restaurant. But the man at the door looks at Soapy's old shoes and says, "You can't come in here. The people in here have money. They have good coats and shoes. Go home. You can't eat here."

Soapy sits down and thinks about his plan again. This time he walks down Sixth Street. He finds an expensive store with a big window. He hits the window with a heavy bottle. Many people—and one policeman—hear the noise and run to the store. Soapy stands near the window and smiles.

"Who did this?" the policeman asks. "Where's the man?"

"Maybe I'm that man," Soapy says with a friendly smile.

"You aren't the man. Look! Down there! A man is running away," the policeman says. He runs after the man. No jail for Soapy this afternoon.

That evening Soapy walks to a street with many theaters. He sees a lot of beautiful men and women in expensive coats and dresses. They are talking and smiling. They are going to have a good time in the theaters and restaurants. Near one theater, Soapy sees a tall policeman, too.

Suddenly Soapy runs in front of the people and starts to dance. Then he makes a lot of noise. He is very friendly. He talks to the important people. "Hello. How are you, my friends? What are you going to see this evening? Can I come to the theater with you?"

The policeman sees Soapy. He looks at him and says to the people, "He's a student from the theater school. They always make a lot of noise, but they aren't a problem. It's a game for them."

Soapy is angry and very unhappy. How can he get into jail for the winter? He walks down the street and sees a man in a big office. The man's pen is on a table near a window. Soapy puts his hand in the window and takes the pen. He walks slowly down the street.

The man runs into the street and says, "Stop! You have my pen!"

"*Your* pen?" Soapy asks. "Then call a policeman."

But the man from the office doesn't call a policeman. He has problems with the police, too. He doesn't want to talk to a policeman. "Maybe it *is* your pen," the man says to Soapy. "Goodbye."

Suddenly Soapy runs in front of the people and starts to dance.

Soapy is going to sleep on the street again today. He sits down and makes a new plan. Maybe he can get a job. Maybe he can have some money and an apartment and good shoes and a lot of food. Maybe he is too old for the street. Tomorrow he is going to find a job. This winter he isn't going to be cold, and he isn't going to be in jail. He is going to be an important man. He's happy with this new plan.

Then Soapy hears a person near him. "Excuse me," a policeman says. "What are you doing here? What's your problem?"

"No problem, my good man," Soapy says.

"What's your address? Where do you work?" the policeman asks.

"No address, no job, but I'm going to look for a job tomorrow," Soapy says.

"No address? Come with me. Three months in jail for you," the policeman says.

ACTIVITIES

The Gift of the Magi and **The Art Game**

Before you read

1 Find the words in *italics* in your dictionary. They are all in the story. Answer the questions.

  a How many *kings* are there in the Christmas story? Why are they *special*?

  b Look at your *watch*. Can you *tell* the time in English?

  c Where can you find a *gold chain*?

  d Do women in your country put *combs* in their hair?

  e What is an interesting *gift* for a *gentleman*?

  f What is the name of an expensive *restaurant*?

  g *Millionaires* sometimes buy *horses* and *art*. What *other* things do they buy?

  h What are your *plans* for the weekend?

After you read

2 What comes first in "The Gift of the Magi"? Number the sentences, 1–5.

  a Della gives a Christmas gift to Jim.

  b Della looks at her money: $1.87.

  c Della and Jim put their gifts away.

  d Jim gives a Christmas gift to Della.

  e Della visits Mrs. Sofronie.

3 Who says this in "The Art Game"?

  a "I don't want to take money from people."

  b "I know a Pittsburgh millionaire."

  c "I can give you $2,000 for your horse."

  d "Now I'm going to have two horses in my bedroom."

  e "Let's go! The train is waiting."

The Troubadour, Money Talks and **Soapy's Winter Home**

Before you read

4 Find the words in *italics* in your dictionary. Answer the questions.

  a Do animals or people live in a *field*?

    b Are *ranches* in towns or in the country?
    c Can you find a lot of *sheep* in Japan or in Australia?
    d Does a *troubadour* tell stories or write them?
    e Are *jails* for good people or bad people?

After you read
  5 Who is it?
    a He lives with his son in a big house.
    b He has a lot of money, fields, and animals.
    c He wants to live in jail for three months.
    d He moves from place to place in Texas and Oklahoma.
    e She doesn't like theater very much.
    f He does a job for $5,000.
    g He had a sister. Her name was Caroline Reeves.
    h He loves a beautiful young woman.
  6 Right or wrong? What do you think?
    a Sam Galloway is a good friend to Mr. Ellison.
    b Mr. Rockwall is a good father.
    c Soapy is going to get a job in March.

Writing
  7 Which story did you like? Why did you like it?
  8 Write about tomorrow morning for the people in one O. Henry story.

The Call of the Wild

JACK LONDON

Level 2

Retold by Tania Iveson
Series Editors: Andy Hopkins and Jocelyn Potter

Contents

		page
Introduction		133
Chapter 1	To the North	135
Chapter 2	The Laws of the Wild	138
Chapter 3	A Bad Fight	142
Chapter 4	The New Boss	149
Chapter 5	A Bad Trip	154
Chapter 6	For the Love of a Man	158
Chapter 7	The Call of the Wild	165
Activities		173

Introduction

And Buck really was crazy now. He had fire in his eyes, and he wanted to kill ... In the end, Buck couldn't stand up. He couldn't see or hear. He was almost dead.

In this way, Buck's new life in the cold north of Canada begins. He has to learn many new things, and the lessons are hard. But Buck is a strong, intelligent dog and he wants to live.

Buck meets dangerous men—and dogs—in this difficult, snowy country. He changes because he has to change. But can he really be happy there?

The life of Jack London (1876–1916) was as interesting as his books. His family didn't have any money, and he wasn't happy with life in Pennsylvania. His great love, when he was a child, was reading.

London left school when he was fifteen years old and he visited other places in the United States. He had many different jobs, but he never had much money. In 1896, he heard about the gold in northwest Canada. He went there because he wanted a new life, and he wanted to find gold.

He met many interesting people and animals. He left the Yukon three years later without any gold, but with the idea for a good story. This was *The Call of the Wild*.

Two of his other books about the cold north are *White Fang* and *The Son of the Wolf*. London was very famous, and he made a lot of money from his books. But he always had money problems, and he drank. He died at the age of forty.

People around the world love his stories about the lives of the people and animals of the north.

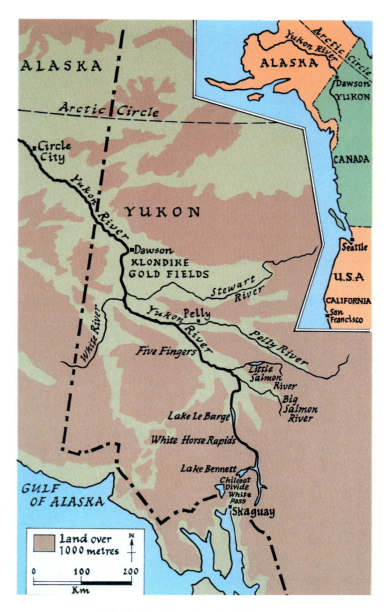

North America: places in this story.

Chapter 1 To the North

Buck was a strong dog with a thick coat. He lived in a big house, Mr. Miller's place, in sunny California. There were tall trees around the house, and there was a pool, too. Buck was four years old, and the Millers were his family. He swam with the boys and walked with the women. He carried the babies on his back, and at night Buck sat at Mr. Miller's feet. There were other dogs at Mr. Miller's house, but Buck was the most important. He was the boss there, and he was very happy.

That year, 1897, was an exciting year. Some men found gold in the cold Arctic north of Canada, and a lot of people followed them there. Everybody wanted gold. And they wanted dogs—strong dogs with thick coats. The dogs had to pull the gold through the snow to towns and rivers.

But Buck didn't know about the cold north, or gold—and he didn't know about Manuel.

♦

Manuel worked for Mr. Miller, but he always wanted more money.

"I can sell Buck," he thought. "He's strong. Somebody will pay a lot of money for him."

One day, Mr. Miller was at work and the children were busy. Manuel put a rope around Buck's neck and left the house quietly. He met a man at a train station, and the man gave him money for the dog.

Buck didn't like this new man, and he started to bark. So the man pulled the rope around his neck very hard. This hurt Buck, and it made him angrier. He tried to fight the man, but the man pulled the rope again. The pain was very bad. Buck fell to the ground and his eyes closed.

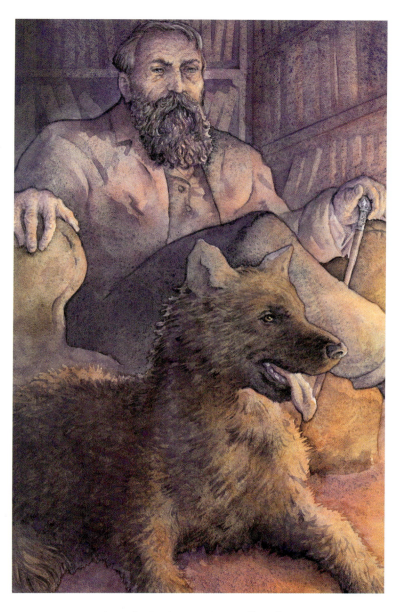

At night Buck sat at Mr. Miller's feet.

He opened his eyes when a loud noise woke him. He was on a train! And there was that man again.

Buck was very hungry and thirsty, and he hated the rope around his neck. He jumped up and tried to attack the man. But the man was quick, and pulled the rope. Buck's neck hurt very badly. Then the man put him in a box.

"Crazy animal!" he said.

When they arrived in San Francisco, the man left Buck, in his box, at a bar.

The next morning, four other men arrived and put Buck in a car. He barked angrily at them, but they only laughed. He was in the box in the car for two days and two nights without food or water. He hated his box, and he hated the men. He wanted to kill somebody.

After a long time, they arrived in Seattle. Four men carried the box to a house and gave it to a man in a red shirt. This man had a club in his hand, and he looked at Buck.

"OK, I'll get you out of that box now," he said. He started to open the box carefully. Buck jumped up and barked. "Now, you crazy dog . . ." the man said.

And Buck really was crazy now. He had fire in his eyes, and he wanted to kill. He jumped at the man: one hundred and forty pounds of angry, crazy dog. But the man suddenly hit him very hard with the club. Buck fell to the ground, and barked. Then he attacked again. Again the man hit him, and again Buck fell to the ground. The pain was very bad.

Twelve times he attacked, and twelve times the man hit him. In the end, Buck couldn't stand up. He couldn't see or hear. He was almost dead.

"That will teach him!" shouted one of the men.

Buck slowly woke up and looked at the man with the red shirt. The man read from a paper on Buck's box.

"So your name's Buck. Buck, my boy," he said quietly, "we had a little fight and now we can forget about it. You know that I'm the boss. Be a good dog, and we'll be friends. I kill bad dogs. Do you understand?"

He brought Buck some food and water. Buck ate and drank quickly. He learned a lesson that day. He learned the lesson of the club, and he never forgot it.

♦

One day, a small French-Canadian man came and looked at Buck. His name was Perrault.

"Wow! He's a big, strong dog. How much do you want for him?"

"Three hundred dollars," answered the man in the red shirt.

"This is a wonderful dog for the cold North," Perrault thought. "He's strong and his coat is thick and warm." He bought Buck and another dog, Curly, and he took the two dogs to a boat. Buck never saw the man in the red shirt or the warm South again.

On the boat, the two dogs met François, another French-Canadian. He and Perrault were kind and intelligent, and they understood dogs. Buck and Curly also met two other dogs, Spitz and Dave. Spitz took Buck's food, so Buck didn't like him. Dave was sad and unfriendly, and wasn't interested in anything. He only wanted to eat and sleep.

Day after day, the weather got colder. Then they arrived in Alaska, and François took the dogs off the boat. Buck walked on snow for the first time in his life.

Chapter 2   The Laws of the Wild

Buck's first day in this new, cold country was very bad. There were a lot of dangerous men and dogs everywhere.

This wasn't a sunny, easy life. Here, there was no rest. Buck had to be careful and he had to learn quickly.

These dogs and men weren't from the South. They were wild, and they followed the law of the club.

Buck's first new lesson, in this cold place, came quickly. Buck and Curly stood near a store, in one of the camps. A new dog walked past them. Curly wanted to be friendly, so she barked quietly. Suddenly, the other dog turned around and attacked her. He hurt her face very badly. Many other dogs saw the attack and ran quickly to the two dogs. They stood and watched quietly. They all looked excited and interested, and Buck didn't understand.

Curly was very angry, so she jumped at this strange, unfriendly dog. But the dog attacked her again and jumped away quickly. Curly couldn't attack the other dog because he was very fast. Suddenly, he pushed Curly over and she fell on the ground. The other dogs ran at her, and Curly barked with pain. But she couldn't stand up and the other dogs attacked her again and again.

Buck couldn't move. Dogs in California never fought in this way. He looked at Spitz, and Spitz laughed. Then François jumped into the center of the crazy dogs and hit them with his club. He and three other men with clubs quickly moved the dogs away.

It all happened very fast, but in those two minutes Curly was dead.

Buck never forgot this attack. Spitz looked at Buck and he laughed again. From that time, Buck hated Spitz more than anything in life.

But then Buck had another surprise. François put a harness on him.

"I know you don't like this, Buck," said François. "I know it's new and strange for you. But you have to wear it. Then you can pull the sledge."

Buck didn't like this new thing around his neck, and he didn't like pulling the sledge. But François hit him when he did something wrong. And Spitz attacked him when he didn't run very fast. François shouted, "*Mush*!" and Buck had to run quickly.

Buck learned to pull the sledge.

He then shouted, "*Ho!*" and Buck had to stop. In this way, Buck learned to pull the sledge.

"These are very good dogs," François said to Perrault, "Buck pulls very hard and he learns very quickly."

In the afternoon, Perrault bought three more dogs—Billie, Joe, and Sol-leks. Billie was a very friendly dog, but Joe was unfriendly. Sol-leks was the same—he wasn't interested in anybody or anything.

That night, Buck had another new problem. He wanted to sleep in a warm, dry place, so he tried to sleep with the men. But Perrault and François were surprised and angry, and they threw plates and cups at him. Buck ran away from them, and went back into the cold.

He was very unhappy; he didn't want to sleep outside. The snow was wet and cold, and the wind hurt him. He looked for the other dogs, but he couldn't see them anywhere! Suddenly, the snow moved under his feet and he jumped back. He started to bark angrily, but then he heard a friendly bark. Buck looked down and saw Billie.

Billie was a little ball under the snow and he was happy and warm. Then Buck understood. He quickly made a little bed under the snow, and he slept very well.

In the morning, Perrault and François bought three more dogs. Now they had nine dogs and they had to begin their trip. Buck was ready, and he was surprised by the excitement of the dogs. But he was most surprised by Sol-leks and Dave.

They were different dogs; suddenly they were happy, excited, and interested. They only loved two things—the harness and the work.

The days were very long and hard. They went past woods and across many large, icy rivers. It was difficult, but Buck worked hard. And at the end of every day he made his bed in the snow and fell asleep very quickly.

Buck was bigger than the other dogs and he was always hungry. François gave him a pound and a half of fish every night, but Buck always wanted more food. Also, Buck didn't eat as quickly as the other dogs, so they often took his fish away from him. After many days, Buck started to eat as fast as the others. And then he started to take other dogs' fish, too. One day, another dog, Pike, took some fish from the food box. Perrault didn't see him, but Buck watched carefully. The next day, Buck did the same thing.

Buck quickly learned the ways of the wild. And now he could live in this cold, unfriendly place. He wasn't the same dog—he was quicker, smarter, and stronger.

He was there, in the North, because Manuel wanted money. And men wanted gold. Now a new life began for Buck. He was a different dog—a wilder dog. On the cold, quiet nights, Buck looked up and howled at the dark sky.

Chapter 3   A Bad Fight

This new, wild animal in Buck was strong, but Buck's new life was very dangerous.

He never fought with the other dogs, but Spitz hated him.

Spitz was the most important dog. He knew the sledge best. He always taught the new dogs to work hard. And the other dogs were afraid of him. He was the strongest, the most intelligent and the most dangerous. He wanted to fight with Buck because every day Buck got stronger and more dangerous. But Spitz had to be the best, so he had to kill Buck.

One cold, windy evening, they stopped next to a river. Buck was very tired and he quickly made a warm bed in the snow. He wasn't happy when François shouted, "Buck, come eat your fish!" He didn't want to leave his warm bed, but he was very hungry. So he ran to the food box and quickly ate his dinner.

But when he turned around, he saw Spitz. The other dog was in Buck's bed. He looked at Buck and laughed. Buck barked at him, and the wild animal inside him went crazy.

He quickly jumped at Spitz. Spitz was very surprised because Buck was never angry.

François was also surprised when the two dogs started fighting.

"Fight him, Buck! You can win!" shouted François. "Get him, get Spitz, that bad dog!"

But the fight never finished, because Perrault shouted. Everybody heard the noise of Perrault's club and the cry of a dog. The camp was suddenly full of strange, thin dogs. There were eighty or a hundred of them, and they wanted food. The two men hit the dogs with their clubs, but the dogs didn't leave.

They found the food box, and they went crazy. The noise was very loud and the sledge dogs were afraid.

The strange dogs finished the food and then attacked the sledge dogs. They hurt them very badly. They hurt Dolly's neck and cut Dub's leg. They took out Joe's eye and almost cut off Billie's ear.

Billie cried in pain and ran away, over the icy river. The other sledge dogs followed Billie, and they all looked for a quiet place to sleep.

In the morning, the dogs walked slowly back to the camp.

"Oh, my friends," said François sadly.

The dogs were in a lot of pain, and they looked very bad.

"Maybe you'll go crazy. Because those dogs attacked you, maybe you're crazy now. What do you think, Perrault?"

"No! They'll be fine," said Perrault. "We have many days of work so the dogs have to be all right!"

But the dogs weren't all right, and one morning, Dolly went crazy. She stopped in front of her harness and sat down. She howled loudly. Then she looked at Buck and jumped at him.

Buck was afraid! He didn't know any crazy dogs. And he liked Dolly—he didn't want to see this. He quickly ran away from Dolly, but she was only one jump behind him. He ran through the trees, across some ice and back to the river. Dolly barked crazily behind him, but she couldn't catch him.

"Buck, come here, boy. Come to me!" shouted François. Buck turned and ran back to the camp. He was very tired now and had a lot of pain in his legs.

"I'll have to help Buck," thought François, and he found his club. Buck ran past him and François's club came down very hard on Dolly's head.

Buck stopped and fell near the sledge. Spitz saw Buck and quickly attacked him. But François saw this and he hit Spitz with his club, many, many times.

"Spitz is a dangerous dog," said Perrault. "He really hates Buck. One day he's going to kill him!"

"But Buck's more dangerous," answered François. "I always watch him, and I know. One day he'll get very angry and he'll eat Spitz for dinner. He'll kill him easily. I know it."

♦

The weather got warmer and the trip got very difficult. The dogs couldn't fight—there was no time. The ice got very thin in some places and the sledge broke through it many times.

One time, when the ice broke, Buck and Dave fell into the icy water. They were almost dead when the two men pulled them out. The men made a fire, and the dogs had to run around it very quickly. They had to get the thick ice off their coats.

Another time, Spitz went through the ice and pulled the other dogs in too. Then the ice broke behind the sledge. Perrault had to climb up a high rock next to the river very quickly. He took the rope from the dogs' harnesses with him. Then he pulled the dogs out of the river, and onto the rock. With the dogs' help, Perrault then pulled the sledge onto the rock. François climbed up after him.

Everybody was very cold and very tired. But they couldn't stay up on the rock; they had to get back down to the river. So they walked to the end of the rock and, slowly and carefully, François and Perrault took the dogs back down. They only went a half of a kilometer that day.

Perrault wasn't happy, because this trip was too slow.

♦

So on the good days, the dogs had to work long hours. But Buck's feet weren't as hard as the other dogs' feet. In sunny California, he never had to walk on cold, hard ice and snow. So now he walked with a lot of pain. One night, he couldn't get up and eat his fish.

François looked at Buck's tired feet. He wanted to help him, so he cut off the tops of his boots. He made Buck four little dog-boots.

"Here, Buck," François said kindly. "These will help you."

Buck loved his new little boots and he was happier after that. One morning, François forgot about Buck's boots. He harnessed the other dogs and then called Buck. But Buck didn't go to his harness and he didn't get up. Perrault and François found Buck and they laughed. Buck was on his back with his four feet up. François put Buck's boots on. Then the dog happily got up and walked to his harness.

"He really is a crazy dog," Perrault laughed.

After many more days on the river, they arrived in Dawson. It was a gray day, and everybody was very tired. There were men and dogs and sledges everywhere. Every day the dogs ran up and down the streets and pulled wood and gold for the men. The dogs worked very hard. They did the same work as horses. And every night, at twelve and at three the dogs howled at the night sky.

The dogs howled at the night sky.

They sang their strange song, and Buck loved to sing with them. It was a very old song—a song from a younger world. And when Buck howled, he howled with the pain of his wild fathers.

♦

Seven days later, they left Dawson. The dogs were strong now, and the fighting quickly began again.

Buck had small fights with Spitz every day, and he always fought him in front of the other dogs. Now Buck was stronger and more dangerous than Spitz, and the other dogs could see this. They stopped liking Spitz. Other dogs began to fight with Spitz, too. They weren't afraid of him and they didn't listen to him. So the dogs began to work badly and they didn't pull the sledge well.

François got very angry at his dogs.

"You stupid dogs!" he shouted, and he hit them again and again. But nothing helped. The dogs didn't stop fighting.

One night, after dinner, a dog found a small animal. The animal jumped up and ran away very quickly. The sledge dogs saw it and they quickly ran after it. Buck was in front of the other dogs. He was very excited. He wanted to catch the animal and kill it. He ran and ran. But the animal was always one jump in front. Buck was very happy.

Spitz quietly left the dogs and ran a different way. Buck didn't see him.

Suddenly Spitz jumped out in front of the animal. It couldn't turn around, and Spitz's big teeth killed it quickly. The other dogs howled and barked. But Buck didn't bark and he didn't stop. He ran at the white dog, and Buck and Spitz began their last, dangerous fight.

Spitz fought very well, and he attacked Buck again and again. Buck tried to push him onto the ground, but Spitz always jumped away very quickly. After some minutes, Buck was in a lot

Buck jumped up and hit Spitz hard.

of pain. He had many cuts, but Spitz was fine. Buck was very tired, and the other dogs watched him carefully. Then Buck jumped at Spitz again. His teeth closed around Spitz's leg, and Spitz cried loudly. With a quick jump, Buck broke Spitz's leg.

Spitz was now in a lot of pain, but he tried hard to stand up. Then Buck started the last attack. He could see and feel the other dogs. They waited and watched. They wanted one of the two dogs to fall. Buck jumped up and hit Spitz hard. Spitz cried and fell. The other dogs quickly attacked him. Buck sat down and watched. He was very tired. But he felt good, because now he was the most important dog.

Chapter 4   The New Boss

"Hey, what did I say? I was right. Buck is a very dangerous dog," François said the next morning. He couldn't find Spitz anywhere, and Buck had many cuts on him.

Perrault looked at Buck's cuts and said, "Yes, but Spitz fought hard."

"And Buck fought harder," answered François. "Now the sledge will go faster. Without Spitz, there will be no more problems. I know I'm right."

Then Perrault put the bags onto the sledge and François put the dogs into their harnesses. Buck walked to Spitz's harness and waited. But François didn't see him and brought Sol-leks to the same place. Buck jumped at Sol-leks angrily, and Sol-leks had to move away.

"Ha!" François laughed. "Look at Buck! He killed Spitz, and now he wants his job! Go away, Buck!" he shouted, but Buck didn't move. Then François pulled Buck by his neck and put Sol-leks in Spitz's harness. Buck barked angrily, but he moved. Sol-leks was afraid of Buck and he didn't want to make Buck angry.

So, when François turned around, Buck easily pushed Sol-leks away again.

François was angry now. "Buck—you bad dog! You move away now!" he shouted, and he took his club. Buck remembered the man in the red shirt and he walked away.

When François brought Sol-leks back, Buck didn't bark.

"OK, now you, Buck. Come here and get into your harness," François said.

But Buck walked away from him. François followed, but Buck didn't stop.

François looked down at the club in his hand. "Oh, I understand. You're afraid of this. All right, I'll put it on the ground—look. Now, come to me."

But Buck wasn't afraid of the club and he didn't go to François. He wanted to be in Spitz's harness. He was the best dog now and he didn't want to go back to his old harness. He walked away again. He didn't leave the camp, but François couldn't get near him.

After an hour, François sat down. He looked at Perrault and smiled. Then he looked back at Buck.

"OK Buck, you win!" And he took Sol-leks out of Spitz's place.

Buck laughed and walked to the sledge. François put him in his new harness.

"*Mush!*" François shouted, and the sledge started to move. François watched Buck carefully. "I don't think Buck can do Spitz's job." François thought. But he was wrong.

After some kilometers, François thought, "Wow! Buck is better than Spitz! He's faster, stronger, and more intelligent than Spitz. Spitz was the best dog, but now Buck is better!"

Buck quickly stopped the fighting between the other dogs.

He was the new boss now, and the other dogs were afraid of him. They listened to him and worked hard for him. François and Perrault were surprised and very happy.

"Buck is the best sledge dog in the North." François said. "Somebody will pay a thousand dollars for him! What do you think, Perrault?"

"Yes, you're right," he said. Perrault was very happy with Buck's work, too.

Perrault was also very happy with this trip. The ice was hard, and there was no new snow. It wasn't too cold. Every day, for fourteen days, they ran 20 kilometers. And at the end of the second week, they could see Skaguay.

But when they arrived at Skaguay, François and Perrault's plans changed. They had to leave Skaguay and the Yukon.

They had to sell the dogs quickly. François put his arms around Buck's neck and he cried. Buck never saw the two men again.

♦

A Scottish man bought the sledge dogs. He and some other men worked for the Canadian Mail Company. They carried people's letters to them. The next day, they took the sledge back to Dawson, and it was hard work for the dogs. The sledge was very heavy and the snow was very thick. Buck didn't like this new job, but he always worked hard. And the other dogs had to work hard, too.

On this trip, Buck only liked one thing. He liked to sit by the fire at night, before he went to bed. He often thought about Curly and his fight with Spitz. Sometimes he remembered Mr. Miller's house in California. But he wasn't sad. He didn't want to go back to Mr. Miller's big house and the warm sun. He had a new home now, and a new life. This life was hard, but good.

After many more days and nights, they arrived in Dawson. Now the dogs were very tired. They were very thin, and they wanted a long rest.

But they only had two days' rest, and then they had to start again. The dogs couldn't run fast, and the men weren't happy. And it snowed every day, so the sledge got heavier and heavier. It was the dogs' third trip back to Skaguay. And day after day, they got weaker and weaker.

Dave had the biggest problem. Sometimes the sledge stopped suddenly, and Dave cried with pain. The men looked at him carefully, but they couldn't find the problem. Something was wrong inside Dave, but they couldn't help him.

After three days, Dave was very weak, and he fell to the ground in his harness many times. The Scottish man stopped the sledge and took him out of his harness. He wanted to give Dave a rest, but this made the dog angry. Dave was in a lot of pain, but he had a job. It was his work, and Dave hated to see another dog in his harness. The sledge started to move again, and Dave ran next to the other dogs. Running was very difficult in the thick snow. He cried and barked with pain.

He was also very weak, and he fell down in the snow. He howled sadly, and started to walk slowly behind the sledge.

The dogs had to have a short rest, so the men stopped. They watched Dave. He walked slowly and carefully to the sledge. He stopped next to Sol-leks and didn't move away.

One man said, "Some dogs die because they can't work. Sledge dogs love their work. And when they can't pull the sledge, they don't want to live."

The Scottish man listened and then said, "I think Dave *is* going to die. But he can die in his harness. Then he'll die happy."

So the men put Dave back into his harness, and the sledge started again. Dave was happy in his harness, but the pain was very bad. He fell many times, and one time, the sledge went over his legs. But he stayed in his harness and night came. The men stopped and made their camp. Dave fell down in the snow next to the sledge. They gave the dogs their fish, but Dave couldn't eat.

In the morning, Dave couldn't get up. He tried to go to his

Dave ran next to the other dogs.

harness, but he couldn't move his legs. The men waited for a short time, but then they had to leave. The sledge moved away from the camp and Dave howled sadly.

The sledge went behind some trees, and the Scottish man stopped the dogs. "I have to help Dave," he thought. "He'll die slowly in the cold snow, and I don't want that. He was a good dog."

He walked back to Dave, and the other men stopped talking. Then they heard the sound of a gun. The Scottish man came back quickly and shouted, "*Mush!*" The sledge moved away fast. But Buck knew, and every other dog knew. They understood the sound of the gun. And now Dave had no more pain.

Chapter 5   A Bad Trip

The Canadian Mail sledge, with Buck and the other dogs, arrived in Skaguay. They looked and felt very tired. Buck was very thin. The dogs' feet had cuts on them and they couldn't run. After thirty days without a rest, they were very weak.

"Come, my friends," said the driver. "This is the end. Now we'll have a long rest—a very long rest."

But there were letters in Skaguay for the men in the North, and the mail sledge had to leave again. The dogs only had a three-day rest. They were tired and weak, and now they couldn't pull the heavy sledge. The men had to buy new, strong dogs, so the Scottish man sold Buck and the other dogs. He didn't ask for a lot of money because the dogs couldn't work very hard.

♦

Two American men, Charles and Hal, bought the tired dogs and their harnesses. Charles was forty-five years old and he had weak, watery eyes. Hal was a younger man of about twenty. He wasn't a kind man. He always carried a gun and a big knife with him. The two men looked strange in the North, and they didn't understand life there.

Hal and Charles took Buck and the other dogs to their new camp. Buck saw a woman, Mercedes, there, and a very large sledge. Hal put the dogs into their harnesses and the dogs waited. The men put a lot of bags and boxes onto the sledge, and it got heavier and heavier.

A man walked past and looked at their sledge.

"You have a very big, heavy sledge there," he said to Hal. "It's too heavy. Do you really think it will move?"

"Of course—now go away!" shouted Hal, and he took out his club. "*Mush*! Go! Move!" he shouted to the dogs. The dogs jumped and tried to move the sledge. But it was too heavy and they couldn't move it.

"You stupid dogs! You aren't pulling hard!" shouted Hal. "I'll kill you!" And Hal started to hit the weak dogs with his club.

Some men came and watched Hal.

"Those dogs are tired. They want a rest," said one man.

"Be quiet!" shouted Hal, and he started to hit the dogs again.

Another man watched angrily. "Those poor dogs," he thought. "That man is very stupid, but I have to help those dogs." So he shouted to Hal, "Break the ice under the sledge. The dogs want to work hard, so don't hit them. Help them, and your sledge will move."

Hal didn't want to listen to the man, but his dogs couldn't move. So he broke the ice, and the sledge slowly moved down the street. But the road suddenly turned left and the large sledge fell over. Bags and boxes went everywhere. Then the harnesses broke from the sledge, and the dogs ran away.

Many nice people came and helped Hal, Charles, and Mercedes. They found their things and brought the dogs back.

One man said, "You'll have to buy more dogs. Your sledge is very heavy."

So Charles bought more dogs, and now they had fourteen animals. They started again, and the men felt happy and important.

The heavy sledge moved slowly down the street. The dogs worked as hard as they could.

The trip back to Dawson was very bad. Hal, Charles, and Mercedes fought every day. They didn't have any plans and they didn't know about this cold country. They started late in the morning and finished early in the afternoon. So they didn't go many kilometers in a day. They hated the cold, the snow, and the Yukon.

They also didn't know about dogs, so they didn't bring much food for them. The dogs began to die because they were tired, weak, and very hungry. In one week, six dogs died, and the other dogs were almost dead.

It was beautiful spring weather. The sun came up early and went down late every day. The birds sang, and the trees were green again. The ice on the river started to break. But through these wonderful days, with new life everywhere, the two men, the woman, and the dogs walked. They didn't enjoy the spring. They thought only of the hard work and the pain.

♦

Buck and the other dogs had no life in them when they arrived, one evening, at John Thornton's camp. When the sledge stopped, every dog fell down in the snow. They looked dead.

"What's the best way to Dawson?" Hal asked Thornton.

Thornton looked at the sledge and thought, "I know these people. They're stupid. I know they won't listen to me. But I want to help those dogs."

"The weather is warmer now," he said to Hal, "and the ice is very thin. Don't walk across this river to Dawson now."

"Some people in Skaguay said the same thing, and we're here.

You're wrong—the ice is thick. We're going to finish our trip. We *will* get to Dawson," Hal answered.

Thornton didn't stop them. They didn't want to hear his words. They didn't understand the North.

Hal shouted to his dogs, "Get up, you stupid animals! Move! Get up, Buck!"

But Buck didn't get up. So Hal took his club and hit him hard. Buck stayed on the ground. Hal hit him again and again. Buck didn't want to get up.

On this trip the ice felt dangerous under his feet. It felt different, and many times on the last river, he was afraid. He was very, very tired and he couldn't get up. The club didn't hurt very much now and Buck started to die. He could hear the club, but now he couldn't feel it.

Suddenly, Thornton attacked Hal. Hal fell to the ground. Thornton stood over Buck and said angrily, "You hit that dog again, and I'll kill you!"

"It's my dog," answered Hal. "Get out of my way or *I'll* kill *you*. We're going to Dawson and you aren't going to stop us!"

Thornton stood between Hal and Buck. He didn't move. Then Hal took out his long knife. But Thornton quickly hit Hal on the hand and the knife fell to the ground. Thornton hit Hal again. Then he took the knife and quickly cut Buck's harness.

Hal couldn't fight Thornton. He was tired, and Buck was almost dead. He didn't want him now.

Minutes later, the heavy sledge, with five tired dogs, Hal, Charles and Mercedes, went down to the river. Buck watched them, and Thornton sat down next to Buck. He felt Buck's legs and his back.

"This animal will have to have a lot of food and rest," he thought. "I hope he doesn't die."

The sledge moved slowly across the river. Suddenly, the thin ice broke and the sledge fell into the cold water. The dogs barked and Mercedes shouted. Then the dogs and the people quickly went under the ice. Buck never saw them again. Thornton looked at Buck, and Buck looked back at him.

"Oh, Buck," Thornton said quietly.

Chapter 6 For the Love of a Man

John Thornton had bad feet from an accident in the winter before Buck came. So his friends made a camp for him, and they left him by the river.

"We're going to Dawson. But we'll be back for you when the weather's warmer. Have a long rest here and get better," they said.

In the camp, Buck sat and watched the river. He listened to the songs of the birds, and he slowly got stronger and stronger. They all got stronger—Buck, Thornton, and his other dogs, Nig and Skeet—and they waited for Thornton's friends. Skeet was a small, friendly dog, and she was a little doctor to Buck. Every morning, after breakfast, she carefully washed Buck's cuts. Nig was a very large, black dog and he was also friendly. They were good friends and they played games every day.

And Buck slowly learned a new lesson. He learned about love. For the first time in his life, he felt strong love—for Thornton. This wonderful man took him away from Hal, and he helped him. He was kind and friendly, and he never hit him. Thornton's dogs were his children and he talked to them every day. Buck loved Thornton's talks with him. He barked at him.

"Wow, Buck," Thornton laughed. "I think you can speak!"

Buck's love for Thornton got stronger and stronger. He loved Thornton more than anything in life.

♦

Buck's love for Thornton got stronger and stronger.

Thornton's friends, Hans and Pete, arrived in the camp with their boat.

In the beginning, Buck didn't like these strange men, but then he saw Thornton's love for his friends.

So Buck walked to them when they called him. And he didn't bark angrily at them. But Buck's love was only for Thornton, and Hans and Pete could see this.

One day, the two men watched Thornton and Buck.

"Buck really loves Thornton," Pete said. "But I'm afraid. You know the men in the North. Sometimes they get angry easily and some men like to fight. And when somebody hurts Thornton, Buck will go crazy."

"Yes," answered Hans. "In Thornton's next fight, Buck will kill the other man."

It was at Circle City, in December, when Pete remembered those words. Thornton and his friends were in a bar. "Black" Barton was in the bar, too. He was a large, angry man. Barton wanted to fight with somebody, so he started to speak angrily to a smaller man. The man was afraid.

Thornton watched the two men. "Oh, no, there's going to be a fight," he thought. "And this won't be a good fight, because Barton is bigger than that other man. I'll have to do something."

So Thornton went to Barton and spoke quietly to him. Barton turned around and hit Thornton very hard in the face.

The people in the bar heard a loud angry bark. Then a large dog quickly jumped up and ran at Barton. Barton put up his arm and Buck attacked it. Buck and Barton fell to the floor. Buck was on top of the man. He was very angry, and he attacked Barton again. This time, he hurt his neck very badly and Barton shouted with pain. Then some men pulled Buck off Barton and they took the dog outside.

A doctor came and looked at Barton's neck.

"He's got a very bad cut, but he's going to live," he said.

A man said, "Yes, but Buck's dangerous. He almost killed that man! We'll have to kill him."

"No, we can't do that!" said another man. "Buck attacked Barton because Barton hit Thornton. He's a good dog, and he helped his friend."

So nobody was angry with Buck. But other people in Alaska heard about this wonderful, strange dog and his great love for Thornton.

♦

At the end of the next summer, Buck showed his love for Thornton again. Hans, Pete, and Thornton wanted to take their boat down a fast river. Hans and Pete stood next to the river when Thornton was in the boat. Buck didn't like this river, and he watched Thornton very carefully.

Suddenly, the boat moved very quickly through the water and it hit a rock. The boat turned over and Thornton fell into the cold river. He quickly went under the fast water, and the river carried him away.

Buck jumped into the water and swam to his friend. When he came near, Thornton put his arms around Buck's neck. Then Buck tried to swim to Hans and Pete. They could pull Thornton out. But the water was very fast, and it pushed Thornton and Buck quickly down the river.

"You can't pull me to Hans and Pete!" Thornton shouted to Buck. He caught a large rock and pushed Buck away. "Go Buck! Go! You have to get out of the river!"

Buck didn't want to leave his friend, but he slowly swam to Hans and Pete.

The two men pulled the wet dog out of the river. They had to help Thornton quickly, so they ran fast to a place above Thornton.

Then they put a rope around Buck and he quickly jumped

into the cold water again. But the water was too strong and it carried Buck past Thornton. Hans and Pete had to pull Buck out of the river again fast, before he hit the dangerous rocks. When they got Buck out of the water, he looked dead. There was a lot of water in his nose and mouth. Hans and Pete hit the water out of him, but he couldn't see very well.

"Help, help! I'm going down," shouted Thornton.

Buck heard his friend's cry and jumped up. He felt very bad, but he had to help Thornton. Hans, Pete, and Buck quickly ran back to the place above Thornton. They put the rope around Buck's neck again, and he jumped in.

The water was very strong and very cold, but Buck didn't stop. Buck swam to Thornton, and Thornton caught him around his neck. Hans and Pete pulled the rope very hard, and slowly Buck and Thornton moved nearer to them. But they went under the water many times, and they hit many hard rocks.

Then, suddenly, they were on the ground next to the river. They looked dead and they had a lot of cuts on them. Buck couldn't move and he couldn't open his eyes.

When Thornton woke up, he wanted to see Buck. He sat up and saw his beautiful dog on the ground near him.

"Is he dead?" he quickly asked Pete.

"No," Pete answered, "but he's in a lot of pain and he can't walk."

"OK," said Thornton quietly, "we can't go down this river now. We'll stay here. And when Buck's well, we'll take the boat down the river again."

After many weeks, Buck got better and they all went down the river to Dawson.

♦

That winter, at Dawson, Buck did another wonderful thing for Thornton.

Buck swam to Thornton.

Hans, Pete, and Thornton were in a bar, one afternoon, with other men.

Suddenly, one man said, "I have a very strong dog. I think he can pull a sledge with two hundred kilos of sugar on it!"

Another man, Matthewson, said, "Ha! That's nothing. My dog can pull a sledge with three hundred kilos of sugar on it."

"Now *that's* nothing," said Thornton. "My Buck can pull a sledge with four hundred and fifty kilos of sugar on it!"

"And walk a hundred meters with it?" asked Matthewson.

"Yes, and walk a hundred meters," answered Thornton coldly.

"Let's see this, and I'll give you a thousand dollars. Or you have to give *me* a thousand dollars. OK?" said Matthewson. He put a large bag of gold on the table. "And here it is. I have a sledge outside, now, and it has four hundred and fifty kilos of sugar on it."

Nobody spoke, and Thornton's face went very red.

"Oh no!" he thought. "Can Buck pull four hundred and fifty kilos of sugar?"

He looked at the faces around him. And then he saw an old friend, Jim O'Brien.

"Can you give me a thousand dollars?" he asked quietly.

"Yes, of course," answered his good friend.

Everybody walked quickly out of the bar. They were excited. They talked about Buck's test and about the money.

Thornton brought Buck to Matthewson's sledge, and put on his harness. Buck looked beautiful. He was young and strong. Thornton sat down next to Buck and put his arms around his neck. Then he put his hands on Buck's face and looked into his eyes.

"Do this for my love, Buck. Do this for me," he said quietly.

Then Thornton stood up and walked away from his dog.

"Now, Buck . . . GO!" he shouted.

Buck jumped up and pulled hard, but it was a very difficult job. Buck pulled and pulled. Nobody spoke. Slowly, the sledge began to move. It moved one centimeter, and then two centimeters. And then it started to move across the snow. Thornton walked behind the sledge and shouted, "That's it, Buck. You're a strong dog. You can do it. Go, go!"

Buck felt tired, but he didn't stop. Slowly, he walked to the end of the hundred meters. Everybody went crazy. They shouted and jumped. They were happy and excited. They talked about Buck, the most wonderful dog in Alaska.

Thornton sat down next to Buck and put his hands on Buck's head.

"I love you, you crazy, wonderful dog," he said happily.

Chapter 7   The Call of the Wild

When Buck walked past that hundred meter line, he showed his strong love for Thornton. But he also won a thousand dollars. And now the three men could begin a new trip. They wanted to go to new and strange places, in the East. They wanted to leave the towns and cities, and to find some gold.

When they said goodbye, their friends weren't happy. "Be careful!" their friends said. "You'll be in the wild for months, and it will be dangerous."

But Thornton, Hans, and Pete weren't afraid. With a sledge, some dogs, and guns, they could live anywhere in the wild. And they could live happily away from other people for a long time.

Month after month they walked. They went down new rivers and slept on new mountains. They felt strange, new winds. Every day they caught fish or small animals for food, and Buck loved this. He loved catching his food and he loved going to these new and exciting places.

One day, they found a road through the woods. But it began nowhere and ended nowhere. Another day, they found an old house in the middle of some trees. They found a gun and an old bed inside, but no people. They saw summer, fall, winter, and then spring again.

And at the end of their trip, they found a wonderful place between two small mountains. There was a small river, and at the bottom of this river the men could see gold.

The men worked hard, day after day. They took the gold from the bottom of the river and put it into large bags. And every day, they got richer and richer. But the dogs had no work, so Buck started to take long walks in the woods.

He didn't understand this new place, but he felt very happy. He started to feel something strange inside, and sometimes he could hear something. It called to him.

One night, he woke up suddenly. He could hear the call loudly, and it came from the woods. It was a long, sad howl and it didn't come from a dog.

Buck jumped up and ran through the camp into the woods. He walked slowly through the trees and, in an open place, he saw a wolf.

He walked slowly and carefully to the wolf. But the wolf was afraid of Buck and it quickly ran away. Buck ran after it and followed it through the trees. After an hour, the wolf understood. Buck didn't want to hurt him.

They started to play. Then they ran for a long time. Buck followed the wolf. He was very happy with his new wolf-brother.

They stopped at a river and had a drink. But when he saw the river, Buck remembered Thornton. He couldn't follow his new brother. He had to go back to the camp. So, he turned around and started to run back. But the wolf wasn't happy. For an hour, he cried and ran next to Buck. But Buck didn't stop. The wolf sat down and howled sadly. But Buck had to leave him.

When Buck saw Thornton in the camp, he quickly jumped on him. He played games with him.

"Where were you, you crazy dog?" laughed Thornton.

For two days and two nights, Buck never left the camp, and he was always near Thornton. He followed him everywhere. Buck was next to Thornton when he slept. He stayed with him when he ate. He watched him at work.

But then he heard the call in the woods again, and it was loud. Buck remembered his wild brother. He couldn't eat or sleep.

Buck started to walk through the woods again, and he tried to find his new brother. But he didn't hear his sad howl again.

Then Buck began to sleep in the woods at night, and he stayed away from the camp for two or three days.

He fished in the river for food, and one day he killed a large, dangerous animal. It was a long and difficult fight but Buck won. He could live in the wild now, and he was strong, young, and intelligent.

"Buck is the best dog in the world," said John Thornton one day to his friends. "Watch him walk."

"Yes, he really is a wonderful animal," said Pete.

"You know, you're right," said Hans.

Buck walked out of the camp.

But Thornton and his friends didn't see the new Buck when he got to the trees. In the woods, he wasn't a sledge dog. In the trees, he was a wild animal—quick and careful. He could catch and kill anything. He killed many times and he always ate the meat of the dead animals.

♦

The weather got colder, and moose started to come into Buck's woods. Buck killed a small moose, but he wanted to kill an older, larger animal. Then Buck found one. He was a very big, strong moose, and he was very angry. He was angry because he had a big arrow in his back. He cried angrily when he saw Buck.

Buck followed the old moose everywhere.

Buck followed the old moose everywhere. Many younger moose tried to attack Buck, but he was fast. They couldn't catch him. When night came, the younger moose had to move away from the trees. They couldn't help the old moose now, so they left him.

Hour after hour, and day after day, Buck followed the old moose. And when the moose tried to eat or drink, Buck attacked him. The moose got weaker and weaker because Buck was always there. At the end of the fourth day, Buck pulled the tired moose down to the ground.

For a day and a night, Buck stayed by the dead animal. He ate and slept. Then he went back to the camp, to his friend, Thornton.

Three kilometers from the camp, Buck began to feel very strange. Something was different and he didn't like it. So he started to run quickly and he stopped outside the camp. He couldn't hear any birds or the sounds of his friends.

Suddenly, he found Nig, his little doctor. Nig had a large arrow in his back, and he was dead. Then he found Hans. He was on the ground and he had arrows in his back. He didn't move—he was dead too.

Buck looked out from the trees. A loud, angry bark came from him, but he didn't hear it. For the last time in his life, he went crazy. He went crazy because of his love for Thornton.

Strange men danced in the middle of the camp. They heard the strange, loud bark. Then they saw a large, angry animal. It jumped at them from the trees. It was Buck, and he wanted to kill them.

He quickly killed the first man, but he didn't stop. He attacked them again and again, and the men couldn't stop him. They tried to kill him with their arrows. But he moved very quickly, so they couldn't catch him. They were afraid, and they ran into the woods.

But Buck hated them more than anything in the world, and he followed them. He killed two more men, but the others ran away.

Then Buck slowly walked back into the quiet camp and he found Pete. Pete was dead in his bed. Buck walked to the river of gold. It was red now. Skeet had his front legs and his head under the water.

And Thornton was also there, under the water. Buck couldn't see him, but he knew. John Thornton was dead.

Buck stayed next to the river all day.

Now he couldn't play with his friend or look into his eyes with love. Buck couldn't howl or cry. He felt a very bad pain inside, and it didn't go away.

But sometimes he looked away from the river and saw the dead Indians. They hurt him, and he killed them. Now he wasn't afraid of men, with their clubs and arrows. Buck felt strong and dangerous.

The sun went down and the sounds of night came to him. He walked to the center of the camp and listened. It was the call, and it was strong and beautiful. And for the first time, he was ready to answer it. Buck only loved one man—Thornton—and now he was dead. Now Buck didn't want the harness or the work of men. He never wanted to live with men again.

Suddenly, a lot of wolves ran into the camp. They stopped when they saw Buck. Buck was larger and stronger than they were. They were afraid.

Then one wolf jumped. But Buck attacked him and broke his thin neck easily.

Three more wolves tried to attack him. But Buck attacked their necks and faces, and they quickly fell back.

Then the other wolves ran at Buck and attacked him. But Buck was very strong and he fought well. They hurt him, but he didn't fall.

After half an hour, the wolves got tired and sat down. A thin, gray wolf carefully walked up to Buck, and he was friendly. It was Buck's wild brother from the woods, and Buck looked at him happily.

Then an old wolf stood in front of Buck and looked at Buck for a long time. He sat down and howled. Buck understood. The call was here, and he had to answer. So, Buck sat down and howled too.

The other wolves came to Buck and barked at him in a half-friendly way. Then the wolves jumped away and ran into the trees. And Buck ran with them, next to his wild brother. He answered the call of the wild.

◆

But the story of Buck doesn't end here. The Indians in the East began to talk about a strange dog. The dog lived with the wolves, but he wasn't a wolf. People were afraid of this dangerous dog. It took food from their houses and killed their dogs. Some people went out and never came back.

Every fall, these people followed the moose into the woods. But they never went to a place between two small mountains, with a river of gold in the middle. That place had a bad name, and people stayed away.

But there was one visitor to the place every summer. He was a great, beautiful wolf—but not a wolf. He came out of the green woods and went to the open place. He stopped next to the gold river and sat for a long time. Then he howled sadly, and left.

But in the long winter nights, he wasn't sad. He ran with his wild brothers, and he howled happily. He sang the song of the wild.

ACTIVITIES

Chapters 1–3

Before you read
1 Which do you like—hot weather or cold weather? Why?
2 Find the words in *italics* in your dictionary.
   a Which of these are words for sounds? When does a dog do these things?
      attack   bark   howl
   b Can you find these in the mountains, in a bank, or in a sports store?
      camp   gold   rocks   rope
   c Put the words below with these word families.
      head, arm, ...   hurt, cry, ...
      bed, sleep, ...   shirt, pants, ...
      woods, mountains, ...   kill, police, ...
      knife, gun, ...
      boots   club   law   neck   pain   rest   the wild
   d Find these in the picture on page 6.
      harness   sledge
   e Do you like *surprises*? How do you feel?

After you read
3 Answer these questions about the story.
   a Why are these people and things important?
      Manuel
      the man with the red shirt
      gold
   b Why does Buck hate Spitz?
   c What happens to Dolly? Why?
4 Discuss this question: Is Buck's life in the North better or worse than in California?

Chapters 4–5

Before you read
5 Will François and Perrault be angry with Buck, because he killed Spitz? Why (not)?

After you read

6 Answer these questions:
   a Why does Buck want Spitz's harness?
   b Dave knows he is very sick. So why does he want to stay in his harness?
   c What happens to Dave behind the trees?
   d Why do Charles, Mercedes, and Hal fight every day?
   e Why does John Thornton want to help Buck?

Chapters 6–7

Before you read

7 Buck has a friend now—John Thornton. Will his new life be easy? What do you think?
8 Find the words in *italics* in your dictionary. Are the sentences right or wrong?
   a A *wolf* is a wild animal. It lives in the woods.
   b A *moose* is a small animal. You can find it under the floors of houses.
   c An *arrow* can kill a person or an animal.

After you read

9 Discuss these questions.
   a What happens to "Black" Barton? Why?
   b What is "the call of the wild"?
   c Is Buck happy at the end of the story?

Writing

10 How is life different for Buck with the family in California and at work in the North?
11 You work for a newspaper. Your company sent you to the North. Write a letter to your boss. Tell him about life and work there. Is it easy/difficult? Why? Would you like to live there? Why (not)?
12 You are John Thornton. Write about your friend Buck. Why do you like him? Do you really understand him?

13 Tell the end of the story through the eyes of the wolf, Buck's wild brother. How did you meet Buck? How did you feel about him? What happened later?

The Last of the Mohicans

JAMES FENIMORE COOPER

Level 2

Retold by Coleen Degnan-Veness
Series Editors: Andy Hopkins and Jocelyn Potter

Contents

		page
Introduction		181
Chapter 1	The Trip Begins	183
Chapter 2	Their First Mistake	184
Chapter 3	By Canoe up the River	186
Chapter 4	The Hurons Attack	189
Chapter 5	Cora's Plan	191
Chapter 6	War Cries	192
Chapter 7	Magua Remembers	195
Chapter 8	Ready to Die	197
Chapter 9	The End is Near	198
Chapter 10	Win or Lose	201
Chapter 11	A Father's Story	202
Chapter 12	The Fight Ends	205
Chapter 13	Follow and Hope	209
Chapter 14	Strange Changes	210
Chapter 15	Love and Hate	216
Activities		221

Introduction

"My son will die one day. Then there will be nobody with Mohican blood. My son is the last of the Mohicans."

Uncas, the last of the Mohican Indians, is with his father and their white friend Hawkeye when they meet Major Heyward and the two young daughters of a British colonel. Magua, a Huron Indian, is also in the woods, and he hates the British. Will the girls see their father again? And can anything save the men?

James Fenimore Cooper (1789–1851) wrote his first book, *Precaution* (1820), at the age of thirty. He wanted to write better books than the English wrote at that time. Later, he wrote the six "Leatherstocking Tales," about Indians and white men. *The Last of the Mohicans* (1826) was the fifth of these six books.

Hawkeye is in each story. In the other books, his name is Natty Bumpo. He cannot live with his people, so he lives in the woods with the Indians. But, he is not an Indian. He is a great fighter and a good friend of the Mohicans.

In *The Last of the Mohicans*, Cooper writes about the fight between the French and the British in North America in 1757. The story is also about the fight between white men and Indians. Cooper wanted women to like his books, so he wrote about love too. Some things in the story did not really happen, but that was not important. Cooper wanted the reader to enjoy a good story. He is one of America's most famous writers.

Chapter 1   The Trip Begins

In 1757, a lot of North America was wild country and the thick woods were often dangerous. Indians fought other Indians. Indians fought white men. The French fought the British because they wanted this country for France. Some Indians helped the British and other Indians helped the French.

The British Colonel Munro and his men were at Fort William Henry, and the Frenchman, Montcalm, and his men were near the fort. The Colonel couldn't fight Montcalm without more men, so he asked General Webb, in the north of the country, for help. Webb sent 5,000 men from Fort Edward. Colonel Munro waited for them, and he also waited for his daughters.

♦

Colonel Munro's daughters, Cora and Alice, arrived at Fort Edward from Scotland. They wanted to visit their father at Fort William Henry.

General Webb told Major Duncan Heyward, "Take the girls to their father. Don't follow the men—it's too dangerous. This Indian will show you the way."

The Indian's name was Magua.

Alice Munro looked at the Indian and his knife.

"I don't like him," she said.

"Don't be afraid. He's a friend," Major Duncan Heyward told her.

"Speak to him," said Alice. "I want to hear his English."

"He doesn't speak English, or he doesn't try," said Major Heyward.

Magua said nothing. He turned and walked away.

"Let's follow him," said Heyward to Munro's two daughters. "Only he can show us the best way to Fort William Henry."

"Cora, what do you think?" Alice asked her older sister.

But Heyward answered, "The French are more dangerous than the Indians. With Magua we will be safe from them. They don't know his way to your father's fort."

They left Fort Edward. The 1,500 men went by road, but Heyward and the two young women followed Magua through the woods.

◆

On that same day, two men sat in the woods next to the Hudson River. They talked in the language of the Mohicans. The white man wore clothes of animal skins. The other man was the Mohican Indian chief, Chingachgook.

"My tribe is the grandfather of all tribes," said Chingachgook. "The Dutch came here and they gave my people fire-water. My people were stupid and they drank it. They couldn't think. They gave our home to the Dutch. Now I am the chief, but I live in these woods. I see the sun only through the trees. I cannot visit the home of my grandfathers."

Hawkeye, the white man, listened and felt sad for his friend.

"My son will die one day. Then there will be nobody with Mohican blood," said the Indian. "My son is the last of the Mohicans."

Chapter 2 Their First Mistake

A sudden noise ended the conversation between Chingachgook and Hawkeye.

They looked up. Uncas, the chief's son, was there.

"Are there Hurons in these woods?" Chingachgook asked him.

"Yes, I think there are about ten," Uncas answered. "They are working for Montcalm and his men."

"My son is the last of the Mohicans."

Chingachgook said to Hawkeye, "We will find them and we will send them out of the woods."

Then the Indian chief put his ear to the ground and listened. He heard white men.

"Hawkeye, they are your brothers. Speak to them."

Then Hawkeye could hear them too.

"Who's there?" he called. He put his gun across his left arm.

"We are friends. We're British," a man answered in English.

"Where are you going?" asked Hawkeye.

"To Fort William Henry. Do you know the way?" asked Major Duncan Heyward.

Hawkeye looked at Magua and laughed. "Did your Huron show you the wrong way? You want a Mohican in these woods. I can show you the right way, but it's an hour's walk from here. It will be night before that. We'll go in the morning."

Heyward looked at Magua and thought, "He's a Huron! He wants Montcalm's men and the other Hurons to find us. They'll kill us!"

Magua saw Heyward's face and understood. He shouted loudly and ran into the woods. Uncas shouted too and started to run after him. Suddenly, there was a loud noise. Hawkeye shot the Huron, but he didn't kill him. Magua ran away.

"We have to leave here," said Hawkeye. "That Huron will bring Montcalm's men here and they'll kill us."

Chapter 3   By Canoe up the River

"We'll help you," Hawkeye told Major Heyward. "We'll take you and the two girls up the river to Fort William Henry in our canoe."

They left the horses and walked down to the river. The canoe was under some trees.

The canoe was under some trees.

Hawkeye told them, "Sit at the front of the canoe. The Indians will go on foot."

He sat at the back, then he pushed the canoe into the Hudson River. The river was wide, fast, and dangerous, and the canoe moved very quickly. Cora and her younger sister were afraid.

"We're going to die in this river," they thought.

Then Hawkeye stopped the canoe and they got out. The two Indians were there.

"Follow us," said the Mohicans.

They took Heyward, Cora, and Alice into a cave.

Inside the cave, the two girls felt safe. The men made a fire. Major Heyward looked at Hawkeye's strange clothes and big gun. He was a very strong man. Then Heyward looked at the young Mohican. Uncas had strong arms and black eyes. He didn't have much hair—only a little on the top of his head.

Alice looked at Uncas too. He looked kind. She said to Heyward, "I'm not afraid now because Uncas is here with us."

"Let's hope that he'll be our friend," said Heyward.

"We can eat now," said Hawkeye.

Uncas gave the girls some food. He spoke a little English to them. When he gave food to Cora, his eyes stayed on her face. He looked at her long black hair and her dark eyes. Her sister, Alice, was younger and very different. She had very light hair. Uncas liked the darker girl, Cora.

Suddenly, a Huron shouted loudly and angrily from the woods. Heyward looked at Alice. She was young, very pretty, and afraid. They heard the Indian shout again.

"Will they find us here?" the girls asked.

Then it was quiet. They listened for a long time, but there were no more sounds. The girls went to sleep. But Hawkeye and the Mohicans didn't sleep. They watched and listened.

Chapter 4 The Hurons Attack

Before morning, Hawkeye said to Major Heyward, "Wake up. We have to go. We'll go up the river in the canoe."

"Cora, Alice, wake up!" called Heyward.

Suddenly, Hurons started to shoot at them from across the river. Hawkeye shot back and killed one of the Hurons.

"They will really want us to die now," said Hawkeye.

Major Heyward said to the girls, "Follow me. You'll be safe in here."

The girls followed him to the back of the cave. It was difficult because it was dark inside.

Then Heyward went back to Hawkeye and the Mohicans. They listened, watched, and waited.

"Maybe they won't come back," said Heyward.

"You don't know the Hurons. We killed one of their men. They won't stop now," said Hawkeye.

Then they saw the heads of five Hurons in the river.

"They're coming for us," said Heyward.

But the river was fast and dangerous. There was a waterfall, and it took one of the Hurons down with it.

Then the four other Hurons climbed up the cliff above the waterfall. Hawkeye shot the nearest man.

"Take my knife! Get that one!" Hawkeye said to Uncas.

Hawkeye shot again and killed the biggest one. Heyward fought one Huron with his hands. But the Huron fought hard and Heyward was afraid. Suddenly, a dark hand with a knife cut the Indian's arm and then pulled Heyward back. The Huron fell a long way down into the river.

The four Hurons were dead. Uncas shouted happily. Then he, Heyward, and Hawkeye ran quickly behind some trees. Chingachgook was there.

Suddenly, a dark hand with a knife cut the Indian's arm and then pulled Heyward back.

Chapter 5 Cora's Plan

The Hurons across the river fired their guns, and Uncas, Chingachgook, and Hawkeye fired back.

Cora came out of the cave.

She said, "Thank you for your help, but I don't want you to die for me and my sister. Go to my father. He has to help us. He has to send more men!"

"We cannot walk away and leave two young women in this dangerous place," said Hawkeye.

But he and Chingachgook spoke in the Mohican language. Then, in English, Chingachgook said, "Yes, good."

He took his knife and tomahawk. Then he jumped into the river and started to swim away.

Hawkeye followed him.

Cora looked at Uncas and said, "Aren't you going to follow them?"

"Uncas will stay," the young Mohican answered in English.

"You have to go to my father. I want you to go," she said.

Uncas looked sadly at Cora's beautiful face. But he jumped into the river and followed his friend and his father.

Cora turned to Major Heyward. "Please go with them," she said.

Heyward looked at the beautiful Alice and she put her hand on his arm. She was young and afraid.

"I will stay," he said.

Chapter 6 War Cries

Cora, Alice, and Heyward went into the cave. They sat and talked. They began to feel happier. Then suddenly, they heard war cries. The Hurons again!

"We'll die now. They're coming nearer the cave!" said Cora.

An Indian shouted, "Hawkeye!" and then more Indians began to shout Hawkeye's name.

They hated him and they wanted to kill him. They looked for him everywhere, but they couldn't find him. Then it was strangely quiet again.

"They went away," Heyward said quietly to Cora. "Alice, we're safe!"

Alice said happily, "We'll see our father. We won't die!"

Then her face changed. Her blue eyes opened wide.

Heyward looked up and saw the angry, dark face of Magua outside of the cave. He took out his gun and fired. The noise inside the cave was very loud. There was a lot of smoke from the gun and for a minute Heyward couldn't see. Magua turned around quickly and ran away.

There was no sound in the woods for two or three minutes. Then, suddenly, loud war cries came from Magua and the other Hurons.

The Indians ran quickly into the cave and they angrily pulled the two girls and Heyward outside. Cora, Alice, and Heyward stood there with the Hurons around them. Then, the Indians smiled. They had the white man and they had the daughters of the British Colonel Munro.

Some of the Indians went back into the cave. They looked for Hawkeye, but he wasn't there.

"Where is Hawkeye?" Magua angrily asked Heyward.

Heyward answered, "He's not here."

Then suddenly, they heard war cries.

"Wait! Do not scalp her!" he said.

"Tell us. Where is he? Is he dead?" asked Magua.

"He isn't dead. He went away," answered Heyward.

"Is he a bird? Can he fly away? Or is he a fish? Can he swim up the river? The Hurons are not stupid," said Magua angrily.

"He's not a fish, but he can swim. He swam down the river, but you didn't see him," answered Heyward. Heyward was angry and not really afraid.

"Why did you stay?" Magua asked. "Do you want to lose your life?"

"A white man doesn't leave women," answered Heyward.

"And where are Chingachgook and Uncas? Did they swim down the river too?" asked Magua.

"Yes," he answered.

The Hurons watched this conversation and waited. Then Heyward finished and Magua repeated it in their language. They shouted angrily. Then they looked with wild and angry eyes at the girls and Heyward.

Chapter 7 Magua Remembers

A dark hand suddenly pulled Alice's long hair. Heyward wanted to stop the young Indian. He pulled out his knife, but an older Indian stopped the younger man.

"Wait! Do not scalp her!" he said. He turned to Heyward and the girls. "Go!" he said.

The Indians took them down to the river, and they got into a canoe.

It was again a dangerous trip down the fast river, but the Hurons knew the river well. Then they got out of the canoe and walked for a long time through the thick woods. At night they stopped. A young Huron killed an animal and they sat down and ate.

Then Magua said to Heyward, "Go to the girl with dark hair. I want to speak to her. Bring her here."

Heyward brought Cora to him and then left her.

She asked, "What does the Huron want to say?" She looked strong and not afraid of the great fighter.

Magua took her arm, but she pulled it away.

"I was born a chief in the Huron tribe," he said. "I did not see a white man before I was twenty years old. Then the white man came. He gave me fire-water. It made me stupid. The Hurons did not want me in their tribe, so I went south through the woods. This Huron chief had to go and live with a different tribe," he said angrily. "Your people did this to me!"

"So, you hate me too?" she asked quietly.

"No," he answered, "you are different."

"Then what do you want?" she asked.

"Later, I fought for the British. I worked for your father. Then again, white men gave me fire-water. Again I was stupid. I was not Magua. The fire-water spoke, not me. Munro, your father, was angry and, in front of his men, he hit me many times."

Cora said nothing.

"See!" said Magua, and he showed her his back. "A Huron does not forget."

She didn't look away from his back, but she slowly closed her eyes—she felt sick.

Cora said quietly, "An Indian can forget. You can be a good man. Take me and my sister to our father."

"No," answered Magua.

"What do you want?" she asked.

"I want good for good and bad for bad," said Magua with a smile.

"You will kill us because my father hit you? Take me, but not my sister. Kill only me."

"No," said Magua. "Come with me. Live with me and be my wife."

Cora's eyes opened wide.

"But, why? You don't love me. You don't want a white woman," she said.

"I want you to cook for me and to bring my water. I want you to work in my home. Munro will sleep with his guns. His daughter will sleep with me."

Cora was very angry.

"You're an animal!" she shouted at him.

He smiled and walked away to the other Indians. Cora walked back to Alice and Heyward. She was angry and unhappy.

"What did he want?" asked Heyward.

"Tell us," said Alice.

Cora put her arms around Alice and said, "Wait and see."

Magua spoke to the Hurons about white men and the home of their grandfathers. He spoke of the great fighters of his tribe and of Hawkeye. Hawkeye's gun killed some of their great fighters, so he talked about the wives and children of those men. Magua's heart was full of hate and his tribe felt this hate also.

"We will scalp more white men!" they shouted.

They were excited and angry and they wanted to kill. They pulled out their knives and tomahawks and ran to Heyward, Cora, and Alice. Heyward quickly jumped in front of the girls. He wanted to stop the Indians, but they pulled him away.

Chapter 8   Ready to Die

Magua shouted, "Do not scalp him. Make a fire! We will put them in it!"

The Indians broke wood from the trees. They were excited.

Magua looked at the daughters of Colonel Munro. Alice looked to Heyward for help. Heyward looked at her, but he couldn't save her.

"The daughter of Munro is better than me? She does not want to live with me? She wants to die?" Magua said quietly to Cora.

"What does he mean?" asked Heyward angrily.

"Nothing," answered Cora. "He's an animal."

Magua said to Cora, "I can send the younger girl to her father. Will you follow Magua? Look! The young girl is crying. She does not want to die! Send her to her father."

"What did he say?" asked Alice. "Can I go to Father?"

"You and Heyward can go to Father. But I . . . I have to go with him! I have to be his wife! What can I do, Alice? Heyward, please tell me," Cora shouted.

"You will not go with Magua!" shouted Heyward.

"What do you think, Alice?" Cora asked her sister.

There was no answer. Alice was quiet.

Then she shouted, "We will die!"

"Then die!" shouted Magua.

He threw his tomahawk and it cut off some of Alice's yellow hair. But it stopped in the tree above her head. Her hair fell to the ground.

An Indian held up his tomahawk. He wanted to scalp Alice. Heyward jumped on him and they fell. The Indian was on top of Heyward and his tomahawk was ready. Suddenly, there was a loud noise from a gun. The Indian's eyes opened wildly and he fell dead on the ground next to Heyward.

Chapter 9   The End is Near

Uncas, Chingachgook, and Hawkeye ran out from behind the trees and attacked the Hurons. They, with Heyward, fought hard. They killed five men with their knives and tomahawks. Then Uncas and Magua fought, and Uncas's knife cut the Huron. Magua fell.

"He's dead!" said Hawkeye.

Uncas, Chingachgook, and Hawkeye ran out from behind the trees and attacked the Hurons.

But suddenly, Magua jumped up and ran into the woods.

"He's only one man—he can go. We won't stop him now," said Hawkeye.

"You saved us," the two girls cried. "Thank you, thank you!"

Uncas and Heyward looked at the two sisters and they felt happy.

"How did you find us?" Heyward asked Hawkeye, a little later.

"We didn't go a long way down the river. We couldn't leave you, so we watched from across the river."

"Did you see everything?" asked Heyward.

"No, but we heard," answered Hawkeye. "We have to go north now. We have to find Fort William Henry. Let's go! It's dangerous here and more Hurons will come."

Heyward, Alice, Cora, Hawkeye, Chingachgook, and Uncas went quickly through the woods. The sisters were very quiet and afraid. Everybody was tired, but they got to the top of the mountain and looked down. From there they saw Fort William Henry, and across the river were Montcalm's men—about 10,000 of them.

"There's your father's fort," said Hawkeye.

"Let's go to him!" said Cora.

"You aren't afraid to die?" asked Hawkeye. "The French and the Hurons will kill us."

They went slowly down the mountain. The weather was very bad and they couldn't see much.

At the bottom of the mountain, they stopped. Hawkeye and the Mohicans left the woods and looked around. They came back quickly.

"We can't walk through there," said Hawkeye.

"Can we walk around them?" asked Heyward.

"I think we can. Let's go," answered Hawkeye.

Suddenly, somebody shouted in French, "Who's there? Stop!" and guns fired at them.

Hawkeye fired back and the French shot again. Men shouted in French. Indians shouted too.

"Run to the fort!" shouted Hawkeye.

Uncas took Cora's arm, and they ran to the fort. The French ran after them.

Then suddenly, they heard a shout, "Wait! Fire when you can see!" It was Colonel Munro!

"Father, Father! It is me—Alice! Save your daughters!"

"Wait! Is that really my daughter?" asked Munro.

His daughters ran to him. The old Colonel put his arms around them and cried.

Chapter 10 Win or Lose

For five days the French attacked the British at Fort William Henry. General Webb's men didn't come. It was too dangerous. Hawkeye went to Fort Edward and spoke to General Webb. But Colonel Munro's men had to fight without them.

Hawkeye's trip back to Fort William Henry from Fort Edward ended suddenly when the French caught him. He had with him a letter from General Webb for Colonel Munro, and the French took it from him.

On the fifth day, Major Heyward went to Colonel Munro.

"It's very dangerous here and our men are tired," he told the Colonel.

Colonel Munro said, "Montcalm wants to talk to me, but I'm going to send you in my place."

So the fighting stopped and Major Heyward went to meet Montcalm. The Frenchman was with three of his men and the chiefs of some Indian tribes. Heyward stopped suddenly when he saw Magua. But then he turned to Montcalm.

"Let's talk," said Montcalm in French, "but I do not speak English."

"I speak a little French," said Major Heyward.

"Good. Your men fight well, but they are very tired," said Montcalm. "I understand that Munro's two daughters are in the fort now."

"They're not afraid. The older daughter can fight too," said Heyward.

"I have more men than you. I have these Indians and they want to attack the British. Don't you want to save lives now?"

"We have more men than you think," answered Heyward.

He wanted to know about General Webb's letter, so he asked Montcalm some questions. But Montcalm didn't tell him anything. The two men said goodbye, and Major Heyward went back to the fort.

Chapter 11 A Father's Story

Colonel Munro was with his daughters.

"Major Heyward!" said Alice, happily.

"Pretty young women in this fort! What will happen next!" laughed the happy father. "Go outside, girls. The men have to talk."

When the girls left, Colonel Munro said, "They're very good girls."

"Yes, they are, sir," answered Heyward. He was happy because Munro liked him. But he wanted to talk about Montcalm.

"Montcalm said . . ." he began.

"That Frenchman and his men can go to . . ." Munro stopped. "He's not the Colonel of Fort William Henry, and he never will be! Webb and his men will arrive and we'll win!" he said loudly. Then, the older man changed the conversation. "Your parents and I are old friends. When I see you look at my daughters, I know a young man's heart."

"Your daughters are wonderful young women, sir. I would like to marry one of them," answered Heyward.

"I would like to marry one of them," answered Heyward.

"Cora is a very intelligent girl, and . . ." said Munro.

"Cora?" said Heyward, "I . . . I . . ."

"Aren't we talking about Cora?" asked Munro.

"No, sir, I'm talking about your other daughter!"

"Alice?" asked Munro.

"Yes, sir."

Munro walked up and down the room for some minutes. Then he said, "Sit down and I'll tell you about my life."

Heyward sat down.

"I was a young man too. I loved a young woman, and I wanted to marry her. But her father said no, so I left Scotland. I fought for my country in other places. I went to the West Indies and I married a woman there. She was Cora's mother. Cora's grandfather was rich, but his wife's family had no money. They worked for rich people and they worked hard. Many white people, many British people, dislike these people. It makes a father angry! And do you too think that Cora is different? Do you dislike the color of her skin?" asked Munro.

"I'm sorry, sir, but . . .," said the young man. He looked down at the floor.

"Your blood is too good for her blood? My daughter is a good woman!" said Munro angrily.

"But Alice is a good woman too, sir."

"Yes, you're right," said the old man. "When I look at her, I remember her mother. My wife died, and I went back to Scotland. There I met the first woman again. It was twenty years later. She waited twenty years, and then she married me. She was Alice's mother. But after Alice was born, her mother died," said Munro. His face looked very old and very sad.

After a minute or two, he stood up and his face changed. "What did Montcalm say to you?"

"He wants to meet you, sir," answered Major Heyward.

"Go to Montcalm, Heyward. Colonel Munro will meet him. Tell him that. But speak to the men, Heyward. They'll have to watch and be ready. We have to be very careful with the French," said the Colonel.

Chapter 12 The Fight Ends

Montcalm and Munro met. Montcalm spoke first.

"Good day," said the Frenchman. "I will speak in French because Major Heyward can speak French and English."

Montcalm looked at his men. They came closer to him. Munro and Heyward saw the dark faces of Indians in the woods.

Montcalm started, "We can fight you and kill you. Or we can stop now. I have many men."

"Yes, you have many men," said Munro, "but we have many men too."

"But they aren't here," answered Montcalm.

He gave Munro General Webb's letter and Munro read it. His face changed suddenly.

The letter said, "I cannot send any men to you. Give Fort William Henry to the French."

Montcalm said, "You have to go. Take your men and guns. Take everything back to England. Write your name on this paper, and then we won't fight again. The French and the British will be friends."

Munro and Montcalm wrote their names on the paper. Then, the old Colonel went back to his fort.

Sadly, he told his men, "We have to leave Fort William Henry in the morning."

The next morning, Munro and his men left the fort. There were 3,000 men, but they were quiet. Some were sick and they walked slowly behind the other men. There were some women and children and they walked behind the sick men. Munro looked tired and old.

"Your father wants to walk with his men," Heyward told Cora. "You and your sister have to go on the horses."

"I'll walk," Cora said.

"But Alice isn't as strong as you, Cora," said Heyward.

"Yes, you're right," she said sadly. Her eyes were red.

"I have to walk with the men. David Gamut will go with you and Alice. You'll be safe with him," said Heyward.

David Gamut was a singer in the church and a music teacher. Cora and Alice liked him because he was a good man.

The French arrived at the fort and they quietly watched the British men, women, and children. The British walked out of the fort and down the road.

Suddenly, about 100 Indians came quietly out of the woods. Cora looked up. She saw Magua! There was hate in his eyes, but he didn't move. Then suddenly, he made the famous Indian war cry.

More than 2,000 wild and angry Indians ran out of the woods with knives and tomahawks! In minutes, hundreds of men, women, and children were dead on the ground and their blood was everywhere. Some Indians drank it.

The British fought back, but the attack was very sudden. Munro quickly got on a horse because he wanted Montcalm. Only Montcalm could stop the Hurons.

Magua's dark eyes looked everywhere for Colonel Munro. He wanted to scalp him this time!

Munro went past his daughters on his horse.

Alice cried loudly, "Father! We're here! Come to us, Father, or we'll die!"

Munro looked at his daughters, but he couldn't stop.

Alice fell to the ground.

Gamut said, "We have to go! Come with me!"

"You can't save us," cried Cora.

Gamut began to sing. An Indian came up behind them and held up his knife. He wanted to scalp Gamut and the girls. But he heard Gamut's song and stopped.

"This man is not afraid," thought the Indian. "I will not kill him now. I will come back for him later." He ran away.

Then suddenly, Magua was there.

"Come," he said. He took Cora's arm. "You don't have to die. You can come and live with me now!"

Magua's hands were red with blood.

"I hate you!" shouted Cora.

"Magua is a great chief!" he shouted angrily. "Will you go to his tribe?"

"Never! You can kill me!" cried Cora.

Suddenly, Magua took Alice in his arms and carried her into the woods. Cora ran after Magua, and Gamut ran after her. He didn't stop singing.

The other Indians didn't stop them.

They thought, "This strange man is not really a man. He can save white women with his song."

In the woods, Cora found Magua and Alice. Magua put the two girls on a horse and Cora put her arms around Alice. Magua took them through the woods and Gamut followed. At the top of the mountain, they stopped.

"Look!" said Magua.

The girls looked down. There were about 1,500 dead men on the ground. Other men waited to die. The Hurons shouted loudly and wildly.

Gamut ran after her. He didn't stop singing.

Chapter 13   Follow and Hope

Munro went back to the place of the great fight. He was with Heyward, Hawkeye, Chingachgook, and Uncas. It was quiet now. They walked around the dead men, and they felt sick.

"Are my daughters here?" asked the Colonel.

Uncas looked at the people on the ground and found some dead women.

"Come. Look here," called Uncas. He didn't want to look. He didn't want to find Cora.

Heyward and Munro looked at the women in a pool of blood. But they didn't find Cora or Alice.

"Maybe they're not dead," they hoped.

Suddenly, Uncas called again. There was a green bag near a tree in the woods. It was Cora's bag.

"My child!" said Munro. He spoke quickly and wildly. "Give me my child!"

"Uncas will try," said the young Mohican.

Hawkeye looked at the ground.

"Uncas, look!" he said. "Cora ran into the woods. Maybe we can follow them. An Indian's eyes can see everything."

They ran as fast as they could into the woods.

"Look here, on the ground," said Uncas.

"What is it?" asked Hawkeye.

"Somebody walked here, and this was not a white man's shoe," Uncas said. He looked very carefully.

"What do you think, Uncas? Who was it?" asked Munro.

"Magua," answered Uncas.

"Magua! One day my gun will stop him," said Hawkeye angrily.

"I hope you're right," said Munro.

"Let's follow him!" said Uncas.

The great woods and mountains were wild. The Mohicans knew these woods very well, but they were dangerous. At night, the men stopped and lighted a fire. Then they slept.

In the early morning they started again. To the Mohicans, the woods were a map, and they could read every tree and every change in the ground. Hawkeye and Munro followed and watched the chief and his son.

Uncas said, "The singer has long legs. Look! He walked here."

"Were my daughters here too?" asked Munro.

"Magua is not very intelligent, but he is not stupid," answered Uncas. "Maybe your daughters followed behind the singer, or maybe the men carried them."

They went slowly and carefully.

Then they stopped because they saw a man near a river.

Hawkeye walked to him and asked quietly, "Sir, are you teaching the animals to sing?"

"They can sing," answered Gamut.

Chapter 14 Strange Changes

"Where are the girls?" Hawkeye asked the singer quickly.

"They're with the Hurons," answered Gamut.

"Are they safe?" asked Munro.

"Yes. They're tired and unhappy, but they're well," said Gamut.

"Where's Magua?" Munro asked.

"He's in the woods. He's shooting animals for food."

"Why are you here?" Hawkeye asked.

"To the Hurons, I'm strange. I'm not a man. So, I can come and go. They don't stop me," said Gamut.

"Why don't you run away?"

"The girls are here. I have to stay here with them," answered Gamut.

"The singer has long legs. Look! He walked here."

"Go to them quietly. Give them hope. We will save them!" said their father.

"I'll go," said Gamut.

"I'll go too," said Heyward.

"Do you want to die?" asked Hawkeye.

"I love Alice and I have to save her!"

Then Hawkeye said to Heyward, "We'll put red and blue colors on your face. The Hurons will laugh. They'll think you're funny. You can go to the girls, but be careful."

Chingachgook carefully put the colors on Heyward's face. The young man had a funny, crazy face and a big smile.

Chingachgook said, "They will not know you. Go—and do not be afraid."

"Go now," said Hawkeye, "but be careful. This is a very dangerous plan, but maybe you'll save the girls."

"I'm not afraid," said Heyward, and they left.

The Indian children saw Heyward and Gamut first. They shouted and laughed. More Indians came and looked at them. They laughed too. The two men walked to the fires. The chiefs waited for them. They looked at Heyward carefully.

Then suddenly, there was a loud cry from the woods. Everybody ran and looked. Two Hurons came out of the woods. They held the arms of a man.

A Huron shouted something, but Heyward didn't understand it. Every Huron man, woman, and child began to shout and run wildly. They had knives and tomahawks in their hands.

The man suddenly pushed the two Hurons hard. He jumped and ran away. He ran faster than a man. A wild animal couldn't run faster. The Hurons couldn't catch him. Then the man stopped high above them, near Heyward, next to a tree. Heyward saw his face for the first time. It was Uncas!

Then one of the Hurons came from behind and quickly caught Uncas by the arm. He took him to the chiefs.

Chingachgook carefully put the colors on Heyward's face.

"You are a young Mohican, but you are a man," said an old chief with gray hair. "Two of my men are following your friend. They will catch him and bring him here."

"Do Hurons have no ears? Didn't you hear my friend's gun fire two times? Your men will never come back!" shouted Uncas.

"You can sleep tonight. Tomorrow we will speak for the last time," said the Huron chief. Then he left.

Heyward carefully went to Uncas, and said very quietly, "Where are your father and Colonel Munro?"

"They are safe. Hawkeye's gun does not sleep," said Uncas very quickly and quietly. "Go now. We cannot talk. I do not know you."

Heyward and Gamut left because they wanted to find the girls. The fires slowly died, and nobody stopped them. They suddenly saw the face of Magua, but Magua didn't see them.

Heyward and Gamut moved quietly. They found a cave and went carefully inside it. There, they saw Cora and Alice.

"It's me—Major Heyward. I'll save you!" Heyward said quietly.

The happy minute came to a sudden end when Magua stood behind Heyward and Gamut.

Then, they heard the noise of an angry animal. There was a wild animal behind Magua!

Magua looked at it and laughed. "Go away, you stupid thing! Go to the children and women. Men have to talk."

The wild animal was not really an animal. It was a man in an animal's skin and Magua knew this. Sometimes Indians wore the skins of animals, and did strange things. So Magua wasn't afraid.

Suddenly, the animal caught Magua in his strong arms. Magua couldn't move. The animal hit him on the head and he fell to the ground.

Then the man took off the animal's head and showed his face. It was Hawkeye!

Heyward, Alice, Cora, and Gamut were very happy.

"We have to go quickly!" said Hawkeye to his friends. "Put

Suddenly, the animal caught Magua in his strong arms.

Alice and Cora in these bags and we'll carry them. The Hurons won't stop us."

Heyward and Hawkeye carried the girls into the woods. There the girls got out and walked.

"Where's my friend, Uncas?" Hawkeye asked. "Can you take me to him?"

"It's very dangerous," said Gamut, "but I can."

"Wait for us. We'll come back for you," Hawkeye said to Heyward and the girls.

Uncas was in a cave. There was nobody with him.

Hawkeye, in the animal skin, and Gamut went to Uncas very quietly.

"Take this," said Hawkeye, and he gave Uncas a knife.

"Hawkeye!" said Uncas happily.

Quietly and carefully they left the cave and went back to Heyward.

Chapter 15   Love and Hate

Suddenly, they heard the loud war cry of the Hurons. The young Mohican was not in his cave, and they were very angry.

Inside the cave, Magua woke up. He wasn't dead! He ran to the Huron chief.

"They will not run away this time. Magua will find them, and they will die!" Magua shouted angrily.

The Hurons ran wildly into the woods. Hawkeye, Uncas, Heyward, Gamut, Cora, and Alice couldn't find a safe place this time. There was no hope. They could hear the Hurons. The Indians came nearer and nearer.

Suddenly, there was the dark face of Magua again. There were Hurons all around them, and this time Hawkeye didn't have his gun.

Magua took Cora's arm and pulled her away.

"She is mine!" said Magua. He looked into Uncas's eyes

He looked into Uncas's eyes and shouted, "Mohican, you know she is mine!"

and shouted, "Mohican, you know she is mine!"

"Please stop. We can give you money. Your tribe will be rich! Don't take the girl!" cried Heyward.

"Magua does not want white men's money!" the Huron shouted.

"Leave the girl," said Hawkeye. "Take me, Magua!"

Hawkeye looked at Uncas and said, "I loved you and your father. Our skins are not the same color, but we're brothers. You'll find my gun under the tree. Take it and remember me." Then he turned to Magua and said, "I'll go with you now."

"No," answered Magua. "I want the girl!" To the Hurons he said, "The other people can go. I want Cora!"

Alice cried and held Heyward's arm.

"Thank you, Hawkeye. You wanted to give your life for me. Thank you," said Cora. She looked at her sister and said to Heyward, "Love her and make her happy. She is a good person."

Cora put her arms around Alice. Then she turned to Magua and said, "Go. I will follow."

Magua and Cora walked away. The Hurons watched.

Suddenly, the great fighter, Uncas, jumped up and ran after Cora.

"Stop!" he shouted.

Cora turned around and looked at him. She shouted at Magua, "I will not go with you!"

Magua looked at Uncas, then at Cora, and said angrily, "Woman, live with me or die!"

Cora looked at Uncas and cried, "I will die!"

Magua pulled out his knife, but he couldn't kill her. So another Huron ran quickly to Cora with his knife in his hand and killed her.

Uncas ran to Cora and fought Magua. Hawkeye ran to his friend, but it was too late. Uncas's blood was on Magua's knife. Uncas was on the ground, dead.

Magua looked at Hawkeye and laughed. "White men are dogs! Mohicans are women!" he shouted.

He jumped to the top of a cliff on the side of a mountain. Then he jumped again, but this time he fell. He fell off the cliff and died.

Hawkeye carried Uncas in his arms and Heyward carried Cora. Gamut helped Alice through the woods. They found Chingachgook and Colonel Munro.

Hawkeye took Chingachgook's hand and said, "I have no family. He was your son and your blood was nearer to his blood. But I will never forget my brother Uncas."

ACTIVITIES

Chapters 1–3

Before you read

1 Find these words in your dictionary. They are all in the story.
   blood   canoe   cave   chief   colonel   fort   general   major
   safe   skin   tribe
   a Which are words for places?
   b Which is higher, a colonel or a major?
   c Which is higher, a colonel or a general?
   d A large Indian family is ......
   e The most important Indian is the ......
   f A dangerous place is not ......
   g A father and son have the same ......
   h An Indian boat is a ......
   i Indians take the ..... off an animal before they cook it.
   j There is a ..... inside the mountain.
2 Look at the picture on page 185.
   a Which man is the chief?
   b What is the name of his tribe?
   c What do you know about his son?

After you read

3 Answer these questions.
   a Chapter 1 is "The Trip Begins." Where are Major Heyward and the daughters of Colonel Munro going? Why? Why don't they go with General Webb's men?
   b Why do the two young women and Heyward lose their way?
   c Why is the name of Chapter 2 "Their First Mistake"?

Chapters 4–9

Before you read

4 Look at the names of Chapters 4–6. What will happen to Cora, Alice, and Major Heyward, do you think?

5 Find the words in *italics* in your dictionary.
  a Which word on the right goes with each word on the left? Why?

cliff	life
fire	climb
heart	hair
hold	gun
save	love
scalp	hand

  b Look at this sentence. Who won, do you think?
  When the Indians *attacked* with *tomahawks*, the white men fired their guns.
  c When did Indians make a *war cry*? Can you make the noise?

After you read
6 Work with another student.
  Student A: You are interested in Magua's life. Ask him questions.
  Student B: You are Magua. Tell your story.
7 How do Cora and Alice feel when they see their father's fort? How does Hawkeye feel? Why?

Chapters 10–15

Before you read
8 Look at the picture on page 203. What do we know about Heyward?

After you read
9 What happens to
  a Fort William Henry and Colonel Munro's men?
  b Uncas and Cora?
10 Cora and Alice are different in many ways. How are they different? Discuss the two young women.

Writing

11 At the end of the story, Alice writes a letter to a friend in Scotland. She tells her friend about Uncas, Chingachgook, Hawkeye, and Cora. Write Alice's letter.

12 Major Heyward wants to marry Alice. Why was Colonel Munro unhappy when Heyward told him?

13 Write about Magua. Who was he? What happened in his life? How did he die?

14 How does Chingachgook feel after Uncas dies? What will he do now, do you think?

White Fang

JACK LONDON

Level 2

Retold by Brigit Viney
Series Editors: Andy Hopkins and Jocelyn Potter

Contents

		page
Introduction		229
Chapter 1	The Gray Cub	231
Chapter 2	White Fang	234
Chapter 3	A Trip up the Mackenzie	239
Chapter 4	The Killer of Dogs	243
Chapter 5	The Great Fight	248
Chapter 6	Love Begins	252
Chapter 7	The Southland	257
Chapter 8	The God's Home	261
Chapter 9	Family Life	264
Activities		269

Introduction

He learned only about hate. Nobody gave him love, so he did not learn about that.

A young wolf, White Fang, is born near the Mackenzie River, in north-west Canada, in about 1893. One day he meets some Indians and they take him and his mother to their camp. They know his mother because she is half-dog. White Fang begins to learn the ways of men—and of other dogs. The dogs hate him, so he hates them. He learns to fight and to kill. It is a hard life, but will it change? Can White Fang learn to love?

When Jack London wrote *White Fang* in 1906, he was a famous writer. In 1903 his book *The Call of the Wild* (also a Penguin Reader) told the story of a dog, Buck. Buck has an easy life in sunny California, but then he goes to the Klondike in the cold north. Here he has to work, and to fight. American readers loved the story.

Wolves were very important to London. They were strong and wild, and they fought hard. He liked this in animals—and people.

Jack London was born in 1876 in San Francisco. His family had little money and he left school at fourteen. In the summer of 1897 he went to the Klondike. The trip was difficult and dangerous, and he had to stay there for the winter. He enjoyed the hard life and the strong people. Later, he wrote about the place in many of his books and stories.

After *White Fang*, London wrote thirty-two other books. He visited Australia, and had a farm in California. He died in 1916.

Chapter 1   The Gray Cub

The two wolves moved slowly down the Mackenzie River. Often they left it and looked for food by the smaller rivers. But they always went back to the large river.

The she-wolf looked everywhere for a home, and then one day she found it. It was a cave near a small river. She looked inside it very carefully. It was warm and dry so she lay down.

The he-wolf was hungry. He lay down inside the cave but he did not sleep well. He could hear the sound of water and he could see the April sun on the snow. Under the snow, and in the trees, there was new life.

The he-wolf left the cave and followed the ice bed of the small river. He wanted food. But eight hours later he came back, hungrier than before. In the wet snow he was slow and could not catch anything.

Strange sounds came from inside the cave. When he looked inside, the she-wolf snarled at him. He moved away and slept at the mouth of the cave.

The next morning he saw five strange little animals next to the she-wolf. They made weak little noises but their eyes were not open. He left the cave quickly. He had to find food for the she-wolf. This time, when he took meat back to her, she did not snarl at him.

Four of the cubs were red, but one was gray. This gray cub was a fighter. He fought his brothers and sisters more than they fought him. He always wanted to leave the cave and his mother had to stop him.

Then, after a time, there was no food. His father did not bring them any meat, and his mother had no milk. The cubs cried, but then they slept.

When the gray cub felt strong again, he only had one sister. The other cubs were dead. His sister slept all the time. Then the fire of life in her died too.

Later, the cub's father died. The she-wolf knew this because she found his body in the woods. Near his dead body lived a large wildcat. The she-wolf found the wildcat's cave, but she did not go inside it. The wildcat was in there, with her babies, and she was dangerous.

One day, the cub left the cave and began to walk. He hurt his feet and he ran into things. He often fell, but he learned quickly.

In the woods he found a very young, thin, yellow animal. He turned it over with his foot and it made a strange noise. Suddenly, its mother jumped on him and bit his neck. Then she took her baby into the trees.

The cub sat down and made weak little noises. He was there when the mother animal came back. He saw her long thin body and long thin head. She came nearer and nearer and then she bit his neck again. He snarled and tried to fight. But the mother animal fought hard. She wanted to kill him.

Suddenly, the she-wolf ran through the trees and caught the mother animal between her teeth. Her mouth closed on the long yellow body. Then she and the cub ate the animal.

After that, the cub went out every day and killed for food. Then one day the she-wolf brought home a baby wildcat. The cub ate it and fell asleep in the cave next to his mother.

He woke when she snarled loudly. The mother wildcat was at the mouth of the cave. She snarled angrily and the hair on the cub's back stood up. Because the mouth of the cave was small, the wildcat had to come in on her stomach. She and the she-wolf fought hard. The cub fought too and bit the wildcat's leg. She hit him hard but he did not stop fighting.

In the end, he and his mother killed the wildcat. But after the

The mother wildcat was at the mouth of the cave.

fight his mother was very weak and sick. For a day and a night she did not move. For a week she only left the cave for water. But at the end of the week she could look for meat again.

For some time the cub could not walk very well, but then he began to look for meat with his mother. He was not afraid of small animals now. He could fight with his mother and kill a large animal.

He liked killing other animals. He also liked eating, running, fighting, and sleeping. He liked the life in his body. He was happy in his world.

Chapter 2   White Fang

The cub ran to the small river. He was heavy with sleep and he wanted to drink. He did not look around him carefully.

Suddenly, he saw them under the trees. Five big animals sat in front of him. They did not snarl or show their teeth. They looked at him and did not move. They were dangerous, but the gray cub could not move. He felt very weak and small next to them.

One of them got up and came to him. When he put his hand near the cub, the cub's hair stood up. He showed his little fangs. The man laughed and said: "*Wabam wabisca ip pit tah*." ("Look! The white fangs!")

The other men laughed loudly. The first man put his hand near the cub again. This time the cub bit it. The man hit him on the head. The cub fell and then cried. The men laughed again.

Then the cub heard something. The Indians heard it too.

The cub's mother ran to him and snarled loudly at the men.

"Kiche!" said one of the men. "Kiche!"

The cub's mother stopped snarling and lay down on the

"Look! The white fangs!"

ground. Why? The cub did not understand. His mother fought everything!

The man came to her. He put his hand on her head, but she did not bite him! The other men put their hands on her head and she did not bite them. The men made noises with their mouths.

"It is not strange," one man said. "Her father was a wolf and her mother was a dog."

"She ran away last year, Gray Beaver. Do you remember?" said a second man.

"Yes. She ran to the wolves because we could find no meat for the dogs."

He put his hand on the cub. The cub snarled and the hand quickly hit him. The cub closed his mouth. Then the man stroked the cub's back and behind his ears.

"His father is a wolf," said the man. "His fangs are white, so his name will be White Fang. He is my dog because Kiche was my dead brother's dog."

The men made more mouth noises. Then Gray Beaver cut some wood from a tree. He tied Kiche to it with some leather. Then he tied the stick to a small tree.

After a time, about forty men, women, and children and many dogs came through the trees. The people and dogs carried heavy bags. A small boy took Kiche's stick and walked away with her. White Fang followed her.

They walked by the small river for a time. Then they came to the large Mackenzie River and the Indians made their camp next to it.

White Fang walked around the camp and looked at everything. A young dog walked slowly to him. This dog, Lip-lip, did not like other dogs, and he bit White Fang badly. White Fang fought him angrily, but Lip-lip was older and stronger. He bit

White Fang again and again, so White Fang ran back to his mother. This was the first of many fights with Lip-lip.

Five minutes later, White Fang left Kiche and looked around the camp again. He saw Gray Beaver and went to him. Gray Beaver sat on the ground near a lot of sticks. Women and children brought Gray Beaver more sticks. Then a strange thing came up from the sticks on the ground. It was the color of the sun. White Fang went near it, and suddenly his nose hurt. He jumped away fast and cried. Gray Beaver and the others laughed loudly.

White Fang ran back to his mother and lay down next to her. His nose hurt and he wanted to go back to the woods. He watched the men in the camp. They were large and strong, and they made fire! They were gods to him.

One of the Indians, Three Eagles, planned a trip up the Mackenzie River. Before he left, Gray Beaver gave him Kiche. So one morning, Three Eagles took Kiche onto his boat. The boat started to move up the river. White Fang jumped into the water and swam after it. He did not listen to the angry shouts of Gray Beaver. He wanted his mother.

Gray Beaver followed him in his boat. He caught White Fang's neck and pulled him angrily out of the water. He hit him hard, again and again. White Fang snarled at him angrily. Gray Beaver hit him faster and harder. Then White Fang felt very afraid. He stopped snarling.

Gray Beaver stopped hitting him. He threw him into the bottom of the boat and kicked him hard. White Fang suddenly felt angry again and bit Gray Beaver's foot.

This time Gray Beaver was really angry. He hit White Fang very hard for a long time. Again, he threw him to the bottom of the boat and again he kicked him angrily. This time White Fang did not bite him.

He caught White Fang's neck and pulled him angrily out of the water.

Later, in the night, White Fang remembered his mother and felt sad. He cried loudly, and Gray Beaver hit him again. After that he only cried quietly when the gods were near. But sometimes in the woods he cried loudly again. He stayed in the camp and waited for his mother.

He was not too sad. Life in the camp was interesting because the gods did many strange things. But the young dog Lip-lip hated him and often started fights with him. The other young dogs followed Lip-lip and started fights with White Fang too.

These fights taught him some important lessons. He learned to stay on his feet in a fight. He also learned to hurt a dog very badly in a very short time. He learned to push the dog off his feet and to bite his neck. He learned these lessons because he wanted to live. He had to be faster, more intelligent, and more dangerous than the other dogs.

One day, he killed a dog in a fight. The Indians saw him and were angry with him. After that, they did not want him near them. They shouted at him angrily when they saw him.

This life turned White Fang into a very angry, dangerous animal. He learned only about hate. Nobody gave him any love, so he did not learn about that.

Chapter 3 A Trip up the Mackenzie

In the fall the Indians put everything from the camp into bags. Then they put the bags into their boats. Some of the boats left and White Fang understood.

He ran out of the camp and through a small river. Then he found a place in the woods and went to sleep. He woke when he heard Gray Beaver. Gray Beaver called his name again and again. Then he stopped calling and went back to the camp.

White Fang played in the woods for a time, but then he suddenly felt afraid. The woods were dark and cold, and the trees made loud noises. He ran back to the camp, but there was nobody there. He sat down and looked up at the sky. He cried sadly to the large night sky.

In the morning he began to run by the river. All day he ran. Sometimes he had to climb high mountains behind the river. Sometimes he had to swim across other, smaller rivers. He always followed the large river on its way. All the time he looked for the gods.

He ran all night and the next day. He felt weak and hungry and his feet hurt badly. Snow began to fall and he could not find his way easily. Then night fell and the snow came down more heavily.

Then he smelled the gods through the snow on the ground. He left the river and went into the trees. He heard the sounds of the gods and saw Gray Beaver near a fire.

He felt afraid but he walked slowly into the firelight. Gray Beaver saw him and looked at him. White Fang went to him and waited. But Gray Beaver did not hit him. He gave him some meat! White Fang carefully smelled it and then ate it. He sat at Gray Beaver's feet and looked at the fire. He felt warm and happy. This was his place.

Some months later, in the middle of December, Gray Beaver went up the Mackenzie River. His son Mit-sah and his wife Kloo-klooch went with him. They took two sleds. Mit-sah's sled was smaller and lighter than Gray Beaver's, but it carried a lot of food.

Gray Beaver and Mit-sah tied White Fang and six other dogs to Mit-sah's sled. Lip-lip ran at the front. All day the other dogs ran behind him. They wanted to catch him, but they could not. Because of this they hated him. In the camp Lip-lip had to stay

He felt afraid but he walked slowly into the firelight.

near the gods because the other dogs hated him. He was not the most important dog now.

At one village, White Fang learned something new. One day a boy cut some meat and some of it fell on the ground. White Fang ate it. The boy ran after him and tried to hit him with a heavy stick. White Fang was very angry. He bit the boy's hand hard. The boy's family came to Gray Beaver but he spoke angrily to them. He did not hit White Fang.

Later that day, some boys from the village began to hit Mit-sah in the woods. White Fang ran angrily to them and they ran away. When Mit-sah told this story in the camp, Gray Beaver gave White Fang a lot of meat. White Fang understood. There were different gods. There were his gods, and there were other gods. His gods were the most important.

They arrived in Gray Beaver's village in April. White Fang was now a year old. He was tall and thin, and his coat was wolf-gray. He walked through the village and saw the gods and dogs from the summer. He was not afraid of the older dogs. He could fight them and win.

In the summer, he saw Kiche outside the village. He stopped and looked at her. He remembered her, but she did not remember him. He ran to her happily, but she bit him in the face. He ran away from her. He did not understand.

Kiche now had new cubs, so she could not remember her older ones. One of her new cubs came to White Fang. White Fang smelled him and Kiche jumped on him angrily. She bit his face a second time. Then White Fang left. This was a she-wolf and he could not fight her.

In the third year of White Fang's life, there was no food on the Mackenzie for a long time. In the summer, the Indians could not find any fish and in the winter they could not find any wild animals. They ate their leather shoes, and the dogs. The old and weak gods died and the other gods cried all the time. Some of the most intelligent dogs understood, and they went into the woods for food. There, the wolves ate them.

White Fang also went into the woods. For months he was very hungry, but he always killed something. Other animals wanted to kill him, but he could run faster than them.

Early in the summer, he met Lip-lip in the woods. He was not hungry, but he snarled at Lip-lip. He pushed him to the ground and bit his neck hard. That was the end of Lip-lip.

One day, White Fang came to the end of the woods. In front of him he saw the Mackenzie and a village. It was the old village, but it was now in a new place.

He left the woods and went to the village. Gray Beaver was not there, but Kloo-klooch gave him a fish. He felt happy because he was with the gods again.

Chapter 4 The Killer of Dogs

When White Fang was almost five years old, Gray Beaver took him on a second trip. This time they went down the Mackenzie, across the mountains and down the Porcupine River to the Yukon River. They stopped in many villages, and in each village White Fang fought the dogs. The dogs often died because they fought in a different way from White Fang.

White Fang liked fighting very quickly. He hated being very near another animal because it felt dangerous. He had to feel free, so he finished his fights very fast. Usually, he won his fights because the village dogs were slower. Sometimes a dog hurt him badly, but these times were accidents. Usually, he was too fast for them.

In the summer, Gray Beaver and White Fang arrived at Fort

Yukon. It was 1898, and there were thousands of people in the town. These people planned to go up the Yukon to the Klondike because they wanted to find gold.

In Fort Yukon, White Fang saw white gods for the first time. A small number of them lived in the town, and other men came from the boats. These boats stopped in the town two or three times a week.

He was very afraid of the white gods because they were stronger than the Indians. But he was not afraid of their dogs. They did not fight well. When they ran at him, he jumped away. Then he pushed them to the ground and bit them in the neck. It was easy.

Sometimes a dog did not get up after a fight with White Fang. Then White Fang left him to the Indian dogs. They jumped on him and killed him. White Fang never killed a white god's dog. He was too intelligent. The white gods were always angry when their dogs died in a fight. They hit the Indian dogs hard with sticks.

White Fang started these fights easily. When the strange dogs left the boat, he went to them. They were afraid of him because he was wild. He was dangerous to them and to their gods so they wanted to fight him.

After two or three of these fights, the white gods always took their dogs back to their boat. That was the end of the game with the dogs from that boat.

After a time, these fights were the only thing in White Fang's life. Gray Beaver had no work for him because he was too busy. He sold leather shoes to the white gods and he was now rich.

White Fang liked the fights, but he was not happy. He did not love an animal or a god, because no animal or god loved him. Everybody hated him.

The white men in Fort Yukon did not like the white men

They were afraid of him because he was wild.

from the boats. These men were from the south, and were weak. The men from Fort Yukon liked the dog fights because the weak men's dogs died.

One man liked the fights more than the other men. He watched each fight. Sometimes when a Southland dog died, he shouted happily. He wanted very much to buy White Fang.

This man's name was Beauty Smith. His name was "Beauty" because he was very ugly and small. He had large yellow teeth and dirty yellow eyes. The thin hair on his head and face was also dirty yellow.

He tried to make friends with White Fang but White Fang hated him. He always showed his teeth to him and moved away.

Then Beauty Smith visited Gray Beaver in his camp. Beauty Smith and Gray Beaver talked for a long time. Gray Beaver did not want to sell White Fang. White Fang was his strongest dog. But Beauty Smith knew Gray Beaver. He visited him often. Each time he took a black bottle with him, under his coat. Gray Beaver began to want more and more bottles. In a short time all his money went on them. Then Beauty Smith talked to him again about White Fang. He wanted to pay for White Fang in bottles, not dollars. This time Gray Beaver listened.

"You catch him, you take him," he said.

After two days, Beauty Smith told Gray Beaver, "*You* catch him."

That evening, White Fang came quietly into the camp. The bad white god was not there. Gray Beaver came over to him and tied some leather round his neck. He sat down next to White Fang and drank from his bottle.

After an hour, Beauty Smith walked into the camp. He stood over White Fang. White Fang snarled up at him. A hand moved down to his head. Suddenly, White Fang tried to bite it. The hand jumped back. Gray Beaver hit White Fang on the head.

Beauty Smith went away and came back with a large stick.

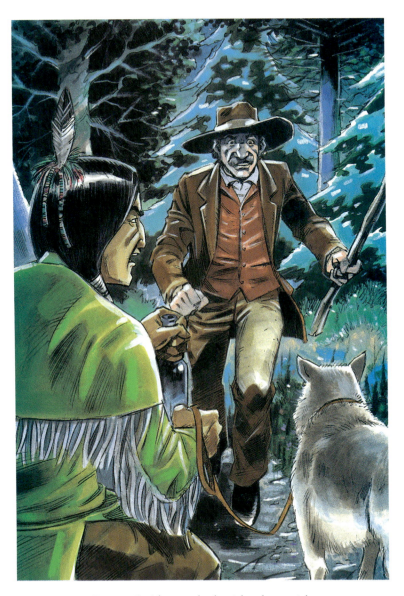

Beauty Smith came back with a large stick.

Gray Beaver gave him the leather and Beauty Smith walked away from White Fang. The leather pulled at White Fang's neck but he did not move. Then he suddenly jumped at the bad god. Beauty Smith did not move away. He hit White Fang hard with his stick. White Fang fell to the ground. Beauty Smith pulled the leather again, and this time White Fang followed him.

In the town, Beauty Smith tied him with the leather and went to bed. White Fang waited an hour. Then he began to bite the leather. When he was free he went back to Gray Beaver.

In the morning, Gray Beaver gave him to Beauty Smith again. Beauty Smith hit him very hard with the stick. He enjoyed hurting him.

Then he took White Fang to the town again. This time he tied him with a stick. In the night, White Fang began to bite the stick. After many hours, he bit through it and was free. He went back to Gray Beaver. He could not leave him.

Beauty Smith came for him again the next morning. He hit him harder than before. When he finished, White Fang was very sick. He could not see and he could not walk easily. He followed Beauty Smith back to the town.

Gray Beaver said nothing to Beauty Smith because White Fang was not his dog now. After a short time, he left Fort Yukon for the Mackenzie.

Chapter 5   The Great Fight

When the first snows began to fall, Beauty Smith took White Fang on a boat up the Yukon to Dawson. He called White Fang "The Killer Wolf" and showed him to people for money. When White Fang slept, people woke him with a stick. They wanted to see an angry wolf.

White Fang was very angry. He hated everything and everybody. He hated Beauty Smith because he hurt him all the time. Beauty Smith wanted an angry wolf because he wanted a fighter.

Sometimes, at night, Beauty Smith took White Fang into the woods outside the town. In the morning, a lot of people and a dog arrived. White Fang fought the dog. Usually, he killed him. He was a better fighter than the other dogs.

After a time, the fights stopped because Beauty Smith could not find dogs for them. Then, in the spring, he suddenly took him to a fight. It was a fight with a very strange dog.

This dog was short and heavy. The people shouted to him, "Go to him, Cherokee! Eat him!"

But Cherokee did not really want to fight. Then a man began to stroke the dog's body from its bottom to its head. Suddenly, Cherokee felt angry and he began to run to White Fang.

White Fang quickly jumped on him and bit him behind his ear. The dog did not snarl. He turned and followed White Fang. Again and again White Fang jumped on Cherokee and bit him. Again and again Cherokee followed him. He planned to do something, but what? White Fang could not understand him. And he could not bite his neck below his head. Cherokee was too short, and his head was too large.

Again and again White Fang tried to push Cherokee onto the ground, but Cherokee was too short and heavy. Then White Fang pushed too hard and fell to the ground. Cherokee bit into his neck. White Fang jumped up and ran. Cherokee's teeth stayed in his neck. White Fang hated this. He hated being near the other dog. He ran around and around.

He only stopped when he was tired. Cherokee pushed him onto his back and sat on top of him. His teeth did not leave

White Fang's neck. Slowly, he moved his teeth up White Fang's neck. Beauty Smith began to kick White Fang angrily.

Suddenly, a tall young man pushed his way through the people to Beauty Smith. He was very angry and his gray eyes were cold. He hit Beauty Smith in the face. Beauty Smith fell to the ground.

"Matt, come here," the young man called.

A shorter, older man went to him and they tried to pull Cherokee off White Fang.

"You can't pull him off, Scott," said Matt. "We have to open his mouth."

Scott took out his gun and pushed it between Cherokee's teeth. Then he slowly opened the dog's mouth and Matt pulled White Fang's neck out from the dog's teeth.

White Fang tried to get up, but his legs were too weak. He fell back into the snow.

Beauty Smith got up slowly and came to him. He looked at him.

"Matt, how much does a good sled-dog cost?" Scott asked.

"Three hundred dollars."

"And how much for this dog now?"

"Half of that."

Scott turned to Beauty Smith.

"Did you hear that? I'm going to take your dog, and I'm going to give you a hundred and fifty dollars for him."

He took out the money.

"I'm not selling," said Beauty Smith.

"Oh yes, you are," said Scott. "Because I'm buying. Here's your money."

Beauty Smith put his hands behind him and moved away. Scott ran after him.

"Take the money or I'll hit you again," he said.

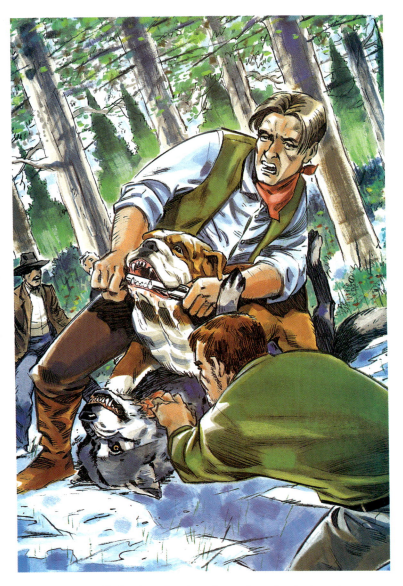

Matt pulled White Fang's neck out from the dog's teeth.

"All right," Beauty Smith said quickly. "But I'm going to tell the police in Dawson."

"Then you'll have to leave town. Do you understand?"

"Yes," answered Beauty Smith and moved away.

Scott turned his back on him and went to White Fang.

Chapter 6 Love Begins

Weedon Scott sat outside his small house in the woods and looked at White Fang. White Fang snarled angrily at Matt's sled dogs.

"He's a wolf, and we can't change him," Scott said to Matt.

"Wolf or dog, he can pull a sled," said Matt. "Look at these lines on his back."

"Can he be a sled-dog again?" Scott asked. He was interested in this idea.

"Maybe. Let's see. Untie him."

Scott looked at him.

"*You* untie him!" he said.

So Matt took a heavy stick and went to White Fang. He untied him. White Fang slowly walked away from him. He could not understand these gods. They did not hit him.

Scott went into the house and came out with some meat. He threw it to White Fang. White Fang jumped away from it and looked at it.

One of Matt's dogs jumped for the meat. Then White Fang jumped on him and bit him. The dog fell to the ground. Matt ran to him, but he was too late. The dog quickly died.

"We'll have to kill him," Scott said.

"Don't kill him now, Mr. Scott," Matt answered. "Maybe he'll change."

"I don't want to kill him," Scott said. "I want to be nice to him."

He walked to White Fang and started to talk to him quietly. He moved his hand near White Fang. Suddenly, White Fang bit it. Scott cried out and White Fang moved away.

Matt ran into the house and came out with a gun. White Fang began to snarl loudly at him.

"Don't kill him! He knows that guns are dangerous!" Scott said. "He's very intelligent."

"All right," Matt said. He put the gun down and White Fang stopped snarling.

"You're right, Mr. Scott. He knows that a gun can kill," he said.

The next day, Scott sat outside the house. White Fang watched him. Scott began to speak. White Fang snarled, but Scott did not move. He spoke quietly for a long time. White Fang stopped snarling and listened to the sound of the god.

After a long time, the god got up and went into the house. When he came out, he sat down in the same place. He had some meat in his hand. White Fang's ears stood up and he looked at the meat. It was good meat, but he did not go near it. He was afraid of the god.

Then the god threw the meat on the snow at White Fang's feet. He smelled it carefully but he did not look at it. He watched the god. Nothing happened. The god did not get up, and he did not hit him. White Fang took the meat and ate it.

The god showed him some more meat in his hand, and again White Fang did not go to him. Again the god threw it to him in the snow. The god repeated this a number of times. But then he did not throw the meat to him. He only showed it to him in his hand. The meat was good, and White Fang was hungry. Slowly, he went near the hand and then he took the meat from it. His eyes never left the god's face, and the hair on his neck stood up. He ate the meat, but nothing happened.

Slowly, he went near the hand and then he took the meat from it.

He waited. The god talked again, quietly and warmly. Then he put his hand lightly on White Fang's head. White Fang felt very afraid, but he also felt happy. He hated the hand, but he liked the warm sound of the words. He snarled, but he did not bite the hand. The god stroked White Fang's head lightly again and again. White Fang began to like it.

In this way, White Fang's old life ended, and his new life began. Slowly, he learned new lessons and forgot old ones. He did not run away, because he liked this god. Then he began to really love him. Without him, he was very sad.

In the early morning, he did not run in the woods, but waited for the man outside the house for hours. At night, when the man came home, White Fang left his warm place under the snow. He wanted to see and hear the god. He wanted to be with him. White Fang did not show his love openly. He never ran to the god. Only his eyes showed his love.

In the late spring, the man suddenly went away. White Fang waited all night for him outside the house, but he did not come. Days came and went. The man did not come back. White Fang was sick for the first time in his life. Matt brought him inside the house. He wrote to Scott:

"The wolf can't work or eat. He wants you. He's going to die without you."

Then, one evening, White Fang suddenly made a quiet noise and got up. His ears stood up and he listened hard. The door opened and Weedon Scott came in. He spoke to Matt and then looked around the room.

"Where's the wolf?" he asked.

Then he saw him near the fire. He called him and White Fang came to him quickly. A strange light shone in his eyes.

"He never looked at *me* that way," said Matt.

Scott did not hear him. He was face to face with White Fang.

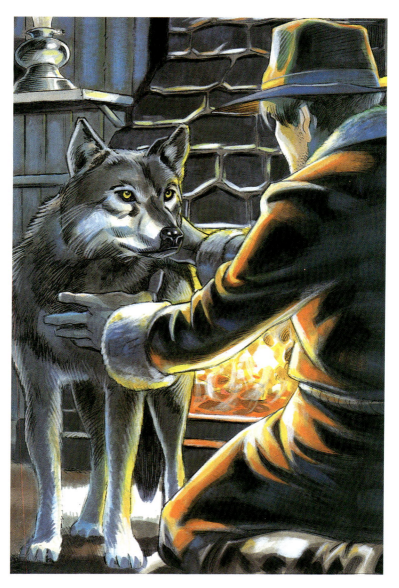

He stroked him, again and again, behind his ears, on his back.

He stroked him, again and again, behind his ears, on his back. White Fang felt a very strong love for him and suddenly he pushed his head between Scott's arm and body. It stayed there for a long time.

Scott looked at Matt. His eyes shone.

"I knew it! This wolf is a dog. Look at him!" said Matt.

White Fang felt better because he was happy again. A day later he left the house and went outside. The sled-dogs jumped on him and he fought them happily. He was well and strong and there was life in him again!

Chapter 7   The Southland

"Listen to that!" said Matt at dinner one night.

Through the door came a quiet, sad noise.

"That wolf knows that you're leaving," said Matt.

"What can I do with a wolf in California?" asked Scott.

A second sad noise came through the door.

"How does he know that you're going?" asked Matt.

"I don't know," answered Scott, sadly.

One morning, White Fang saw Scott's open bags on the floor of the house. Scott and Matt came and went all day. Sometimes Scott put things in the bags. White Fang could not eat. That night he cried loudly outside the house. The next day he felt very afraid. He followed Scott everywhere.

Two Indians arrived and took Scott's bags. Scott came to the door of the house and called White Fang inside. He stroked White Fang behind his ears and spoke to him sadly.

"I'm sorry," he said. "I'm going a long way, and you can't come with me."

White Fang pushed his head between Scott's arm and body.

From the river came the sound of a boat. Matt and Scott got up and left the house quickly. They shut the front door and the back door, and they went down to the river.

"Be good to him, Matt," said Scott. "Write and tell me about him."

"I will," said Matt. "Listen to him!"

White Fang cried loudly in the house behind them.

On the boat the two men said goodbye. Suddenly, Matt saw White Fang! He was on the boat!

The two men went to him and they found cuts on his face and body.

"We forgot the window. He jumped through it!" said Matt.

Scott thought quickly.

"Goodbye, Matt, old man. About the wolf—don't write. I—"

"What! You mean—?"

"Yes! *I'll* write to *you* about him!"

Later, when White Fang arrived in San Francisco, he felt very afraid. There were a lot of people, and he could not look at them. The noise in the streets hurt his ears and the houses were very large. He stayed near his god all the time.

The god took him to a small room and left him there for a long time. The room was full of bags. When the god came back, they left the city. They were in quiet country now.

A man and a woman came to his god, and the woman put her arms around his neck. She wanted to fight him! White Fang jumped at her and snarled angrily. His god stopped him.

"It's all right, Mother," Scott said. "He'll learn."

The woman laughed, but her face was white. She was afraid.

Scott spoke quietly to White Fang, and then more loudly: "Down! Down!"

White Fang lay down.

Scott put his arms around his mother, and watched White Fang.

White Fang jumped at her and snarled angrily.

"Down!" he repeated.

White Fang watched them. This time he did not jump up at the woman.

The gods got into a carriage and drove away. White Fang ran behind them. After fifteen minutes the carriage turned into a small road between two lines of trees.

Suddenly, a dog stood between White Fang and the carriage. Its eyes shone angrily. White Fang ran to it but stopped. He could not fight it because it was a she-dog. She was afraid of him so she jumped at him. She bit him, but he did not hurt her. He tried to move around her but she stopped him.

"Here, Collie!" called the strange god in the carriage.

Weedon Scott laughed.

"It's all right, Father. White Fang will have to learn many things. He can start learning now."

The carriage drove away, but Collie did not move. White Fang ran around her and she followed quickly. Suddenly, he turned and pushed her to the ground. Then he ran after the carriage. She followed but she could not catch him.

The carriage stopped at a large house. When White Fang came to the house, a large dog suddenly ran to him very fast. It pushed him to the ground. White Fang jumped up and almost bit the dog's neck. But then Collie angrily jumped on him. Again White Fang fell to the ground.

His god came and stroked White Fang. Another god called the other dogs to him. Under his god's hand White Fang felt better.

The carriage left and more strange gods came out of the house. Two of them put their arms around his god's neck, but White Fang did not move.

The gods walked into the house. White Fang followed Scott.

"Take Collie inside and leave Dick and your dog outside. They'll fight and then they'll be friends," said Scott's father.

"Dick'll be dead in two minutes!" answered Scott. "The wolf will have to come inside."

Chapter 8   The God's Home

White Fang learned quickly about life at Sierra Vista, Scott's home. He was not friendly with the other dogs, but he did not fight them. Dick wanted to be friends, but White Fang always snarled at him. In the end, Dick did not come near him. Collie always wanted to fight him because he was a wolf. When White Fang saw her, he turned away. When she bit him, he walked away slowly and carefully.

He learned about his god's family. There was his mother, his father, his wife, his two sisters, and his two children, Weedon and Maud. White Fang did not like children, because they always hurt him. But these children were very important to his god, so he did not snarl at them. After a time, he began to like them. He did not go to them, but he waited for them. When they left him, he was sad.

After the children, White Fang liked his god's father best. When he read the newspaper, White Fang sat at his feet. Sometimes Scott's father looked at him and said something. But White Fang only sat with him when his god was not there. When *his* god was there, White Fang was not interested in the other gods. He never looked at them with love, and he never put his head between their arm and body. He only did this with his god.

One morning, White Fang found a chicken outside the chicken house. He killed it and ate it. It was fat and good, and White Fang wanted more.

Later in the day, he saw a second chicken outside the chicken house. This time a man ran and hit White Fang with some leather. At the first cut of the leather, White Fang left the chicken for the man. He jumped for his neck. The man put his arm over his neck and White Fang bit his arm.

Suddenly, Collie jumped on White Fang. She was very angry. She ran around him again and again and in the end White Fang ran away from her.

"He'll learn about the chickens," Scott told his father, "but I'll have to catch him with them."

Two nights later, White Fang climbed into one of the chicken houses. He killed every chicken in it.

In the morning, Scott found him. He put White Fang's nose next to the dead chickens and spoke to him angrily. He hit him lightly on the neck. Then he took him inside another chicken house. White Fang wanted to kill the chickens, but the god's words stopped him. He did not kill chickens again.

In this way, Scott taught White Fang about life at Sierra Vista. Sometimes Scott hit him lightly. This hurt White Fang very much because of his great love. When Gray Beaver and Beauty Smith hit him, he felt angry. But when Scott hit him he felt very sad. Usually, Scott did not hit him. He spoke to him, and White Fang understood.

White Fang learned about life in the town too. There was meat in the stores, but he could not eat it. There were cats in some of the houses, and dogs everywhere, but he could not fight them. There were people everywhere, and they often wanted to stroke him. He did not snarl at them. It was not easy, but he learned the ways of the Southland.

On the way to town, three dogs always jumped on him when they saw him. Each time some men in the street shouted at the four dogs because they wanted to watch a fight.

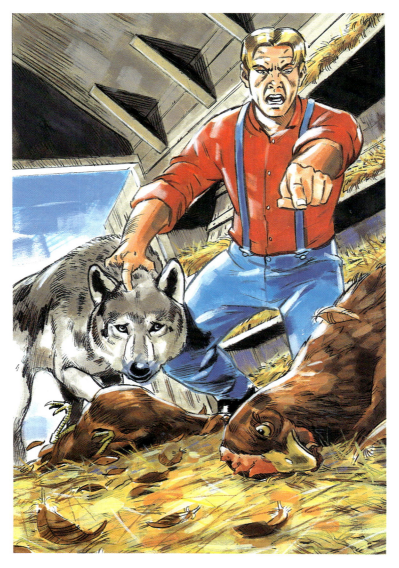

He put White Fang's nose next to the dead chickens and spoke to him angrily.

One day, they shouted at the dogs and the god stopped the carriage.

"Go to them," he said to White Fang.

White Fang looked at him.

"Go to them," he repeated. "Eat them."

White Fang did not wait. He jumped on the dogs, and quickly killed them all.

After that the dogs in the town did not jump on him.

Chapter 9   Family Life

The months came and went. There was a lot of food and no work in the Southland, so White Fang was fatter than in the Northland. Life was not dangerous, and White Fang was not afraid of anything.

The only problem in White Fang's life was Collie. She snarled at him all the time and followed him around the farm. She could not forget the dead chickens. When he looked at a chicken, she was very angry. Then White Fang lay down and closed his eyes. She went away when he did this.

The gods were good to him, so he was happy. Sometimes his god laughed at him. White Fang could not be angry with his god, but he had to do something. He tried not to move his face, but his god laughed harder. In the end, White Fang's mouth opened and his eyes shone with love. He laughed!

He also played with his god. They fought in a friendly way. He snarled at his god, but he never bit him. At the end of the game, the god always put his arms around White Fang's neck.

The god often went out on his horse and White Fang went with him. One day, his god fell from the horse and could not get up. White Fang jumped angrily at the horse's neck, but his god stopped him.

"Home! Go home!" he said.

White Fang did not want to leave him. He walked away, but then came back. Scott talked to him quietly and White Fang listened carefully.

"Go home and tell them, wolf. Go home!" he repeated.

White Fang understood "home" so he ran back to the house. The children ran to him, but he pushed past them. He turned to his god's wife and took her dress in his teeth. He snarled and snarled.

"I hope he isn't going crazy," said Scott's mother. "Maybe it's too hot for him here."

"He's trying to speak, I think," said Beth, Scott's sister.

White Fang snarled again.

They all stood up and followed him to Scott.

After this, Scott's family loved him more.

In the second winter in the Southland, Collie changed. When she bit him, her teeth did not really hurt. She sometimes wanted to play with him.

One day she ran into the woods. White Fang's god was on his horse. He wanted to leave the farm with White Fang. But White Fang had to follow Collie. He ran with her through the woods for a long way.

One night after this, White Fang woke suddenly. He was inside the house, near the front door. He smelled a strange god and heard a strange sound. He made no noise, but got up. He followed the strange god to the bottom of the stairs. The stranger began to climb the stairs. At the top of the stairs was the bedroom of White Fang's god.

White Fang did not snarl—he quietly jumped on the man's back and bit him. They fell to the floor. White Fang jumped at him again and bit him again.

Tables, chairs, and glass fell and broke. The noise woke the

But then he closed his eyes and went to sleep in the sun.

family. There were the sounds of a gun and a man's loud shouts. Then the noise stopped.

Weedon and his father came down the stairs. A dead man was on the floor, under the chairs and tables.

They turned to White Fang. He was on the floor too. Scott's father called the doctor.

The doctor worked for an hour and a half on White Fang.

"He's very sick," said the doctor. "I think he's going to die."

But White Fang was strong and did not die. He slept and slept. In his sleep he lived again the days with his mother, Gray Beaver, and Beauty Smith.

Then one day he got up. It was difficult, but he stood up. The gods watched him.

"Take him outside," said the doctor. "He has to walk."

They all followed White Fang outside. He felt very weak. He had to lie down outside the house for a long time. But then he began to walk again, and he started to feel stronger

At the farm he saw Collie. Next to her were six fat little dogs. She snarled, so he did not go near them.

His god pushed one little dog next to him. Collie snarled again. White Fang was interested in the little dog and watched him. He put his nose next to the little dog's nose and washed its face.

Then he felt weak again and lay down. The other little dogs ran to him and climbed over him. Their bodies felt strange. But then he closed his eyes and went to sleep in the sun.

ACTIVITIES

Chapters 1–3

Before you read

1 The words in *italics* are all in the story. Find them in your dictionary.
   a Look at the pictures on pages 3 and 5. Find these animals and things in them.
      cave   cub   fangs   wolf
   b Put these words in the table.
      bite   lie down   smell   snarl   stroke   tie

People do this	Animals do this

   c Answer the questions.
      Where does *leather* come from?
      What does a *sled* move on?
      What can you do with a *stick*?
      What, in your *body*, do you use when you eat?
   d Put these words in the sentences.
      camp   god   neck   village
      My ..... hurts, so I can't turn my head.
      Our family lived in this ..... for twenty years.
      They made a ..... for the night near the river.
      People killed animals because they wanted the rain ..... to bring rain.
2 White Fang is a wolf. What do you know about wolves?

After you read

3 These chapters tell the story of the first three years in White Fang's life. What can he do at the end of them?
4 Is White Fang's life better with or without the Indians? Why? What do you think?

Chapters 4–6

Before you read

5 Look at the names of Chapters 4–6. What is going to happen to White Fang, do you think?

6 Where do you find *gold*? Find the word in your dictionary. Why did a lot of North Americans look for it in the 1890s?

After you read

7 Why does White Fang lose the fight with Cherokee?

8 Work with another student.
   Student A: You are Beauty Smith. You visit Weedon Scott and you ask for White Fang back. Why do you want him?
   Student B: You are Weedon Scott. Answer Beauty Smith.

Chapters 7–9

Before you read

9 Chapter 7 is about the "Southland." Where do you think this is? How will it be different for White Fang? What will he do there?

10 Find the word *carriage* in your dictionary. What pulls a carriage?

After you read

11 Talk to two other students.
   Students A and B: You are Scott's mother and father. Scott is in the South again. Ask him about White Fang. How will he live in your house?
   Student C: You are Scott. Answer their questions.

12 How does White Fang help
   a Weedon Scott?   **b** the Scott family?

Writing

13 Write about the fight between White Fang and Cherokee for a newspaper.

14 You are somebody in Weedon Scott's family. Write a letter to a friend a week after Weedon comes back. Tell them about White Fang.

15 White Fang is sick. You are Weedon Scott. Write a letter to Matt. Tell him about life at Sierra Vista with White Fang.

16 It is a year later. What is White Fang doing now, do you think? Write about a day in his life.

Answers for the Activities in this book are published in our free resource packs for teachers, the Penguin Readers Factsheets, or available on a separate sheet. Please write to your local Pearson Education office or to: Marketing Department, Penguin Longman Publishing, 5 Bentinck Street, London W1M 5RN.

BESTSELLING PENGUIN READERS

AT LEVEL 1

The Adventures of Tom Sawyer

Amazon Rally

The Barcelona Game

Jennifer Lopez

Leonardo DiCaprio

Little Women

Prince William

Ricky Martin

Run for Your Life

Teen Stories - Blackmail

Teen Stories - Mystery Girl

Teen Stories - The Plan

THE BEST WEBSITES FOR STUDENTS OF ENGLISH!

www.penguinreaders.com

Where the world of Penguin Readers comes to life

- Fully searchable on-line catalogue
- Downloadable resource materials
- First ever on-line Penguin Reader!
- New competition each month!

www.penguindossiers.com

Up-to-the-minute website providing articles for free!

- Articles about your favourite stars, blockbuster movies and big sports events!
- Written in simple English with fun activities!

CHECK THEM OUT!

NEW from Penguin Readers
Your favourite titles on Audio CD

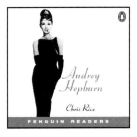
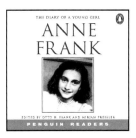
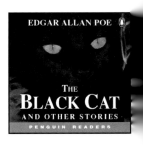

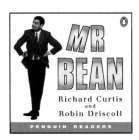

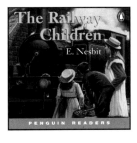

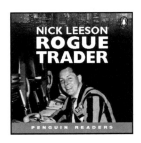

www.penguinreaders.com

THE JUDAICA IMPRINT
FOR THOUGHTFUL PEOPLE

in conjunction with **Aish HaTorah**

Like Water on a Rock

True stories of spiritual transformation

Edited by
Nechemia Coopersmith
and Shraga Simmons

© Copyright 2011 by Shaar Press

First edition – First impression / November 2011

ALL RIGHTS RESERVED
No part of this book may be reproduced in any form, *photocopy, electronic media, or otherwise without* written *permission from the copyright holder, except by a reviewer who wishes to quote brief passages in connection with a review written for inclusion in magazines or newspapers.*
THE RIGHTS OF THE COPYRIGHT HOLDER WILL BE STRICTLY ENFORCED.

Published by **SHAAR PRESS**
Distributed by MESORAH PUBLICATIONS, LTD.
4401 Second Avenue / Brooklyn, N.Y 11232 / (718) 921-9000

Distributed in Israel by SIFRIATI / A. GITLER
6 Hayarkon Street / Bnei Brak 51127 / Israel

Distributed in Europe by LEHMANNS
Unit E, Viking Business Park, Rolling Mill Road / Jarrow, Tyne and Wear, NE32 3DP/ England

Distributed in Australia and New Zealand by GOLDS WORLD OF JUDAICA
3-13 William Street / Balaclava, Melbourne 3183 / Victoria Australia

Distributed in South Africa by KOLLEL BOOKSHOP
Ivy Common / 105 William Road / Norwood 2192, Johannesburg, South Africa

ISBN 10:1-4226-1175-2 / ISBN 13: 978-1-4226-1175-3

Printed in the United States of America
Custom bound by Sefercraft, Inc. / 4401 Second Avenue / Brooklyn N.Y. 11232

וְלִמַּדְתֶּם אֹתָם אֶת בְּנֵיכֶם לְדַבֵּר בָּם (דברים יא,יט)
You shall teach them to your children
to discuss them (Deuteronomy 11:19).

In honour of the simchas Bar Mitzvah
of our dear son

Aryeh Leib

May you always be fulfilled by your
Yiddishkeit and inspired through
your learning of Torah.

**Stuart & Andrea Hytman
and family**

Table of Contents

Introduction 9
Acknowledgments 12

Drops of Discovery

The Jew From Kuwait 17
Sleepless in New Jersey 23
The Jewish Prince of Persia 29
In My Boots 36
My Converso Family 40
Encounters with Elijah 48
The Torah in Our Church 55

Drops of Faith

She Is Pure 63
My Barber, Morris 68
Standing Before God 73
The Buried Seder Plate 77
A Photo from Dachau 81
The Mother of All Miracles 86
God and I 90
The Music of Recession 94

Drops of Challenge

When Cancer Came Knocking 99
What Every Parent Dreads 108
Almost Normal 117
A Leg to Stand On 122
Anorexia: Starving in the Land of Plenty 127
Stop the Loneliness 135
NICU 137
Person First, Disability Later 141

Drops of Inspiration

Skeleton Key 147
Every Note Counts 152
My Kidney Sister 157

I Can Do It	167
The Day Before My Wedding	170
The Telemarketer	174

A Drop of Sadness

The Heartrending Cry	179
Mournful	185
The Rabbi and the Professor	190
The Life and Death of Yoseph Robinson	195
Better or Bitter	201
Meatloaf for Mourners	208
Time of Death	211
Shocked Into Silence	215

A Drop of Humor

Deep Center	221
The God of Large and Small	226
The Rabbi and the Cabinet Minister	231
Salami and Shiites	237
Six Ways to Attain Misery	244
A Button's Life	247

A Drop of Wisdom

The Greatness of Rabbi Noach Weinberg *zt"l*	255
I Am a Wall	260
In An Instant	265
Oblivious to the Music	268
Hacked	271
The Lights on the Tree	274

Drops of Love

Father of the Bride	279
My Enemy, My Friend	283
True Romance	287
Stepmother	290
Confessions of a Jewish American Teenager	295
My New Dad	298
In the Blink of an Eye	302
A Stone's Throw	305
Forgiving My Father	308
Stairway to Heaven	312

Introduction

It is one of the most inspirational Talmudic stories, related in *Avos D'Rav Nosson*. Rebbe Akiva was a shepherd, a laborer, an *am ha'aretz* — religious in observance, but ignorant of Torah knowledge. At age 40, he didn't even know how to read the *aleph-beis*.

One day Akiva was out by a brook, and noticed a steady trickle of water hitting a rock. It was only a drip, but it was constant — drop after drop after drop. Akiva observed something incredible: A hole had been carved out by that steady drip of water. He wondered: How can that be? Then he was reminded of the phenomenon stated in the verse, "Water wears away stones" (*Iyov* 14:19), and he concluded: If something as soft as water can carve a hole in solid rock, how much more so can Torah — which is hard as iron — make an indelible impression on my heart.

And the rest, as they say, is history. Rebbe Akiva committed himself to Torah study, and went on to become the greatest sage of his generation, with 24,000 students learning under him at one time.

What is the message of Rebbe Akiva and those life-transforming drops of water?

On one level, this story shows how every Jew, if given the chance, can achieve great heights.

On a deeper level, the story of Rebbe Akiva teaches that every drop of Torah, even if undetectable, makes an impact. Torah, as the word of the Almighty, has unparalleled power to effect change. Sometimes we do not perceive it, and the results are not apparent until years later. But if one keeps at it, the majesty of Hashem's Torah will penetrate. Drop after drop after drop, it will carve into your *neshamah* and transform you.

Indeed, that is the Jewish view of spirituality. Achieving great heights comes not so much through dramatic bursts of insight and inspiration. Experiences are fleeting; once they are over, the connection quickly dissipates. Rather it is the consistent striving to live with Torah values — the small triumphs of the soul — that add up drop after drop, to ultimately create true spiritual transformation.

Rabbi Noah Weinberg *zt"l* used the story of Rebbe Akiva as the inspiration for his pioneering *kiruv* organization. Drawing from the words of the Prophet Yirmiyahu (23:29), "Are not My words like fire, says Hashem?" (see *Kiddushin* 30b), Rabbi Weinberg added a new dimension to Rebbe Akiva's deduction: If something as soft as water can carve a hole in solid rock, how much more so can Torah — which is like fire that can melt iron — make an indelible impression on my heart. Rabbi Weinberg therefore named his organization Aish HaTorah ("Fire of Torah").

This theme became Rabbi Weinberg's calling card: Torah wisdom is the deepest way to change people. No preaching, just showing how *Toras Chaim* — the life-giving and life-affirming source — illuminates one's life and, drop by drop, imperceptibly enters one's essential core.

It was that stalwart conviction in the power of Torah that gave Rabbi Weinberg the confidence to reach out to every Jew. For decades Rabbi Weinberg taught tens of thousands of eager souls to understand what the Almighty is saying through the words of Torah, and then to live their lives with this knowledge.

This book, in its own humble way, is an illustration of Rebbe Akiva's principle.

Each essay is like a single drop of water, showing how Jews from varied walks of life are grappling with Jewish ideals and applying them to everyday life. There is struggle, determination, and consistent focus. There is failure, and there is success. Yet captured in every essay is that moment of impact where another drop of Torah penetrates, producing a subtle yet permanent transformation.

Aish.com, the website where these essays first appeared, has been remarkably successful in disseminating millions of drops of Torah. Our mandate is to use this God-given gift of technology to reach Jews across the globe. We connect to Jews wherever they are — at home, in the office, on the road. And with our websites in English, Hebrew, Spanish, and French, we speak in their language.

More than 400,000 people around the world are subscribed to Aish.com's weekly email update. Every time someone visits the site (it happens over one million times per month), another drop of Torah seeps into the world. The vehicle may be an essay offering Jewish "wisdom for living" on spirituality, career, parenting, Israel, or current events. It may be in the form of a complex Torah essay or a short video. Whatever the case, the slow drip penetrates and makes its impact on the Jewish soul.

A 2011 survey showed that among non-observant Jews, 86 percent say that Aish.com gives them a better understanding of Judaism, and 59 percent say that Aish.com has increased their Jewish observance. (Similarly, 82 percent of observant respondents say that Aish.com has deepened their sense of Jewish pride.)

Drop after drop, this impact of online Torah study creates a genuine transformation. Through Aish.com, countless numbers have profoundly deepened their understanding and commitment to Torah learning and observance. Many have taken on observance of Shabbat, have begun regular Torah study, are attending synagogue, and are now affiliated with vibrant Jewish communities. For others, Aish.com was their entrée to learning in yeshivah.

With the Almighty's help, this collective impact will continue to grow, contributing to a historic renaissance in the Jewish world.

We hope these stories will inspire you, providing the drops of water that together add up to a powerful impact, setting ablaze every Jewish soul.

Acknowledgments

Aish.com is recognized as one of the leading Jewish websites thanks to the efforts of many. Our endless gratitude goes to:

Jack Kalla, for his unwavering dedication, keen insights, and deep fount of creativity. In bearing the heavy load of resource development, he personifies the dictum of *Ein kemach, ein Torah*.

Our crackerjack programming team of Shraga Botwinick, Dovid Rosenfeld, Hersh Seibert, and Chaya Richmond, whose expertise and precision make the engines run.

Nir Grinberger, Meir Rosenberg, Yigal Guinerman, and Itamar Avnon, for their devotion and skill in expanding Aish.com in Hebrew, Spanish, and French.

David LeVine, for deftly charting the course in our crucial formative years.

Yitzhak Attias, for his stunning graphics that accompany each article and video, and Seth Aronstam, for his elegant site design.

Benyamin Buxbaum, for masterfully juggling the infinite details of our email lists, and Mendel Newman, whose dedication helps sustain the site.

Rabbi Pinchas Waldman and Rabbi Mordechai Younger, our scholarly "Ask the Rabbi" team.

Rabbi Kalman Packouz, whose Shabbat Shalom Weekly and Western Wall Camera remain two of Aish.com's flagship features.

Micah Smith, the director of many of our viral films, whose talent behind the camera is matched by his passion to impact the Jewish people.

All the Aish.com writers, whose drops of Torah create a tsunami of inspiration. In particular we thank our regular columnists Yaakov Salomon, Lori Palatnik, Emuna Braverman, and Sara Yoheved Rigler for their ceaseless dedication and constant flow of insights.

The many financial supporters of Aish.com, whose donations — whether $18 a year or much larger amounts — keep the ship afloat. Without you, Aish.com would cease to exist.

Our hundreds of thousands of loyal readers, whose feedback, enthusiasm, and support remain instrumental in helping to refine and expand the Aish.com vision.

The administration of Aish HaTorah Jerusalem, for helping to make our job easier.

The excellent staff at ArtScroll. It has been a pleasure working with Miriam Zakon and Shmuel Blitz.

Our wives and families, who support us every step of the way and offer invaluable feedback and advice.

Rabbi Hillel Weinberg and Rabbi Eric Coopersmith, who believe in the power of Aish.com to nudge the Jewish world, one click at a time, toward its goal of *tikkun olam*.

Rabbi Noach Weinberg *zt"l*, for his breadth of vision, his depth of Torah, for his warmth and love, and for having the confidence in us that we can truly make a difference.

And finally Hashem, Who makes all things happen.

Nechemia Coopersmith and Shraga Simmons
Jerusalem, Kislev 5772

Drops of Discovery

The Jew From Kuwait

My Muslim background left me unprepared for this shocking discovery.

Mark Halawa

Growing up in Kuwait, I had the best of everything. My father owned a successful construction company and provided us five children with amenities like piano lessons, swimming, calligraphy, and trips all over the world. Although we were Muslims like everyone else, we were totally secular and my father always aimed to shield us from religious people, whom he described as crazies.

I grew up being told that Israelis and Jews were the lowest type of creature in existence, put on Earth only to kill us Arabs. In math class the teacher would say, "If one rocket killed X number of Jews, how many would six rockets kill?"

My father was rabidly anti-Israel. He was a product of Nasser's school of thought: secular from a Muslim point of view, yet deeply dedicated to the idea of pan-Arab unity. Israel, he believed, was an American proxy in the post-colonial Middle East.

My father was a supporter of the PLO since the 1960s when Yasser Arafat (who founded the PLO while living in Kuwait) was

---

Mark Halawa, now known as Mordechai, was born in Kuwait and grew up as a Muslim in a non observant family. Today Mark is an observant Jew who is studying full-time at Aish HaTorah Yeshivah in Jerusalem.

raising money from wealthy Palestinians working in Gulf States. As an engineer, my father participated in a program where the engineering association in Kuwait would deduct money from his monthly salary to be sent directly to the PLO. He insisted that war and resistance was the only way to deal with Israel.

In the summer of 1990, when I was 12 years old, our lives changed completely. We were on vacation when Saddam Hussein invaded and annexed Kuwait. My father's business — along with much of the country — was ravaged. Our savings became worthless pieces of paper. We could not go back to Kuwait, so we immigrated to Canada. My father did manage to sneak back in for a few days to retrieve important business documents that would later be useful in recovering compensation from a United Nations fund.

Praying in the Dark

Of my family, I'm the only one who stayed in Canada. My father never really adjusted to life in the New World, and he had good business contacts back in Jordan, so my parents returned there. All my siblings also moved back to the Middle East.

One evening in 2003, I was studying at the university library in London, Ontario, when I happened to notice an older man. From his chassidic garb, he looked like a religious Jew. My curiosity was aroused, so I approached him and asked, "Are you Jewish?"

With a gentle smile on his face, he said, "No, but I like to dress this way." I didn't know whether he was joking or not. All the religious people I had come across in the past were pretty scary. Are Jews supposed to be funny?

His name was Dr. Yitzhak Block, a retired professor of philosophy. We exchanged a few words and then he asked about my background. My family history is pretty complex, and I get a headache every time I have to explain it all. So I simply told him that I'm an Arab from Kuwait, and mentioned that my grandmother from my mother's side is Jewish.

My mother's parents met in Jerusalem when my grandfather, an Arab from the West Bank, was serving in the Jordanian army fighting the Zionists. He was 18 years old and my grandmother was 16. Her father ran a school in Jerusalem — the same school where she would jump off the wall to meet my handsome, uniformed grandfather. They fell in love, got married, and lived for a number of years in Shechem (Nablus).

After my grandfather was discharged from the Jordanian army, the family moved to Kuwait, where oil profits were fueling huge business and construction projects. That's where my mother met my father and got married.

Knowing about my grandmother's Jewish background always made me curious about Jews. Whenever we were on vacation in Amman, Jordan, I used to constantly watch the Israeli channel — when my parents weren't around. My favorite was the Israeli national anthem, and I would stay up late waiting to hear them play it at the end of the TV transmission.

Standing there in the university library, this religious Jew, Dr. Block, looked at me and said, "In Muslim law, you're considered Muslim, since the religion goes by the father. But according to Jewish law, you're Jewish, since Jewish identity is transmitted by the mother."

My head started to spin and memories of my childhood in Kuwait began to surface. I recalled how my grandmother had a funny name on her documents, Mizrachi, which I never heard before. She also had a small prayer book with Hebrew letters, and she prayed in the dark crying. (I thought the Wailing Wall was so named because crying was a part of prayer.)

Aside from a vague family legend, my grandmother never mentioned anything about being Jewish — but now the pieces were fitting into place. I thanked Dr. Block for the conversation, and ran home to tell my roommate what I heard. He smiled and said, "So you're a Mus-Jew!" I was not amused.

I went to my room and called my mother. She rebuffed the story, saying, "Don't listen to people like that. We are Muslims and that's that."

I decided to call my grandmother myself and bring up the subject.

I beat around the bush a bit — after all, she'd been denying it for the past 50 years — and then finally blurted out, "Grandma, are you Jewish?"

She didn't answer the question directly, but she started crying and spoke about the years of Arab-Israeli conflict. She told me how her brother Zaki had been killed in Jerusalem before the rebirth of the State. To me that was sufficient confirmation of her Jewishness and I decided to leave it at that.

Over the next few months I avoided the whole issue of Judaism, mainly for the sake of not upsetting my mother. Besides, I was just finishing university, and career was my main priority. I was content with telling myself that I belonged to a mixed-faith family.

Streaming Tears

About a year later, I was rollerblading one day in my neighborhood when I took a hard fall and badly sprained my wrist. The road was smooth so I couldn't figure out why I had fallen. I couldn't stop thinking that it seemed like a push from Above. These thoughts caught me by surprise, since I wasn't into spirituality and I never had any religious connection. I was a bodybuilder, had tons of friends, and was on the heels of a successful career as a foreign exchange trader. So why had this happened?

Because my wrist was heavily bandaged, I was forced to take off from work for a few days. Dr. Block had mentioned the name of his synagogue, so that Saturday morning I decided to go check out the scene. I was hesitant at the thought of everyone being from European background and me the only Middle Easterner, but I decided to go anyway.

I called a cab and got dropped off at the synagogue. As I walked in, the first person I saw looked Indian. He shook my hand, said "Shabbat Shalom," and handed me a *kippah*. Then I saw a black man, which really surprised me. And Dr. Block was there, too.

I was handed a prayer book, shown the proper page, and before I knew it everyone was singing, *V'Shamru*:

"*And the Children of Israel shall keep the Sabbath, to make the Sabbath an eternal covenant for their generations. Between Me and the Children of Israel, it is a sign forever that in six days God made heaven and earth, and on the seventh day He rested and was refreshed.*"

Something hit me and I felt as though I knew this song. I just stood there taking in the sounds, the smells, and the sights. Everything felt whole and perfect. It was the opposite of everything I'd ever heard about Jews or Judaism. At this point my tears were streaming in freefall.

After the services finished, I met everyone over Kiddush. I spoke with an Egyptian couple and we shared our personal stories. Jews from all backgrounds were gathered together and I was another piece of this puzzle.

After Kiddush, I accepted Dr. Block's invitation to join him for lunch. I told him: "I can't believe I'm here, singing and praying in Hebrew. I could never have imagined it."

He smiled and said, "It's not so hard to believe. Every Jew is born with a little Torah and a little Menorah inside." He then pressed his shoulder up against mine and said, "All it takes is for another Jew to bump into him and light it up."

Dreams of Peace

My interest grew from there, and I began studying Torah and keeping Shabbat. Last year I spent a month in Israel touring and studying on Aish HaTorah's Jerusalem Fellowships program. It was a great "homecoming."

I still keep in close contact with my family and old friends. They're wonderful people and I love them very much. Yet it's hard to relate to them on many levels. In the Arab world there are tons of misconceptions and misinformation regarding Israel.

Another issue I'm trying to address is how the Arab world is filled with Holocaust denial. This past summer I went to Auschwitz, and I am working to produce the first-ever Arabic documentary about the Holocaust. I want to explain to Muslims in their own language exactly what happened.

The other issue that needs urgent attention is intermarriage in Israel. Unfortunately, a story like my grandmother's is not so rare. Many young Jewish women are wooed by Arab men and brought back to live in their villages. The children and grandchildren are never told the truth, especially with political tensions and the emotional unrest this would cause a family. As a result, many Jews are lost to our people. My mother has five sisters, and from there I have a few dozen cousins who are all Jewish — all living as Muslims in the Middle East. I recently met a seventh-generation Israeli whose cousin married a Palestinian and went to live in Saudi Arabia; her descendents are Jews living in Saudi Arabia.

All my relatives know that I'm practicing Judaism, and for the most part they're accepting. I can talk to them about Judaism and they're politely interested. We love and respect each other. My father is resistant, however, given that secularism and war against Israel are the two ideological pillars of his life. When I first became interested in Judaism, I didn't tell him straight out. We were having a political discussion and I mentioned that I support the State of Israel. That ignited a big clash and I've learned to only discuss these matters with him in an indirect way. I always know when I've crossed the line; he gets angry and calls me a "Zionist."

The other big exception — not surprisingly — is my grandmother. I've asked her a number of times for more information about her family background, but she refuses to talk about it. Maybe one day I will find the key to opening her up.

Growing up, I was taught that Jews were the source of all evil, descended from monkeys and pigs. On the other hand, I had the image of my grandmother holding her small prayer book with the Hebrew letters, praying with tender devotion. She is the sweetest person I know and there's no way she came from a bloodthirsty gang of murderers. She gave me a Jewish soul, and in her own way, it was she who kept my Jewish spark alive.

Sleepless in New Jersey

What if living out the dreams of your ancestors keeps you up at night?

Allison Josephs

Growing up, I remember hearing stories about two of my great-grandfathers, both of whom left behind tradition in pursuit of the American dream.

Grandpop Sam, my father's grandfather, was an avowed capitalist, even as a child. So at the ripe old age of twelve, when Communism began to sweep through Eastern Europe, he left his entire family behind in Russia — along with his religious lifestyle — never to see either again. He arrived penniless and parentless, hardly knowing a word of English, and not a decade later graduated from the University of Pennsylvania. After graduation, he got married, opened a cigar factory, and was soon buying a new Cadillac for himself every two years.

My mother's grandfather, Abraham, did not fare as well in America. Although he did everything in his power to provide for his family

---

Allison Josephs is the founder and director of JewintheCity.com, which breaks down misconceptions about religious Jews and offers a humorous, meaningful look into Orthodox Judaism through the power of new media. Allison has been involved in Jewish outreach for over a dozen years and is a sought-after speaker on inspirational Jewish topics. She received her Bachelor of Arts in Philosophy from Columbia University and lives with her husband and four children minutes from the George Washington Bridge.

(including keeping his haberdashery open on the Sabbath), Grandpa Abraham died at 36 from leukemia, leaving behind his young wife and three children to struggle through unyielding financial hardship at the start of the Great Depression.

Along the way, both of these great-grandfathers shed their Jewish observance in order to make a better life here in America. Three generations later, I was quite representative: upper middle class, assimilated, and living in Northern New Jersey.

Our comfortable lifestyle was founded on our great-grandfathers' sacrifices. My father was a doctor. We had a pool in our backyard, a vacation house in the mountains, and we attended private school. My mom had us in more after-school activities than I can remember: dance, gymnastics, ice skating, tennis, baton twirling, piano lessons, and Hebrew school, to name a few. On Saturday mornings we'd climb into bed with my parents for tickle-wars with my father, followed by a waffles-and-bacon breakfast prepared by mom. And we rarely missed our Thursday family night out for Chinese food.

Despite all the wonderful things I had in my life, it occurred to me one day, at around the age of eight, when I was well into collecting Garbage Pail Kid cards, though still regularly conducting Barbie weddings, that there was something enormous missing from my life. No, not a sense of fashion; everyone in the late 80's was wearing their hair big and tall, with rhinestone-studded baggy shirts and slouch socks. What I was missing, rather, was something profound and yet so basic: *I didn't know why I was alive.*

This realization was brought on by a discussion my father and I were having about infinity. He was trying to explain that not only do numbers go on forever, but that there's also an infinite amount of space between every integer. We then started talking about how the universe has no end either. (One might wonder why a father would burden his young child with such knotty concepts, but my dad is a natural-born numbers guy who hadn't a clue at the time how his seemingly harmless banter would come to wreak havoc on my psyche.)

This notion of infinity started messing with my little eight-year-old brain, and I began staying up at night, trying to wrap my head around these concepts.

Then a tragic event exacerbated my worries about infinity and launched me into years of insomnia, panic attacks, and existential angst. As the story was retold in whispers by my classmates on a cold December morning of my 4th-grade year, a horrible murder took place and my schoolmate Angela and her siblings were dead.

Now, I grew up in a sleepy suburban town where things like this just didn't happen. So when something like this did happen, I was forced to confront the fact that I too could die at any moment, and that life was not nearly as stable and predictable as I had always assumed. This got me thinking about the eternity of death — how I'd be either somewhere or nowhere forever. Then I realized something even more disturbing: I had no idea what I was supposed to do with the time I'd been given before I had to confront that unknown eternity.

I approached my parents one day — I was almost nine — and casually asked, "Why are we here?"

"Where?" they responded, sharing quizzical looks.

"You know," I persisted, "living. What are we here for?"

Clearly, my parents didn't know how to slam shut the philosophical Pandora's Box I had just opened. "Um," was about all they could muster in response.

Their inability to answer my question upset and surprised me. They were the ones who brought me into this world. How could they not know what they were doing in it? It seemed irresponsible of them to have gotten me tangled up in this mess of existence when they hadn't bothered to figure it out for themselves yet.

Desperately, I began asking other people this question — friends, family, teachers, anyone who might have a clue. But no one seemed able to answer what I had assumed to be a very basic question.

Eventually I came to think that life was not much more than people staying so busy that they never had time to consider what they were staying so busy for in the first place. But I was never able to keep myself distracted for very long. During the day, when I was tied up with school or other activities, I could push away the big questions that haunted me. But late at night, when all the noise was gone and I was left alone with my thoughts, I was tortured. *Why did the day I just lived even matter? Why should I bother waking up tomorrow to do it all over again?*

I never once considered the possibility that there simply was no purpose. The world seemed too detailed and complex, human beings too full of talent and abilities, to have it all be used for nothing. But each day that passed without finding an answer brought me one day closer to the end, and I was painfully aware that once my time ran out, I would get no more.

Over the next eight years, I would suffer from off-and-on insomnia and panic attacks. I would get a nauseous, empty feeling in the pit of my stomach as my mind would fixate on the fact that there was no way of escaping the eternity that awaited me. I would repeat over and over again to myself, "Oh my God, Oh my God, Oh my God," until someone (usually my older sister) would pull me out of my state.

Hawaiian Epiphany

In my junior year in high school my family took a winter break trip to Hawaii. We stayed right by the shore in Maui for a week, and my father — good old numbers guy — told me to listen to the waves. So I did. I listened in the morning, in the afternoon, and in the evening. I listened to them when I went to sleep, and when I woke up the next day I heard them again. It occurred to me that waves had never stopped crashing. I ran to my father to announce my discovery.

He looked at me as if I had gone mad. "Waves don't stop. So what?"

But I challenged him to do the math, and we figured out that if the world was a million years old, the waves on that shore would have crashed 10 to 12 trillion times, without once ever stopping. And not just on that one shore — but on countless shores across the planet.

And then it hit me: If I had spent 16 years taking something so profound for granted, I must be missing so much more. I spent the rest of my vacation trying to appreciate the natural world like I never had before. But it wasn't until the last day of the trip that my life would change forever.

My family and I were hiking through a breathtaking tropical rainforest called the Road to Hanna. In the middle of the hike, we came upon some bamboo shoots whose bark was covered in green and gold vertical stripes

"Did someone paint these on here?" I wondered aloud.

Everyone in my family had an opinion on the matter. Some said painted, some said natural, but my father came over to settle the confusion. "These lines are too straight and flawless to be natural," he assured us.

But when I looked up, I saw that the shoots towered over us 50 feet in the sky, with stripes all the way to the top.

"*Wow*," I muttered to myself, "*God has quite a paintbrush.*"

I took a few more steps and shook off the wonder of the moment, only to stop in front of the most incredible tree I've ever seen. It had a smooth bark, lavender background, and was covered in pink, blue, and green swirls. There was no doubt in my mind: Some nutty artist was painting the trees in this forest. It was the only thing that made sense. But when my mother told me to look up, I saw that the color continued to the top of the trunk. And for a brief moment, it was as though I understood the entire universe.

The best way I've been able to describe my experience is that I had a moment of clarity during which I tapped into a greater sense of harmony in existence. And in an instant I went from intense doubting to intense belief in God.

The nauseous, empty feeling that used to occur in the pit of my stomach as I'd contemplate my own demise was suddenly filled with warmth and light. What I realized in that moment was that from every comet to every caterpillar, everything in the universe was in its exact right place and time, including me and my life.

Of course, I was petrified to leave Hawaii. I doubted — in all of New Jersey's ugliness — if I'd ever experience such transcendence again. But when I got back home and continued with the Jewish studies classes I'd begun not long before, I began to understand that it is not occasional moments of spirituality that provide a sense of meaning and purpose. Yes, those moments give us inspiration and often point us in the right direction. But it is through day-to-day study and observance that a person builds a lasting connection with that awesome force that I sensed in the forest in Hawaii.

My great-grandfathers sacrificed everything to pursue the American Dream. Three generations later, I retraced a path back to their Jewish roots and returned to a place of tradition and observance that had been all but forgotten within my family. I learned that everyday actions can transcend our transient lives, and connect us to something greater and more permanent. Now I live my life with that knowledge, which has finally — and thankfully — put my mind at rest.

The Jewish Prince of Persia

The Shah of Iran's descendant tells his story from Jerusalem.

Sara Yoheved Rigler

Moshe* looks like any other religious Jewish man in Jerusalem — dark hair, dark beard, wire-rimmed glasses, poring over a Talmudic tome in a yeshivah. No one would suspect that he is the great-great-grandson of a former Shah of Iran.

Moshe's life has had more dramatic twists than a Disney movie. He is a scion not of the Pahlavi dynasty, which was deposed by the Islamic Revolution after two generations, but rather of the Qajar dynasty, which proudly ruled Persia for ten generations. He remembers visiting his

---

Sara Yoheved Rigler is the author of three bestsellers: *Holy Woman, Lights From Jerusalem,* and *Battle Plans: How to Fight the Yetzer Hara* (with Rebbetzin Tziporah Heller). She is a popular international lecturer on subjects of Jewish spirituality and a popular featured writer on Aish.com. She has given lectures and workshops in Israel, England, South Africa, Mexico, Canada, and over thirty American cities. A graduate of Brandeis University, after fifteen years of practicing and teaching meditation and Eastern philosophy, she discovered "the world's most hidden religion: Torah Judaism." Since 1985, she has been living as a Torah-observant Jew in the Old City of Jerusalem with her husband and two children. She presents a highly-acclaimed Marriage Workshop for women [see www.kesherwife.com] as well as a Gratitude Workshop. To invite her to your community, please write to slewsi@aol.com.

great-grandmother, the daughter of Mohammed Ali Shah Qajar, whom they called the "Little Princess" until her death at age 99, who used to regale him with stories of growing up in the palace, in the shadow of the Peacock Throne. He also remembers escorting his great-uncle into a room of Persian expatriates in Europe; everyone bowed to his uncle and called him, "shazdejeun, great son of the king."

Moshe's grandmother was married off to an aristocrat whose fiefdom was far from Tehran. "In great aristocratic families, it's not good to work," explains Moshe. "All his life, my grandfather didn't work, but he gambled and did opium." One fateful night, when Moshe's mother Mina was nine years old, her father gambled away everything he owned — his palace, his landholdings, his stable of Arabian stallions. The family was cast out of their home with barely food to eat.

It was the first of three times in her life that Mina would lose everything in a single night.

The family retreated to Tehran and was given an apartment in the palatial home of the Little Princess, Mina's grandmother. The family had lost its wealth, but not its prestige. "People in Persia are very proud of their origin," comments Moshe. "People respected my mother because she was high-born. Even if you lost all your money, you are still respected. Persians are very proud, and if you are aristocracy, it's even more so."

But at age 17, Mina risked losing even her status. She fell for Charles, a European Christian living in Tehran. When she revealed to her mother that she intended to marry this man who was neither Persian nor even Muslim, her mother threatened to disown her. Mina did not back down. At the end of a raging argument in which her mother told her she never wanted to see her again, the door was closed behind Mina, leaving her on the street with a single suitcase.

Charles, at age 22, was a budding scientist and a man of eloquence and charisma. He went to Mina's mother and eventually convinced her to accept the marriage. Although Mina had a strong belief in God, like most of the Persian aristocracy she was a lukewarm Muslim. She converted to Christianity and the couple had three weddings: civil, Christian, and Moslem.

Childhood and the Revolution

They lived in Tehran and Charles launched a company based on his scientific discoveries. In 1971, their second son Henry (later to become Moshe) was born. Strangely enough, his grandmother insisted on having him circumcised on the eighth day. He was also baptized as a baby. He was not given a Persian name, nor did his father permit him to learn to read and write Persian. Charles wanted his son to feel that the world was his home; his fate was to grow up with no home.

Charles's business was successful, and Henry was raised in the lap of luxury: his own horse, skiing every weekend, vacations in European capitals, and an Occidental school attended by the upper class. He remembers the privileged precincts of North Tehran as "a paradise for children. People were extremely good and friendly, we had a huge family, and I watched English television."

His idyllic childhood was ended by the Islamic Revolution of 1979. "People were killing each other in the streets," Moshe recalls. "I used to go to my school in a school bus. One day one of the school buses was blown up by a rocket. All the children on the bus were killed. Two days later my brother and I were in Europe."

They arrived in their new boarding school in the European countryside in a chauffeured Rolls Royce. None of the locals had ever seen such a sight. They thought the boys were from the family of the fleeing Shah.

During the first phase of the Revolution, Iranians across the political and religious spectrum were united in their desire for liberty and to get rid of the Shah. Had Mina been a Pahlavi, she would have been executed. Instead, she was from the revered Qajar dynasty. Like many of the aristocracy, she made an amiable alliance with the new government. A year later, she brought her sons back to Iran.

For Henry's family, the national chaos was exacerbated by personal tragedy. Unscrupulous Western concerns had been trying to buy Charles's innovative technology, but he had repeatedly refused. Finally, two Harvard men came to Tehran and over a period of a few months implemented a carefully plotted scheme to win Charles's confidence. One night they plied him with liquor and got him to sign his business away. Overnight, the family lost everything. A broken Charles went to Europe, where he tried to start over again. A few months later, the family was notified that Charles was found dead, apparently of a heart attack.

Protégé of the Ayatollah

Mina was now alone, but undaunted. She approached a company that had been associated with her husband and asked to work for them. They offered her a lowly position as a salesperson. She converted a room in their small apartment into an office, and started from scratch. Her efforts, however, were undermined by rampant government corruption.

Mina went directly to Ayatollah Khomeini. Henry remembers the servants in his home during his halcyon childhood speaking of the coming of the Messiah. When Ayatollah Khomeini returned to Persia at the outset of the Revolution, virtually the entire populace regarded him as the Messiah. Mina, shrewd and secular, was an exception. But when she spoke directly with him to complain about government corruption, she became star-struck. Khomeini would not look directly at a woman's face. Nevertheless, by the end of the interview, Mina had become his faithful protégé. Upon arriving home, she received a phone call saying, "Any time you have a problem, just call the office of Ayatollah Khomeini and he will take care of it."

For the rest of Khomeini's life, even during the most violent days of the regime, Mina enjoyed his personal protection. "The government feared my mother," asserts Moshe. Several years later Mina had become a fantastically successful businesswoman.

Meanwhile the Revolution had entered a repressive phase. The religious zealots began to kill off all the other factions. Moshe remembers watching a movie in the home of the first Minister of Justice after the Revolution. Two years later, that Minister was murdered by Islamic radicals.

"Tehran became like the Chicago of the 20s," remembers Moshe. "People with machine guns were gunning down other people in the streets. They closed the Occidental school my brother and I attended."

Mina wanted her sons to become educated, cosmopolitan people. She decided that they had no future in the new Iran. A year after bringing them back, she again sent them to Europe, this time for good. Henry was nine years old when he bid his final farewell to the only home he would know until he created his own in Jerusalem.

The boys attended a Christian boarding school. They were completely alone in a foreign country. They had no contact with their father's relatives, who had failed to attend Charles's funeral; Mina had severed all ties with them. Mina visited two or three times a year, taking them on vacations to the United States, Vancouver, Hawaii, Spain, etc., but even on vacation her attention was on her business.

For high school, the boys attended the International School of Valbonne on the French Riviera. Known as "the school of geniuses," it was the academy of choice for the sons of heads of state from every continent.

Throughout his teenage years, Henry engaged in a quest to find ultimate Truth. He read copiously in literature and philosophy. He dabbled in spiritualism, Epicurean philosophy, art, and theater. He experimented with Zen meditation; after just a few months he attained "a sort of Nirvana." With shoulder-length hair and all black clothing, he walked barefoot around Valbonne's campus.

His quest for Truth did not take him to religion. Having been raised by monks in Christian schools, he did not take Christianity seriously. Having been exiled by Islamic zealots, he had no respect for Islam. His quest was intellectual, not religious, and God played no part in his life.

Then one day while he was in college, Henry had a mystical experience. He was suddenly, powerfully gripped by a consciousness of God as real and immanent. This state, which was not drug-induced, lasted a fortnight. After it ended, Henry wanted nothing else as much as to re-experience that God-consciousness. As an intellectual, he trusted his mind and knew that what he had experienced was an unadulterated dose of Reality. But where could he find God again?

Discovering Judaism

One evening while in law school, some of his secular Jewish friends mentioned that they were going to a Jewish class that evening. Henry invited himself along. As Henry attests, "Everything the rabbi said, I felt, 'This is what I have been seeking.'" His Jewish friends soon stopped attending the weekly class, but Henry continued. He resonated completely with the teachings. In a bookstore, he found some classic Jewish texts, such as the *Kuzari* and *The Path of the Just*. Reading them, he was overwhelmed by the sense, "Yes, this is what I want."

The Path of the Just, an 18th-century text describing the ascending levels of character refinement and spiritual attainment, became for Henry a map back to the God-consciousness he had known and lost.

After law school, Henry decided that it was not enough to study Judaism; he had to live it. He made up his mind to convert to Judaism, but when he tried to make an appointment to initiate the conversion process at the city's Beit Din (Jewish court), he was ignored. Finally he phoned the Beit Din and asked to speak to the Chief Rabbi "about something very important and private." The secretary asked what he wanted to speak about, but Henry insisted it was private. He was given an appointment, but as soon as he told the Chief Rabbi why he had come, the Rabbi told him, "I have ten minutes, not one minute more, to give you." An hour later, he was still engaged in an intense conversation with Henry. At the end, the Rabbi told him, "Come back in one year. In one year, I will accept you."

Henry understood that it was a test of his sincerity and persistence. The Rabbi did not know that he was dealing with the undaunted Qajar breed. A year later, Henry came back. After two years of studying how to be a Jew, Henry converted at the age of 28. Six months later, he married Noa, and they made aliyah to Israel, where he studies in yeshivah.

Converting to Judaism meant forfeiting his aristocratic prestige, his mother's approval, and all connection to his extended family. "For an aristocratic Persian, becoming a Jew is the most awful thing you can do," declares Moshe. "It's simply unimaginable. It's shameful."

During the long conversion process, he never became discouraged by the prospect of losing all the privileges of his birth and upbringing. "I believed something," Moshe attests. "I believed that Torah is the Truth, and I wanted to have it. I didn't want to just learn about it. I wanted to reach the spiritual heights described in *The Path of the Just*."

After his conversion, Moshe had a conversation with his brother. "Why don't you convert?" Moshe asked him. "You know Judaism is true."

Moshe's brother replied, "I know it's true but I can't convert. I love luxury and comfort too much."

Sitting in his simple Jerusalem apartment, surrounded by his wife and children, Moshe ponders the trade-off he made in choosing truth over comfort. Did he get more than he lost? Moshe's answer is a broad smile.

In My Boots

What's a nice Jewish girl like me doing in a place like this?

LTJG Laurie Zimmet, US Navy

I'm sitting at my desk in one of the former palaces of Saddam Hussein, well into the fifth month of my second tour of duty in the war in Iraq. What I want to share with you may seem silly at first, but it has hit me like a ton of bricks. This is not easy for me ... okay, enough stalling, here goes: I have been wearing the same combat boots day in and day out since I was called to active duty in August.

Doesn't sound like much to you? Well, it is to me. Allow me to explain.

My boots have walked through the kind of sun and heat most associate with scorpions and death in all those Sahara movies from the 1940's, and my boots have trounced through water and mud,

---

Lieutenant Junior Grade Laurie Zimmet was born in Simi Valley, California and lives in a Los Angeles suburb. She attended EYAHT — Aish HaTorah's women's seminary in Jerusalem — in 1993, and has taught at several Jewish Day Schools in the Los Angeles area. She has lectured throughout the United States on her Jewish experiences during her first tour of duty in Operation Iraqi Freedom, including observing a clandestine Shabbos, and what it was like to lead the Passover Seder on an island in the Persian Gulf.

lots of mud. I'm looking at my boots and the one thing I can't shake loose from my mind is how in the world did I end up this way — still single, no children, serving in a war, again? Why am I wearing these boots?

Please don't misunderstand me. I am honored to serve my country, proud to wear the cloth of my nation, and mine is an exciting job. Once again, as in 2003, I am assigned to an Intelligence unit — a unit that goes after truly evil people. I do feel like I'm doing good for God, especially since these same people we go after not only harbor a disdain for America and all she holds dear, but not surprisingly, abhor Israel as well, and most especially the Jews.

I should feel good about that, right? And how about this: I'm able to serve in this war while keeping kosher, and as a side assignment working as an unofficial lay leader to Jews here at my FOB — Forward Operating Base. I even organized a giant menorah lighting ceremony in Saddam's Palace and made 100% kosher latkes for everyone at the ceremony. Many Jews here are still stunned that we pulled that off.

Still think I should feel good? I would too if I were reading this about someone else. But I'm not. It's me, not someone I've never met that I've labeled "hero" in my mind.

The truth is that I always wanted to be married and have children. Since I was a young girl I've thought it the noblest endeavor of any woman. Sure, I could go into my past, discuss each date with you, explain this and that about why it didn't work, but that would take volumes of writing with chapters and subheadings, perhaps even footnotes. Besides, I'm convinced prior to anyone reading it they would already be of the mindset that I was too picky or had other issues that precluded me from realizing that I'll never find that perfect person. They'll say, *see, she used the word "perfect," right there I can tell you that's her problem.* I don't want to do that; I don't want my life dissected. I cherish my dignity too much and until someone has actually walked in my shoes, been on my dates, I would appreciate it if they would give me the benefit of the doubt.

I'm a teacher by profession and I felt it such a privilege to teach children in cheder how to read, write, do arithmetic, and learn social skills; I never really felt like I was making any sacrifice. My friends have always explained to me that that's a big part of marriage and parenting, your time is not your time, every decision you make is based on the needs of the family. You're part of this grand team, all sharing the same name, like all teams — you know, the Dodgers, the Lakers, the Goldbergs, the Weinsteins, etc. This team builds a home, a family home, a Jewish home.

I'm human; I've had that need too. I wanted to feel I was sacrificing myself for some grand purpose to redeem our world, to be a part of something bigger than myself, to serve a greater good. I didn't want my decisions in life to affect only me. Thus, I answered a billboard ad and joined the United States Navy Reserve. And I suppose, in some ways, I have found a kind of family, not building a home but saving and protecting our homeland.

Still, I sit here and I stare at my boots. Forgetting already what it was like to feel like me, wearing a pretty skirt and blouse. Taking out my finest on Shabbos, surrounding myself with *mentschlich* friends who don't use curse words like they better hurry and say as many as possible before they're no longer allowed. I miss hearing the children *daven* at the *cheder*, those sweet voices that remind me that God is still hard at work on our behalf. I miss telling lonely children that they are never alone, that God knows him, that He is always with her, and that I love them too, and that I believe in all that they can be. I miss my rabbis and rebbetzins. Oh, I know they are only a phone call away — when I can get a line out — but it's not the same. And, I miss my friends, the ones who know me best, who know how much I've ached all these years to be a part of a different team, the one my husband and I would forge into the world praying all the while that we were indeed fulfilling God's goal for our lives.

With eight to nine months still ahead of me in Iraq, I sit and stare at my boots. Where will they go? What will they look like when, God willing, I return to Los Angeles, to my home?

Why am I writing this? I guess to vent, and I suppose I have another agenda. If you're reading this and you're married, raising children in a home, a Jewish home, with access to rabbis and rebbetzins, a variety of kosher food, and yes, for that matter — indoor plumbing — I can only share with you this: please don't ever think it is glamorous to go to war, perhaps something more exciting than the life you lead back home. The military, this war is very necessary, but it is anything but glamorous or romantic. I'll allow Hemingway to get away with such a description of war, but only him.

I implore you to appreciate your uniform in God's army — your kippah and *tzitzis*, your modest dress, your holy speech, your Shabbos table, your children's *cheder*, your Jewish life, your *Yiddishkeit*. You don't need world travel, adventures, or medals on your chest to feel a life fulfilled. You're already a hero.

And yes, I do continue to pray that my original goals in life not be forgotten. That God willing, I'll return home soon and that He will grant me the blessing of joining a different team, sharing a different name, wearing pretty shoes.

Please forgive me, I'd like to write more. I have more to vent, to share, but I've just received an order to take my boots on yet another mission, and I wonder — what will my boots look like tomorrow? Glamorous? Romantic? Nope, not even close.

My Converso Family

Becoming a Jew was my greatest act of defiance.

Reyna Simnegar

The day of my conversion to Judaism was the ultimate cosmic link between my past, my present, and my future. Although it was 12 years ago, I remember it as if it happened a few hours ago. I can still feel the acceleration in my heart, the knot of tears trapped in my throat, along with the nervous breathing from the overwhelming commitment I was undertaking. I can still hear the words "kosher, kosher, kosher" echoing in my mind and the warm waters of the mikveh embracing me, transforming me into a new being.

Catholic School

Sometimes reality is stranger than fiction. I grew up in the city of Caracas, Venezuela, in a wonderful, close-knit family surrounded by

---

Reyna Simnegar was born and raised in Venezuela. Her family history dates back to the Spanish Inquisition when her family fled from Spain and ultimately arrived in Venezuela. Reyna moved to the United States in 1995 to pursue higher education in Interior Design. She is very happily married and lives with her wonderful husband and vivacious five boys in Brookline, Mass. And by the way, she did end up getting her Bachelors degree in International Management and Economics from the University of Massachusetts with honors.

cousins, aunts, and uncles. I was raised with excellent family values, tremendous respect for authority, and a great fear of heaven. I was also raised as a Catholic.

My parents sent me to Catholic school for almost my entire life. I was always a deeply religious person. At school I gladly participated in mass and prayed fervently every night with the only tools I was taught by my mentors. But many questions hovered in my mind as I was growing up. Catholic school was a great place for the complacent soul; it turned into a nightmare for my seeking soul. Whenever I had a question in the class, if I dared to ask, I was looked down upon because I was to accept what I was being taught with my heart, not with my mind. For the most part questioning the faith was seen as an act of defiance.

Some nuns were very nice; others were incredibly unreachable and scary. There was a huge focus on dressing modestly in the school. We could not wear makeup, nail polish, or dye our hair. We had to wear a very modest uniform. But at home we were allowed to wear whatever we wanted, as short as we wanted. Venezuela is known for its beauty pageants and beautiful women. It is the dream of every young girl to be considered pretty enough to participate in the Miss Venezuela pageant. I was no exception to the rule and gave my parents much pride by winning various beauty pageants, from first grade on, and by being the homecoming queen in high school.

This mixed message made me more confused. Why would any of us want to follow the nun's example of modesty if we got so much more attention being immodest? Why did the nuns preach modesty and then organize beauty pageants to celebrate the culmination of the school year? Why would I strive to be modest when there was never an explanation given for it?

Growing up in this bewildering environment made me question authority even more. Sometimes I would stare at the nuns at school and ask myself, *Why are you dressed like this? What do you have that makes you spiritually closer to God than I am? How do you know what God wants from you? What kind of mother would you have been?* I needed answers to my questions. I needed to know there was a way to reach closeness to God without having to become like them. I *needed* freedom to talk to God directly. I needed truth.

So I started searching for more. Somehow I was always fascinated with Judaism. I didn't know anything about it, but I wanted desperately to know more. I only knew about the Jews from the Old Testament but I knew these people still existed. I started reading and learning about Jews on my own, convinced they would have an answer. Little did I know that this search would take me so far — all the way back home.

My Converso Family

The first time I saw a Jew was one Saturday as we were driving to see my paternal grandparents. We saw several men with black hats, black coats, and beards walking in the streets of my grandfather's neighborhood. "Who are these men?" I asked my father. "They're Jews." He then mentioned that my grandfather's house was in the Jewish community. I always felt apprehensive around my paternal grandparents. There were very old and strict, especially my grandfather, who just sat in his "special" chair where no one else was allowed to sit. My sisters and I were not allowed to get up from the couch and run around like normal kids.

One day I asked my Aunt Sarah, who lived with my grandparents, if she knew their house was located in a Jewish community. Her answer changed my life forever. She said in a whisper, making sure my grandfather would not hear, "Of course I know our home is in a Jewish community. After all, our family is of Jewish origin. Our last name had been changed from Peres to Perez."

I could not believe my ears. "What do you mean our family is Jewish? What are you talking about? I have never heard of this!"

She told me that the family had come from Spain a few hundred years after the Spanish Inquisition and settled in Venezuela. They changed their name to blend in and avoid persecution. "You mean you never wondered why all of our names are Jewish names?"

I had to sit down to recover. Hundreds of images and situations flashed in front of my eyes. All the strange things my father's family did were not idiosyncrasies; they were mere family traditions dating back to the time of the Inquisition. I had found the lost piece of the puzzle. I was closer to the truth than I had ever been. I had a reason to embrace the fascinating religion with which I had become obsessed. I was going in the direction of truth. After all, my family was Jewish. Or was it?

I immediately started researching and reading about the Inquisition. I learned that the Jews in Spain had been tremendously affluent and relatively accepted in the early years, under the Muslim rulers in the early 10th century, but suffered during persecutions by Iberian Christians, including pogroms in Cordoba (1011) and Granada (1066). These attacks continued as the "Reconquista" became full blown, and by the 14th century the Christians had taken most of Spain from the Muslims. Many Jews decided to escape these attacks by converting to Catholicism. These Jews were the most affluent and did not want to give up their social and commercial status. They were called "conversos."

Many of these conversos practiced Judaism in hiding, pretending to be Catholics on the outside. They lived side-by-side with their Jewish brethren and some even remained active in the Jewish communities. At first this solution proved beneficial and many conversos became very successful. But inevitably, this very success sprouted jealousy among Catholic Spaniards, who reported unfaithful conversos to the authorities. Many conversos practiced certain customs that, for the Catholics, were definite signs that these people were not true converts and were still spiritually linked to their Jewish past. These conversos were then called marranos (pig in Spanish), or crypto-Jews, and were to become the main focus of the Inquisition's agenda.

My research about "marranos" made me realize that my family was one of them. I always wondered about the rare customs of my father's family. Unlike most Venezuelans, my grandmother was keen for making all kind of eggplant dishes, in particular fried eggplants. Although the Arabs introduced eggplants to Spain, it was the Jews of Spain who became exceptionally fond of it, later bringing this vegetable to South America after the expulsion (around 1650). Spanish Jews were so fond of eggplants that the satirical poetry of the day made reference to it. She also made desserts called "Cabello de Angel" and "marzipan," both a staple for converso families. Sadly, thousands of marranos were murdered because of adhering to their culinary customs. In fact, the Inquisition Trial Documents (still available after all these years) are crammed with testimonies from maids or neighbors testifying in court against conversos making these dishes.

Speaking to my relatives, I discovered more information. My grandfather had a house in the town of Zaraza, Guarico State, the first town in which my family settled. They came by boat in the 1700s from the River Unare that leads into the Caribbean Sea. I have in my possession today one of the family's precious pieces of fine china, which they brought with them to the New World. It is a sauce dish dating back to 1767. My father recalls that in the house in Zaraza there were two paintings that always puzzled him. One was a painting of Queen Esther pointing at Mordechai and another called "La Plegaria de Esther" (Queen Esther's plea). The story of Purim has no real relevance in the Catholic religion. I didn't even know this story existed until I became Jewish! I discovered that Queen Esther was the heroine of the converso Jews because she was the quintessential hidden Jew.

I also have my grandmother's precious candelabras, made of extremely old Baccarat crystal, that sit next to my Shabbat candles. Every Friday I get goose bumps just imagining my relatives lighting these old candelabras with a hope that one day they could practice Judaism in public.

One uncle remembers seeing a Chanukah menorah and even kippot in the Zaraza home. Many people recall how my grandfather had a midnight private wedding ceremony where only a few were invited, perhaps because this ceremony was to remain a secret for the rest of eternity. Many converso Jews "sacrificed" a family member to the church to become a priest in order to not bring any doubt that the family was indeed devoted to Christianity. And many celebrated mass in their home, lead by the "family priest." And indeed, one of my father's uncles was a priest who later in life gave up priesthood, and many times there was a private mass held at my grandmother's house.

It wasn't until my grandfather passed away when I was 15 that many other secrets came to light. My grandfather kept locked in his room many pictures and documents that helped the family reconstruct the past. The names of my ancestors and even of family members today are mostly Jewish names. We not only have converso family in our genealogy but also European Jewry (my great-great-grandfather's first wife was Carmen Martin Rosenberg). My grandfather was General Guillermo Isaac Perez Telleria. He was given the honorary title of General for financing part of the Venezuelan independence war (Venezuela used to be a Spanish colony).

One of the most amazing yet macabre finds were several art works made with hair from the deceased. My family was always obsessed with keeping a lock of hair from a loved one. I still remember a lock of my grandmother's hair framed and hung in the wall of my uncle's home. My cousin and I both own one of these art works, which date back to the early 1800s. They are depictions of the burial of a family member, without any Christian devotional object. (In fact, I recently discovered that the family's mausoleum in Zaraza was originally built without any Christian symbols; only an open book and the names of the deceased.) The depictions in the art are incredibly delicate, made with the strands of hair of the departed. The date of birth of the family member in the artwork is 1802. Considering the Inquisition was abolished in 1834, it is possible her family felt she could not have a public Jewish burial.

I remember going to the cemetery with my father to visit our late relatives. Instead of bringing flowers we would search for little rocks to put on the top of the graves. I always wondered why we did this; I don't think my father even knew. I now know this is a Jewish custom.

In 1480 the Inquisition began to spy on the conversos. In the course of 12 years, thousands of conversos were tortured and burned at the stake. In the year 1492, King Ferdinand and Queen Isabella, aided by the Catholic Church, decided that as long as there were Jews remaining in Spain there would be conversos trying to keep Judaism in secret. Therefore, they determined that all Jews must leave Spain or convert. The Alhambra Decree (also known as the Edict of Expulsion) was issued on March 31, 1492, ordering the expulsion of Jews from the Kingdom of Spain and its territories by July 31, 1492.

The punishment for any Jew who did not leave or convert by the deadline was death.

The only Jew permitted to stay under any circumstances was Don Isaac Abarbanel, a leading Torah sage who served as the Finance Minister of Spain. He was too valuable to the kingdom to spare. Abarbanel used his clout and money to try to convince the monarchs to revoke the edict, offering them so much money that the King actually hesitated. However, the evil Torquemada, Inquisitor-General of Spain, convinced the monarchs otherwise. Abarbanel only managed to get the deadline extended for two more days. Hence, the date of expulsion fell on August 2, 1492 (the ninth of Av, 5252), the anniversary of the Temple's destruction, a day of Jewish tragedy.

There is disagreement regarding the exact number of Jews who left Spain, but the figures vary between 130,000 to 800,000. A primary source, the *Me'am Lo'ez* (written in Ladino, the language of the Jews of Spain) in its section on Tishah B'Av mentions that a third of the Spanish Jewish population died for their faith, a third converted, and a third went into exile. It is said that the Jews who left Spain that day, including Don Isaac Abarbanel, departed singing songs of joy and uttering prayers of thanksgiving to their Creator for having withstood the test and not submitting to conversion. They were allowed to take their belongings, except gold, silver, and money. The crown and the inquisitors confiscated all their properties.

At the date of expulsion, 50,000 to 70,000 Jews had converted to Catholicism and remained in Spain. Historians estimate a cumulative 100,000 to 200,000 Jews converted during the Inquisition.

My family tried very hard to keep living as Catholics while keeping many Jewish customs in the privacy of their home. It was never safe because many Spaniards turned in conversos to the authorities. My family practiced Judaism in secret for more than 100 years before leaving Spain to Venezuela. Many conversos felt they would be able to live a full Jewish life by leaving, but the Inquisition followed them to the Americas. It was not until the year 1834 that the Spanish Inquisition was finally abolished. Unfortunately, many conversos were lost and ultimately embraced the religion which oppressed them.

Reigniting the Spark

After so many years, whatever was left of the "spark" of Judaism in my soul has risen from the ashes and embraced the Torah. There are times I wish my family had fled Spain, leaving everything behind. How I wish they had not "given up." How I wish I had Ladino in my lips instead of only Spanish! After all, what kind of message did they give their children when they submitted to conversion? With what authority could they have expected their children to observe Judaism when they were not strong enough to give up wealth and status for Torah? They paid a high price for trying to make the Torah "fit" their lifestyles instead of embracing their heritage and trusting that God would ultimately take care of all the details.

But I choose to focus on the positive things my ancestors did accomplish. I feel the very reason I am today a Jew must be because ultimately they did something right. I have no doubt that it was because of the merit of my ancestors dying *"al Kiddush Hashem,"* sanctifying God's Name, that I have the privilege to become a full-fledged Jew.

I can never judge my ancestors decision for converting to Catholicism. But the fact is that many of their descendants ended up not being Jewish. Among my family I am the only one who "returned" to embrace Judaism. This leaves me with a great responsibility, to make sure my descendants remain strong, proud Jews. Whenever I make my grandmother's converso dishes I feel I am performing an act of defiance and triumph. When I eat this food on Shabbat I rejoice; the Inquisition is gone, but I remain! There is nothing better than seeing my children with *tzitzit* and *kippot,* indulging in marzipan!

I feel proud that even though many of my family members died *"al Kiddush Hashem,"* today my children are living *"al Kiddush Hashem!"*

Encounters With Elijah

"Elijah the Prophet" showed me what it means to be a Jewish Princess,

Rea Bochner

I met Elijah the Prophet in Phoenix.

    I suppose I shouldn't have been surprised that he showed up — it was Passover, after all — but at age 12 I had sat through enough Seders to know that the prophet we opened the door for after dinner didn't make a habit of appearing in the flesh. Mostly, I thought of Elijah as the Jewish version of the guy in the red suit and giant gift bag: a sweet entertainment for gullible children. The Ghost, if you will, of Seders Past.

    So I wasn't expecting much of a show that night, at the Arizona resort where non-observant families like mine could spend their Passovers adventuring at the Grand Canyon, catching a Suns game and jeeping atop the red mesas. In fact, I expected to spend my

---

Rea Bochner is a writer and musician who lives in Massachusetts. She holds a BA in Film at Emerson College and a Master's in Special Education from Montclair State University. Rea has worn many hats in her life, including: a tour guide at the Disney MGM Studios, a story developer at Universal Studios and later, and as a teacher of students with special needs. These days, Rea is wearing her "Mom" hat, happily raising her kids while writing for various publications, whipping up gourmet sugar-free muffins, and studying to become a midwife.

evening bored to tears as my father retold a story I'd heard a hundred times. The only thing keeping me in my chair that night was the promise of the five-star dinner I knew would eventually come.

We trudged through the Haggadah and ate our fabulous gourmet meal until we were stuffed to the seams. We searched for the Afikomen, and after I found it we prepared to open the door for Elijah. Everyone stood, singing a song of welcome, but as my brother pulled the door open, everyone froze. What I saw sent a shiver through me.

In the doorway stood a round, jolly man with a bushy beard and wearing full Chassidic garb: black jacket and *tzitzit* swinging, and hat askew, as if he'd just blown in on the desert wind. We stared at him as he waddled into the room.

"Gut Yontif!" he said, his voice a bubbly giggle. "I'm Itzik."

We were silent.

"I'm the hotel *mashgiach*," he said, identifying himself as the person who ensures the kitchen is kosher. "I just wanted to make sure everything was good for you here." His high-pitched English was a curious garble of Israeli and Brooklyn accents, with a dash of the Old Country for good measure.

"Everything is wonderful," Dad said. "We just thought you were … we just opened the door for Elijah the Prophet and you were standing there."

Itzik made a strange whispering sound, Psshhh … and burst into laughter.

Okay, so the prophet hadn't magically shown up in Chassidic garb. We all laughed the tension away. But I was still on guard. Ghost or no, Itzik was still an "ultra-Orthodox" Jew, and my experience had shown that his type would be quick to judge us for our lack of observance. I had spent my childhood studying in an Orthodox school where I was the only Conservative kid in my class. My *treif* (non-kosher) lunches and secular lifestyle was not exactly a good fit. If I wasn't good enough for them, chances were I wouldn't be good enough for this Itzik — who by now we'd learned was Rabbi Itzik — either.

After a few minutes of chatting, Itzik made to leave. "You're my last table. I have to start my Seder now, before it gets too late."

"By yourself?" Dad asked.

Itzik shrugged.

"You shouldn't have a Seder alone. Come join us."

My father, fired up by prospect of a bona-fide Chassid at his Seder table, scrambled to get Rabbi Itzik a chair.

"But you're almost finished," Itzik demurred. "I need to have Seder from the beginning."

"Then we'll start again," Dad replied.

What?

It was already 11 o'clock! I'd sat through one Seder already; I'd even extended myself to read a paragraph or two aloud from the Haggadah. There was no way I was doing it twice in the same night.

But that was exactly what happened. Horrified, I looked on as Dad ushered Itzik into a seat and flipped his Haggadah back to the beginning. They sang, they drank, they told stories deep into the night, while the rest of us fell asleep across rows of dining room chairs.

At three in the morning, when my mother woke me to return to our room, their second Seder was still going strong.

I took one last look at my father and his new friend sitting catty-corner at the table, engrossed in their Haggadahs. They were in their own world, I saw, when Dad didn't even look up to say good night.

Cinderella at the Bat Mitzvah

After our Passover escapade, we returned to New Jersey and life as usual. Preparations for my bat mitzvah were in full swing. Dad taught me how to lead the Shabbat services while Mom ironed out the details for my big bash: color schemes, catering menus, and, of course, The Dress: a white, poufy-sleeved concoction that screamed "Cinderella!"

During those months, Rabbi Itzik took his place as a quirky supporting character in our family folklore. He would come to visit us from Brooklyn with plastic containers of *shmaltz*, chicken fat, which he smeared with delight over challah and crackers. As he ate with gusto, he would chuckle at our horrified faces and wave off admonitions about watching his weight. A black-hatted Chassid was an anomaly in our suburb, but he made himself right at home in our kitchen. We couldn't help but welcome him; he was such a character, with his ready smile and twinkling eyes, constantly late, but always with an entertaining reason for being so. Eventually, the Brooklyn trappings fell away from view and all we saw was Itzik.

And yet, I waited for him to look askance at our modern clothing or lack of attention to Jewish law. I suspected eventually he would start snooping around our drawers and poke his head in our fridge to discern our level of kashrut. I waited for the day he would shake his finger in our faces and tell us we were doomed if we didn't observe the Sabbath. But that day never came.

My bat mitzvah day finally arrived. The affair was a smashing success — and I had the mountains of presents to prove it.

When Itzik arrived at the party (hours late, of course) the festivities were already winding down. Bidding goodbye to the last of my guests, I went to him, with my hand stretched out. I was pulled up short when he didn't reach back.

He would not touch me.

Suddenly, the true import of the day struck me, full-force. I was a woman now, according to Jewish law, and off-limits to men to whom I was not related. The sense of transition from one stage of life to another resonated with me more deeply in that moment than any other throughout my bat mitzvah celebration. I had spoken before an entire congregation and amassed a thick wad of checks, but only now was I shaken by real grief at the loss of my childhood. At the same time, I felt a keen sense of hope and anticipation about my future as a grown woman. Without saying a word, Rabbi Itzik had woken me up.

A Real Princess

Some time later, Rabbi Itzik was marrying off his daughter. I was surprised we'd been invited to the wedding in Brooklyn; I didn't think we were the kind of friends Rabbi Itzik would want to advertise having. Our appearance at the wedding — most likely, I assumed, a drab affair in a mildewy hall with prehistoric wallpaper — would probably be as welcome as a tuberculosis patient in a sterilized lab. Despite my misgivings, I tagged along with my parents, curiosity outweighing dread.

We arrived in the middle of the *Kabbalat Panim*, the pre-ceremony reception, where at least a thousand guests had come to greet the bride. From the first moment, it was like entering a foreign country: a sea of black hats and expensive-looking wigs, an animated buzz of thick New York accents sprinkled with Yiddish. Whereas I had anticipated walking into a room full of sneers, our arrival barely caused a first glance, let alone a second.

Hungry for some glamour, I scanned the room for the bride. When I finally saw her, my breath stopped. Dewy and pink-cheeked, she smiled graciously at her guests from a high-backed, wicker chair. Her dress was a simple white, high-necked and long-sleeved, and she brimmed with an ethereal glow that reached me from across the room.

Forget Cinderella; this was a real princess.

As my parents brought me over to say hello to her, I could barely speak. It was like meeting a movie star. She smiled into my eyes and told me how happy she was that we were there. Although we had never met before, I could see she meant it.

Everyone poured out to the street for the *chuppah*, the wedding ceremony. At every other wedding I'd been to, people were silent during the ceremony, but that evening, the street buzzed with small talk. As the bride circled her groom seven times, two women swapped kugel recipes and argued over where to find the best price for a whole chicken. I jumped at the ecstatic chorus of "Mazel Tov!" as the new husband stepped on a glass to mark the end of the ceremony.

The reception was wild, the room thrumming with electricity. Every guest danced with joy as if they themselves had stood under the *chuppah*. Peeking through the *mechitzah* from the women's side, I saw a swell of men dancing in circles, circles within circles, eyes squeezed shut in what looked like a hypnotic state. Somehow I found my father in the crowd, his arms thrown around the shoulders of men I didn't know, his red face slick with sweat. There was an abandon in him I had never seen before. My father, I realized, was happy.

Riding home, images from the evening played over and over again in my head: The swarm of people, the glowing bride, the kind hellos and wishes of Mazel Tov. There had been no finger-pointing or whispers behind palms, only smiles of welcome. I fell asleep to the echo of music, the lights along the Lincoln Tunnel throwing shadows across my face.

Searching for Answers

Over the next decade, life evolved for all of us. My memories of Brooklyn quickly faded as I launched onto the treadmill of high school and college, fueled by a desire to make my mark. I traveled the world, lived in exotic cities, worked at some of the world's most influential companies. And yet, a longing followed me wherever I went, a need for something deeper than the bells and whistles of modern life. I tried it all — New Age Philosophy, Eastern religions, Transcendental Meditation — but instead of answers, I just found more questions. Once in a while, memories of my friend Itzik and his world would resurface, and I would wonder if they knew something I didn't. Then I would bat those thoughts away like a mosquito. I could stand on my head and spout mantras for hours, but those Orthodox Jews were nuts.

And yet, my travels eventually landed me in Jerusalem.

As an alumna of Birthright Israel, I'd been invited to study at a seminary for a few weeks. I knew nothing about the school, its philosophy, or where it was located, but it didn't matter; the trip was basically free. Which is how I found myself standing in one of the city's most charedi neighborhoods, wearing pants and a T-shirt.

Amidst black-hatted men and long-skirted, hair-covered women, I stuck out like a sore thumb. A few of the women gave me the up-down while the men didn't look at me at all. It was awkward, uncomfortable, even terrifying: I was sure a tribunal would be formed on the spot to have me stoned in front of the seminary. I couldn't stand it; I was grabbing a cab back to airport and going home now.

But something stopped me: Memories of a long-ago wedding, the smiles, the dancing. And of Itzik, with his funny stories and the love he always showed us, just because.

Was it possible, by assuming these people were judging me, that maybe, just maybe, I was judging them? If Itzik could have accepted me just as I was, there might be a chance that someone in this seminary would do the same.

It was just a few weeks.

I gathered my strength and walked in.

✳✳✳

It was a beautiful occasion filled with family and friends, delicious food and words of Torah. Of course, it was no surprise that Itzik arrived just as everyone was leaving, something about ending up in Long Island when he should have been in Teaneck. And yet, it was just as it should have been, the way it was at my bat mitzvah, when he'd shown me the true meaning of being a Bat Yisrael; at my wedding, where he'd come to greet me while I sat in my own *bedekin* chair; and now, today, celebrating the *brit milah* (circumcision) of my first child.

With his bright smile and happy laughter, Rabbi Itzik had come right on time.

The Torah in Our Church

The amazing story of our church that en masse decided to convert to Judaism

Yosef Juarez

I was born in Honduras 23 years ago, the oldest of four children. I lived in a neighborhood with all my cousins, on a street named after my mother's ancestors. We attended a church that is non-denominational, but with a strong evangelical bent.

When I was three years old, I fell from the second story of my house and dropped head-first onto the concrete, fracturing my skull. I was rushed to the hospital and wasn't moving at all, just gazing off into the distance. The situation was very grave. But then something strange occurred. The next day, it was as if nothing had happened. The doctor ordered new x-rays, and there was no sign of any damage — no fracture, not even a scratch.

Yosef Juarez was born in Honduras, and grew up in Houston Texas. After converting, he attended Yeshivah Aish HaTorah in the Old City of Jerusalem for seven months and upon returning to the United States, he learned at Yeshivah Ohr Somayach in Monsey.

He and his wife Tzipora Perel, a native of Tunisia, are the proud parents of Tzofia Emunah. He and his wife, who has an amazing story of her own, share their stories with Jewish audiences across North America. Their dream is to make *aliyah* in the near future and learn Torah in Eretz Yisrael.

Due to this, our family grew in our religious observance, and throughout my life I was focused on the service of God.

When I was eight years old, we moved to America, which offered better financial opportunities. We settled in a suburb of Houston and looked around for a church to attend, but nothing seemed as good as what we had back in Honduras.

Our old church was based in Honduras, but has branches in U.S. cities that have a sizable Central American and Hispanic population. So together with one other family, we requested that the church send us a minister. They sent us a man named Hector Flores, who at the time was still training to be a minister. And that's how our Houston church started — in one room in a house.

Minister Flores was fascinated with the Holy Temple, and its predecessor the Tabernacle (Mishkan). He had access to books and resources, and he started teaching Torah ideas that were unique in a Christian setting. We would spend months and months delving into aspects of the Torah.

Our membership grew steadily, as we were very outreach-oriented. The city was divided up into districts and groups, and we would literally go out into the streets and preach to people. During high school, I studied in my church's discipleship program, where they train young people in leadership skills and how to preach. We'd bring people into the church and provide them with family counseling and programs for all ages. It functioned very much like a family. And we would train the new members to reach out and bring more people to church.

Of course, people who came to our church for the first time would wonder why we were discussing so many Jewish topics. But Minister Flores continued on his unique path, and the church eventually split into two congregations. We got our own building and bought land to expand.

One of the unique customs of our church was something Minister Flores called "festivals of consecration." These were patterned after the festivals in the Torah, but in our church people would bring large donations on the "festivals" to fund our activities. From there it was constant small steps toward Torah observances. We took upon ourselves the obligation to tithe, and we'd give 10 percent of our income to church activities. After a while our festivals got assigned Jewish names, like Purim and Shavuot, corresponding to the Jewish holiday they fell close to.

This was definitely not consistent with mainstream Christianity. And the closer we got to Torah, the more some congregants became uncomfortable and started to drop out. It was a filtering process.

Unbeknown to us, behind the scenes, Minister Flores was going through an intense personal transition. After much research, he discovered many inconsistencies and contradictions in the New Testament, making the tenets of Christianity untenable.

Minister Flores started secretly going to a rabbi, to pester him with questions. Then he'd come back and teach us, slowly getting us closer and closer to Judaism.

Soon after, Minister Flores made the decision to convert to Judaism. But he struggled to find a way to tell us, as he didn't want to tear down Christianity without being able to offer us an alternative. So he kept teaching Torah, but in a way that was as subtle as possible. He gradually peeled away many of the things that were wrong and got us closer to Torah. Our songs became Hebrew songs. We began to incorporate real Jewish traditions into our festivals, and we even got a Torah Scroll for the church.

At that point we resembled more of a Jews for J— group, in the sense that we were Christians with a lot of Jewish traditions. The difference, of course, was that we were moving in the direction toward authentic Judaism, not the other way around.

During this process, our biggest resource for information was Aish.com and its Spanish sister site. At one point the church printed out reams of Aish.com articles on all the holidays, and gave a binder of these articles to each family.

Some of the church members became resistant to all these changes, and a number of people dropped out. There were occasional confrontations where people would question the minister, "How far are you going with all this?" And he would simply answer, "As far as the Torah takes us."

Revelation

About six months after Minister Flores made the private decision to convert, my mother had been at a Jewish bookstore and bought the book, *The Real Messiah* by Rabbi Aryeh Kaplan. This book lays out all the evidence for why Jews don't believe in the teachings of Christianity, in a very scholarly and convincing way. We found that a lot of Christian teachings were based on mistranslations or taking biblical verses out of context.

So my mother suspected there was more to this "Torah teaching" than the minister had been letting on.

Every Sunday after services, the entire congregation would go together to the park. One Sunday, my mother confronted the minister: "You know more than you're telling us, don't you." He would never lie or deny such a direct question, so he saw this was the right time to reveal his plan to convert. That Sunday, we all stayed at the park for hours and hours, discussing and explaining, until long after dark.

At that point, about 100 people wanted to keep studying with the possibility of conversion. But many others took the choice of becoming Bnei Noach, following the seven pillars of human civilization that the Torah presents for non-Jews to observe. Minister Flores explained that any human being who faithfully observes these laws earns a proper place in heaven, and this was an appealing alternative for many church members.

My mother, however, wanted to stick with the group who was interested in conversion. So we kept on learning, and eventually our group decided to attend Shabbat services. One Saturday morning our entire congregation showed up at the United Orthodox Synagogues. It was a bit of a shock to the community, because such a huge influx upset the social balance. But the leader of the synagogue, Rabbi Joseph Radinsky, was like an angel to us; his kindness and sincerity is clear to anyone who knows him.

When they saw things were serious, the Houston community sent a Spanish-speaking rabbi, Jose Gomez, to help each family clarify the right path. (He himself had converted 10 years earlier in Houston along with his entire family — parents, siblings, aunts, and uncles.)

As expected, all of this caused a real stir in the Christian community in Houston.

Minister Flores was among the first to convert, and since then many of our church members have converted, while others are in the process. My own conversion was finalized a year ago, and my mother and siblings are still in the process. I chose the name "Yosef" because in the Bible, Joseph was the first of his family to go down to Egypt. He established himself and was able to help bring the rest of his family along. My mother says that in our path to conversion, I have been sent ahead as our family's "Yosef."

After my conversion, I came to Israel and was really amazed. I saw a variety of Jews, and a whole different side of Judaism. There was something special about everything. I even found myself taking pictures of grass and rocks!

I started doing research into my roots, because I knew that this awakening to Judaism comes from a very deep place. I found out that on a voyage to the New World in 1502, Christopher Columbus reached the Bay Islands on the coast of Honduras, which became part of the Spanish empire. Jews undoubtedly came to Honduras at this time, on the heels of the Spanish Inquisition when many Jews "converted to Christianity" but secretly remained Jewish. I'm anxious to find out more about my ancestors, but it's very hard to track.

So where am I today? I am studying at the Aish HaTorah Yeshivah in the Old City of Jerusalem and I love it. I'm so enthusiastic about everything that I learn, and cannot wait to share it with all my friends and family back home. At this point, my plans for the future are pretty open. I want to continue to study Torah, finish my undergraduate degree, and see what opportunities develop.

But one thing I know for sure: I am committed to reaching out to my fellow Jews. If I was fortunate enough to discover this gold mine of spiritual wealth and fulfillment, then those who were born Jewish surely must be given that opportunity. And who knows — just as Aish.com spurred my Jewish growth, maybe this article will be the spark that someone else has been waiting for.

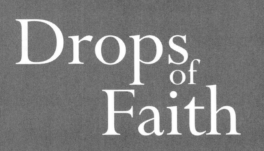

Drops of Faith

She Is Pure

*Preparing a Jewish woman
for her final pilgrimage.*

Andrea Eller

When I got the call, I was unprepared. I'd forgotten that I'd expressed interest in observing a *taharah* — preparing the deceased for burial. What had I been thinking? But I felt silly refusing the invitation given my initial enthusiasm, so I agreed. I tried to convince myself (it wasn't easy) that here was the perfect opportunity to explore the mitzvah with no quid pro quo. *From the sidelines.*

An hour later Phyllis, the friend who had piqued my interest in the *Chevrah Kadisha*, picked me up, reaffirming our agreement that nothing was expected of me and that only were I to change my mind would I assist the *taharah* team, and only under her tutelage. Short odds on that. I didn't say much on the way to the funeral chapel, and when we arrived I retreated even more into myself. I walked in and instantly tears caught in my throat, pleading for a ladies' room haven.

Andrea Eller attended EYAHT, the women's division of Aish HaTorah, for a year and a half. She is a writer and English teacher who also sings and acts professionally. Her latest one-woman-show is called *Shidduchim and Survival, A Ba'alas T'shuva's Tale,* the story of her transition from the secular to the observant and the search for her soulmate. (She has been happily married for six years.)

The terrain summoned still-fresh sorrow for my father's unexpected passing a few months earlier. But there was a task to be performed here. I would hold off my own pain for later.

We took the stairs down to a dimly lit parlor furnished in worn Victorian. At the back, the sad room opened to a corridor flanked on the far end by a heavy metal vault-like door. There three other volunteers waited — René, Lara, and Miriam — all friends of mine, who, with Phyllis, would comprise the *taharah* team.

Greetings were brief. We each donned a full-sleeved hospital gown of yellow gauze, over it a bibbed white plastic apron, a pair of firemen's boots to be worn over shoes, and two pairs of surgical gloves. A faded sheet with softened and torn edges was taped to the outside of the door; each of us silently read from it a prayer that God help us perform this deed with the right intentions and facility. *Help us? Not me. Help them. I'm just an onlooker.*

Subdued and qualmish, I followed them through the door into an open, bright, white-tiled room. There on a spotless white gurney lay a stilled woman. Swaddled in white sheeting was Sarah bas Avraham, a woman well into her eighties. Her metal bed was waist high, slightly angled toward its foot over a trough built into the floor. There were metal buckets and plastic buckets in the corners of the room, push brooms, hoses, and white cabinets filled with supplies: gauze, scissors, tape, sheets, strange-looking liquids, toothpicks, acetone, towels …. Each labeled item had its labeled place. After we washed our hands at the sink — right hand, left hand, right, left, right, left — I backed into a corner with the brooms.

Phyllis led the team. She began by murmuring the closest thing to conversation I was to hear for the next hour and a half. "Sarah bas Avraham, please forgive us if anything we do here as the *Chevrah Kadisha* offends your dignity in any way."

Silently, carefully, she began cutting away Sarah's encasement. As it fell away, Lara and Miriam inspected the body for wounds that might require stanching lest the burial clothing, which must be kept spotless, become stained. The only sounds were the clip clip of scissors and René's whispered prayers for Sarah. Reading from a laminated, timeworn sheet, she said a prayer at each step of the *taharah*.

I was afraid to look at Sarah's face, but my eyes were pulled to her. I never saw her fully, as care was taken to keep her face covered. The Kabbalists tell us that although the eyes of the dead cannot see, exposure of the face in such a setting of helplessness is a source of humiliation to the *neshamah*, the soul. They say that the *neshamah* hovers about the body in confusion and pain until burial is completed.

Now the silence was broken by the quiet splash of water running down the gurney and into the trough as Phyllis, Miriam, Lara, and René gently and methodically cleansed Sarah, section by small section. Only the part of her being washed was exposed at any moment; all else was kept covered by a clean white sheet. The women took care to save any cloth that had absorbed even a drop of Sarah's blood — blood that had been the source of her life. These cloths would be included in Sarah's casket.

I had inched over to the gurney and was facing Phyllis, when by way of hand gestures she asked me if I cared to remove Sarah's nail polish. There must be as few physical obstructions as possible between the body of the deceased and its ultimate home, and even nail polish is considered an obstruction.

"No way!" I thought as my head nodded yes independently.

My throat turned to dust. This would be the first time I'd ever touched someone who was not alive. But I was distracted from panic as Phyllis beckoned me to the head of the gurney. There she handed me cotton swabs saturated with acetone. It was odd. Why hadn't she just reached over the gurney and given me the swabs? I didn't know then that it is an insult to the deceased to hand articles over the body as if she were a thing, as if she and her body had not been the vessel for a soul. Any exchange of objects is therefore conducted beyond the deceased, in deference to the body and soul that God had wed.

I forced myself to pick up Sarah's right hand. It was surprisingly heavy and cool, frozen in a graceful curve. The experience was not at all macabre. My timorousness became wonder. What had she done with these hands? Had she cooked for a husband and children? Had she written letters? Played piano? Sown gardens? Carried grandchildren? Had she erred with these hands?

With my own right hand I daubed the pink away, feeling an unexpected warmth for this stranger whose face I could only glimpse. And I felt a sense of privilege that would recur each time I would perform this step of a *taharah*, helping to prepare a Jewish woman for her endmost pilgrimage.

All tasks up until this point had been in preparation for what was to follow. The team moved Sarah slightly, positioning wooden planks under her to lift her body from the metal bed. Then in one swift movement Phyllis swept off Sarah's sheet, and Miriam, René and Lara engulfed her in an unbroken watershoot from the buckets. "*Tehorah hi* (She is pure), *Tehorah hi, Tehorah hi*," said the team, and it seemed to me that had the sanctifying waters spoken they would have answered, "Yes. Pure is She, Pure is She, Pure is She."

Miriam quickly shook out a fresh, dry white sheet and re-covered Sarah.

The dressing process was very beautiful. Sarah was enshrouded in immaculate white cotton pants, undershirt, tunic, and bonnet, in that order, each garment secured with three-loop bows. The loops represent the three tines of Shin, the Hebrew letter beginning one of God's Names. I took it upon myself to see that the bows lay spread out, flat and pretty — another detail I would eventually make mine — while the other women beseeched Sarah bas Avraham in poignant Yiddish to remember herself as a *Yiddishe tochter* (Jewish daughter), and to recall her Hebrew name while on her final course.

Ensconced in a simple, unvarnished pine box lined with fresh and fragrant straw, Sarah looked clean, warm, and cared for. We closed the casket and gathered around to ask her pardon had we inadvertently performed any of our work without full and proper respect. We spoke of our hopes that in the world of the living she had paid any debt of pain or suffering, and that her journey henceforth be one of reward. Backing away slowly out of the room we faced the casket in final tribute to the body and soul of Sarah bas Avraham.

I found the lavatory, and there I wept deeply. I cried in the retro-hope that the *Chevrah Kadisha* tending to my father had done for him what this *Chevrah* had done for Sarah, that they had treated him with the same care. And that he finally lay as clean and cared for as Sarah now lay.

Waiting for me in the dark sitting parlor my friends gracefully refrained from comment when I joined them. We left the chapel. We washed our hands to rid ourselves of the spiritual impurity of death: right, left, right, left … .Then, emotions not quite spent, a flood of love for this mitzvah washed over me, and an even greater bond with these women of the *Chevrah* was forged. But most remarkably, and I'm so grateful for this, I felt a strengthened security in God Who commands this *Chesed shel Emes*, this altruistic kindness. It was security born of an internal quieting making me truly less afraid, somehow, of the passage of death.

My Barber, Morris

After discovering my local barber's secret, no haircut has ever been the same.

Mordechai I. Twersky

There was something about my barber, Morris.

I was always drawn to this affable Mr. Hooper look-alike with the Popeye laugh, who greeted me with a smile each time I entered his popular Bronx barbershop along with my father and younger brother.

The adult customers who flocked to him — Jews, Italians, Irish — sat in cream-colored, vintage barber chairs. Children had other amenities: an elevated, gleaming red fire truck and a box forever filled with candies.

I may have been only six years old, but Morris made me feel like a grown up.

"*Nu, calega'le*, how do you want the neck? A square-back or natural?" he'd ask, invoking the affectionate Yiddish word for colleague. Then he'd wrap the white-cloth smock around my neck, close the snaps, and remove my yarmulke.

Mordechai I. Twersky, a freelance writer and broadcast journalist, is a doctoral student in Jewish History at Bar-Ilan University in Ramat Gan, Israel.

"Careful with the *peyis!*" my father, who was Morris' rabbi, would warn him, while directing the haircut like a movie scene. Morris would then clip my side-locks precisely at the cheekbone.

The mere touch of Morris' loud, vibrating electric razor at the base of my neck would tickle my funny bone, triggering fits of hysterical laugher. *"Nu, zai shtil!"* Morris would whisper, in a futile attempt to get me to stop fidgeting.

Then, in the haircut's final moments, he'd bring out his secret weapon — what he dubbed the "hot comb" — in a semi-successful attempt to tame the two stubborn cowlicks at each corner of my forehead. "Horns," I called them.

The rest of the time Morris would converse with my father in Yiddish. I couldn't understand a word, but the deep sighs and long pauses spoke volumes.

And all the while there were the perpetual, almost haunting, sounds of Morris' scissors.

Aside from my regular visits to his barbershop, I would see Morris at my father's synagogue when he'd come to recite the *Yizkor*, or Memorial Prayer, during the holidays.

On those occasions I would notice a different man. Morris didn't mingle with his fellow congregants, nearly all of whom were his customers. He'd sit in the back row and stare blankly into his prayer book, sometimes straight ahead, seemingly into nowhere.

Over time I would learn that Morris, along with my father and nearly the entire congregation, shared something in common: they were survivors of the Holocaust.

I would learn that the off-blue "KL" tattooed onto Morris' right forearm — the mark I stared at for years — was from a concentration camp, and I would take note of the repeated references to Nazis in Morris' Yiddish conversations with my father.

I would learn that my name wasn't *merely* biblical: I was named for my paternal grandfather, who was murdered together with one of his sons and more than 50 Jews in July of 1941.

For me, Morris' lonely, sad, and detached synagogue demeanor overshadowed his barbershop persona. In a congregation of Holocaust survivors who seemed otherwise happy and well adjusted,

Morris somehow stood out. His sighs could move mountains.

But I did not dare approach him.

Unraveling the Mystery

During my high school years, as I drifted away from home, I drifted away from Morris. With my adolescent desire for "space" came the desire to replicate my friends' perfectly layered, designer haircuts. The bangs were combed back. The barbershop on White Plains Road was replaced by a trendy Manhattan salon with pulsating music, free of parental direction, Yiddish, and signature sighs.

Over the years I would see Morris in synagogue and feel guilty. He would look at my assorted holiday haircuts — one year he saw a perm gone awry — and ask: "Who's giving you haircuts? *Er hut tzvei linkeh hendt* (He has two left hands)!"

It was not until I was a 31-year-old graduate student in journalism in search of a documentary subject that I had my first in-depth encounter with Morris. I sought out this man — who had since retired but continued to cut his rabbi's hair at our home — determined to unravel the mystery of his past.

"What would you like to know?" he replied in his heavily accented English. "Come up to the house and we'll talk."

Several days later I visited Morris and his wife at their Bronx apartment. A faded, black-and-white picture immediately caught my eye: that of a baby girl in a carriage.

"You've grown," said Morris, who hadn't seen me as often since my move to Manhattan. His wife, Fela, emerged from the den with an old color photo: it was from my brother Isaac's traditional first haircut at age three. The year was 1969, and pictured with my brother was Morris, holding his trademark scissors.

"I had a child, once," he began. "Her name was Rivkaleh. She was only five years old when they took her from me."

Then, Morris, who must have been 80 years old at the time, held out his hands.

"You see these?" he asked. There was a slight tremor in his hands, which were thick, tinged with red, with hardly a wrinkle. "These kept me alive."

"I don't understand," I politely replied, hoping he would elaborate.

"The Nazis needed barbers in the ghettos and in the camps," he said matter-of-factly. "Why else would they keep me alive?"

As I sat there, my mind raced. I imagined Morris some 50 years earlier in a striped prison uniform. I stared at his hands — the very same hands that for years caressed my face, offered me candies, and shielded my eyes when he trimmed my bangs. My thoughts turned to others who sat in his barber chair during the war in Poland: German SS officers who came for their daily shave, and countless Jews whose hair was sheared before entering the gas chamber.

Over the course of two hours Morris described the harrowing tale of his daughter's murder. He said he dreamt of her often and still wonders whether she could have been saved.

"A Polak once begged me to give him my girl," he recalled. "He wanted to raise her. She had blonde hair and didn't look Jewish."

He told of his experiences in five concentration camps, his liberation from Dachau, and his arrival in the United States with his first wife, who by that time was ill and could no longer have children. She died in 1970.

"Doss iz iss," Morris said in Yiddish, summing up with a deep sigh. "That's the way it is. There was nobody to cry to for help."

I learned how he prolonged the lives of fellow inmates by sharing with them the food rations he earned as a barber. And I learned of his encounter with his daughter's murderer when he testified against him at a war crimes trial in Germany.

"I spit him in his face, that Nazi murderer," Morris said, in his only visible display of emotion.

In the year following my interview with Morris I returned to him, making sure to be present at my parent's home every time he cut my father's hair.

Now I wanted Morris to cut my hair.

Following my *aliyah* to Israel I maintained contact with Morris, speaking with him before the Jewish holidays. He would emerge from retirement to give the traditional first haircuts to each of my brother's four sons.

My father and Morris have since passed away, and no haircut has ever been the same.

More often than not, the barber chair feels cold. My memory drifts back to the Bronx, to the voices and images of two men who shared their past and their pain in a bi-monthly series of conversations that spanned 40 years.

I can still hear the scissors.

Today, Morris' old barbershop is a stationery store. The legacy of that space, receded into history, is unknown to a new generation of residents. But for me, the light in the store still burns. The barber's pole on White Plains Road beneath the elevated subway line still turns.

"What's it gonna be?" a bilingual barber in his forties asks me before beginning a recent haircut in Jerusalem.

"Give me a square-back," I reply. "And — "

"Yes?" he asks.

"Careful with the *peyis*."

Standing Before God

43, never married, no kids: I was having a tough time getting up the enthusiasm to pray for these same things once again

Diane Faber Veitzer

Two years ago, I approached the High Holidays with a certain sense of "here we go again." Having just turned 43, never married, no kids, I was having a tough time getting up the enthusiasm to pray for these same things. How many times can you ask for the same thing, and get the same answer?

In shul Rosh Hashanah morning, I saw that two of the young women in our community were standing up throughout the repetition of the Mussaf service. These two girls, Sara and Tova, were the daughters of close friends my age. Both about 18 or 19, they were each just back from a post-high-school year studying in Jerusalem, and now, according to our community's custom, "ready to get married." I knew that these girls would be praying fervently to find their basherts (soul mates) quickly and easily.

I had some understanding of why they stood through Mussaf. It is an especially long prayer service, and one is not required to stand throughout, but it is considered meritorious to do so. I imagined that

---

Diane writes from Los Angeles, California.

in this important year for them, these young girls wanted to stand out before the Almighty in piousness and sincerity, with the hope that their prayers to get married that year would stand out as well.

As I sat there behind these two girls, the only ones standing among the seated multitude as the service progressed, I envied their youthful innocence, their steadfast belief that doing something extra could make a difference in the heavenly sphere. I envied their high chances of marriage that year to young men of their choosing. I envied their physical stamina for the hours of standing, and I envied their perseverance, to stand throughout the long service while everyone around them remained seated.

How different their outlook is from mine, though we pray for the same thing, I thought to myself. How better their chances. How lucky they are. I wish I had what they have; I wish I could do what they do, with their faith. From my seated position, I envied their prayers and I believed that their prayers would be answered, and that mine, again, probably would not.

They don't want to be married any more than I do, I thought to myself from the comfort of my chair. Their prayers are not more worthy than mine. They are just younger and stronger than I am, I told myself.

And then I did something I did not expect.

I stood up.

I stood up to show the Almighty that my prayers were as deeply felt as theirs, that my desires were as real and sincere. To show the Almighty that I am not too tired, nor too old, to embrace the responsibilities of marriage and family. Perhaps to remind myself that I can do more, be more, and that it could be possible for my prayers to be answered.

I looked at the others who were still seated comfortably around me. I made the choice again to stand. Each time the congregation stood and then sat again, I remained standing. During the songs I swayed, during the silent prayers I wept. I pushed myself physically, emotionally, spiritually.

Later, during that same year, Sara, Tova, and I were married within six weeks of one another — two very lovely young ladies, and one woman old enough to be their mother. I planned my wedding as my two dear friends planned their daughters' — we shared caterers, photographers, and a lot of laughs as a season of planning for joy enveloped us, and we danced together at Sara's, then Tova's, and finally my own wedding reception.

An Unanswered Prayer

Last year, as the High Holidays approached, I still had one prayer left unanswered. I understood the statistics, the physical realities, the unlikelihood of success, but I was married now, and like most married Jewish women, I hoped for a child. Was my desire any less because my body was old? *In fact*, I thought, *at 44 my desire is greater: if I am ever going to have a child, it probably has to be this year.*

I wondered whether I could summon the inner strength and the physical strength to stand through the service again. Sara and Tova were no longer there to unknowingly inspire me; both were far away, living with their husbands who were learning in yeshivas in Baltimore and Jerusalem. *I will be on my own this year,* I thought. *Do I have the commitment to persevere?*

I tried. I made it through the Rosh Hashanah service. I felt good; I was determined. Anything is possible, I thought. But on Yom Kippur, my physical strength failed me. I stood, and I stood, and I stood, and then I just had to sit down. I felt so wiped out I thought I might pass out.

As I took my seat, I felt a terrible sense of despair. *You know what? I'm not as strong as a 20-year-old; I don't have the stamina; I can't do it on my own,* I thought. I knew that standing wasn't required, but over the past year I had come to believe for that year, at least, standing had made the difference.

At the closing prayers of Neilah, the whole congregation was standing, and I was on my feet again, along with them. I knew so many matters were being decided at that moment, and I wasn't sure I had done all I could. Just before the very end of the service, I leaned forward to a close friend, and whispered in her ear, "Could you ask for just one more *neshamah* (soul) this year?" And then I burst into tears, fearing that I had failed.

A few weeks later I learned why my physical strength had failed me on Yom Kippur: I was expecting. Months later, I learned that Sara and Tova were also expecting, our "due dates" lining up close together in the order we were married. My two dear friends were about to become grandmothers for the first time.

This year, Sara, Tova, and I became mothers. My husband and I were fortunate to share yet another season of joy with my two good friends, and their daughters and sons-in-law ... and their new grandchildren.

As the High Holidays approach this year, I wonder if I will even make it to services. I'm exhausted from night feedings. I worry that my baby daughter will disrupt the service for others whose prayers are still unanswered. And I'm contented in so many ways. But I'll try to make it anyway, if only to express my deepest gratitude for prayers answered so completely.

When I look back at the changes in my life over the past two years, I realize what a powerful opportunity those Rosh Hashanahs and Yom Kippurs gave me — the opportunity to stand before God and to plead my deepest desires to Him, and the courage to hope, once again, for a different response.

The Buried Seder Plate

The tragic fate of one survivor's remarkable heirloom

Rabbi Benjamin Blech

Remember that you were once slaves in Egypt ....

The Exodus and the miracles of the Passover story happened a long time ago, but they are still part of our contemporary consciousness because of the power of memory. But not everyone remembers, and, tragically, some choose to forget, as demonstrated by the incredible incident I had with Shmuel's Seder plate.

A few years ago I was browsing in an antique store on the East Side in New York when I spotted an all-too-familiar object. I recognized it immediately, even before I spotted the family name clearly etched on its border. How could I not know what it was when I had been so involved in its story? After all, my eulogy of Shmuel, a miraculous survivor of the infamous Auschwitz concentration camp, focused on it.

Rabbi Benjamin Blech is the author of 12 highly acclaimed books, including *Understanding Judaism: The Basics of Deed and Creed*. He is a professor of Talmud at Yeshiva University and the Rabbi Emeritus of Young Israel of Oceanside which he served for 37 years and from which he retired to pursue his interests in writing and lecturing around the globe. He is also the author of *If God Is Good, Why Is the World So Bad?* and of the international bestseller, *The Sistine Secrets*.

What a tale it had been. The Germans had rounded up all the Jews in his little town for deportation. Some believed that they were merely being transported to another site to be used for labor. But Shmuel knew that they were meant to be murdered. He understood that the Nazis wanted to eliminate every Jew as well as every reminder of their religious heritage.

So Shmuel took a chance. Had he been caught, he would have paid with his life. But he did what he had to do so that something might remain — so that even if not a single Jew in the world stayed alive, someone might find it, reflect, and remember. He paced off 26 steps, corresponding to the numerical value of God's Name, from the apple tree alongside his house and carefully buried his treasure — a silver Passover plate.

He wished he could have hidden much more. How he wanted to preserve a Torah Scroll. But he had so little time, so little space for concealing an object of value. His choice, in retrospect, seemed almost divinely inspired for its symbolism — the key vessel used to commemorate the festival of freedom.

From that day forward not a day went by in the hells of the concentration camps that his mind did not return to his Seder plate in its special hiding place.

Shmuel could never explain how he, out of all his family and friends, survived. In his heart of hearts, he once confided to me, he felt it may have been because he viewed his continued existence on earth as a holy mission — to go back to his roots and uncover his own symbol of survival.

Incredibly enough, in ways that defy all logic and that Shmuel only hinted to me, this escapee of 20th-century genocide was reunited with his reminder of deliverance from age-old Egyptian oppression. Shmuel journeyed back to his home, found his tree, counted off his steps, dug where he remembered he had buried it, and successfully retrieved his Seder plate. It became a symbol of his own liberation as well. With it he celebrated dozens of Passovers, until his death.

In almost total disbelief, this was the Seder plate that I saw in the shop for sale.

Where was it from, I inquired. What was it doing for sale when it carried with it so many precious memories? "I want to buy it," I assured the dealer, "but I need to know how you happen to have it."

"It was part of the sale of the contents of an estate by the children," the dealer replied. "You see, the deceased was religious but his descendants aren't. So they said they don't really have any need for items like these.'"

The symbol that sanctifies memory could only have been discarded by those who forgot their past.

If you have a loved one who suffers from Alzheimer's, you know how horrible it can be to live without an awareness of events that came before. We don't have a name for a similar condition that describes ignorance of our collective past. Yet the voluntary abandonment of historic memory is equally destructive.

How I wish that the unsentimental harshness of Shmuel's descendants was just an aberration, a remarkably unusual demonstration of insensitivity not likely to be duplicated by others. But the sad truth is that we are part of a "throwaway" culture that gives equal weight to used cars, worn furniture, and old family treasures. What has served the past is of no interest if its sole claim to value is its gift of associations.

Memorabilia have lost their allure because we no longer revere the meaning of memories. So what, I am often asked, if my grandparents used this every holiday? We have no space, we have no need for it. As if utilitarian function is the only rationale for holding on to something that enables us to preserve our past!

The ring with which I married my wife may not be the most expensive but I pray it remains in my family as a legacy of the love we shared, perhaps to be used again by my grandchildren. The cup with which I usher in the sanctity of every Sabbath may reflect the poverty of my youth, but I hope it is passed on to the future as a testament to the importance of religious values in our household. If objects that we treasured are held sacred by our children, then perhaps what we lived for will also be reverentially recalled.

"Unless we remember," the English novelist Edward Morgan Foster put it so beautifully, "we cannot understand."

That's why I weep for my friend Shmuel, whose family has become an orphan in history, severed from its past.

And that's why I keep retelling Shmuel's story on Passover, because I believe it captures the essential message of this holiday. God commanded us to remember because it is only by treasuring the messages of the past that we can understand the present and hope for a more blessed future.

A Photo From Dachau

Was that my father standing behind the barbed wire?

Rabbi Tzvi Nightingale

My father has three birthdays. Yes, three. His biological birthday is May 10, 1924. When he came to Canada after the war, he was too old to qualify as an orphan, so he had to rearrange his age a bit and make himself younger. 5/10/24 became 10/5/27 and he was now born on October 5, 1927. (Please don't tell the Canadian government about this. I would hate to see him deported at this stage of his life.) Oddly, our family has been

---

Rabbi Tzvi Nightingale is Director of Aish South Florida. Tzvi grew up in Toronto, Canada, home of the perennially losing Toronto Maple Leafs ice hockey team. He attended Aish Jerusalem in the summer of 1979, determined to gain access to great Jewish works and thinkers such as the Talmud and Maimonides. Little did he know that it would take far longer than two months; he ended up staying in Israel for nine years. He received rabbinic ordination in 1985 and met his wife Karen, who grew up in London and is the great-granddaughter of the former chief rabbi of Meshed, Iran. As can only happen in Israel, Canadian-Polish-Jewish became intertwined with British-Israeli-Persian. Rabbi Nightingale has been involved in Aish South Florida since 1989 and has been Executive Director since 1993. During that time he has met over 20,000 people who have attended Aish programs, but he does not remember all of their names. In the meantime, watching his beloved Maple Leafs not win a championship since 1967 has taught Rabbi Nightingale the importance of patiently waiting for the arrival of Mashiach.

celebrating this completely fictitious birthday ever since.

But it is his third birthday that he speaks about with the most emotion; the one that carries the most meaning for him. He spent years in various forced labor and death camps after his town of Staszow, Poland was liquidated by the Nazis in 1942. He was finally liberated on April 29, 1945 from Dachau concentration camp in Germany. My father has never been one to speak at length about his experiences as a survivor of the Holocaust, but he does talk about this one particular day. Among other things, I have heard him praise the American army for quickly delousing the inmates soon after they freed the camp. Being free from the Nazi hell and from the lice that infested his body for so long gave him a new lease on life.

The day after Yom Kippur I went to my office and did what I do after every Yom Kippur — not much. Not only am I tired from the fasting and teaching, but truth be told, I find the next day to be a bit of a downer. After intensely thinking about life, God, goals, and being a better person, and trying to inspire 150 people who come to our Aish center for services, I am just not up to the everyday mundane grind that comes rushing back. So trying to recapture some of the seriousness and meaning of Yom Kippur, I found myself on the computer and typed in "Dachau" in the search box. The top of the list was a film called *Dachau Concentration Camp Liberation*.

It was not a sophisticated piece, by any means. It consisted of photos slowly being panned to the background music from *Schindler's List*. There were photos of soldiers approaching the camp and arresting surrendering Nazis, a bird's-eye view of the camp, and photos of the main entrance and a gate with the infamous *Arbeit Macht Frei*.

A picture appeared of an American soldier walking on a wall perpendicular to a building, and I wondered, *If my father were to see this short film, would he remember some of the structures and buildings?* I briefly thought of showing him the film but knew I would not follow through due to his extreme sensitivity whenever the subject of the Holocaust comes up. In all the years I have known my dad, I have only heard snippets here and there.

At 1:50 into the film, a photo appeared that made me hit the pause button. It was a relatively clear photo, a close up of sorts, of three inmates behind barbed wire, all smiling and waving — presumably at their saviors. The short man on the left has an overcoat, obviously given to him by one of the soldiers. The man on the right with the moustache is taller and appears to be saluting. They are wearing the familiar striped concentration camp garb.

And the man in the middle looks like my father.

I began to stare intently and analyze every detail of the physical features to see if they match my dad's. The widow's peak hairline, the shape of the face, the somewhat larger ear, the gap between his front teeth — all were consistent with his look. *Could it be? Could this really be him?* I kept asking myself. But the trait that made me think it was him the most was the shape of his waving hand. I have always noticed this about my father, how his index finger curls and seems slightly raised higher than his middle fingers and how his thumb comes to almost meet them. Today, thanks to his arthritis, his hand is almost frozen in that position, and this was the shape of the hand of the man in this photo.

I immediately emailed the link to my three brothers in Toronto with the subject line, "Something very weird" and told them to pause the film and tell me what they think. By next morning, they agreed that this could indeed be our father in the photo.

Then things got a little complicated. We were faced with the dilemma of showing this photo to my father. Will it bring back too many painful memories? Should we subject him to an image of himself from so long ago of the most horrible time in his life? What effect would possibly seeing himself in Nazi prisoner garb have on his psyche?

My oldest brother, Reuben, has always been closest to my father ever since he went to work for him in his meat packing plant at the age of 15. My dad gave him the most noxious job there to discourage him from working at Grace Meats, but packing tripe did not turn Reuben away. They have been very tight ever since. Reuben felt that we should think this through and "sit on it" for a while. "He has not seen the photo for all these years, another day or so will not change things."

Sid, the next oldest brother and the peacemaker in our family, agreed. Murray and I wanted to show it to him but for the time being we deferred to the elder siblings. But the following day Murray came up with a Solomonic solution: Let's show the picture to my dad's one surviving sibling, Henya, who was with him in the camps earlier in the war and would be able to recognize if this indeed was him.

Murray called me that morning on his way to Auntie Henya. I told him to call me on my cell as soon as he spoke with her. Murray called me at 12:30 pm. "She was unequivocal — it's him. And not only that, but the man standing next to him with the overcoat was his childhood friend, Herschel D."

With that Murray then called my dad and asked if he wished to see a photo of himself on the day of his liberation from Dachau. He did. Murray went up to his condo and showed him the picture. With tears in his eyes my father declared, "Yeah, that's me."

❋❋❋

On April 29, 1945 a handful of photos of the liberation of Dachau were taken by Robert Spring, an x-ray technician serving with the 59th Evacuation Hospital of the U.S. Army Medical Corps. There were 32,000 inmates on that day and most of the photos taken by soldiers were of men too skeletal to discern their identities, too grainy to see any specific faces, or group shots taken from far away. But Mr. Spring decided to take one photo of a random group of nameless survivors whom he would never see again. To the Nazis, the man in the photo was prisoner number 147 963 and for 64 years and five months it was a photo of a nameless prisoner experiencing freedom for the first time in many years.

On the day after Yom Kippur in the year 5770, Tuesday September 29, 2009, it was discovered that the smiling inmate in Nazi prisoner garb was not just prisoner 147 963, and he was not a random nameless survivor that a heroic soldier happened to capture on camera. He was born Icek Nachtigal, Yitzchak Dovid ben Reuvain, and he goes by the name of Irving Nightingale. He was born on May 10, 1924 but he will tell you that his real birthday is April 29, 1945.

And he is my father.

Mother of All Miracles

Becoming a mother left me speechless.

Freidl Liba bas Chava

Silence.

There is simply overwhelming silence.

I've been meaning to write for months now, to share the enormous joy, to tell people that a miracle happened — that, after three years of a new marriage, new stepmotherhood, and, alas, two miscarriages, I became the mother of a healthy, sunny-natured, delicious baby girl.

After two thwarted pregnancies, this one was largely uneventful. We went with a "high risk" obstetrical practice, but it turned out that it was a routine nine months (though I — gratefully, gleefully — threw up several times a day until nearly the last month). The real risk, it seems, was the fear and apprehension that shadowed me at every moment, like background music set so low that it can barely be discerned consciously.

It wasn't until a few weeks ago that it even seemed *real*. I was waddling around like a modestly dressed hippo, and yet, when one of my doctors told me that, after that point, if anything went wrong they'd deliver the baby, I stared at him dumbly: "You mean there's

---

Freidl Liba bas Chava is an Israeli writer.

really going to be a baby?" It really was likely that I was going to end up with a live baby, rather than medical bills, haywire hormones, and crumpled hopes.

And so, not so long ago in an American hospital room kitted out like a fancy hotel suite, I met the little girl whom I'd been waiting for for almost a year. She was big and healthy, and incredibly alert (I fear for her teen years). I'd wondered for so long what the experience of birth would be like, and how I'd react to the momentous occasion of meeting my parents' grandchild. Now I found out: My husband wept, and I made some crack about her looking Pakistani, which was highly unexpected, given my husband's and my extreme Caucasian-ness.

And there she was, in this world.

Someone holier-than-I-am had told me that labor is a particularly auspicious time for prayer and so, as I lay surrounded by nurses, my doula was yelling, "Remember Yael! Think of Yael!" As I brought this beautiful baby *into* this world, I tried (somewhat inarticulately) to concentrate on taking something horrible *out* of it at the same time — the cancer that has attacked one of my oldest friends, a 39-year-old mother of three who lost her too-young father to another form of that disease only a few years ago.

To me, this moment perfectly represented this unredeemed world — the co-mingling of joy and pain; that we cannot explain why we are showered with joy at one moment and sorrow the next; why God chose that this daughter's soul was meant to come into this world while her two siblings were not; nor why Yael and her family must, again, be tested so harshly; why amazing, beautiful men and women suffer through unwanted singledom; why my brother's son had to battle leukemia; why some children are born into families flush with love while others wither in families cursed with a poverty of love. My daughter carries the name shared by my great-aunt, who tried and tried but never had children, and my husband's grandmother, who shepherded her two sons through the horrors of the Holocaust.

And so my silence.

What can I say?

We might have called her Ora for the way she poured *ora v'simchah* — light and happiness — into our already blessed family. We are all helpless at her chubby little feet — her parents, her grandparents, her siblings (my stepkids are the most loving siblings any mother could ever wish for her child). And yet I can't believe I am here.

When she was a few days old, I took her on a walk. I put her in the stroller, put a hat on her, and ambled around for a few blocks in the sun. At the end of the first block, it hit me — am I really here? Am I really, now, a *mom*?

I'd been, I liked to quip, "providing maternal services" to my stepkids for a few years now, even though I am not their biological mother. And it irritated me every time someone made reference to me *now* finally having children — but I *have* children, already, I felt, even if they're not mine. And they are no less a part of my family than is my baby.

And yet, there I was — pushing a stroller, looking down at a smiling baby, and it took my breath away.

A teacher of mine, Rebbetzin Rivi Brussel, taught me that a mother is like wall around a city. But unlike city walls ringed with sentries looking for threats coming from the outside, a mother encircles her family, looking inward — looking to see who each member of the family is, what he needs to become the best version of himself.

Being a stepmother teaches that, however amazing your kids are, you know that they did not come — biologically — from you. So when people compliment me on how gracious, kind, independent, and interesting my stepkids are, I usually smile and say that I had nothing to do with it — I'm just the stepmom.

But now I see that it's the same with this baby. Just as her siblings came to me with their own unique sets of strengths and weaknesses, charms and annoying tendencies, she came out with a sunny, funny disposition. She came somewhat implacable, hard to ruffle, and very, very communicative. I wonder at her every day. And I am reminded of my teacher's words: My job is to watch her carefully, as I watch her siblings, and help her harness the gifts God gave her and work on the challenges He set out for her.

And this job is a clear gift. It's a blessing that takes my breath away, that defies description (even for a wordy woman like myself), that humbles me, that makes me so aware of how incredibly blessed

I am. Sure, our family faces many challenges (there's no point listing them, but we have them in spades), but how can I not feel *drenched* by all this? By my husband, my stepchildren, my family, my daughter, our relative health ....

But, somehow, I am also keenly aware of the suffering everywhere I look: Fighting cancer; marriages and families unraveling; people struggling to pay bills; loneliness; mental and physical afflictions; women and men weeping because they want desperately to be husbands and wives and mothers and fathers and God, for whatever reason, says — for now — not yet. And that's not even getting into famine, war, and the like.

So when I see images from post-tsunami Japan, or see a family struggling to stay intact, listen to a teenager tell me of her feelings of abandonment and isolation, or hear about my neighbor trying to keep his house out of foreclosure, all I can do is reach out for my children — all of them — and hold them close, and hope that I can be worthy of my role and teach them how to live — joyfully, faithfully, righteously — in a world filled with pleasure and with pain, and to reveal the Great, Loving, and Merciful God Who is often hidden from us in this world, but Whose love is overwhelming.

God and I

My conversion to Judaism

Cindy Johannsen

My father has been an atheist for most of his life, although he was brought up as a Protestant. My mum was raised Hindu although she has not observed any practices since she was 18.

My parents always told me and my sister that they didn't feel it was their place to impose a religion on us (mainly because they were from such different backgrounds), but that we would be free to choose ourselves. Religion was seen as being something that other people did, but I was always encouraged to think about faith.

Until the age of 16 or so I didn't think about belonging to a religion. I believed in something, but I didn't know what. I always felt that there was something bigger than me that I was not able to comprehend. I remember lying in bed as a child and talking to God, and I was always curious about religion.

I went to a Christian school until the age of 14 but became very close to a Jewish girl there. When her father sadly died when we were nine, I remember being struck by the process of sitting *shivah* and the

---

The above essay was written by a woman currently undergoing conversion with the London Beth Din.

enormous support her family received from the community. As someone brought up in a community of four (!), it was something which touched me tremendously. However, I had no structure to my beliefs, and no way of expressing them. My dad has since reminded me that I was fascinated with Judaism for many years; I had assumed that it was not until much later that I started to look toward Judaism to give me that structure. However, we recently spoke about how much I used to talk about Judaism and the Jewish people, and he found an exercise book in which I had written about Succot and the Exodus at age 11!

For a few years while I was a teenager I became very angry with God. We had a very difficult time as a family, and I went through the experience of losing two family members who had been very religious (although they were not Jewish, obviously). At this point I remember questioning for the first time whether there was a God, and whether I had been kidding myself by feeling that I was being watched over. I remember this very angry period as a dark and difficult time.

I'm not sure what changed for me, but I vividly remember visiting Auschwitz-Birkenhau when I was 16 on a school trip. As I walked down the railroad tracks in Birkenhau behind my classmates, the sky suddenly turned completely black and I felt an enormous connection to the people who had walked there 50 years before. It was the first time in my life I had felt such a strong connection to a community other than my immediate family, and it was astonishing for me. After returning from Poland, I decided to begin exploring this further and wrote my A Level History project criticizing Holocaust revisionism.

Around this time, I became acquainted with a Jewish boy and he began telling me about his religion. I remember being struck by how openly he talked about his relationship with God, and how firm his belief was. Previously, the concept of God had always felt very private to me, and almost embarrassing, but he was so proud to believe and to see himself as having a close personal relationship. I began to feel that perhaps I could be entitled to such a personal relationship as well, and I started repairing the relationship that I had felt with God when I was younger.

That was, I suppose, the start of the journey that has brought me to where I am now. About five years ago, I decided to test my ideas about "rules" being restrictive. I started to eat only kosher meat and stop mixing meat and milk in order to see what effect that might have on me. I was surprised at how broadly it affected my life.

Firstly, simply having to think about the food I was preparing and eating encouraged me to consider where it had come from and the special significance I could give to food by having to think about it in this way. I did a lot of research at this time about kashrut and the emphasis on compassion really struck a chord with me. It also had the unexpected effect of making me think about my identity. I had always been aware of my mixed-race identity, but that felt like it singled me out from others. Now I felt an affinity to a community, just through the way my actions set me apart from other people. At this point, I was still eating in non-kosher restaurants (ordering vegetarian food), and I was struck by how much I had to think about my identity even just looking at a menu or going to the supermarket. Rather than feeling limited, as I would have expected when I was younger, I felt somehow special, and I enjoyed feeling that the simple act of eating could encourage me to be so reflective.

Finally, changing the way I ate also had the effect of changing my identity to other people. I found myself shocked at the strong reactions I received. Many of my friends questioned why I would change my lifestyle at all. This was the first of many times I would have to explain my actions, and it had the dual effect of encouraging me to think about my reasons for doing it, and increasing my affiliation with the Jewish People.

Following this decision I spent a long time reading on my own, and thinking a lot about how I felt about religion, and what it would mean to be Jewish. The more I read, the more I found views which I felt described the values I already had, such as being hospitable to others, being careful with one's words, the separate roles of men and women, being charitable, and so on. I was particularly struck by ideas of God as being present in the world but hidden, and being an incomprehensible concept that we could never fully understand. This seemed to really put into words what I had always felt, and it was a relief to find an idea of God which was so separate from humanity, so broad and encompassing, and yet still personal and close.

Around this time I started experiencing my life quite differently. The only way I can describe it is that I felt "accompanied." As I was reading and thinking about whether to try to become Jewish, a number of things happened which made me feel as if God was listening to me and telling me that I was on the right path. At times I put this out of my head, thinking "I'm just one person, why would He care?" but the feeling persisted and gave me a lot of comfort. Even now I have found that when times are difficult, something always happens to let me know that I am on the right path and that I should persevere.

Feeling this growing personal relationship with God has not only given me strength and comfort, but I think it has also had a huge effect on my relationships with other people. Shira, who is tutoring me in Jewish studies, told me some time ago that I should make my decisions thinking about what God would want me to do. I find that this underpins a lot of my thinking now. I feel that it has made me more forgiving, more determined to see the best in people. I am constantly thinking about whether I am "doing the right thing." This has at times meant that I have made difficult choices, but I get a lot of strength from feeling that I am trying to live my life in this way.

Going to synagogue for the first time was a very moving experience for me, and I am eternally grateful that we chose Yom Kippur as my first experience of shul; listening to that first *Kol Nidrei* service is something I will always remember. Incorporating prayer into my daily life has created a foundation for me to make the most of every day; saying *Modeh Ani* and thinking about starting my day "like a lion" always makes me jump out of bed in the morning! Praying every morning, saying blessings throughout the day, and reflecting in the evening remind me to be thankful and give me pause to consider what I am doing, how I should go about my day, and how I can improve the next day.

It has been quite a journey. In many ways though, it feels almost like I have done a lot of traveling and come full circle, coming back to the close and pure relationship I had with God when I was a child talking to Him before falling asleep. It is a great source of strength to me to once again have that feeling of being watched over.

The Music of Recession

Sometimes life is so hard, you just have to sing.

Goldy Rosenberg

My father built a sweater factory in the employment-starved Catskills, creating job opportunities in a locale that didn't have many. Then along came the seventies with its sharp-dropping economy and wiped out the factory. All that my father had left was unplugged machines and a shell of a building. He, who had created jobs for others, had no business and no job of his own. So my father sought employment in the nearest metropolitan area, three hours away from home.

The recession-time job market was slim. The situation was desperate as my father had a family to support. He took the first job available, that of night mechanic in someone else's factory. Pay was minimum wage.

A dozen mouths to feed. A mortgage to carry. All on minimum wage. The budget numbers just didn't add up, which is why my father became adept at cutting corners and making do without. The first thing he cut was personal transportation, giving up driving his car.

Goldy Rosenberg has written for several publications and is the author of *Clouds of Glory* (ArtScroll/Mesorah). She is working on trying to figure out how her life can become her magnum opus.

Yet even bus fare from New York City to our home was a strain on an already strained budget. So my father decided to stay in the City all week and only come home for Shabbos. Since he wanted to stretch his meager earnings even more, my father would hitchhike home.

One Thursday night, my father stood on the side of the New York State Thruway trying to catch a ride. No one stopped. It was cold. Time passed. Sleet started to fall, drenching my father. Each passing car sent a shower of icy water cascading toward him.

As my father told me the story, he said, "It was so bad, I just had to sing."

"Say again?!" I wasn't sure I heard right.

He smiled and told me, "Sometimes it is so bad, you just have to sing to God."

Music is an odd invention; it always employs force. Think about it. The drum is a skin stretched to its tightest which you then pound away at with the drumsticks. The guitar is strings pulled taut, which you then pick or strum at, exerting pressure on the right string. The piano works more or less like the guitar, with strings being stretched and then hit. The flute, the clarinet, the oboe — they take breath pushed strongly through it and constrain it into a narrow space so that there is pressure on that breath, until it escapes through an opening.

All instruments are pressure concepts. As soon as you take away any tension, your instrument won't work. It needs pressure.

David was a shepherd boy spurned by kin and countrymen alike. Alone he grew. Alone he forged his character. Through the pressures of daily teasing, through the tension of being hounded near unto death, David became King David, author of *Psalms*. From the ultimate pressurized childhood came the timeless songs of David. Pain can make music.

My father realized that only individuals strong enough to withstand tension become the instruments of song in the world. In a world so finely tuned, his moment of pressure must have been orchestrated for a response. So he met every challenge head-on. Were he to buckle from the pain, my father felt he would have failed, like the guitar string that snaps under tension.

That's why in that moment of pain my father sang, bringing his unique music into the world.

Life can get incredibly hard, so I've learned. And my father taught me that if I'm in pain, I'm being asked for a response. I can feel worthy of being picked to be played. And like my father and King David, I can take each pressure, pain, or tension and sing a song to the world.

Sometimes life is so hard, you just have to sing.

Drops of Challenge

When Cancer Came Knocking

Everyone dies, some sooner than later. It's how we choose to live our lives that matters.

Mandy Gaziel

Cancer came knocking. We didn't want it to but it barged in, uninvited, unwelcome.

My husband, Danni, and I were in our mid-30s with two young children and we suddenly had to deal with words and concepts that had no place in our young lives. Death and sickness had always been vague, far-off concepts that happened to other people.

When the oncologist told us that the cancer had already spread from the left lung to the other side of Danni's chest, and that he had a 4 percent chance of survival, we began to live a new reality. Living with fear and uncertainty, yet not allowing it to overtake us and destroy our lives. Not allowing this unexpected disease to rob us of our joy for life, our hopes and plans for the future.

Living with fear and the unknown, yet not wanting these feelings accessed by anyone, not even our closest family and friends. We felt that we had to put on a front, to show that we were strong. How

---

Mandy Gaziel has a BA in English Literature and Judaica. She lives with her family opposite some rolling hills in Ramat Beit Shemesh, Israel.

could we admit that we ourselves were frightened? So in keeping up a brave and positive face, we learned to ignore negative thoughts and not allow them to control our lives. We remained happy and positive people, and our strength helped these beloved people to cope as well.

Danni started chemotherapy, and I started researching alternative treatments. Our life's motto became: We are 100% going to be in that 4% survival category. There was no way that this disease was going to get us!

Unbelievably, we actually learned to enjoy our new reality; there were so many good things coming out of it. Danni and I were spending so much more time together and our marriage got stronger. In facing death our relationship became deeper and more meaningful.

Danni is the type who is always doing something. Instead of lying on the couch and feeling sorry for himself, he would do as much as he could without over-exerting himself. The company I worked for was very understanding and allowed me to take off whatever time I needed, but I still had to work. Often when I got home the laundry would all be done, the house all tidy.

Danni never saw himself as an invalid. He just got on with life, kept busy, and looked so well people couldn't believe he had life-threatening cancer. With such a great attitude and amazing inner strength, it was easy to focus together on getting well.

Danni's illness opened up a huge outpouring of *chesed*, selfless giving. We were inundated with calls, emails, offers to help, money, you name it, from both friends and strangers. The fact that I did not have to prepare supper or Shabbat meals for a very long time took a huge burden off of me, and knowing that people were praying for Danni was a tremendous comfort.

At first we didn't want to accept any help. I felt we didn't need it. We were coping fine and I could not bear the thought of becoming objects of pity. A wise friend told me: "You have to let people help you. God has given you an opportunity to bring *chesed* into the world." I realized that people needed to express their pain and concern for us into something concrete. Our acceptance of their *chesed* would help them feel better, and of course, it would also help us too!

Before Danni got sick, we had purchased a new home, budgeting down to the last cent. After we signed the contract there were big changes in the dollar/shekel exchange and we ended up losing a lot of money. Our financial worries were enormous, but after cancer came knocking, money became the absolute lowest priority.

The extravagance of eating expensive ice cream became a daily ritual: Since chemotherapy recipients often lose extensive weight, Danni's cancer nutrition specialist told him to indulge in the ice cream with the most calories every day. As a supportive wife, I certainly could not let him eat on his own! Danni managed to keep his weight steady, and as for myself, no comment!

In the Eye of the Storm

When Danni first got sick we didn't publicize it, feeling that it was something private to be shared only with the closest family and friends. However, after discovering that the cancer was so advanced and that the chances of survival were so small, we decided to go public and get as many prayers as we could. Everywhere I went I felt eyes on me; sympathetic, aching, heart-sore eyes. It was very hard. I appreciated their concern, but I couldn't bear their pity. What I really needed was to have a good laugh, to forget even for a short time what was happening in my home. I needed to forget my husband, once virile and full of life, now lying pale and wan on the couch (albeit with a smile on his face). I needed to forget my four-year-old daughter's nightmares, my eight-year-old's questions on life and death. Of course I realized that people just cared about us, and essentially it was very much appreciated.

I felt myself as the pillar of the family, holding everything together. I knew that if I collapsed, I would bring everyone down with me. I had to keep strong, positive, and upbeat.

I knew inherently that this was God's plan for me; that this was the best thing that could happen to me. I couldn't understand why, I certainly didn't like it, but I knew that the Almighty was testing me, giving me the opportunity to develop my strengths and become a better person through my experience. Every now and then when things got too much I would close my eyes and say "God, please help me, I can't anymore," and I would hear a voice saying "You can. I am with you," and I would be strengthened and could carry on.

Spinning in a whirlwind, it took all our effort to stay centered in the eye of the storm. We did manage to find a sense of equilibrium and tranquility by working hard to focus on the good that God had blessed us with, and not thinking or ruminating on the negative. Thankfully there were so many things to be grateful for, so many blessings in our lives.

Metastatic cancer is a life-changing experience. No one can live with serious illness and stay the same. You become defined by how you deal with your illness; are you swallowed up in self-pity, or have you turned into a conqueror? That first year changed us tremendously and I think it is fair to say we, as a family, were in the category of conquerors.

Dragged to Hell

After a year of various chemotherapy treatments and radiation, incredibly we got the all clear from the doctor. It was nothing short of miraculous. I felt that now we could handle anything.

Our joy that the tumor had vanished was doused by the fact that Danni would have to undergo major surgery, cutting out the lobe of left lung where the cancer had been. A lobectomy is known to be a terribly painful operation but we were ecstatic that Danni was alive to undergo it. Our surgeon had told us that almost no one with Danni's medical history has this operation — they either have too many medical complications or die before they can be operated on.

And then I was dragged into the dark hole of hell. God had plans that twisted and squeezed every bit of sparkle out of me. What is hell? Hell is seeing your beloved husband wracked in horrific pain. Hell is knowing that you need to be with your husband in the hospital because he can't function alone, yet your children need you too. They are sure their father is going to die, and you want to be with them to hold and reassure them. Hell is being the recipient of your husband's frustration, anger, and pain, yet not being able to retaliate because you know he is in a terrible place and is lashing out in desperation, not in nastiness. Hell is seeing your children's anguish when they hug you after a quick visit, before you return to the hospital.

Danni has a huge scar from the side of his chest going round to the back. They opened his entire chest cavity from the side, slashing all the sensitive nerve endings, hacking muscles and breaking ribs in order to access the lung. The surgeon told us that the operation was very difficult. Usually he operates on much older people and their bodies melt like butter when he cuts in. Danni's body being young and strong objected to the onslaught and he paid the price in terrible, ongoing pain for months afterwards. Painkillers only took the edge off, doctors couldn't help, and nothing alternative seemed to work.

Massive doses of drugs altered Danni's personality. My nice husband disappeared and an irritable and aggressive man moved in. This man took out his frustration mainly on me, but also on the children. He was numb, barely aware of what he was doing. I found myself trying to be a supportive wife, yet also defending the kids against their father. They didn't deserve to be shouted at for the tiniest thing, yet Danni didn't have the strength to control himself — he was so weak and sick. I had to explain to my children that their father was not himself, that he was unwell.

It was also extremely difficult for my in-laws to see their son like this. They were very needy and I had to strengthen them too. On top of all this, I had a job. I was torn in many different directions.

At the time my youngest daughter was five years old. Her screams at night from her ongoing nightmares were draining. She was convinced her father was going to die, but couldn't tell me, not wanting to burden me more. I saw her angst and took her to a psychologist where things came into the open. We explained that he was not going to die, that the operation would make him better. Intellectually she understood but couldn't comprehend why he was behaving so roughly. Nor could her older sister. For that matter, nor could I. I turned to the surgeon, our oncologist, our family doctor, desperate for help. They all said the same thing: the painkillers were chemically affecting Danni's brain, causing personality changes. They assured me that these were temporary and would cease when he stopped the drugs.

This was one of the worst periods of my life. I was walking though a poisonous fog where every gulp of air was painful, but I had to breathe to stay alive. I spent a lot of time mulling over the concept of suffering. We don't ask for suffering. We obviously don't want to suffer. But things happen to us, unpleasant, unwanted. While we can't choose our suffering, we certainly can choose how to accept God's plans for us. We have the free will to collapse and cry all day, or alternatively to say this is God's will, and I know and accept with a whole heart that all that God chooses for us is what we need to go through. We have the free will to hold our heads up high, and smile and laugh (and even cry), but know that we can and will be strong no matter what happens.

Throughout this period the Almighty was a constant presence I turned to. There were times when I felt that I could barely get out of bed, and although I went through the motions for the sake of my family, in my mind's eye I was curled up, fetus-like, hurting and unhappy. At those times I would gather my strength and invoke the blessing *"Blessed are You, Lord Our God, Who raises up those who are bowed down,"* and I'd imagine God's finger gently uncurling me, raising me up, helping me to lift up my head and be strong, and I then could carry on normally.

Repeat Visitor

Very slowly, things began to improve. Danni started coming back to himself, and the loving husband and father that we missed so much returned to us. After hell came healing, and the whole family managed to shift back to normality. Life was wonderful again. We had beaten cancer; it was over! While we were certainly aware that the tumor could come back and never stopped praying; we just did not think about it.

About one year later, a new malignant tumor was discovered in Danni's lower left lung. We were distressed, but grateful it had not spread. Danni was immediately scheduled for a complete pneumonectomy (removal of the entire lung).

So we were plunged into hell all over again, this time even worse than before. Because Danni's body had been through so much trauma, it fought against the surgery and there were complications. Danni was in hospital over three weeks, sicker and weaker than ever before. I won't go into all the details — suffice it to say that God works wonders in helping us to forget difficult situations, and I thank Him for giving me the strength to be able to get through that period, leave it behind me, and move on.

Danni got well again and hell faded away. We picked up the pieces and life was enjoyable again. We thought we'd closed the chapter. There was no more left lung. Goodbye cancer! And so, you can imagine what a big shock we got when another malignant tumor was discovered in Danni's right lung only seven months later. We somehow never expected the cancer to come back on the other side. On the outside I was calm, but in my mind a mantra was resonating: "My husband is going to die, my husband is going to die," and yet another voice was shouting, just as loud "No! No! No!" It took a lot of work not to give in to negativity this time. We were still so frail but we hadn't come this far just to give up. So our family went into battle mode again, determined to win.

But this time there was one major difference. While running to doctors and second opinions, trying to decide the best course of treatment, a new life was stirring. I was expecting a child.

I was so thankful. Thankful that the cancer was contained in this one tumor and hadn't spread throughout Danni's body. Thankful to live in a developed country with advanced medicine, including many types of chemotherapy that could help Danni to prolong his life. Thankful for a wonderful doctor who really cared about us. Thankful for supportive family and friends. Thankful for so many blessings that I felt all around me, but mostly thankful that after five years of waiting, I would finally be able to hold a newborn in my arms. We had chosen to live, and this baby was a confirmation of that fact.

With surgery deemed too dangerous, conventional drug therapy was the best option for Danni. Chemo was, relatively speaking, a breeze. Once again we were a team marching forward toward the enemy, strong and courageous, determined to triumph.

I'd walk into the oncological day room in my maternity clothes, feeling the eyes of every single person in that room following me, some of them smiling in approval, others looking at us as if we were downright crazy.

Our precious son Brachya (which means *a blessing from God* or *God blessed us*) entered this world exactly one year after Danni's second surgery, on February 28, 2007. The baby brought so much happiness and light into our family. When he wasn't feeling well after his treatments, Danni would lie on the couch holding our little blessing with such joy. His older sisters just adored him, and having a new baby brother took their minds off Danni's illness. He made us all forget our suffering and indeed, to this day, Brachya is illuminating our home with his delightful sunny personality.

The next CT performed a few months later showed a huge reduction in the tumor and Danni was deemed "healthy". Once more we began the process of rebuilding, picking up the fragments of our lives, and trying to move forward into normality.

Our respite ended rather abruptly a half year later with the oncologist's announcement that the tumor was back. Once again we were thrown into the "now what do we do" arena. Doctors, specialists, second opinions, and reassuring our girls that "it's going to be okay" occupied all our time. In the end it was decided to proceed with a special type of 3-D radiation only available overseas. We packed up and went to Munich, Germany, all expenses paid by our medical aid. My sister who lives in Berlin drove down with her family to meet us, and notwithstanding Danni's treatment, we managed to have a wonderful holiday in the Alps, and thereafter in the States, where we went for Danni's recuperation.

Choosing to Live

In the last CT before this article was written something suspicious was found again. Although everyone who heard the news was totally distraught, Danni and I were not; probably because we have reached the stage of just accepting whatever happens and not getting upset by it. Danni did a biopsy, and thank God it wasn't anything to worry about.

Although Danni is "clean" now, we don't really think it's over (we'd like to think so!). Cancer is part of our lives, and the brutal truth is that we are just playing for time.

I once asked our oncologist if it wasn't depressing to work with sick and dying people all the time. His answer blew me away. "Everyone is going to die," he said, leaning forward over his desk, "some sooner than later. It's how we choose to live our lives that matters. My job brings me into the company of wonderful people who, despite illness and suffering, have chosen to live. I can't think of any job more rewarding than that."

It really is all about how we choose to live. So many times over the past few years people have told me that they are amazed at how positive we are. And I tell them, "It's just a matter of attitude. We can choose to sit, cry, and give in to depression, or we can say, Okay, this is my life, and I'm going to live it as best as I can!"

So we are carrying on with our life, pushing cancer to the back of our minds and hoping that it doesn't come knocking again. Hoping that it doesn't ruin our plan to sit together on the porch in our rocking chairs, watching our grandchildren play. And if it does come back, then we'll keep fighting because with the help of God, nothing is going to destroy our hope to have a wonderful future together.

With great sorrow we regret to inform you that Danni Gaziel passed away on Oct. 3, 2010, Tishrei 25, 5771. May his soul be bound in the bond of eternal life.

What Every Parent Dreads

It was 10 p.m. when we got the call: "Your son was in a car accident. The situation is very serious. Come to the hospital immediately."

Rabbi Ephraim Shore

At around 10 p.m. we got the phone call that every parent dreads. I knew it was bad when I saw my wife's knees buckle and her hand grasp the wall for support. She handed me the phone.

"We think your son may have been involved in a traffic accident. We can't release any details until you identify him as your son. You should both come to the hospital immediately where a social worker will meet you. The situation is very serious."

On that incredibly long journey to the hospital, through my tears, I warned my wife to prepare for the worst. I was quite convinced that our 21-year-old son, Yaakov, was dead.

I can't imagine any other scenario where hearing that my child is undergoing emergency brain surgery would be a relief, but in this

---

Rabbi Ephraim Shore is one of the directors of Aish HaTorah Jerusalem, and the Israel Director of HonestReporting.com and the Hasbara Fellowships network of pro-Israel campus activism. Prior to making *aliyah*, he was Executive Director of Aish HaTorah in Miami and Toronto.

case it was. We were devastated, but there was hope.

For two more hours they refused to tell us anything until our son emerged from the first of his two skull surgeries of that endless night. They finally told us that Yaakov had been hit by a car on a major road while rollerblading. He sustained a severe head injury as well as broken bones. They were working to relieve the pressure from bleeding and swelling in his brain.

Yaakov was just completing his army service. He had served as a combat soldier in the Nachal Charedi, an Orthodox unit in the IDF. When home, he loves going on long bike and rollerblade rides around Jerusalem, discovering every nook and cranny of the beautiful city. He is a master rollerblader and an avid athlete.

We asked the usual questions: "How bad is it? Will he live? If he lives, will there be permanent damage? Will he ever walk or talk again? Will he have the same personality?"

The answer to all these questions was the same: We don't know. And we won't know for a long time.

We felt like the car had plowed into us.

The one thing they did know was that the first three days were critical for his survival. In those first 72 hours the brain continues to swell in reaction to the trauma, putting additional pressure on the brain which can lead to irreversible injury.

Since then, my wife has hardly left his side. He lies in ICU in an induced coma to keep his brain pressure down, with a hundred pipes leading in and out of almost every part of his body.

We thank God that he has now passed the critical danger point and the pressure has begun to slowly go down. But our eyes still run a constant circular track, darting from the book of *Psalms* or Torah that we read to him, to his angelic quiet face (now growing a young man's fuzzy beard), to the menacing monitors constantly changing their frightening numbers.

We still don't know what Yaakov's outcome will be. We've learned that knowledge of the brain is very minimal and the experts have no way to assess damage or repair. The body (read: God) does the work. Doctors merely create the environment to allow the body to repair itself. Until the body starts to do something like talking, no one can guess if it will. All they can tell us with any surety is that it will take a long period of patience and therapy.

I have never known such pain in my life. I didn't know this caliber of pain even existed. I've read about it, but it was tucked away in the realm of imagination, where it belonged. It had no part of my secure world.

Shock is a big part of it. Overnight I went from a "normal" family man with a busy professional life to a "father of a boy fighting for his life in ICU with possible permanent brain damage." We went far too quickly from being parents terrified by a child's high fever, to parents dancing for joy when our son moves his hand three inches, which thank God happened yesterday for the first time.

It takes time.

The anguish, fear, terror, sadness, guilt, anger rolled over me in colossal, confusing waves. Numbness would periodically make a merciful visit, an automated defensive response to prevent the approaching, seemingly inevitable shattering of my fragile being. I was defenseless against the onslaught. The mind struggled to sort out the feelings and make sense of the raging offensive unfolding inside me but it was in vain, like a traffic cop holding up his pathetic little hand as a 10-ton truck smashes into him.

Coming Together

The biggest surprise to us has been both the unimaginable outpouring of love and support — and just how much a difference it makes. Around the world people are praying and doing mitzvot and good deeds, beseeching God that Yaakov ben Esther should have a full and fast recovery. Thousands of emails, millions of prayers, groups getting together to complete the Book of *Psalms*, Torah classes, publications have been dedicated for his merit. It was as if a massive machine came together within hours, mobilizing thousands of disparate parts into an integrated international effort to storm the heavens for Yaakov's recovery, and to strengthen us in our desperation.

People in Miami, New York, Costa Rica, Switzerland, and Mexico, Jerusalem and Tel Aviv, Australia and Toronto. A busload of widows prayed for him at the graves of the righteous in Israel. People I lost track of literally 20 years ago reconnected to express their solidarity. Religious and secular have joined together in a united prayer, tangibly (for me) climbing to the heavens. Friends kicked in to take over our busy household: transportation to schools, babysitting, food, shopping, laundry, cleaning, even stuff I never get around to doing. It has been an incredible whirlwind.

With everyone coming together to help, we've seen that the Jewish people truly are one unit. That was the prerequisite for receiving the Torah at Mount Sinai. Because unity is what allows miracles to happen.

During the first terrifying night, at 3:00 in the morning a friend showed up, somehow finding us in the bowels of the hospital near the surgical suites. His family had survived a major car accident which included many brain traumas and he came to reassure us that there was hope.

Don't Blame, Don't Complain

So what can you do to help?

It is a great merit for a sick person when others are inspired by him to improve their own lives.

Two of Yaakov's excellent character traits are worthy of all of us to emulate, and by doing so, he will God willing benefit as well.

First, no matter what happens to him in life, he never complains. For someone his age, he's had a relatively tough life. We never heard him grumble or whine; he stoically accepts his challenges and moves forward. His army buddies said that even during the most difficult tasks (like 60 km mountain marches wearing massive backpacks and heavy rifles), when everyone else was maxing out on kvetching, he would never join the pity party.

After receiving the Torah at Sinai, the Jewish people (unfortunately) do a fair bit of moaning as they wander through the desert. At first glance they look like real crybabies. But when you think about it, they were traveling in a hot, dry desert, faced with major problems like no water and no food! What do we expect them to do if not complain?

Rabbi Noah Weinberg, my rabbi, answered that they should have asked, "God, why aren't You giving us water? We know You love us and we know You can give it to us easily, so what do You want us to learn or change? Please help us understand Your message." That's legitimate; complaining is not. We complain when we choose the comfort of suffering our lot rather than embracing the effort to try and improve it.

And Yaakov never blames. Believe me, he's had good cause. Blaming is a handy mechanism to remove any personal responsibility for one's fate. When we avoid blaming, we have to face our challenges head on, something human nature desires to avoid at all costs.

In Yaakov's merit, we are asking everyone to try raise their sensitivities in these two areas: DON'T BLAME AND DON'T COMPLAIN.

Blaming and complaining create negativity and drive people apart. Making the conscious effort during your day to eradicate them is a practical way to build unity in your home and workplace. We suggest you print signs for your home and office — DON'T BLAME AND DON'T COMPLAIN — to serve as reminders to bite your tongue and start seeing things in a more constructive manner. It will certainly make your life better and hopefully Yaakov's as well, and for that we thank you from the bottom of our hearts.

Epilogue: Rebirth

Six weeks ago, our son, Yaakov, was hit by a car while rollerblading in Jerusalem. After two emergency head surgeries, he lay unconscious in the ICU of Hadassah Hospital, growing thinner and paler, with tubes coming in and out of just about every part of his body, for two weeks.

We didn't know if he'd make it out of the hospital. The terror of those days was thick and black and forever. The unrelenting beeps of the countless machines attached to him were all we had to remind us of the passing hours and days as we sat by his side, praying, reading him Torah, holding his hands.

Finally, Yaakov's brain pressure went down to levels the doctors felt were safe to begin the process of allowing him to wake up. It took four days to slowly wean him off all the heavy drugs. With trepidation, we waited for him to awake. Would he recognize us? Would he know how to talk, or had the brain been damaged in that area, as the doctors feared? Would he remember anything of his past? Would he have the same personality? Would he ever again be able to walk, taste, read, or do other basic things? Life was one giant question mark. The doctors could not reassure us.

All we could do was pray with all our hearts to the Master of the universe: "Please bring us back our Yaakov!"

With the Shavuot holiday coming, some of Yaakov's army buddies offered to stay with him those 24 hours so my wife and I could be at home with our other children — to gain some rest, some perspective, and to experience the full impact of the holiday.

When God revealed himself to the Jewish People on Mount Sinai and gave us the Torah 3,800 years ago, tradition tells us that all the sick people were healed: the lame walked, the blind could see. On each Shavuot, the anniversary of that event, the same power of healing returns.

As the holiday finished, we received a call from Yaakov's army buddies who had sat at his side for 24 hours. "Come quick! He's awake! He recognizes us and he understands."

With tears in our eyes, we rushed to the hospital. On the surface, it looked like a repeat of that same awful route two weeks before, driving and crying to the hospital. But this was so different: our tears were primal expressions of relief, of joy, and of thanks. When we stood at Yaakov's side and saw him smile at us, his eyes glassy but shining with recognition and life, we once again had trouble standing.

He couldn't talk, and he could hardly even open his eyes, but when my wife bent over to kiss him, he somehow found the strength to reach out his hand to caress her cheek to say, "I love you." It was heaven opening up. When his friend said goodbye, Yaakov slowly took his hand and drew it to his mouth to kiss it, and then he winked. With those small movements he was able to let us know that our Yaakov was back.

We have witnessed something few people have the opportunity to see: a miracle.

But actually, we've seen lots of miracles. Almost daily. Rabbi Dessler explains that the only real difference between a miracle and "nature" is its frequency. Is manna appearing with the dew each morning for 40 years in the desert any more miraculous than rotting seeds transforming into stalks of wheat or mango trees? But since we see that all the time, we lose touch with the marvel of it. The same goes with every aspect of our body's wondrous functions.

I know that the words "everything is a miracle" sound trite. But when you see creation appearing before your eyes, trite is not trite anymore. It is profound.

We have beheld what can only be described as a rebirth of a human being. At first he was an immobile blob of flesh. Then his eyes opened and he began to recognize things. Over the next days, he started to breathe by himself again, and slowly to move his hands, his legs. Later, our joy knew no end when he was able to sip a popsicle, and soon after, to drink by himself. It took a while, but soon he could even hold a water bottle himself!

A few days later, he painfully forced out his first words and our ecstasy was beyond expression. Then he began to eat solids, and to tell us what he needed. Like a baby's umbilical cord, they gradually removed him from the myriad pipes which had supported every aspect of his bodily functions.

Each morning upon waking, we say a beautiful prayer of thanks before we even climb out of bed: "I thank you, living God, for returning my soul into me in kindness …." Judaism describes sleep as "one-sixtieth of death." Our Yaakov was in a state that was more like 59 sixtieths of death, but God returned his soul. Almost every day we see more of him coming back home from somewhere far, far away.

Each day we fought the lurking, awesome fear of "What if this is as far as he's going to go? Maybe it will stop here!" We drew upon every drop of optimism and forced ourselves to be "convinced" that he was going to move further along. We found ourselves (and still do) torn between an immense sense of gratitude for how far he has come, and our uncompromising yearning for Yaakov to regain all his abilities, memories, and self.

Positive thinking has a potent impact on the outcome of things. In fact, Judaism demands optimism. We have a loving God Who has infinite power to help us. He's got a great track record: just as He's helped us in a million ways until now, we can surely count on Him to help us going forward. We should be shocked and amazed when things don't go the way we want them too. Shocked enough to ask what lesson He is trying to teach us in His love.

After one more week in the ICU, Yaakov was moved to the neurological ward of the hospital, and a few days later, with his tracheotomy pipe still sticking out of his throat, he was transferred to a rehab hospital.

As we were leaving, saying good bye to our new friends, the staff of the ICU, a social worker shared with us that everyone who leaves this place leaves with two very special gifts. First, they have a newfound perspective on what really counts in life. Petty problems are just that, petty problems. Secondly, they take with them a realistic appreciation of the incredible miracle that is life. Every one of the hundreds of things we do each day is simply amazing. When you see your child without that ability, and you imagine what life will be like for him without it (eating by himself, talking, going to the bathroom, reading, walking, holding, understanding, remembering things), you know how appreciative we all must be. "These gifts are for you, the family," she told us. "Your son won't remember what he went through, but you will."

On one of those first days of reawakening, Yaakov was in tremendous bodily pain, shaking all over, suffering terrible headaches and enveloped in a huge fog. He got a glimpse in a mirror of his shaved head, huge scar, pale, thin face, and he began to cry. I hugged him hard and cried with him, but I told him, "Yaakov, you might be crying from pain, and I'm really sorry that I'm not more sympathetic. But I am crying tears of joy. I don't expect you to understand yet, but seeing you alive, feeling and aware, is so huge that all I can do is cry." He understood, and he was calmed.

At first he didn't know his name or age, where he lives, or how many kids are in our family. Today, Yaakov is out of most of his pain and he's communicating (in both Hebrew and English) beautifully. He still has a long way to go in a lot of areas, like a painful leg, broken jaw, more surgery, and holes in his memory, but we see more and more faculties returning almost daily.

He's returned to many of his wonderful traits, like not blaming and not complaining. Despite his present disabilities, he's almost always happy and he lights up when his next visitor shows up. Yesterday, we found more glass embedded in his arm, but he didn't complain or blame.

We've encouraged ourselves and people all over the world to work on these two important traits — not blaming and not complaining — and we've heard from hundreds of people about how they are working at it, just how difficult it is to change our negative habits, and the huge difference a little bit of awareness has made in their lives.

One of my rabbis, a young father who was diagnosed with life-threatening cancer, was treated and went into remission, shared with me something I've never forgotten. "If someone had offered me $10 million to go through this experience, I would never have taken it. But now that I've gone through it, if someone offered me $10 million to take it away from me, I would never give it up."

Now I understand what he meant. The agony, the deep, unimaginable fear and heartache of these last few weeks are something I would not wish on anyone. But the lessons my wife and many of our friends and family have learned from this are so precious; it's hard to imagine going back and living life without them. These are just some of the gifts we have received: my appreciation for the beauty and the miracle of life, my understanding of the power of kindness, love, and friendship; the life-altering impact of small (and large) caring gestures; the intimacy with God that comes with tears and heartfelt prayer; the strength and comfort of community; and the earth-shattering lesson in unconditional love for a child, with no expectations or judgments.

For all of these treasures, and for Yaakov's return to us, I will be forever grateful.

Almost Normal

> *I always considered "being normal" the most important quality in a person. Then I had a baby with Down syndrome.*

Dina Coopersmith

When I was growing up, I considered "being normal" the biggest compliment. Moving to Israel at a young age and switching schools every year or two implanted in me a basic yearning just to fit in and be like everyone else.

When I became a young adult, I still thought "normalcy" was the overriding, most important quality in a person. I associated a lot of things with "being normal" — being emotionally healthy, balanced, relatively confident, down-to-earth, religious but not fanatical, spiritual but not flaky. In short, someone more or less like me — preferably more.

At some point "normal" became synonymous with being successful and having a relatively trouble-free life. Being a failure or burdened with problems would be pathetic, the very worst possible thing to be.

Dina Coopersmith has a Bachelor's in Education and a Master's in Jewish History. She teaches in a number of seminaries in Jerusalem, where she lives with her husband and children.

People frequently confirmed to me that I was, in fact, "extremely normal." As a teacher of young women, I became my students' friend and confidante since I was "so normal." I never ended up being the butt of any "Purim spiel" jokes; the students couldn't find much to make fun of — no radical quirks or weirdness — which worked just fine for me.

I got married to a super-normal guy at the normal age of 22 — not too young, not too old — and had my first baby — a girl –less than two years later; not too soon, not too late.

I think that was the last very normal event in my life.

Things began to take a turn for the "unusual" a couple of years later. Suffice it to say that having children wasn't coming as easily for me as it did for everyone else. After a few long breaks we somehow, thank God, managed to have three terrific kids spaced about four years apart, and I was ready to get back to the business of being a "normal" family.

This wasn't as easy at it sounds. We live in Jerusalem, in a densely populated, religious neighborhood. By densely populated I mean mostly by children. The average number of kids per family seems to be a dozen. Okay, maybe not a dozen, but seven or eight, and the moms who have only two or three are not much older than 20, and all three kids are under the age of two and a half.

So I wasn't quite as normal as I had always hoped to be. I compensated by idealizing the particular life-style I had as a result of not always needing to be at home with kids. I had an enjoyable part-time teaching job that kept me intellectually and spiritually stimulated. I took parenting courses to try and become the best mother I could be, and convinced myself and others that I wouldn't enjoy dealing with babies day after day, year after year. I told myself that quality was so much more important than quantity (and my kids were, after all, the brightest and most beautiful in the neighborhood!).

So I was certainly not to be pitied. God forbid anyone should consider me a *"nebach,"* pathetic. Oh, no. Everything was exactly how I wanted it to be. I still had it all together and was super-normal. Everyone said so.

When I was expecting my fourth child and everything seemed to be going well, I finally began to breathe more easily. Things were going to be just fine now. I'll be a "normal" mommy with baby in tow, a stroller with which to walk my daily fast-paced jaunt to town, and with which I could now frequent the playground with my other children as well. And four kids is pretty normal, isn't it?

Then my baby boy was born. And he had Down syndrome.

Out went the visions of carefree afternoons in the park, chatting and exchanging witty anecdotes about our children with the other young mothers. In came the horrifying thoughts of the neighbors' pity, my parents' sadness for my sake, my friends and relatives feeling bad for me, and the label "*nebach*" in big, bold letters.

Almost secondary to all these thoughts were the real concerns and worries about raising a child with special needs — the time and effort this would entail and how much of a change I would need to make in my life.

At my son's *bris*, all I could think was, "Act normal and happy like nothing's wrong. Smile, go through the motions, and don't let anyone have reason to feel bad for you."

As some of my neighbors were leaving, one said, "You know, you truly are amazing." All the others nodded in agreement as I cringed inside. Didn't they know that's exactly what I didn't want to be? "I just want to be normal!" I wanted to scream.

Now, eight months later, this remains my greatest challenge. Yes, I totally love with my adorable little boy and I find caring for him as stimulating and fulfilling as for any of my other kids, if not more so. Each sign of progress is met with cries of excitement and celebration, and at times I even feel exhilarated. But I still haven't let go of the normalcy dream. To a certain extent, I still haven't accepted the fact that my Yehuda Meir and, by proxy, my family and I, will never be "normal."

Sometimes I avoid mentioning it to people who know I had a baby but don't know about the Down syndrome. I figure they can find out from someone else and I can avoid having to deal with their reaction. That fleeting shadow of horror that crosses their faces before it's replaced by a half-smile of pity and concern, or a piece of well-meaning advice or consolation, like, "I heard they can be concert pianists — they're very musical," or "God only gives challenges to great people who can handle them."

I find it difficult associating myself with other parents of kids with disabilities. What in the world am I, queen of normalcy, doing in a room full of people like this? It can't be that I belong here, can it? I will occasionally find a long-discarded, quickly-jotted phone number of someone to call "when you're ready to talk" scrunched up at the bottom of our messy kitchen drawer. Who was I kidding? I wasn't about to join a support group or anything so obviously pathetic!

I grasp at any compliment such as: "He's so cute, you can't even tell he has Downs" or "He's doing everything a regular kid his age does," to confirm to myself once again that hey, we are the most normal people in this abnormal group.

I am forced to live with the realization that to be "normal" is something entirely different from my original misconception.

Just about all the people I've encountered through the shared reality of having a child with disabilities have been extremely impressive. Typically they are caring, driven, intelligent, and emotionally balanced, going to heroic lengths to do what's best for their children. Adjectives like "weak" or "pathetic" don't even enter the picture.

I realize that to be truly "normal" is to be confident enough with yourself and the situation you have been given by the Almighty that you are able to ask for help and advice if you need it, and to openly admit that you may not have it all together all the time. And that it's arrogant to think otherwise ... maybe even a little pathetic.

"One who flees from honor, honor runs after him" (Babylonian Talmud, *Eruvin* 13b).

If a year ago someone would have told me that I was going to become a mother of a child with Downs, I would have laughed it off as impossible. "The Almighty knows that I could not handle that!"

Well, I guess God, in His infinite wisdom and humor, has greater expectations of me than I of myself. He is not going to let me run away from one of the primary issues I need to work on.

I still hate it when I sense people's pity, and to be honest it's hard to see that changing any time soon. But as I integrate the reality of my particular abnormal situation, perhaps someday I will acquire the necessary humility to be truly "normal."

Postscript, 7 years later

I have come to realize many things about myself and my family and the mission we are in this world to accomplish. God has given me my particular set of tools, strengths, and circumstances with which to fulfill a unique purpose that no one else can fulfill. We each have a unique path to bring good and holiness in to this world. I still believe there is value to being competent, confident, and emotionally stable, but those are just means to help you achieve your purpose more effectively. There is certainly very little value in being like everyone else, just for the sake of being normal. That's just boring!

My son Yehuda is seven and a half now, fully integrated in to a regular second-grade class in the *cheder* my other sons attend. He reads and writes, speaks both English and Hebrew fluently and rather clearly. He has friends his age, some younger than he is and some older. He is generally a sensitive, friendly child, sometimes shy and introverted. He is sometimes stubborn and misbehaves, but often he is hard-working and well-behaved. He usually likes to please and seeks approval, and sometimes he has had it and just refuses to listen. He loves food and can almost always be bribed to act appropriately with sweets as an incentive.

He is basically a normal little boy. Well, almost normal.

A Leg to Stand On

At 13, Yitzy Haber decided to have his cancerous leg amputated. He's never looked back.

Andrea Kahn

Yitzy Haber is the kind of guy you'd want to be stuck with in a broken elevator. Infectiously upbeat, he has a knack for making the best of every situation. He's had a lot of practice.

In the suburbs of Jersey, Yitzy was a typical boy. He loved the Mets, model airplanes, and playing sports. Despite a stout physique, he was the fastest runner in his class. He had a thick, unruly mop of dark, wavy hair, and an irresistible smile that charmed him out of many a mishap. Life was good.

But during Little League practice when Yitzy was 11, he suddenly felt pain in his right leg. When it worsened, doctors put him on crutches, thinking perhaps one leg was growing faster than the other. Then came more tests and x-rays. Finally, boy and parents received the diagnosis: cancer. He had osteosarcoma — one of the most common bone cancers in children.

He knew his mother was upset by the mascara streaking her face. But he didn't take it too seriously; what did he know about cancer?

Andrea Kahn is a former reporter for the *Los Angeles Times* and editor for *TEEN* magazine. She currently lives in New York, where she continues to freelance for a variety of publications.

"I thought I'd maybe have a week off of school, lying in bed, watching TV, popping a couple of pills," says Haber, now a trim, bearded 30 year old who still wears an irrepressible grin. But nothing could prepare him for what was to come: multiple surgeries, and a year of chemotherapy and all its side effects — hair loss, excessive vomiting, infections. Throughout the ordeal, he and his family were kept afloat by support from their Teaneck, New Jersey community, and from Chai Lifeline, an international organization that provides countless services for children with cancer and their families at no cost.

"Chai Lifeline paid for tutors, and they had visitors coming round the clock," Yitzy remembers. "They provided social workers for me and for my parents, who were going through torture, and even for my siblings. My brother was only six and no one thought he understood what was happening. Then he asked the social worker, 'Is Yitzy going to die?'"

Yitzy's treatment, meanwhile, was anything but clear; an allograft (donor bone), more surgeries, more infections, pins, rods. He felt like a puppet. The doctor gave the now 13 year old three choices: insert another allograft from the knee down, leaving his entire leg straight forever; replace his knee and bone with a metal knee and rod, which would leave him at a high risk of infection and require more surgeries to replace the implants as he grew (and which could easily crack, severely limiting any normal-boy action); or amputation from above the knee down. Yitzy's parents left the decision up to him.

"I decided on the amputation. I wanted to be able to dance, to play sports. I wanted to be normal."

Making such a momentous decision was one thing; the shock of waking up one day without his leg, quite another.

"I remember clearly the last time I had my leg. And then not having it," he recounts. "I can't even describe the feeling — it was just a shock. But then, in the cancer ward, I saw this gloomy, depressed woman in a wheelchair, and I thought, if you walk around like that, for sure you're going to die. But if you're happy, I told myself, your body will want to fight it, and you'll win. I had always been upbeat, but at that point I became really focused on being happy, even *without* a leg. I've never looked back."

Of course, all the optimism and determination in the world couldn't begin to erase the countless challenges. For years Yitzy experienced phantom sensations where his leg once was — from the benign, as if he were wiggling his toes, or an inexplicable itch on a part of his leg he could not locate, to the excruciating, with a searing ache where his calf or ankle once was. The phantom pain has mostly disappeared, but to this day, if he trips in a way that would have caused a sprained ankle, he'll automatically start limping. "But now," he says, "I can tell myself that it doesn't hurt, that there's no ankle there, and I can stop myself from limping."

As an adolescent, Yitzy had to begin the arduous process of learning to walk anew, and even how to fall "right," so he wouldn't hurt himself. Through it all, he found ways to amuse himself and others. At Chai Lifeline's Camp Simcha, a free two-week camp-extravaganza in the Catskills for kids with cancer, the mischievous Yitzy loved putting one over on his bunkmates. "I would say, 'Whoever can put one foot on the floor and one foot on the ceiling at the same time is the head of the bunk,'" he recalls. "They'd all try it and fall over, and then I'd take off my prosthesis and touch the ceiling. I still use that one."

Yitzy spent five summers at Camp Simcha and eventually became a counselor, learning how much he actually had to offer others. "I had been on the taking side for so long, and it was an amazing feeling to finally be on the other side," he says. "I knew from real-life experience the living nightmare these kids were going through. I could see that I really made a difference to them, and I gave them hope. And that gave me strength, too."

A Full Life

As Yitzy grew into a strapping young man, he began thinking about marriage. His parents were concerned — would there be a woman who would accept him? But he never worried. "Maybe I was just naïve, but I never thought it would be an issue, and I had my share of dates. Then again, maybe no one wanted to be known as the girl who turned down the one-legged guy," he says with a wink. Now married with two young children, his leg — or lack thereof —

has never presented a problem. "My older son will say, 'Daddy, put on your leg so we can play.' They don't have a point of reference for anything different."

With the help of his parents, grandparents and others, Yitzy had finally built a full life for himself. But there was more tragedy to come. When he was 20, his mother, Deena Haber, whom he credits with keeping his family together during the worst of his crisis, became sick — with cancer. She had taught Yitzy to appreciate every moment, and now she lived that way throughout her own personal ordeal. One day, he came home from yeshivah and he found her eating a huge ice cream sundae, with sprinkles, chocolate syrup, even a cherry. "I asked her, 'What's the occasion?' And she said, 'It's my year anniversary of still being alive.' She meant it. She really celebrated her life." After battling the illness for three years, Deena died a year after Yitzy's wedding.

In many ways, the physical challenges of losing a leg to cancer have been simpler than the emotional. It can be tough relating to those who have never been through any kind of life-changing trauma. "When we first got married, sometimes it was hard for me to understand some of the things my wife got upset about," he relates. "I didn't see the big deal. Or when my friends were dating, and one would say that he wouldn't go out with someone because she had red hair. I couldn't believe how superficial people could be, how petty." Many cancer survivors have a difficult time adapting to life after, and Yitzy is now involved with a new support group through Chai Lifeline, or, as he calls it, a "post-treatment-figure-things-out group." He does what no social worker can — he offers a living example. "When someone is scared, and says to me, 'How will I ever get married?' or 'How will I ever fit in?' I encourage them; I show them it's possible."

No Laughing Matter

Yitzy is not only determined to nurture and cherish the joy in his own life, he is relentlessly driven to awaken that joy in others. Or, as he puts it, "to get a laugh or a smile, no matter what it takes." And he's not joking. He turned an interest in magic that he developed when he was sick, into a high school hobby entertaining at birthday parties, into a profession, and he now works about 100 bar mitzvahs a year as a brightly clad "motivational dancer," encouraging tweens (and otherwise lethargic adults) to get up and celebrate. He parlayed his innate charisma and physicality into doing exactly the thing that nourishes his body and spirit.

"I think all of us, if we look hard enough, can see the good in what happens to us," says Yitzy, his ever-present smile momentarily fading. "I didn't love throwing up, or the surgeries, or losing my leg — but if I had to do it all again to guarantee I'd be where I am now, I would do it. It's not that I consciously think 'I had cancer so now I'm going to appreciate life,' but that is what I've internalized. I never asked 'why me.' It just was me, so now deal with it.

"I have a dream about building a giant, magic one-way mirror. Anyone who is upset about something small — their kid didn't say please, or their house isn't perfect — would look in the mirror and see a person like themselves whose life has been turned upside down due to illness or an accident. To make them see and appreciate how much they really have, and how things can change in an instant. If I had a dream, that would be it."

Anorexia: Starving in the Land of Plenty

Five years ago, without warning, anorexia kidnaped my 15-year-old daughter.

Efraim Jaffe

It all began so subtly that I didn't even realize she was missing. She was restricting her food intake. She used to eat a sandwich for lunch; now she came home from school with her lunch intact. She was too busy to sit and eat with the family. I noticed her catching frequent nervous glances into a full-length mirror from various angles.

My wife noticed the changes right away; she had been trained to work as a nutritionist with patients who had eating disorders. But I wasn't worried. It was hard to imagine these quirks developing into a full-blown crisis. We agreed to send Rachel to a therapist, and I drove her to weekly appointments with an "expert" in the field, expecting my daughter to be quickly cured. She didn't like the therapy, complaining that it was stupid and besides, she didn't have a problem. But she reluctantly went every week.

As the weeks and months went by, she got worse, although she developed a remarkable ability to camouflage her behavior: she

---

Efraim Jaffe was born and raised in Portland, Oregon. He attended Aish HaTorah in the late 70's, along with his two brothers. He has resided in Passaic, New Jersey, since 1987.

happened to be busy at meal times, she had headaches at meal times, she picked at the food on her plate. It was like a giant vacuum cleaner was draining her brain cells and depriving her of the ability to think and act normally. Her sunny disposition turned sullen and moody. She was losing the battle — worse, she didn't act like she wanted to win.

Rachel had never been skinny, nor was she overweight. Now she was starting to look really "good," Hollywood style. Friends and neighbors began to take notice. "Rachel! You look great!" "Rachel, how did you get so skinny?" The Thin Worshipers heaped on the praise.

Why was this happening? What could we do to reverse the growing momentum?

Anorexia is a type of eating disorder that mainly affects girls and young women. A person with this disorder, according to the U.S. Department of Health and Human Services:

- Refuses to keep a normal body weight
- Is extremely afraid of becoming fat
- Believes she's fat even when she's very thin

Anorexia is more than a problem with food. It's a way of starving oneself to feel more in control of life and to ease tension, anger, and anxiety that frequently erupts around adolescence. Girls as young as eight or nine can become anorexic. Causes of anorexia may include the following:

- Biology. Genetic factors contribute to the onset of this disorder, according to some recent studies.
- Culture. The popular culture idealizes extreme thinness as a model of physical beauty.
- Overly permissive or overly controlling parents.
- Perfectionists and obsessive-compulsive behavior frequently characterize anorexics.
- Personal feelings. An anorexic may have poor self-esteem and hate the way she looks, or feel unable to meet pressures from family or social expectations.
- Stressful events or life changes. A new school or new job may trigger anorexia.
- Families. Having a mother or sister with anorexia increases the chances of developing the disorder.

Parents who think appearance is important, diet themselves, and criticize their children's bodies are more likely to have a child with anorexia.

What are the signs of anorexia?
- Looks a lot thinner
- Uses extreme measures to lose weight
- Makes herself throw up
- Takes diet pills
- Exercises excessively
- Weighs food and counts calories
- Moves food around plate without eating
- Weighs herself constantly
- Distorted body image; sees herself as fat
- Acts moody or depressed
- Wears baggy clothes to hide appearance
- Doesn't socialize
- Talks about food all the time
- Won't eat in front of others

Anorexia denies the body the nutrition it needs, making it slow down to compensate. Bone loss, dry skin, hair loss, swollen joints, heart palpitations are a few of the symptoms. If effective and timely treatment is not received, the mortality rate is alarmingly high.

Rachel had always been popular in school, but by eighth grade her A.D.D. was getting worse and her grades went from passing to failure, in a rapid descent. She started to drift away from her classmates and began to rebel against her Jewish identity. She had lost 20 pounds, from her normal weight of 135 lbs. down to 115. The more we talked, the worse the disorder became. As a family, we were about to enter a five-year war, literally battling for Rachel's life.

You can scream at a disorder, but that doesn't make it go away. Rachel's grandparents, recently deceased, survived the Nazis and their biggest thrill was to feed their grandchildren. Their only granddaughter was now wasting away in the Land of Plenty. Mercifully, they didn't live to see it.

I learned that an "eating disorder" is not about eating, any more than an alcohol problem is about alcohol. The disorder is a refuge, a friend, an all-consuming identity, and a glorious victory over the laws of nature. Rachel chewed gum non-stop, did sit-ups to the brink of exhaustion, cooked gourmet meals for the family without taking a bite, did all of our grocery shopping, took several hot baths daily to warm up, isolated herself in her room, and her mood swung wildly from reasonable to impossible. She started several jobs but would abruptly quit from exhaustion after a few weeks.

We decided to take Rachel, despite her strident protests, to an in-patient residential facility located on a former country estate outside of Philadelphia where she was supposed to stay for several weeks. The in-patient placement is designed to supervise caloric consumption, make sure that the anorexic is not involved in the bulimic practice of vomiting after meals, and provide counseling andtherapeutic group activities. We left her in tears, begging us not to leave her.

For the next three days she called us day and night, sobbing and swearing that the program was unbearable. On the fourth day, a car service showed up at our front door. Rachel had exercised her right as an 18-year-old to check herself out, paying a taxi $400 in cash that she had secretly brought with her.

Fading Away

"One thing that really shocked me is that the experts say that it takes about four to seven years to recover from an eating disorder," said Lauren Greenfield, whose documentary film *Thin* (and book by the same name) chronicles the lives of four women with eating disorders. "Yet, the average insurance policy pays for three weeks of treatment. That's a huge disconnect. That kind of stress took away from the quality of the treatment because they were so worried whether or not they can continue. Some of the girls would be on the phone, begging their insurance carriers for just one more day of treatment."

Rachel was released several times from a hospital after a two- or three-week stay. She immediately began to deteriorate and return to her disorder upon release from the hospital.

Watching Rachel starve created an ongoing dilemma: Should we encourage her to eat, triggering her anger and denial, and an even more severe round of restriction and isolation? Or should we not intervene, as all the professionals had advised us, because this is "her problem and only she can solve it"?

The tension of seeing Rachel in the kitchen, eating lettuce and diet salad dressing while family members pretended not to watch, was like walking in a mine field. "You don't have a right to do this to yourself, or to us," I would tell her. My words echoed in my head. Do they help? How can I stand by idly and watch? My workday was increasingly consumed by research into finding a solution and going with Rachel to psychologists, psychiatrists, treatment centers, and family sessions.

The urge to explain to Rachel the compelling need to eat properly was overwhelming, and every so often I would try to reason with her. "I know you think you're fat, but you must trust everybody when they tell you that you're not!" The problem is that the anorexic looks in the mirror and all she sees is fat, fat, fat. Anorexics have been known to cut a raisin in half, food for two meals. If a person has cancer, depression or any other disease, they'd like to be rid of it. But the anorexic's main fear is being cured!

Living with Rachel meant not knowing if at any moment she would collapse, have a heart attack, or even, God forbid, die.

Unconditional love is easy to give when things are going well. The Rachel that I unconditionally loved was all but gone, and I wanted to scream, "Eat! Enough! You win! You're ruining our lives too! What gives you the right?"

I prayed for Rachel, but it wasn't working. How could it work if she didn't want it to? I found little cups of yogurt opened with one tiny spoonful missing. Rachel's bones rattled beneath her loose-fitting clothes like a museum skeleton hanging to dry in the wind. How does one pray to bring dry bones back to life?

Hope and Courage

Hope is a fleeting emotion. I never completely lost it, but at times felt it slipping away like the last warm summer day.

One day my son called from his school in Israel to tell us about an eating disorders program at the New York State Psychiatric Institute. (His friend had been treated for a substance abuse problem in the same program.) This research program was publicly funded and wasn't restricted by insurance company rules.

After a month of seemingly futile attempts to gain admission, Rachel was admitted, a skeletal 65% of her "ideal body weight," dehydrated, and in serious danger.

The hospital research protocol emphasized gaining weight in a strictly controlled environment with the objective of regaining 100% of ideal body weight. Rachel's vegetarian regime was not allowed; the program believed that all restrictive eating habits had to be broken. Rachel hadn't had meat or fish for years, after witnessing chickens being slaughtered on a school outing. I was nervous that she would be out of compliance and be disqualified from the program.

Amazingly, she ate the meat and survived her first major test of recovery. Hope returned like a bird singing on a spring day. She survived the first two weeks of the program, gradually increasing her calories from 1800 to 3000 per day, eventually consuming 4000 per day. A family member or her good friend would visit every day to offer encouragement.

She constantly complained that the other patients picked on her and were reporting her minor infractions to the "authorities;" she was caught chewing gum or throwing unwanted food into the garbage, and became hysterical with anger and resentment. Rachel would lose privileges, like a daily visit to the hospital coffee shop or the enclosed outdoor area. (The locked unit made forays to the outside world impossible without some kind of pass.) The prison walls were closing in. Could a jailbreak be close at hand?

The call came while I was at work. "Mr. Jaffe? This Is Mrs. N. at the New York State Psychiatric Institute. I just want to tell you that Rachel has signed herself out. Her brother is picking her up. We can only keep her here until after lunch."

I felt like a freight train had flattened me. But I knew I had to think fast and do something. We had about one hour. "Just keep her there as long as you can. I'm on my way over," I responded. My wife and I were determined to keep Rachel in the program at all costs. We didn't want to see her die.

The hospital is about a 40-minute drive from my office. I called my son, Rachel's confidant, from the car. He had been persuaded by Rachel to pick her up. She had already checked out, she told him, and if he didn't come she would just have to find her way home on her own. "Stall her," I told him. I was so nervous that I took the wrong exit and got lost in Newark, before getting back on track. My plan was to get to the hospital before she left and figure out some way to get her to stay.

Rachel was still there when they let me into the locked unit. She was hysterical, desperately shaking and crying. "Don't you see it won't work?! Don't you see it's not for me!?"

I tried to remain calm and told her and the social worker that we won't take her back home. Refusing to take her back home meant that the hospital would not release Rachel in such an endangered condition without going to court. No matter how hard she screamed, I wasn't going to blow what might have been be her last best chance at recovery. I left Rachel screaming and shaking in the locked unit.

Miraculously, Rachel recovered after a few days and met a girl who would become her inseparable friend and remains so to this day. She began to see the possibility of completing the program and even to see recovery as a possibility.

A week after the crisis, I received the following letter:

"Dear Daddy: Happy Father's Day. Where do I begin? Thank you so much for being my constant rock for the past month. I know it's been hard on you to make me stay here and watch me struggle, but you made that decision with my best interests at heart. Looking back, I can appreciate how difficult that must have been for you to leave me here crying. I have come a long way since then, and I wanted to thank you for saving my life that day, by not letting me leave and not giving up on me. But most of all, just for being there whenever I need you, and loving me unconditionally."

Hope lives!

A month later, longer than any previous hospital stay, Rachel had gained "leave" privileges and was able to leave the hospital for hours at a time, a major morale boost. After two months, she was allowed to come home for overnight stays. Her release was scheduled to be two weeks away. While it seemed that she had turned a corner, in our family therapy sessions Rachel repeatedly stated that she still felt like an anorexic, had no desire to work or go to school, and had no confidence that she could maintain her progress after her impending discharge from the Psychiatric Institute.

Almost four months have now passed since Rachel came home. The first two weeks were nerve-wracking for all of us, but Rachel soon found an out-patient support team and has consistently made the effort to maintain her weight and her will to tackle life head on. She got a job at Starbucks and works 30 hours a week. The struggle goes on and her mood swings and anorexic thoughts still haunt her, but life is good again and Rachel's smile has returned.

Welcome back Rachel! We missed you so much. To all parents and friends, husbands and boyfriends, sisters and brothers: don't buy into the lie that thin is beautiful. If a woman is starving herself, give her empathy and get her help. Make an appointment with an eating disorder team that includes a therapist, a nutritionist, and a psychiatrist. There is not a moment to lose.

Stop the Loneliness

Don't let what happened to me happen to one more single person

by A Lonely SFJ

I do not know how it happened, but I am approaching 50 and am still single.

And I have given up. I know that I will never marry and have children. I do not write this article for me, but for those who still believe and have hope for a normal life.

I grew up in the typical, normal religious home. My parents were Holocaust survivors. My father was lucky. Having come from Europe directly after the war, he was taken in by an uncle who had moved to California two years before the war began. This uncle took my father under his wing, educated him, gave him a good job, and found him a wonderful partner in life, my mother. My mother was very young when she came to America and was therefore able to blend in quite well.

They had six children. All of us were close and had a wonderful childhood. I am the second to youngest. I saw all of my siblings marry wonderful spouses and had high hopes that the same would

---

The author wishes to remain anonymous. The initials SFJ stand for Single, Female, Jewish.

happen to me. Year after year went by and nothing happened. I'd like to say that I know why, but in all honesty, I can't. I was bright, attractive, from a wonderful family and have what everyone calls a good personality. I wasn't one of those girls who are overly picky. Yet, something went very, very wrong.

In the beginning, I didn't feel much pressure. I was young, working, had many friends, and was enjoying being single. But as my friends and family were getting married, one after the other with seemingly little effort, I started to get nervous. I went to rabbis for blessings, took trips to Israel to pray at the holy sites of our forefathers, and dated anyone and everyone.

But now I have given up. I am lonely beyond words, and worst of all, I will never know the joy of motherhood.

I write this article not for me, but to help those who are still searching. My words are not directed at them, but to those of you who have found your *bashert*, your soul mate. DO SOMETHING. Those of you who are married and have families have an obligation to those who don't. When one is sick we raise money for treatment. When one needs blood after surgery, we rally and donate. When a family loses a parent, we volunteer our time and try to help.

Well, the biggest disease of this generation is the thousands of singles, sitting in their homes alone and crying out to God for help.

You are in the position to do make a difference. DO SOMETHING ABOUT IT NOW. Don't let what happened to me happen to one more single person. I cry at how lonely I am and beg you to help.

Make it part of your life to fix up any and every single you know. This will save more lives than you'll ever know.

Don't sit silently and let our tears of loneliness fall without lifting a hand to help.

NICU

Love's vital ingredient

Yael Mermelstein

My first moments of motherhood are etched in my brain in indelible print. Sitting by my son's incubator day after tedious day, I tried to glimpse his body through the tangled wires and machinery. When the Huggies newborn diaper covers your baby from head to toe, it's enough to make any new mother wonder if she got more than she bargained for.

And so I sat, and sat, and sat. I was not allowed to hold him due to the line that he had running into his umbilical artery through his microscopic bellybutton. Instead I moved aside the tangled rainbow of wires, and tried to find a fuzzy place to stroke. I had read that massaging premature infants was a stimulant for them and this kid sure could have used some of that.

When he reached a stage where he was ready for food, we were jubilant. Feeding meant sending a few drops of my mother's milk down a tube that started in his nose and ended in his stomach cavity.

Yael Mermelstein is a wife, mother, writer, editor, lecturer, and writing coach. Her recent and upcoming releases include the novel *Second Chances* (ArtScroll / Mesorah), the teen novel *Switched* (ArtScroll / Mesorah) and the children's book *Izzy the Whiz and Passover McClean* (Kar-Ben). Yael was the recipient of the Sydney Taylor Manuscript Award. She lives in Israel with her family and her pet computer.

My husband held the tube, and I held the baby (finally!). It was the closest thing to mother/child bonding you could find in the neonatal intensive care unit.

Midnight was weighing and bathing time. We learned to do it all ourselves, rendering the nurses extraneous (almost). We burned the midnight oil night after night in that hospital, like truckers guarding a big haul.

He was our child, and through many weeks of intensive care we staked that claim over and over again. Like a pioneer explorer sticking his post in a mound of dirt, I claimed my little slip of a life, through a stroke of the cheek, an original lullaby, and a drop down the feeding tube.

Love was in the air.

The Nature of Love

In his treatise on kindness, Rabbi Eliyahu Dessler makes a groundbreaking statement on the nature of love. He posits that a relationship based upon giving is one in which love will grow ad infinitum. Why? Because love is an outgrowth of the giving process.

My students often had a bone to pick with this theory. In a loving relationship, isn't giving a natural outgrowth of love? It was a matter of which came first, the chicken or the egg, but the implications were far reaching. In their eyes, love was an electrical impulse that translated into giving. According to Rabbi Dessler, the more you give, the more electrical current you create in your relationships. He puts the steering wheel in our hands, instead of leaving it up to some inexplicable force.

I must admit, I empathized with my students' point of contention. As a new mother, I knew that my love for my child was just that — intangible and beautiful, unforced and uncultivable.

Approximately two years after our first child was born, I found myself sitting in the same neonatal unit with son number two. This one was a "hefty" 33-weeker. We were miles past son number one. Sitting there after delivery, I watched his wan face redden as he tried to cry, but emitted no sound, as the respirator was suppressing his larynx. He was not ready for food yet, and I stored God's precious elixir in little bottles in the NICU freezer.

It was all the same. The grey tweed upholstered chairs, the nurses in their one-piece pinks, and the pungent smell of antiseptic soap. I felt as if I were watching a re-run of a medical drama.

I was discharged without my child, and again that old familiar feeling of stepping over the threshold of our home without the tiny life that I had to leave behind. I knew, though, what the next few weeks heralded. I would be there the next morning.

My loyalties were painfully divided over the next weeks between my emotionally needy toddler at home, and the tiny bundle lying supine in his incubator. I ran to the hospital each morning to fulfill my duty, and then rushed back to pick up my eldest from playgroup. Whenever feasible, I returned a second time in the evening, but I had to go back and relieve my husband so that he could visit as well. I felt as if some very core part of me was torn in half, somewhere deep inside where my brain didn't seem to reach.

My husband went to the hospital often to check on our baby. He brought me back reports, some of which I relished. Others I would have preferred not to hear.

I knew things were different within me that first Shabbat afternoon that son number two was in the hospital. "Yael, do you want to walk over to see the baby?" my husband asked.

"Nah. You go. I'm tired. I need to build up my strength. I'm still just after birth." (That never stopped me before.)

My husband just kind of raised his eyebrows and looked at me askance. He went. I stayed. Cocooned in my blanket, I could almost pretend that my life was on cruise control.

I did what I had to do. I did not in any way neglect my responsibilities as a parent to either of my children. That is why I am not sure why it took me for a spin when someone offhandedly remarked later that week:

"You must really love that baby!"

I must really love that baby. I mean, of course I must. Which mother does not love her child? I thought of him for a moment, with the little gauze strip covering his eyes to protect him from the bilirubin lights.

He looked like he was tanning when I saw him this morning.

"I mean, obviously," I replied.

I went back to my dishes, scrubbing away bits of residue with a vengeance. *Do I love my child? My baby? Is there anything more inglorious than a mother who doesn't love her child? Am I that type?*

A few weeks later we brought him home. This strange child that I had been visiting all this time was now sleeping in my bedroom. The indispensable nurses were dispensed of. At three in the morning I awoke from my half-sleep to his cry. I picked him up — a four-pound butterball, and I nestled him in my arms. I breathed in the fresh scent of Johnson's baby bath and I ran my nose softly along the rim of his scalp. I watched him open and close his little mouth, looking, looking for me. He needed me. *He needed me!*

I gave myself to him.

And love was in the air.

Rabbi Dessler was right.

Person First, Disability Later

My daughter is a unique individual, not a diagnosis.

Robin A. Meltzer

It is Yom Kippur, one-thirty in the morning. A young Jewish couple is in a hospital delivery room, minutes away from becoming first-time parents. Anticipation mixes with the holiness of the night. This child will be another link in the unbroken tradition leading all the way back to Sinai. And then she is born. The parents are elated. But the nurses fall silent; the doctors look uncomfortably at the floor. Because the baby has Down syndrome. And that young Jewish couple is informed that their daughter, their precious firstborn child, is some sort of mistake.

I was the mother on that delivery table. And on that Yom Kippur, in the middle of the night, I learned that being Julia's mother meant being her advocate.

My job started immediately. My basic philosophy has remained constant over the past nine years: Julia is a unique individual, not

---

Robin Meltzer is an attorney with the federal government and a genealogist. Originally from Syracuse, New York, she lives in Silver Spring, Maryland with her husband and children and their highly energetic English springer spaniel.

a diagnosis. She must be given every opportunity to develop her capabilities. She is a full member of the Jewish community, entitled to the birthright of Torah and a Jewish education.

After the reception she got at the hospital, I hoped that the Jewish community would be more welcoming. And generally it was. But there is a lot of fear and misinformation.

The first issue we resolved was that according to Jewish law, Julia was obligated in mitzvah observance. Our rabbi explained that the basic cognitive standard obligating a person in commandments is discerning that a coin is valuable while a rock is not. The issue of whether or not a particular individual is generally obligated to observe the mitzvot is complex and requires consultation with an experienced rabbinic authority.

Yet, many people we encountered were certain that the diagnosis of Down syndrome, regardless of Julia's capacities, automatically exempted her from mitzvah observance. This damaging misconception could lead to eliminating any need for a Jewish education or for the community to provide that education. As the Passover Haggadah tells us, even if a child has no capacity to inquire, we are obligated to teach him the commandments. The Talmud (*Eruvin* 54b) relates that the great sage Rav Preida had a student that needed his lessons repeated 400 times. One day, it was necessary to double that. And for those 800 patient repetitions, God rewarded Rav Preida with a long life and granted him and his entire generation the World to Come.

To our great dismay, we also discovered that some confused and frightened parents are advised to abandon their babies with Down syndrome in the hospital. While it is true that not all parents are capable of raising a child with special needs and that placing a child for adoption is sometimes the only choice, many more parents would take their baby home if those they respect did not inveigh against it. Too often, these misguided assessments are viewed as a merciful response to the family's fear and misinformation about people with Down syndrome, and not based on true Torah principles. New parents need support to work through the initial shock of diagnosis. They need time to get to know their baby, to hold her and rock her and sing some lullabies. If given the chance, most parents will realize that they love their baby very much and are quite able to raise her.

Furthermore, there should be no fear regarding marrying a child from a family that has a member with Down syndrome. The geneticists we consulted assured us that siblings are at no increased risk of having a child with Down syndrome.

Even positive attitudes must not distract us from seeing people with Down syndrome as people first. We were told that the Chazon Ish would rise when a person with Down syndrome came into the room in recognition of an elevated soul. Other rabbis claim that people with Down syndrome are in some way angelic, or perhaps reincarnated *tzaddikim* (righteous people) whose souls require only minor repair.

These are profound spiritual ideas. But we should not focus so hard on spiritual mysteries that we miss the real person sitting in front of us. Has anyone ever answered the preschool application question, "Is there anything else we should know about your child?" with "Yes — he is a reincarnated *tzaddik*"? It is far more relevant whether a preschooler can sit in circle time and eat a graham cracker. Julia did fine with both. And she was a very cute singing dreidel in the Chanukah play.

As Julia began to accomplish more and more, it became clear to us that full academic inclusion would be the best thing for her. We did a lot of research and talked to many parents and professionals. When we first approached our neighborhood day school, there were a few awkward moments. Actually, there were a whole lot of awkward moments. But we worked through them. We kept the focus on Julia the little girl, not Julia the "Downs child."

Instead of getting stuck in "what if things go wrong," we concentrated on what we knew she could do right. With optimism, realism, and persistence, she made it through kindergarten. And then first grade, second, and third. She took her turn as class *chazzanit*, wrote a book report on Marco Polo and made a stamp album featuring all seven continents. Now in fourth grade, Julia is an avid reader and enthusiastic Torah student. She does her homework every night. And she loves to eat pizza with her friends.

This is what can happen if Jewish communities see people with Down syndrome as people, real people who are worthy of friendship and respect. This is what can happen when Torah values like kindness, fairness, and *ahavat Yisrael* — loving your fellow Jew — get put into action.

Many communities have made a lot of progress in school, shul, and social inclusion. More and more Jewish schools are welcoming students with Down syndrome. But the added tuition can be prohibitively expensive. And most communities will not cover the cost, despite several well-known halachic decisions that hold that Jewish education for children with special needs is a community obligation. We need to take the next step and make Jewish education a reality for all our kids.

It is true that a person's value is not determined by his or her capabilities, and that we need to appreciate the intrinsic worth of one's Jewish soul. But at the same time, if we really valued people regardless of their limitations, we would do all we can to include Jews with Down syndrome into community life. Because that is the Torah way.

Drops of Inspiration

Skeleton Key

Gratitude opens every door.

Sara Yoheved Rigler

One of the most moving scenes I ever witnessed took place at Gate B2 of the Baltimore airport. In a chair-studded corridor leading from Security to the departure gates, I had set down my carry-on and taken out my prayer book in hopes of reciting my morning prayers. A denizen of dozens of world airports, I suddenly heard a sound I had never before heard in any airport: applause.

Are people greeting a rock star? I wondered. *Don't rock stars fly in private jets?* The applause subsided, and I continued with my prayers. Two minutes later, however, I again heard clapping, accompanied by cheers and ululations. I suppressed my curiosity and tried to concentrate on my prayers. The noise died down, but a couple of minutes later another wave of applause and cheers picked me up and carried me to Gate B2.

A crowd of about 30 people was gathered at the gate, facing the entrance to the jetway. Some were waving American flags. Lined up against the wall leading from the jetway were five uniformed sailors and several civilians, including a TSA official. A new

---

For a biographical note on the author, please see page 29.

round of applause and cheers roared through the area. I weaved my way through the crowd to glimpse the object of all this adulation. At the entrance to the jetway I spotted him: an old man in a wheelchair.

The fellow pushing the wheelchair stopped to let the man absorb his rousing welcome. The man smiled and weakly lifted his right hand to acknowledge the crowd. As the wheelchair slowly moved past the receiving line, the sailors saluted, the others nodded, and the TSA official stepped forward, shook the old man's hand, and said in a heartfelt voice, "Thank you for your service."

The wheelchair moved past, a quiet lull ensued, and then another round of applause for the next deplaning passenger: another old man, standing wobbly on his own legs, leaning on a cane. He paused, looked up in surprise at his hero's welcome, as if not quite understanding all the hullabaloo, and then continued his limping gait, past the saluting sailors and the waving flags. He stopped only when the TSA official stepped forward, grasped his hand, and said, "Thank you for your service."

"What's going on here?" I asked the young woman beside me. "Who are these men?"

"They're World War II veterans. They've come to see the monument in Washington, D.C. that commemorates their service."

Sixty-six years had passed since these men, then mere boys, had come home from the war, having seen their buddies die, perhaps being wounded themselves. Sixty-six years, and here at Baltimore airport, a few dozen cheering Americans, most born long after the war, were still grateful for their service.

I joined the crowd, clapping loudly as each old man, most of them in wheelchairs, paused at the jetway entrance for his moment of glory. My eyes filled with tears. Something profound was taking place here at Gate B2.

When the last wheelchair rolled off toward baggage claim, I approached the TSA official. "I want you to know that I was very moved at how you thanked each and every veteran," I told him. "We all clapped, but you were the only one who put the gratitude into words. And words are very important."

He appreciated my appreciation. "Well," he said humbly, "I myself served, so I know what they've been through."

Opening Doors With Gratitude

Gratitude is the skeleton key that opens every door: faith, love, joy, even success in marriage. Gratitude is what distinguishes a mensch from a wretch.

Madelyn Weiss, a Miami lawyer specializing in divorce mediation, took a post-graduate seminar on the subject of divorce. At the first session, the professor went around the room and asked each student, "What is the main cause of divorce?" Some students answered, "Finances." Others answered, "Infidelity." Finally, the professor shook his head and declared, "The main cause of divorce is ingratitude."

"When the husband isn't grateful for all that the wife does for him," Madelyn explained to me, "or when the wife isn't grateful for whatever the husband does, despite his faults, the marriage just spirals down into criticism and backbiting."

In Jewish thought, gratitude is so essential that the Torah records that in Egypt at the time of the Ten Plagues, God instructed Moses to tell Aaron to strike the earth with his staff in order to initiate the plague of lice. Our sages explain that it would have been wrong of Moses himself to strike the earth because decades before the earth had benefited him when he used it to bury the body of the Egyptian taskmaster he had killed. The sages infer that if Moses had to show gratitude to the earth, an inanimate object that had involuntarily helped him one time decades before, how much more so must we all show gratitude to every human being who helps us voluntarily, even once, even long ago.

"*Yehudi*," the Hebrew word for "Jew" is derived from the root word meaning, "to thank." The essence of every Jew is the ability to be grateful.

But that ability exists only in potential. Gratitude, like gymnastics, is an acquired skill. Even if you're agile, if you don't work hard at it, you'll never be a gymnast. Even if your mother told you a million times, "Say, 'thank you,'" you'll never be a grateful adult unless you

develop your gratitude muscle. The aerobic exercises for developing gratitude are:
- Recognizing the good.
- Perceiving everything as a gift.
- Expressing gratitude.

Recognizing Good

The Hebrew term for "gratitude" is "*hakarat hatov*," which literally means, "recognizing the good." With many people and situations, it's as hard to find the good as to find Waldo amid 200 tiny figures. Gratitude requires:
- Entering the three-star hotel room your spouse reserved for your anniversary and focusing on the beautiful view instead of the seedy furnishings.
- Noticing all the toys that your child *did* pick up rather than the five Duplo pieces that he didn't.
- Focusing on how well your housecleaner cleans the floors and windows even if she's a little lax with the dusting.

For those who object that noticing the good while ignoring the bad is a Pollyanna-ish failure to see the whole picture, let's be humble enough to admit: No one ever sees the *whole* picture. Human beings are complex. Even if you have lived with a person for decades, you cannot see all of his depths or all the secrets of his past (let alone his past lives). As I learned in Perceptual Psychology 101: Human beings see what they want to see. Choosing to see the good—*recognizing the good*—may be the best choice you'll ever make.

The Entitlement Poison

Nothing kills gratitude like a sense of entitlement. If I'm entitled to quiet neighbors, then I'll never be grateful for the tranquility in our building until the noisy new neighbors move in — and then I'll be irate at their loudness. If I'm entitled to good health, then I'll never be grateful to God for the flawless functioning of my myriad cells and systems until I get a bad diagnosis — and then I'll ask, "Why me?"

The antidote to a sense of entitlement is a sense of gift. The person to whom every sunset, every wonder of the body, every bag of groceries packed up by the supermarket bagger is experienced as an unearned gift will always be happy.

Developing a sense of gift requires:
* Being grateful to the taxi driver for getting you to your destination even though you paid for the ride.
* Being grateful to your spouse for doing the laundry or dishes, even though you agreed that that was his/her job.
* Being grateful to God that you can see to read this article, even though you've always had the gift of sight.

Expressing Gratitude

Unexpressed gratitude is like a gift purchased and wrapped, but never given. Once we've noticed the good and experienced it as undeserved, we have to express it in words.

Recently I asked my teenage son to put away two cans of spray paint he had used in a project. Five minutes later I walked by and saw that the cans were indeed put away. I called out to my son, "Thank you for doing what I asked the first time I asked you."

He replied, "Thank you for saying that."

With a jolt I realized how rarely I thank my children for doing "what they're supposed to do." His gratitude for my gratitude woke me up and made me want to express my appreciation much more often.

That's why I expressed appreciation to the TSA official for his saying, "Thank you for your service" to each veteran. As I ran off to catch my flight at Gate B9, I passed two young soldiers in grey camouflage fatigues. I stopped and said to them, "Thank you for your service."

Why should they have to wait 66 years?

Every Note Counts

Creating eternity, one line at a time.

Rabbi Yaakov Salomon

He was a speech pathologist by profession, but far more than that he was a soul that was truly searching. Despite the fact that he had never learned Torah until now, he was not deterred. Every summer morning he would leave his modest bungalow in Woodridge, NY, ArtScroll Talmud in tow, and park himself in the study hall of nearby Camp Morris. I suppose he wanted to keep company with some of the world's greatest Torah scholars, perhaps hoping that by osmosis some of their erudition would rub off.

It didn't take long for Rabbi P. to notice him. Sitting in the back of the noisy auditorium, Richard was the epitome of humility and sincerity. He would study the Talmud (Tractate *Kiddushin*) with the

---

Rabbi Yaakov Salomon, CSW is a noted psychotherapist, in private practice in Brooklyn, New York for over 25 years. He is a Senior Lecturer and the Creative Director of Aish HaTorah's Discovery Productions. He is also an author for the ArtScroll Series and a member of the Kollel of Yeshiva Torah Vodaath. Rabbi Salomon is co-author, with Rabbi Noah Weinberg, of the best selling book *What the Angel Taught You; Seven Keys to Life Fulfillment* (ArtScroll/Mesorah), and the author of *Something to Think About* and *Salomon Says: 50 Stirring and Stimulating Stories*. His speaking, writing, and musical talents have delighted audiences from Harvard to Broadway and everywhere in between. Rabbi Salomon shares his life with his wife, Temmy, and their unpredictable family.

Aramaic translated into English, and he never seemed to care that by the time he left he had advanced not more than just a few lines. Quality and direction took precedence over quantity, he would reason.

And every so often Rabbi P. would sidle up to the empty chair beside Richard and together they would plow through the ancient text, ever still relevant and resonant.

"Don't spoon-feed me, Rabbi," he would say, "I may go slowly, but I've got to get through this on my own."

It wasn't long before the two became friends. Torah has that power. It can meld personalities and create a bond that withstands the vicissitudes and tribulations that life inevitably brings.

It was during one of their daily encounters, eight summers ago, that Richard felt comfortable enough to confide in his younger friend.

"Rabbi, you might as well know ... I'm quite ill. I have cancer of the liver. The best doctors do not offer me much to hope for."

Rabbi P. was as surprised as he was saddened. Richard's upbeat countenance and zest for life belied his deadly prognosis.

"Over 25,000 Americans are diagnosed with liver cancer every year," Richard continued. "Most are over 65, twenty years older than me. But that's God's will. Very few survive. I have abandoned all conventional treatments in favor of a more radical, holistic approach. And I pray."

The summer passed far more quickly than it should have and, as happens all too often, the two friends went their separate ways.

It was ten months later, on a stifling Friday morning in July, that they reunited on the Camp Morris lawn. Score some points for holistic medicine. Tucked under Richard's arm was an ArtScroll Talmud, still Tractate *Kiddushin*.

"I'm up to page 10a," he declared. "I'm not exactly speeding."

The two spoke for a while, catching up on news, and studied a few lines together. Lunchtime arrived. In the past they had shared an occasional quick meal, but today Richard begged off.

"Don't wait for me," he said.

Rabbi P. detected a certain heaviness in Richard's tone and demeanor. It just didn't feel like the Richard he remembered and admired. He inquired ... and Richard confirmed his suspicions.

"I'll be honest with you. I've been giving this learning thing some thought lately. I come here to Camp Morris. This is a very special place. Few institutions can boast scholars of this level of excellence. And I look around and ask myself. *What am I doing here?* I'm a struggling *ba'al teshuvah*, barely comprehending a few lines of ancient writings here and there. A virtual flounder in an ocean of mighty whales and sea giants.

"What possible purpose could my learning have? Why would the Almighty really care about my puny contribution to His sizable flotilla of scholarship and intellect?"

Rabbi P. heard the questions, but more than that he understood that his response could very likely have a profound impact — positively or negatively — on this man's life and future.

There are times when we hear a fleeting whisper or experience a moment that appears almost inconsequential, but coincidences are not in the Jewish lexicon. God's fingerprints are everywhere if we open our eyes.

It was just 15 hours earlier that Rabbi P. was sitting in his car, making his routine trek from Brooklyn to the Catskills. It was a trip he had made dozens, if not hundreds of times before. One of the more difficult tasks of the trip is simply staying awake and alert. Rabbi P. noted his eyelids surrendering to gravity, so he reached out and flipped on the radio. It was a talk show. A man was talking about classical music; not a topic that Rabbi P. had much knowledge of or interest in.

The man was speaking about Arturo Toscanini, one of the most acclaimed musicians of the late 19th century and 20th century. He was renowned for his brilliant intensity, his restless perfectionism, his phenomenal ear for orchestral detail and sonority, and his photographic memory.

Toscanini was sitting one day with one of his biographers. Together they were listening to a recording of a certain overture. The piece was a complicated one — many movements, complex arrangements, and sophisticated orchestration. The two men listened silently, concentrating on every note and every emotion.

When the recording was finished, the maestro turned to the

author and remarked, "Did you notice anything unusual about what we just heard?"

He had not. The rendition had been stirring, perhaps even exceptional, but the writer could not imagine what the genius was referring to.

"I have no idea," he confessed. "But I am curious. What was so unusual about this piece of music?"

Toscanini explained. "My familiarity with this overture is great. Believe me, I know what it is supposed to sound like. There should, in fact, be exactly 14 violins in that orchestra. But in this particular recording of this overture, I only heard 13 violins. One violin is missing. I am certain of it."

The biographer knew better than to chuckle in front of the great conductor, but he was mystified. How was it possible for Toscanini to discern that one violinist was missing? And how could he dare to be so certain? It made no sense.

The next day the man began to do some research. To his amazement, he discovered that Toscanini was precisely correct. One of the violinists had indeed been absent when that recording was made.

Rabbi P's mind raced as the details of this providential story flooded his thoughts. He suddenly understood why he had tuned in to that particular station at that particular time last night.

"Richard," he said, "have you ever heard of Arturo Toscanini — the great conductor?"

Rabbi P. proceeded to recount the remarkable story to his discouraged friend.

"Richard, the layman does not detect nuance. No one listening to that symphony would be able to realize that one measly violin was missing. But *The Master*, He can hear everything. He knows *exactly* how that piece of music is supposed to sound. That's what makes him so great.

"In our study hall, there could 50, 75, or 100 voices studying Torah at the same time. To the untrained ear it is just a cacophony of sound and clamor. But to The Master, every single utterance is part of a grand overture, a symphony of cosmic proportions, a holy harmony that pierces the heavens and makes angels sing. Only you can provide that, Richard. Without you, the concert just isn't the same."

Richard smiled. He seemed at peace. The two walked off together.

Summer flew by again that year. Autumn brought bad news. Richard's soul was returned to The Conductor in October. But not before he had given many more performances … slowly, sweetly, one simple note at a time.

I never met Richard. But I think I can still hear his music.

My Kidney Sister

Why I donated my kidney to someone I didn't know.

Lori Palatnik

If you really want a conversation stopper, tell someone you are planning to donate a kidney and you don't even know who you're giving it to.

That's what's been going on in my life.

It all started three years ago in Denver when my husband's good friend needed a kidney. None of his family matched or was able to donate for various reasons. If you have any history of kidney disease, have had certain illnesses like cancer, or possess the wrong blood type, you're out.

One night I was up late and I did some basic research on kidney

---

Lori Palatnik is an author and Jewish educator who has appeared on television and radio and has lectured on five continents, illuminating traditional practices and lifestyles for our contemporary world. She and her husband, Rabbi Yaakov Palatnik, live in Washington, D.C., where she is Executive Director of the Jewish Women's Renaissance Project. Lori is the author of *Friday Night and Beyond — The Shabbat Experience Step-by-Step*; *Remember My Soul*, which explains the Jewish concepts of soul and the afterlife and a guide to anyone who has ever lost a loved one; and *Gossip—Ten Pathways to Eliminate It From Your Life and Transform Your Soul*, featured on "Dr. Laura" and FoxNews.com. Her popular video blog, *Lori Almost Live*, is featured every week on Aish.com.

donations. I just wanted to see what our friend was going through. There was a lot of information out there, and I began to see that based on the requirements and restrictions, I was actually a very good candidate to donate a kidney.

My blood type is O Positive, which in the world of kidney donations makes me a universal donor. I can only receive from an O, but I can give to anyone. Many blood types can only give to their own type. Some, like AB, are universal receivers. They can only give to their own type, but can receive from anyone. I was a universal donor, and I liked the sound of it. Now I had to see if I could live up to the title.

The idea of donations on the medical front always appealed to me. There are restrictions in Torah law regarding this, and one needs to consult a competent authority in Jewish law to find out what exactly is permitted and what is forbidden.

Years ago in Toronto I ran bone marrow drives for a young man from New Jersey who was looking for a match in order to cure his leukemia. I learned a lot about that type of donation/transplant, and became a strong advocate for people to register in the bone marrow bank.

A couple of years later I was called in as a possible match for someone. I was disappointed to be disqualified after further testing.

So now the idea of donating my kidney crossed my mind. After speaking to my husband and our rabbi, I decided to offer our friend my kidney. He was extremely grateful and touched, and we began the process of medical testing. Immediately into the process his medical team felt that since he was so much bigger than I was, my kidney would never be able to sustain his body. I was rejected and so disappointed.

A few months later we relocated to the Washington D.C. area to work for Aish. I saw an email that had gone out through the internal Aish system about a very sick five-year-old boy who needed a kidney. I replied, explaining to them that I had already done the research and felt I was a good candidate to give a kidney.

A few days later I received a reply that said it turned out that the boy was too sick for the transplant, but would I be willing to be tested for some other people?

The person who wrote me was Chaya Lipschutz, an observant

Jewish woman from New York. She had given her kidney to someone years ago, and her brother, Yosef, did the same. Now she was devoting her life to helping others.

That was my first moral dilemma. For our friend, yes. For a little boy, yes. How could I say no to someone else just because I didn't know them?

I filled out the forms and began the process of testing again. There were three women from New York that I was being tested for, in their 30s and 40s, each with several children. All three were very sick and in desperate need of a kidney.

I passed the first stage, and they accepted me as a candidate to be an "altruistic donor" (someone who has no connection to the recipient). Now I had to discuss it with my husband.

I told him that I did not really know why I wanted to do it, but I did. I explained that the tests could rule me out at any time. He was not enthusiastic and wanted to speak to our rabbi about it, but we agreed to go forward.

Very few people at this stage knew what I was thinking of doing. The reactions of those who did were, by and large, uniformly negative. How could I put my life at risk? I had children and a husband and responsibilities. What was I thinking? What if I needed a kidney one day? What if one of my kids needed one and I couldn't give it?

I tried to explain to them that for the donor the risks are very low, about the same as any surgery where there is general anesthetic. The recovery time is about the same as a Caesarean section (without a newborn baby to take care of 24/7). Yes, I was thinking, and had done extensive research. If you donate a kidney, and for some reason down the road you need one yourself, instead of waiting on a first come, first served list (which in New York State is an average of eight years), you are bumped to the very top of the list. Now *that's* insurance. (The Kidney Donor Clinic at the Montefiore Medical Center had only one such case in the 20 years they had been doing transplants.)

I did ask Pat, the wonderful woman who runs the clinic, what if one of my kids or one of my parents needs one down the road? She told me that six months after taking the job running the transplant clinic, her own brother got sick and needed a kidney. She was able to give him hers and save his life. Years later she developed cancer, which she beat. She explained to me that if she had hesitated and waited to give him her kidney, she would nowbe disqualified as a donor because of the cancer. In other words, God runs the world, and when presented with a mitzvah, an opportunity to save someone's life, grab it. It may not come again. To hold back and live in a world of "What if ...?" could cost lives.

I also explained to people that I felt so much more comfortable giving my kidney to someone I didn't know, as opposed to someone I knew. Imagine if I gave a friend a kidney and months later I ask my friend to do me a favor and cover my carpool. She says she is too busy to do it. And what will I be thinking? *I gave you my kidney, you can't cover my carpool??*

Testing, 1-2-3

Through emails and phone calls, the kidney clinic gave me a long list of medical tests I had to pass in order to make this all happen — mammogram, CAT scans, renal scans .... They told me I could be eliminated at any time. I still had not told my extended family. I did not want them to worry, and what if it didn't pan out?

Some of the tests I had done locally, but some had to be performed at Montefiore, which was located in the Bronx. On a trip home from Israel I had a plane connection there, so I arranged to stay on for two days and get as many tests done as possible.

My friend, Rebecca, who had traveled with me to Israel on my annual women's mission, stayed with me in New York. She had been very apprehensive about this whole "kidney thing" as she called it, but is such a good friend that she agreed to tag along for moral support.

In the end it was more than just moral. One of the procedures was a 24-hour test that restricted me to the couch, lest any movement impact the test results. So Rebecca had to go out searching for kosher food and wait on me for 24 hours.

But the most intense part of the two days was when we arrived. We had just traveled across the world from Israel after finishing a whirlwind tour and we needed a good shower. We landed at JFK early in the morning on a day a freak tornado had touched down in Brooklyn.

The city was in chaos and traffic was a nightmare. It took us *five hours* to get from JFK to the Bronx in stop-and-go traffic. On the trip we tried to encourage our driver, who seemed more exhausted and nauseous than we were. He clearly did not want to be on the road that day, and I was afraid he was just going to pull over and say forget it, so I played the "kidney card" in hopes of gaining his sympathy.

He was quite fascinated and asked me, "Why would God give us two kidneys if we only needed one?" I replied, quoting Dr. Greenstein, an observant doctor at the clinic, "He gave us one to keep and one to give away."

When we finally arrived, disheveled, exhausted, and weak, groaning under our mass of luggage, the transplant coordinators came to the hospital lobby to greet us. They took one look at Rebecca and asked her, "Are you the recipient?"

I spent the afternoon giving blood and taking tests, while Rebecca settled us into the apartment-hotel room provided for us around the corner from the hospital. Later that night we laughed about how they mistook her for the recipient of my kidney.

"You know, Rebecca," I said, suddenly serious, "if you did need a kidney, I would give you mine."

"Yes," she said. "I know."

"Then how can I not give away my kidney, just because it's for someone I don't know? *Somebody* knows them. They are someone's wife, sister, friend and daughter."

"Okay," she said. "I get it."

From Tests to Transplant

I continued to pass through the myriad of tests, thankful to get to the next stage. It was also comforting to know that I was, thank God, healthy from head to toe. They told me that there had been many times that a potential donor's life was saved, as they had discovered things wrong that had gone undetected.

My husband was still not fully on board. He was doing his own research, had spoken to a nephrologist and our rabbi. The doctor told him that people can live a perfectly normal and healthy life with one kidney. Our rabbi told him that saving a life was a very big mitzvah and he should support me in every way. Finally, my husband traveled to the clinic, met the transplant team, and gave me 100% support.

The transplant clinic called to let me know that the recipient had been told that she indeed had a kidney donor and the transplant was to be in two weeks. They wait until the last minute to tell the recipient — it can be devastating to think you have a donor and, for whatever reason, it falls through.

What are the reasons? The most common is that people back out due to their own doubts and fears and the negative pressure they sometimes feel from family and friends. On two separate occasions I had well-meaning people sit down with me and try to convince me not to do this "kidney thing." If I hadn't done so much research to refute their fears, and if I didn't feel completely committed to what I was doing, I would have caved in as well.

The clinic wanted to know if I wanted to speak to the woman who would be my recipient. "Yes … no … yes!"

Clearly I had mixed feelings. What if I didn't like her? What if she was judgmental? Or, as one friend cautioned, what if she was taking drags on cigarettes in between sentences? I was more concerned about it being just incredibly awkward.

In the end I decided that I did want to speak to her, but only if she felt comfortable speaking to me. I told them to give her my number, but she shouldn't feel obliged to call.

For the next two days I kept my cell phone on, even when I was teaching. My heart leapt each time it rang, but it was never her. Finally, on the third night, as I was walking into a class, my phone rang. It was the woman who would be receiving my kidney.

We made up to speak in an hour, after my class was over. Completely distracted, I taught, and then went into my office and received her call. We talked for four hours.

"There are no words." she began.

At one point she asked me, "Who *are* you?"

"Are you at your computer?" I asked. "Go on to Aish.com."

I guided her to *Lori Almost Live,* a weekly video blog I do for Aish.com. "That's me."

We wanted to know everything about each other's lives — our kids, our work, everything. It was one of the most significant conversations of my life.

She was an extremely brave woman. She was an observant Jew with seven kids, and was one year older than me. A year and a half earlier, during routine blood tests to correct a hernia, she found out she had a deadly kidney disease, KPD.

A kidney transplant is the only cure. Dialysis, which can only sustain a person for five to seven years, destroys a person's immune system and chains them to a grueling life. Approximately 70,000 people in the United States are currently waiting for a kidney. And the list grows each year. Only 6,700 kidneys become available each year through cadaver (after death) and live donations. Live donation kidneys give a person twice the chance of recovery, since it is healthy and fresh. And if a person receives a kidney before going on dialysis, their chance at recovery also doubles. Thousands each year die waiting.

I traveled to New York for the transplant with Rebecca, who volunteered to come with me so my husband could take care of our kids on the home front. Our community of students and friends rallied and organized meals and carpools so I would not have to worry. So many people were now on board and being so supportive.

The surgery was scheduled for a Thursday. They needed me there three days before for more tests. On the Monday that we arrived the recipient of the kidney called and invited us to her home for dinner that night. I was excited and nervous at the same time. I felt like I was about to meet a twin sister separated from me at birth.

We had the most incredible evening with her and her husband. We were so alike in so many ways, and her husband even reminded me of my husband! Clearly this was a match made in heaven.

She made us the most incredible, healthy gourmet dinner, and of course she could not eat a morsel. The only way she was able to stay off dialysis was to be vigilant in her diet. Since the day she was diagnosed, she had not had a gram of protein, dairy, citrus, potassium, and so many other foods. She told me lunch for her was a rice cake with lettuce. For a treat, she would put a bit of mayonnaise on it.

The meeting was awkward in some ways, but it was also very inspiring. In the year and a half she had been sick, she married off three children. She showed me the wedding albums, and later I asked her what she was thinking at the weddings, knowing that time was running out. "With each wedding I knew that this child would be all right. They had married a good person. If I were to die it would be difficult for them, but they could go on. I just wanted to live long enough to marry off my last two children. Then I could go."

I couldn't even imagine being so strong. In the face of her dire situation, she always had a smile on her face. Her faith in God never wavered; in fact, it only strengthened. She continued to work full time, and was clearly the energy force of her family.

The night before the surgery she called me to tell me that I didn't have to do this. "Lori, you are taking a risk and I want you to know that you can absolutely change your mind. I will completely understand."

I was so moved, but reassured her that I would be there the next morning at 6 a.m. at the hospital as planned.

I called my parents and siblings that night to tell them for the first time what I was doing. They were surprised but incredibly supportive. I apologized for springing this on them at the last moment, but I did not want them to worry.

My Kidney Sister also told her children at the last moment. Months before they thought they had a donor, but two days before the surgery it was called off. They had found protein in the urine of the donor, which eliminated the possibility of the transplant. The family was devastated.

The Big Day

Many people have asked me if I ever had any doubts. There was only one moment where I hesitated. It was when I was walking with the nurse to the operating room. There was a semi-sterile vestibule that we entered before entering the actual OR. "Here we go," she said.

"Hold on," I said. "I need to say a prayer."

I said the *Shema* and asked God to let me live, that the operation should be a great success, for both me and the recipient.

"Okay," I said, "I'm ready."

And then she opened the doors to the OR I was shocked to see so many people there, everyone running around doing all kinds of things with equipment and machines. I saw the lights, the long operating table with straps, and I froze. *"What am I doing?"* And then I closed my eyes and said to myself, *"Just do it. Just do it."*

I lay down on the table, and the next thing I knew I was in recovery and they were telling me it was a success and everything was all right.

It was over. But really it had just begun.

The Life It Gave Me

The surgery was laparoscopic and I was in the hospital for just a few days recovering. During that time, the grown children of my Kidney Sister and her extended family streamed into my room, crying and thanking me for saving her life. When I was feeling better, I would walk down the hall to visit her. She was doing great, and she told me again that there are no words. The only way she could describe her feelings was that she felt that a truck was hurtling towards her full force, and I had stepped in front of her from out of nowhere and put my arms out, stopping the truck.

God gave me the opportunity to give her life, and the gratitude she and her family feel towards me is immense. I learned that I should have that same gratitude to my parents, who gave me life. It was humbling to realize how casually we accept that we are here, and how little regard we have for the people who made it possible.

I am still processing the whole experience and feel very small in the face of the enormity and fragility of life and death.

Giving away a kidney is not for everyone. Some people literally cannot do it because of personal or family medical history. But as one person told me just before I left for New York, "Lori, I may not give away my kidney, but because of what you are doing, I will now be more of a giver."

Thank God I am back on my feet and planning to drive carpool tomorrow, easing back into my life. I speak to my Kidney Sister almost every day, and she is doing great. The marker for kidney patients is their creatinine level. If you are a 10, you must be on dialysis. Going into the surgery she was a nine. Twenty-four hours after the transplant, she was a two. The day she left the hospital she was a 1.6. God made our bodies wondrous. It is difficult for me, and for her, to see people eating junk food or smoking. How could we possibly abuse a body that is so miraculous and precious?

Human beings made a huge dialysis machine to filter out the impurities that our kidneys cannot. It can only do 15% of what a four-ounce kidney that God made can do.

Take pleasure in your life, and take care of the life that you have. And please do what you can to help others do the same.

I Can Do It

I conquered because someone believed I could.

Rabbi Shraga Simmons

We've all heard about the sociology experiment — better known as the Pygmalion effect — where a schoolteacher is given a class of "under-achievers" and told that it is the honors group. Then, by treating them as "advanced," they actually become so.

It's hard to believe that the mere power of suggestion could create such a dramatic turnaround. So I was always skeptical about this story.

Until it happened to me.

It started out like any regular day in Jerusalem. My afternoon appointment was in an unfamiliar neighborhood, so when I got to the general area, I parked my car, got out, and stopped someone to ask for directions.

Rabbi Shraga Simmons spent his childhood trekking through snow in Buffalo, New York. He holds a degree in journalism from the University of Texas at Austin, and rabbinic ordination from the Chief Rabbi of Jerusalem. He is the senior editor of Aish.com and the director of JewishPathways.com. He is also regarded as an expert on media bias relating to the Middle East conflict, and was the founding editor of HonestReporting.com. Rabbi Simmons lives with his wife and children in the Modi'in region of Israel.

"Go down one block, turn right, and then take your first left," said a nice, religious man.

I said "thanks" and was about to run off, when he gently took hold of my hand and said:

"I can't help but mention what a great mitzvah you've done."

I was startled. "What do you mean?"

He looked straight into my eyes, and for a split second I froze. "The mitzvah of honoring your parents," he said. "I can read faces, and I see this mitzvah clearly in you."

I felt as if the wind was knocked out of me. He was right on target.

Only weeks before we had moved my father's grave from the United States to Israel. My mother had very much wanted to do that, as it is considered a great merit to be buried in Israel. I undertook the responsibility for making all the arrangements — which was time-consuming and emotionally draining. She was extremely grateful, and hopefully my deceased father was, too.

Still, I was skeptical about this stranger's comment.

"Thank you," I said, "but I'll bet you say that to everyone!"

"No," he protested. "I'll never see you again, and I have no reason to flatter you. It's simply true what I said."

I figured he'd made a lucky guess. And since I anyway take compliments with a grain of salt, I had the perfect comeback:

"Okay, fine. But can you tell me about the *bad* things I've done?"

He hesitated for a moment, as if not wanting to insult a stranger. But he saw that I truly wanted to hear. So he continued to hold his warm, soft hand in mine, and said:

"Actually, I do see something." He proceeded to name a negative behavior that I'd been particularly struggling with, and was threatening to become truly problematic.

He continued:

"You were struggling with it. But then you fixed it."

Fixed it? Hah! I thought to myself. This man isn't so smart after all. Sure, he pinpointed my outstanding good deed. And sure, he zeroed in on my precise point of struggle. But he was wrong on one very important count — I hadn't fixed it!

I went off to my appointment, and continued to think about my encounter with the mysterious face-reader.

And after much pondering, I reached a conclusion:

This man was so special, so caring, so sincere. And he thinks I fixed my problem. So how can I disappoint him? I can't just shrug off his hopeful, positive energy and continue with my negative behavior.

So I decided: He believed in me, and I'll prove him right! I'll stop my negative behavior right now. Cold turkey.

And just like that, I fixed it.

I thought about the schoolteacher with the class of underachievers. It's true. If somebody truly believes in our ability, they can convince us to believe in ourselves, too.

And then I thought about how the Almighty deals with us as well. He believes in us. He knows we can do it. And He cares so deeply. How can we dare disappoint Him?

Sure, we sometimes get caught in a rut, a pattern of negative behavior. Yet we have the freedom to flick the switch, to turn 180 degrees to the path of good.

And so often in life we have the choice whether to put someone down, or to encourage them. An employer, a child, a friend, a spouse. Which way do we go? The words we say and the message we convey can make all the difference between someone spiraling downward in negativity, or soaring skyward.

It's a power we all hold. Even if we can't read faces.

The Day Before My Wedding

We were on opposite poles: her life was drawing to a close and mine was about to begin.

Yael Mermelstein

It was late afternoon, the day before my wedding, and I sat at the dining room table, tapping my foot impatiently against my chair.

"Calm down," my mother said as she filled out yet another cream-colored place card. "We'll get there. We'll get there."

I stared out the window as a car trundled down the block. I had so much to do. Would I be able to sleep tonight? I was getting married tomorrow!

I shook my pen and filled out another card with my best curlicue handwriting. Then I threw my pen down. I couldn't do this anymore.

I closed my eyes and breathed deeply, the room a flurry of activity around me as my parents and my sisters gathered together gowns and shoes, petticoats and hair ornaments. Tomorrow night I would dress in white like we do every year on Yom Kippur and I would fast all day. Tomorrow my prayers would take on new definition and

---

For a biographical note on the author, please see page 137.

would hold a special place next to God. Tomorrow I would be starting my life as a Jewish married woman.

"I'm going out," I said.

"Crazy bride," I thought I heard someone murmur. Then laughter. I grabbed the car keys and closed the door behind me, breathing in the freshness of April. I had too much to do and too little time. Where should I go? There were things that needed to be picked up from the cleaners. I could run over to Rite Aid and pick up the lipstick the make-up lady had recommended for me. And I needed bobby pins for my veil. Oh, I had almost forgotten that I needed inserts for my white satin bridal shoes. I would slip right out of them while walking down the aisle if I didn't get those. What should I do first?

I looked up at the sky as if waiting for an answer and I watched the sun spin copper-colored ribbons across the sky. It was getting late. Soon I would need to get back to my *shomeret*, a woman who traditionally accompanies a bride so that she is never alone during the 24-hour period before her wedding.

Tomorrow. Me. Married. A new Jewish home. Thank you, God.

I suddenly knew exactly where I needed to be.

I grabbed an invitation from the trunk of the car and I tucked it into my purse. Then I drove the five miles to The Pembrook Nursing Home. I rode the elevator to the fifth floor.

"Which way to Mrs. Ackerman's room?" I asked.

The nurse pointed me in the direction of her room. I hadn't been to visit her here yet, though I had been to visit her so many other places.

Mrs. Ackerman was the wife of the candy-man in our synagogue. He had passed away when I was a young girl and a loyal group of girls made sure to visit her every Shabbat in thanks for the sweets her husband had doled out. Over the years, the girls had gone in so many different directions, but Mrs. Ackerman always remained in the same place, in her squat little house on the corner of 180th Street.

Eventually, there were only two of us left visiting her. And just as eventually, Mrs. Ackerman, in her late nineties, became ill. When she was hospitalized for the final time, it was only Esther and I who remained from our original group of visitors. I sat by her bed in the hospital and read to her from *Oliver Twist*, watching her smile as the story unfolded. I poured her a drink and I wiped her lined cheeks. I brought my future husband to meet with her and I received her smile of approval. When we got engaged, she rejoiced from her hospital bed.

But then things got busy. The wedding was getting closer — our engagement had been less than three months. Esther called me and told me that our dear Mrs. Ackerman had been moved to Pembrook. I filed the information away in the corner of my brain, somewhere between "dress fitting" and "florist."

I walked down the corridor on tiptoes so as not to disturb the hush. I rapped gently on her door and then let myself in. She was asleep, an oxygen mask on her face, her hands folded gently atop her baby-blue blanket. I reached out and touched her hands, the sparkling diamond on my finger catching the warm yellow of the lamp by her bed. She opened her eyes.

"Yael," she mouthed, for she was too weak to speak.

I reached into my purse and pulled out the invitation. "I'm getting married tomorrow," I said. "I . . . I know you can't make it. I wish you could. But I'm going to be thinking of you." I laid the invitation across her hands, then awkwardly took it back again to read aloud its contents. She turned her face towards me just a bit, her lips cracked at the edges, the irises of her eyes covered by a thin film of age. And she smiled.

"Thank you," she mouthed.

And just then, I had nowhere to go that was more important than this room with its faded pink curtains and its tepid pitcher of water on the nightstand. I sat with her, prattling on about the navy gowns my bridesmaids would be wearing and the flower bouquet which I hadn't even cared enough to choose on my own. I watched her drinking in the world with her eyes as she clutched my hand. We were on opposite poles of the earth, with her life drawing to a close while mine was only about to begin. And yet, like a magnet to iron, we were drawn together by that ephemeral feeling that can only be experienced by those just on the cusp of some wondrous journey.

Mrs. Ackerman passed away shortly after my wedding. And my life since then has been a steady whirlwind of bringing up a large family. I race up and down the roller coaster, with barely a pause to breathe.

But the day before my wedding, I had all the time in the world.

The Telemarketer

Sometimes, you have to throw away the script.

Yael Zoldan

I was working my way through college doing telemarketing, a job despised by almost everyone with brain cells. But it was easy and it paid by the hour.

The room was crowded, divided into small cubicles and filled with young people like me. We were fundraising for various Jewish charities, calling numbers from a national list, usually during dinner time. With bright, cheery voices, we faked intimacy with the unsuspecting person on the other end of the line. We read smoothly from a pre-written script, reminding people of their previous year's commitment and looking for a larger one.

To make ourselves sound as non-denominational as possible, all the girls were told to say that their names were Rachel Cohen and all the boys called themselves David Levine. It was a ridiculous farce, but that's the way it was done and there was a bonus every time you

---

Yael Zoldan is a freelance writer whose work has been published in print and on-line. Her children's book, *We Can Do Mitzvos from Aleph to Tav* (Feldheim, 2009) features a delightful array of mitzvos corresponding to letters of the Hebrew alphabet. The book is currently available in Jewish bookstores. Her latest book, *When I Daven* (Feldheim), helps small children learn to understand and enjoy prayer in an easy and exciting way. It is due out in bookstores in Fall 2011.

got someone to commit to a high dollar amount. I wanted the bonus.

Magda Schein was the next name on the list and I rehearsed the charity's script in my head as I waited for the connection. The phone rang shrilly.

"Hello?" an unused voice quavered over the line.

"Hi there, Mrs. Schein! This is Rachel Cohen," I chirped, bright as a mirror and equally false. "How are you this evening?"

"I am very well," she answered carefully with that old European accent I knew so well from my own grandparents. I heard the years of etiquette training kick in as she added, "And yourself, how are you?"

"Fine, thanks," I answered briskly. "So, anyway, as I said my name is Rachel Cohen and I'm calling on behalf of ..."

"Rachel who?" she interrupted.

"Rachel Cohen," I answered enunciating loudly in case the poor old woman was hard of hearing. Then, unwilling to be swayed from my script, I continued, "And I'm calling on behalf of ..."

"Rachel Cohen," she said in a wondering voice, "I'm sorry, I don't know any Rachel Cohen and I ... Oh! Wait, Wait a minute, Rachel! Yes I think I remember now, little Rachel! I didn't hear from you already such a long time!"

Then with a warmth I didn't deserve, "Rachel, darling, how are you?"

"I'm fine, thanks," I answered carefully, trying to figure out how to barrel ahead, get back on track, make the sale. "So anyway, I just called to ..."

"Of course I know why you called, darling," she said with a little laugh. "You just called to *vinch meer un*, to wish me a good year. *Ach*, Rachel, you were always such a good girl."

I was startled for a minute. *Was I always such a good girl?* I didn't think so.

I looked at the script but there was nothing there to help me. I had lost my words.

"I didn't hear from you such a long time already," Mrs. Schein continued happily. "I didn't hear from nobody a long time already until you called now. I was just sitting here looking out the window. It's silly I know, so much to do before Yom Tov and me just sitting!"

Her voice burbled on and on like joyful waters released from a dam and I imagined her apartment with the dark wooden chairs on delicate clawed legs and the faded maroon velvet couch and the doilies. I saw the cherished sepia photographs and breathed the smell of things that were clean but not quite fresh.

"So what's going on with you Rachel? How's your mommy? How's your bubby?"

I could hear her eagerness, her joy at the call and it made me want to cry. Instead, I reached for the script on the desk in front of me and pushed it away.

"I'm good, Mrs. Schein," I said leaning back into my seat and injecting a warmth into my voice. "I'm good and my mother and grandmother are too. I'm sorry I haven't called for so long."

"Darling! Don't apologize, you're busy! All the young people are very busy."

"Yes, busy," I agreed. "But not so busy and I just couldn't let another day pass without calling you up and wishing you happy new year — a *gut, gebenscht yor*."

"And to you!" she said quickly, "I should have said before! A year for you and yours, of health and happiness, and *nachas*. A year of *alles gut,* all the good things!"

"Amen, Mrs. Schein."

"And a year filled with good friends like you!" she added.

"Amen," I said again, ashamed.

We talked a few minutes more about Yom Tov recipes and how quickly the weather had turned. Then we hung up the phones. I stared at the receiver for a while wondering about the impossible loneliness of the elderly and how little we understand about the greatness of small gestures. Then I reached for a pad of paper and a pen and I carefully wrote down her number and put it in my pocket.

To call later.

A Drop of Sadness

The Heartrending Cry

How is it possible to mourn something that happened 2000 years ago?

Keren Gottleib

Every year when Tishah B'Av came around, I would have a dilemma. This is supposed to be a day on which we mourn the destruction of our Temple. It is a day when we do not eat, drink, or wear leather shoes and follow varied and unique mourning customs.

Every year I would arrive at the synagogue to hear the Book of *Lamentations*, which bemoans the destruction of Jerusalem. However, every year I would end up daydreaming about totally unrelated things. As the cantor would be reading about the Temple, I would completely disconnect, planning my summer vacation, celebrating the end of my exams, or just hoping that the fast would go well this year.

It was difficult to be truly mournful over something that took place 2000 years ago — something that I'd never seen and didn't really feel lacking in my daily life. But all that was about to change.

Keren Gottleib is a social worker who worked for many years with kids and youth at risk and guided new immigrants from Ethiopia. She was sent by the Jewish Agency to various countries to promote Jewish interest among Jews in the diaspora. She currently resides with her family in Moshav Bnei-Darom, where she also spent her childhood years.

The Turning Point

I was working in the Bat Hatzor caravan site located near Gedera. The site held 700 caravans, which housed thousands of new Ethiopian immigrants. In the mornings I taught immigrants at the Yad Shabtai School in Ashdod. In the afternoon and evening hours I served as a counselor on the site.

This was shortly after Operation Solomon in 1993, during which roughly 14,500 Jews from Ethiopia were airlifted to Israel. It was a special and moving operation, and the entire Israeli population was surprised to see that suddenly there were Jews walking around who had been severed from our nation many generations ago.

They observed Shabbat, were familiar with some of the holidays, and lived in a devout and pious manner. But it was clear that the separation they had undergone throughout all those years had influenced their system of traditions. They had never heard of Purim or Chanukah — none of the historical events that took place subsequent to their break-off from the Jewish nation.

I realized that unless I concentrated on filling these gaps of knowledge, their adjustment in Israel would never be complete. I decided to allot a considerable amount of time each day to teach them about Judaism.

Passover and Ascending to the Temple

The month of Nissan had arrived and I started teaching about the holiday of Passover. My class consisted of 20 students, 3rd – 6th grade. (They were placed according to their reading level rather than chronological age). These children had come to Israel only a few months beforehand and more than anything else, they loved to hear stories, mainly because they didn't have to read or write in Hebrew, which was still quite a difficult task for some of them.

"Today is the first day of Nissan and Passover is celebrated in this month," I began. "Passover is one of the three festivals when the entire Jewish people used to go to Jerusalem, to the Temple."

At this point, a student jumped up, cutting me off in mid-sentence. "Teacher, have you ever been to the Temple?"

I smiled at him, realizing that he was somewhat confused. "No, of course not. That was a very long time ago!"

My student was insistent, and a few more pairs of eyes joined him. "Fine, it was a long time ago. But were you there? Were you at the Temple a long time ago?"

I smiled again, this time slightly confused myself. *"Doesn't he understand? Perhaps my Hebrew is too difficult for him,"* I thought.

"No, of course not. That was a *very* long time ago!"

Now the rest of the students joined him. "You've never been there?" "Teacher, what's it like being in the Temple?" "What does the Temple look like?"

I tried calming everyone down. "Listen, everyone — there is no Temple! There used to be a Temple many years ago but today we don't have a Temple. It was destroyed, burned down. I have never been to it, my father has never been to it, and my grandfather has never been to it! We haven't had a Temple for 2000 years!"

I said these words over and over, having a very hard time believing that this was so strange for them to hear. *What's the big deal? This is the reality with which we've all grown up. Why are they so bothered by it?*

The tumult in the class was steadily increasing. They began talking among themselves in Amharic, arguing, translating, explaining, shouting, as I lost total control over the class. When the bell rang they collected their things and ran home. I left the school exhausted and utterly confused.

Next Day's Surprise

The next morning I was hardly bothered by the previous day's events. In fact, I had nearly forgotten all about the incident. That day I had planned to just teach math, geometry, and other secular subjects.

I got off the bus and leisurely made my way toward the school. As I neared the gate the guard approached me, seeming a bit alarmed. "Tell me," he said, "do you have any idea what's going on here today?"

I tried recalling a special activity that was supposed to be going on, or some ceremony that I had forgotten about, but nothing exceptional came to mind.

"Why do you ask?" I asked him. "What happened?"

He didn't answer. He only pointed toward the entrance to the school.

I raised my head and saw a sizeable gathering of Ethiopian adult immigrants — apparently, my students' parents. *What are they doing here? And what are they yelling about?*

I went over to them, attempting to understand what was the matter from the little Amharic that I knew.

As I came closer, everyone quieted down. One of the adults whose Hebrew was on a higher level asked me, "Are you our children's teacher?"

"Yes," I answered. "What is the matter, sir?"

"Our children came home yesterday and told us that their teacher taught them that the Temple in Jerusalem no longer exists. Who would tell them such a thing?" He looked at me in anger.

"I told them that. We were discussing the Temple and I felt that they were a bit confused. So I explained to them that the Temple had been burned down thousands of years ago and that today, we no longer have a Temple. That's all. What's all the fuss about?"

He was incredulous. "What? What are you talking about?"

I was more confused than ever. "I don't understand. What are you all so angry about? I simply reminded them of the fact that the Temple was destroyed and that it no longer exists today."

Another uproar — this one even louder than before.

The representative quieted the others down, and again turned to me. "Are you sure?"

"Am I sure that the Temple was destroyed? Of course I'm sure!" I couldn't hide my smile. What a strange scene.

The man turned to his friends and in a dramatic tone translated what I had told him. At this point, things seemed to be finally sinking in.

Now, however, a different scene commenced: one woman fell to the ground, a second broke down in tears. A man standing by them just stared at me in disbelief. A group of men began quietly talking among themselves, very fast, in confusion and disbelief. The children stood on the side, looking on in great puzzlement. Another woman suddenly broke into a heart-rending cry. Her husband came over to her to comfort her.

I stood there in utter shock.

I felt as if I had just told them about the death of a loved one. I stood there across from a group of Jews who were genuinely mourning the destruction of the Temple.

Tishah B'Av

A few months later it was Tishah B'Av. I was on my way to college, and my experience with the Ethiopian community seemed as if it had been such a very long time ago.

As I did every year, I went to synagogue. Everyone was already seated on the floor, as is customary for mourners, and I was waiting to hear the Book of *Lamentations*. I had expected, as in previous years, for this to be a time for some daydreaming and hoped I wouldn't get too hungry.

The *megillah* reading began.

"Alas, she sits in solitude … like a widow … She weeps bitterly in the night and her tear is on her cheek. She has no comforter … all her friends have betrayed her …."

Suddenly that first day of Nissan began replaying in my mind. The angry looks of those children. The parents' screams. The mothers' crying. The men's pitiful silence. The shock they were overcome with as they received the terrible news, as if I had just told them about the death of a loved one.

At that moment, I understood.

I understood that this was exactly how we are supposed to mourn the Temple on Tishah B'Av. We are supposed to cry over the loss of the unity and peace throughout the entire world. We are supposed to lament the disappearance of the Divine Presence and holiness from our lives in Israel. We are supposed to be pained by the destruction of our spiritual center, which served to unify the entire Jewish nation.

We are supposed to feel as if something very precious has been taken away from us forever. We are meant to cry, to be shocked and angry, to break down. We are supposed to mourn over the destruction of the Temple, to cry over a magnificent era that has been uprooted from the face of the earth. The incredible closeness that we had with God — that feeling that He is truly within us — has evaporated and disappeared into thin air.

Now when Tishah B'Av rolls around, I go back to that incident and try to reconnect to the meaningful lesson that they taught me — what it truly means to mourn for the loss of the Holy Temple.

Mournful

A bereaved mother's perspective on the Three Weeks.

Naomi Cohn

I had a family. Four beautiful children. A strong marriage. An open home filled with guests all the time. A wonderful relationship with my parents and siblings. Enough money to pay the bills. Health. My life felt so perfect. So complete.

There was this sense of calm perfection to everything. My kids were adorable. Two boys, two girls. Everyone would say how cute they were and how well behaved. I went to bed at night feeling so proud of what I had.

After living in a small Midwest city for over a decade, we'd be moving our family to the warm, sunny south. My husband was taking a new position down in Florida and I looked forward to building a new, fun life for our family. Dreaming of taking walks with my son while the others were in school. Swimming in our pool year round. It was a hopeful, seemingly perfect time.

We were knee deep in packing tape and boxes as the school year was coming to an end. The Sunday before our big move we took a break from the packing and traveled to Chicago for a close friend's

---

Naomi Cohn has a master's degree in Human Resource and Business Administration. She and her husband are very involved in NCSY. Currently pursuing her dream of owning her own commercial real estate management company to be named after her son, when not carpooling or at the gym, Naomi enjoys writing and has been published on Aish.com.

wedding. My toddler got a little fever and started crying on Sunday afternoon as I shopped for a dress for my older daughter to wear that night. I was worried that he might have an ear infection and thought about the bad timing, being that the moving truck was coming on Thursday. Some baby Motrin took care of his pain and he fell asleep. He was resting so deeply and comfortably that I left him at my sister's house while we went to the wedding instead of dressing him up and taking him along with a sitter. We came home well past midnight. He was asleep. I couldn't sleep very well; he was making noises that sounded as if he was having a bad dream.

It was a bit before 8 o'clock in the morning, and I'd given up on sleeping, so I went to take him out of bed. It was dark in our room, so I couldn't be sure but he didn't look right. He was definitely sick, I decided, but something seemed more alarming. I woke up my husband. "Does he look funny to you?" I asked.

"This boy needs to get to a hospital," said my usually under-reacting husband We ran upstairs, leaving our two oldest kids sleeping in the basement and my nieces in charge.

The next few minutes, hours and days seem like slow motion …. Asking my niece for the keys to the car. Deciding that we couldn't drive with him in this condition. Calling 911. Waiting what seemed like a very long time before hearing sirens as the ambulance approached the house. Sitting outside the house with paramedics. His blood sugar was too low. His head was turned to the side and he was staring to the left. My uncle, a doctor, running up the block in response to my frantic phone call minutes earlier. The ambulance finally heading to the closest ER. The ER doctor was quite worried. Blood tests. IV's. MRI's. Sepsis? Meningitis? Infection? Holding him on the stark white stretcher and just waiting. He seemed to be calming down a little, closing his eyes to rest, but then startling himself awake. His tired body was giving in and giving up. But at least he was startling himself awake to breathe, a good sign to me. Little did I know that it was the damage to his brain stem beginning to show.

Transferring to the Children's Hospital. I realized that we might not be going home that day. I realized that something might be very wrong. I called my mother in Israel. Please pray for him. I reminded myself that God doesn't give us what we can't handle and I knew I couldn't handle losing my son. So it would be okay, right? But that gnawing feeling that this was the beginning of his end. I couldn't ask God for anything. I just knew that He'd do what was right and just and deserved.

Waiting and waiting for the pediatric ICU doctor to talk to us. Another brain scan. No activity. "We'll know more tomorrow." Still no activity in the brain and stem. It's a matter of time. "Say your goodbyes," he said.

Just a virus that got into his spinal fluid, they said. No cause, no reason. We couldn't have done anything different. It was no one's fault ... but I knew that it must be mine. I must not have valued the lives that I created, and so now He was taking one away. I knew that he'd never wake up again. All those wires and tubes and the beeping. Holding him after waiting all that time, being careful not to move his breathing tube. He didn't feel like mine anymore ....

And nine days later, he was gone. Still in Chicago, in unfamiliar apartments and houses. Our home was packed up and sent along to Florida without us. Our cars were driven to us by friends. Following his casket, not allowing myself to think about the little boy who lay inside. Sitting in a velvet-covered chair. Shocked. Listening to my husband read the eulogy we'd written the night before. Hearing people crying behind me. Watching me watching them bury my son, thinking of their own healthy children. Mine was gone.

My once full, happy, satisfying life was empty and sad. The constant yearning inside of me for the familiarity of being complete threatened to turn the most basic daily motions into tears of desperate sadness. Like picking out vegetables at the store or switching a load of laundry. I was overwhelmed with despair. I was forever incomplete. My purpose of life snatched away from me as I sat in my house for eight hours a day waiting for my other three children to come home from camp and school so I could reclaim my role of Mommy that was gone all day long.

It's been a year now since my toddler died. A year that was mostly spent remembering only that he was gone and not so much on thinking about his amazing personality. I let myself remember him two weeks ago on his first *yahrzeit*. I remember holding him and how he'd pat my shoulder the way we do to our babies. I remember his chubby hands taking hold of my cheeks and planting a big messy kiss on my lips. I remember him dropping food off his tray and saying "Uh-oh." I remember him signing for more food or a drink. I remember the almost boastful pride that I felt pushing him and his older sister in the double stroller to shul. Or down the aisle at the grocery store. I remember spoiling him, giving him a taste of whatever I was eating. Letting him stay up past everyone else's bedtime so I could spend some time playing with just him. Nursing him. He was gorgeous, with his blond hair and blue eyes peeking over the side of his car seat when I walked around to his door, playing his own version of peek-a-boo.

I was very strong when he was in a coma. I was even stronger when God took back his precious soul. After the *sheloshim,* the 30-day period of mourning, it got harder to feel positive. After we moved to Florida I was too sad to function. I'd cry to relieve the painful pressure that I felt in my chest but no relief would come. I was too sad to continue my life. I felt like I was just going through the motions every day. I reminded myself to be a good mother to the other kids. I didn't want them to lose their brother and their mother, even if I was still here physically. I played the role of "coping" well. I seemed to be doing fine. Talking or thinking about how I really felt was just too hard, too painful, too lonely.

Somehow I got through the year. Taking trips without buying him a ticket. Taking carpool without having to count his seat as occupied. Buying three Shabbos treats instead of four. Thinking in "fives" instead of "sixes" for making reservations and setting the table. His birthday. His *yahrzeit*. And somehow the strength worked its way back in. I am functioning. I love being a mother to my older three. I pray better. I turn to God more often. And He has helped me make it through.

Feeling the Loss

For as many years as I can remember, the Three Weeks were always a strange time for me. I observed all the customs of mourning

— I didn't take a haircut or go shopping for clothes. I didn't listen to music. But it seemed rather rote and not as meaningful as it should. I tried to imagine what we are missing with not having the Temple so I'd be mournful that we were still in exile, but it was hard to do with my perfect family, my lovely home, and my nice clothes.

This year is different. No more perfect family, no more lovely home. And my nice clothes are meaningless to me without my son here to complete the picture. I now realize that this is what it must have felt like 2000 years ago to lose the Temple. We had a home in Jerusalem — a place of security, safety, and comfort. Walking down the street as a Jew brought pride, the same way strolling down the street with my kids filled me with pride. And now the home is gone. Chained up and burned to the ground. We can go to the Kotel and feel a hint of the closeness of what used to be there, the same way I can hold his blankie and remember my son. But what we really need and yearn for is the real thing.

I know that with the coming of Mashiach and the rebuilding of our Temple, I will also get back my completeness. My son and so many other beautiful souls will return to us. We will all be whole. We will all feel the comfort and the security that we need. So this year, I feel it. I feel the raw pain of being stripped of what makes me complete. The raw pain of being a Jew without a home. I no longer struggle to yearn for something I never knew, to mourn for something that I never loved or held dear. Because I've suffered the unimaginable, unbearable loss of my son I understand a little bit of how I should feel as a Jew during this time. I yearn so much more for the Final Redemption. I only wish I didn't learn to yearn by losing my son.

A toddler dies with no sins and joins the Almighty at a level higher than the greatest tzaddikim. So as much as I want to say that I write l'iluy nishmas my son, Menashe Koppel A'H, I really know that anything I do in his merit is really salve for my own pain. But I do hope that the merits that are credited to Koppie become merits for the healing of other sick children.

The Rabbi and the Professor

"They are all holy."

Rabbi Ari Kahn

Many years ago, when I was a relatively young yeshivah student, I had the opportunity to study with one of the great rabbis of the previous generation. His name was Rabbi Yisroel Zeev Gustman and he may have been one of the greatest rabbis of the 20th century. He was certainly the greatest "unknown" rabbi: While he fastidiously avoided the limelight and was therefore unfamiliar to the general public, he was well known to connoisseurs of Torah learning.

His meteoric rise from child prodigy to the exalted position of religious judge in the Rabbinical Court of Rabbi Chaim Ozer Grodzinski at around the age of 20 was the stuff of legend — but nonetheless

---

Rabbi Ari Kahn graduated from Yeshiva University with a BA in psychology, an MS degree in Talmud, and rabbinic ordination where he studied with Rabbi Yosef Dov Soloveitchik. He is Director of Foreign Student Programs at Bar-Ilan University in Israel, and a senior lecturer in Jewish Studies. Rabbi Kahn is Vice President of Migdal Ohr Institutions in Israel, and a senior educator at the Aish HaTorah College of Jewish Studies. He has published two books, *Explorations* on the weekly *parashah*, and *Emanations* on the Jewish Holidays. Rabbi Kahn combines the mystical explorations of kabbalah and chassidism with psychology, literature, and Jewish history for a broad-minded approach to Torah study. He has lived in Israel since 1984 with his wife Naomi and their five children.

fact. Many years later, I heard Rav Gustman's own modest version of the events leading to this appointment: A singular (brilliant) insight which he shared with his fellow students was later repeated to the visiting Rav Chaim Ozer, who invited the young student to repeat this same insight the following day in his office in Vilna. Unbeknownst to Rav Gustman, the insight clinched an argument in a complex case that had been debated among the judges in Rav Chaim Ozer's court — and allowed a woman to remarry.

One of the judges adjudicating the case in question, Rabbi Meir Bassin, made inquiries about this young man, and soon a marriage was arranged with his daughter Sarah. When Rabbi Bassin passed away before the wedding, Rabbi Gustman was tapped to take his place as rabbi of Shnipishok and to take his seat on the court. Although Rav Gustman claimed that he was simply "in the right place at the right time," it was clear that Rav Bassin and Rav Chaim Ozer had seen greatness in this young man.

While a long, productive career on the outskirts of Vilna could have been anticipated, Jewish life in and around Vilna was obliterated by World War II. Rav Gustman escaped, though not unscathed. He hid among corpses. He hid in caves. He hid in a pigpen. Somehow, he survived.

For me, Rav Gustman was the living link to the Jewish world destroyed by the Nazis. I never had to wonder what a Rav in Vilna before the war looked like, for I had seen Rav Gustman, 35 years after the war. At the head of a small yeshivah in the Rechavia section of Jerusalem, Rav Gustman taught a small group of loyal students six days a week. But on Thursdays at noon, the study hall would fill to capacity: Rabbis, intellectuals, religious court judges, a Supreme Court justice and various professors would join along with any and all who sought a high-level Talmud *shiur* (class) that offered a taste of what had been nearly destroyed. When Rav Gustman gave *shiur*, Vilna was once again alive and vibrant.

One of the regular participants was a professor at the Hebrew University, Robert J. (Yisrael) Aumann. Once a promising yeshivah student, he had eventually decided to pursue a career in academia, but he made his weekly participation in Rav Gustman's *shiur* part of his schedule, along with many other more or less illustrious residents of Rechavia and Jerusalem.

The year was 1982. Once again, Israel was at war. Soldiers were mobilized, reserve units activated. Among those called to duty was a reserve soldier, a university student who made his living as a high school teacher: Shlomo Aumann, Professor Yisrael Aumann's son. On the eve of the 19th of Sivan, in particularly fierce combat, Shlomo fell in battle.

Rav Gustman mobilized his yeshivah: All of his students joined him in performing the mitzvah of burying the dead. At the cemetery, Rav Gustman surveyed the rows of graves of the young men, soldiers who died defending the Land.

On the way back from the cemetery, Rav Gustman turned to another passenger in the car and said, "They are all holy." Another passenger questioned the rabbi: "Even the non-religious soldiers?" Rav Gustman replied: "Every single one of them." He then turned to the driver and said, "Take me to Professor Aumann's home."

The family had just returned from the cemetery and would now begin the week of *shivah* — mourning for their son, brother, husband, and father. (Shlomo was married and had one child. His widow, Shlomit, gave birth to their second daughter shortly after he was killed.)

Rav Gustman entered and asked to sit next to Professor Aumann, who said: "Rabbi, I so appreciate your coming to the cemetery, but now is time for you to return to your Yeshivah." Rav Gustman spoke, first in Yiddish and then in Hebrew, so that all those assembled would understand:

"I am sure that you don't know this, but I had a son named Meir. He was a beautiful child. He was taken from my arms and executed. I escaped. I later bartered my child's shoes so that we would have food, but I was never able to eat the food — I gave it away to others. My Meir is a *kadosh* — he is holy — he and all the six million who perished are holy."

Rav Gustman then added: "I will tell you what is transpiring now in the World of Truth in *Gan Eden* — in Heaven. My Meir is welcoming your Shlomo into the *minyan* and is saying to him 'I died because I am a Jew — but I wasn't able to save anyone else. But you — Shlomo, you died defending the Jewish People and the Land of Israel.' My Meir is a *kadosh*, he is holy — but your Shlomo is a *shaliach tzibbur* — a Cantor in that holy, heavenly *minyan*."

Rav Gustman continued: "I never had the opportunity to sit *shivah* for my Meir; let me sit here with you just a little longer."

Professor Aumann replied, "I thought I could never be comforted, but Rebbi, you have comforted me."

Rav Gustman did not allow his painful memories to control his life. He found solace in his students, his daughter, his grandchildren, and in every Jewish child. He and his wife would attend an annual parade where children would march in Jerusalem. A rabbi who happened upon them one year asked the Rabbi why he spent his valuable time in such a frivolous activity. Rav Gustman explained, "We who saw a generation of children die, will take pleasure in a generation of children who sing and dance in these streets."

A student once implored Rav Gustman to share his memories of the ghetto and the war more publicly and more frequently. He asked him to tell people about his son, about his son's shoes, to which the Rav replied, "I can't, but I think about those shoes every day of my life. I see them every night before I go to sleep."

On the 28th of Sivan 5751 (1991), Rav Gustman passed away. Thousands marched through the streets of Jerusalem accompanying Rav Gustman on his final journey. As night fell on the 29th of Sivan, 9 years after Shlomo Aumann fell in battle, Rav Gustman was buried on the Mount of Olives. I am sure that upon entering Heaven he was reunited with his wife, his teachers, and his son Meir. I am also sure that Shlomo Aumann and all the other holy soldiers who died defending the People and the Land of Israel were there to greet this extraordinary Rabbi.

On December 10th 2005, Professor Robert J. Aumann was awarded the Nobel Prize in economics. I am sure he took with him to Stockholm memories of his late wife Esther, and his son Shlomo. I suspect he also took memories of his Rabbi, Rav Gustman.

May it be the will of God that the People of Israel sanctify His Name by living lives of holiness which will serve as a light to the nations — and may no more children, soldiers, or yeshivah students ever need to join that holy *minyan* in Heaven.

Postscript:

The last time I saw Rav Gustman, I was walking in the Meah Shearim/Geulah section of Jerusalem with my wife and oldest son, who was being pushed in a stroller. It was Friday morning and we saw the Rosh Yeshivah, we said hello, wished him "Good Shabbes." Then I did something I rarely do: I asked him to bless my son. Rav Gustman looked at the toddler, smiled and said "May he be a boy like all the other boys."

At first, my wife and I were stunned; what kind of blessing was this? We expected a blessing that the boy grow to be a *tzaddik* — a righteous man — or that he be a *talmid chacham* — a Torah scholar. But no, he blessed him that he should be "like all the boys."

It took many years for this beautiful blessing to make sense to us. The blessing was that he should have a normal childhood, that he have a normal life, that he have his health .... Looking back, I realize what a tremendous blessing Rav Gustman gave, and why.

(This article is based on a combination of first-hand knowledge and a composite reconstruction of events as retold to me.)

The Life and Death of Yoseph Robinson

The slain rapper turned observant Jew teaches a lesson in the power of redemption.

Jenny Hazan

The first time Yoseph Robinson stared down the barrel of a gun was 15 years ago, when the Bronx drug dealer was betrayed by a colleague in crime. It changed his life. Robinson, then 19, quit life on the street filled with drugs and crime and embarked on a path that would eventually guide him from his post as a successful Hip Hop recording exec in L.A. to Orthodox Judaism. On August 19, the 34-year-old father of four was shot a second time, this time fatally, in Flatbush, Brooklyn, at the MB Vineyards kosher liquor store where he worked.

"It's like his tragic death closed a circle," says owner of MB Vineyards Benjy Ovitsh, 39, Robinson's employer and close friend, who was on vacation when the crazed gunman entered the store and

---

Jenny Hazan is an expat Canadian journalist and editor living in Tel Aviv.

shot Robinson in the chest and arm for protecting the woman he was dating, Lahavah Wallace, 37, from the robber

Ovitsh and Robinson met two years ago, when Robinson first returned to Brooklyn from L.A., where he had converted to Judaism, married, and divorced.

The pair met through a mutual friend at Khal Zichron Mordechai synagogue in Brooklyn. Soon after, Robinson began working at the store, where he quickly became a fixture.

"People used to come into the store just to see him. He was warm and open, always up for a good conversation or debate," Ovitsh told Aish.com. "He really made a *Kiddush Hashem* (sanctification of God's Name) every single day. He affected everybody."

Ovitsh is confident that Robinson himself would see his own tragic demise as some sort of poetic closure, since that is how he viewed his life in general and his path to Judaism in particular. Robinson saw his conversion, at age 23, as the culmination of a series of seemingly unconnected events that inspired him to conclude, as Ovitsh says, "that he didn't choose Judaism, Judaism chose him."

Another close friend of Robinson's from Brooklyn, Shais Rison (aka MaNishtana), 28, a fellow "Jew of Color," concurs. "Yoseph's faith was extremely strong and he always believed that everything that happened was from Heaven. He didn't believe in coincidences," he says. "If something didn't go the way he'd have liked, he'd sometimes spend hours trying to figure out the good in it, or why it might have happened. He really embodied the maxim *gam zu l'tova* — this too is for the good."

Chester's No Exit

Robinson's journey to Judaism may have begun as early as birth. Apparently his paternal grandfather was a Jew, a fact that meant little to Robinson throughout most of his life, but eventually became very significant to him. It was an Orthodox Jewish family from Borough Park, for whom Robinson's mother worked as a nanny, which sponsored his immigration papers to the U.S. at the age of 12, from his birthplace in Spanish Town, Jamaica. When he arrived in Brooklyn his first after-school job was delivery boy for a kosher grocery store, which brought him in close proximity with the community he would eventually become part of.

After his brush with death, the high school dropout, born Chester Robinson, turned from his life of street crime and violence and moved to California, where he became CEO of No Exit, a record label in L.A. He found material success, drove a Lamborghini, and had all the bling one could want. But he quickly grew disenchanted with the materialism of the Hip Hop lifestyle and continued his search for something deeper.

Ovitsh tells the story of Robinson's first conscious encounter with Judaism. It all started with the botched delivery of Robinson's plasma screen TV, which inspired him to take up reading instead. One day, he went book shopping and accidentally wandered into a bookstore in San Fernando Valley.

Robinson had decided to read the Bible, after seeing copies of it in the many hotels he would frequent throughout his career in the music industry. When the clerk asked if he wanted a copy of the New Testament or the Old Testament, Robinson didn't understand the difference and settled on the Old Testament, since it sounded more authentic.

"That was it. He was inspired by what he read," says Ovitsh. "This was one of many little connections to Judaism throughout his life."

As he showed more signs of curiosity about Judaism, a Jewish friend bought him a prayer book and Robinson began attending services at a local shul. Finally, in 1999, Robinson converted under the auspices of the Los Angeles Beit Din, a process that took two-and-a-half years.

The process was not without tumult for Robinson. He faced some challenges transitioning to the Jewish community as a black man, and dedicated much of his time to bridging the gap between Jews and blacks, via community outreach and speaking engagements at local synagogues and schools, activities, which he continued when he moved back to Brooklyn from L.A.

As he wrote on his website, "In Judaism, it's the soul, the *neshamah,* that constitutes the person. The concept is spiritual and can embody any vehicle or physical body. Once people are able to accept the idea that spirituality is not physical and is not bound by space or time, then a black Jewish man is easy to accept."

"He was very proud of being Jewish, and very proud of being Jamaican, and he didn't see them as contradictory," comments Ovitsh.

All the details of Robinson's Jewish journey were to appear in his memoirs, *Jamaican Hip Hopper Turned Orthodox Jew*. Ovitsh, who was helping him with the book, still hopes to get it published. "I would like to do that, as an honor to his memory," says Ovitsh.

Rabbi Shlomo Rosenblatt met Robinson at Rabbi Moshe Tuvia Lieff's shul, the Agudah of Avenue L, where Robinson often attended weekday services.

"He was a member of the community. He was well-loved throughout the entire community. Everyone enjoyed his company tremendously," says Rabbi Rosenblatt, who recalls with fondness the Shabbasos, Succot, and Rosh Hashanah festivals Robinson spent with his family. "He was a very warm, spiritual, charismatic person, positive, always smiling and upbeat. We were honored to have him as a family friend."

Rabbi Kenneth Auman of Young Israel of Flatbush, where Robinson often took in Shabbat services, says Robinson touched so many people in the community because of his openness, and his attendance at all types of synagogues throughout the Flatbush community.

"You couldn't pigeonhole him," says Rabbi Auman. "He fit in everywhere."

Minyan in Jamaica

On his death, the outpouring from the community was overwhelming. Hundreds of people showed up at his memorial service. In addition, with the help of Borough Park's charitable burial organization Chesed Shel Emes, 10 men from the community flew to Jamaica to ensure the presence of a *minyan* at Robinson's funeral in Spanish Town.

Robinson's family insisted he be buried in the backyard of his childhood house, alongside his grandmother Pearl, who raised him until he left for the U.S. Although Jewish community members preferred he be buried in a Jewish cemetery, they respected the family's wishes, and agreed to hold as kosher a ceremony as possible under the circumstances.

"This is the fulfillment of *'meis mitzvah,'* when a Jew passes away and there are no Jewish next of kin to take care of the burial," explains Rabbi Auman, one of the 10 *minyan* members. "Many people from the community contributed generously to send us. That just goes to show how people felt about this and about him."

Rabbi Auman's fondest memory of Robinson is how he behaved during services. "I have this image of him standing in the shul. He always sat in the same spot. He stood there so proud, and prayed with such intensity. He took the service very seriously. This is how I will remember him."

Ovitsh recalls how Robinson once found an unmarked envelope full of cash in the liquor store. Robinson insisted he put it aside and wait for someone to claim it, even though according to Jewish law it was *hefker* — legally ownerless.

A few days later, an elderly non-Jewish customer came in, asking about the envelope. When Robinson handed it over, the man was moved to tears. Robinson explained to him that it is a mitzvah, a valued deed, for Jews to return lost objects to their rightful owners.

"That man will forever see Jews in a special light," says Ovitsh. "Yoseph was a man of great honesty and integrity."

What Rabbi Rosenblatt remembers most about Robinson is his generosity. "Our job in the world is supposed to be giving, and he lived to give," says Rabbi Rosenblatt, who recalls a happy time when Robinson came over to their house with bags of fresh ingredients to share his famous jerk sauce recipe with the family. "He loved to share with others and give to others. He was really a giver and that's how he left the world — with one final act of giving."

"Yoseph's life shows that you really can change, that you are not stuck with the hand you are dealt," says Rabbi Auman. "You can rise above whatever difficulties and challenges you have. His life was an example of that."

Rison agrees. "He was extremely proud telling of the trouble he'd gotten into and been around — not for the sake of bragging about how bad he used to be, but as a source of pride for how far he'd come," he says. "Yoseph was a pillar for black men, a pillar for Jews, a pillar for Jews of color, and a pillar for our generation."

"Yoseph wanted to demonstrate that a person can change, regardless of who you were or what you did," said Ovitsh in his eulogy at Robinson's memorial service in Borough Park. "He transformed himself, emotionally and spiritually, into the person he wanted to become. That's what makes him so unique. He was flawed, as all of us are flawed, but he tried to improve himself. And he succeeded, day after day, to become a better human being. He lived his life according to standards of ethics and integrity that few of us can ever attain."

Better or Bitter

Five-year-old Lily shows us how to get through life's challenges.

Slovie Jungreis-Wolff

"Sometimes it really hurts when the doctor puts a needle in my arm."

I am visiting five-year-old Lily, whose mother attends my parenting classes. Last summer, Lily had some awful headaches. One night, they became so terrible that Lily woke up her parents in middle of the night. The shock upon receiving a diagnosis of a brain tumor was beyond imagining.

Lily's initial treatments included six weeks of radiation and chemotherapy, and then some more chemotherapy. Except on treatment days, Lily never complained or even missed a day of school. This summer, Lily has just been put on a clinical drug trial.

We are sitting across from each other, beautiful Lily, her incredibly gracious mother, Felicia, and I. Lily is chatting and busy coloring a white *tzedakah* box that I had brought over.

Slovie Jungreis-Wolff is a freelance writer and a relationships and parenting instructor. She is the daughter of Rebbetzin Esther Jungreis, founder of Hineni International. Slovie has taught Hineni Young Couples and Parenting classes for more than fifteen years. Her book, *Raising a Child With Soul*, has just been released by St. Martin's Press.

She stops for a moment as her soft voice grows serious. "Sometimes it really hurts, you know. And I get scared."

Felicia leans toward Lily. "That's okay sweetie, we sometimes all get scared. I'm scared of spiders, did you know that?"

Lily's eyes open wide.

"And I'm scared of big bugs," I add. "Not only that, but one of my children jumps from loud thunder and lightning. It's okay to sometimes be afraid."

Lily giggles. I want to scoop this precious child into my arms and kiss all her fears away.

Driving home, I cannot get Lily out of my mind. I am trying hard to find some profound thoughts to come away with. While spending time with Lily and Felicia, I feel as if I've been privy to a most priceless moment in time. I am moved by this child and her sweet innocence as she confronts a most difficult challenge.

Our Choice

There is no life that will be spared adversity. True, some challenges are more arduous than others, but for each person, their challenge is a battle. Health issues, financial problems, marital stability, difficulties while raising children are just a few of the struggles that may come our way. We cannot choose our life challenge. But we can choose how to get through the challenge. Will we become better or bitter? That is up to us.

The Hebrew word for challenge is *"nisayon."* The root of the word is *"nes,"* which can also be defined as "miracle" or "banner." My mother, Rebbetzin Esther Jungreis, once explained to me that as we go through our *nisayon*, our life test, and then emerge stronger and wiser, we have created our own personal banner. We have unearthed a part of ourselves that until now remained concealed deep within us. We've discovered our hidden potential.

Our banner is our legacy through which we are remembered. When going through difficulties, instead of being miserable and sinking into despair, let us ask ourselves — Did I choose to create a banner filled with colors of faith, courage, and strength, or did I pull up the covers and become overwhelmed with my sadness? Did I reach out to others in my life despite, or perhaps because of, my challenge, or did I only have room for myself?

A Kindness a Day

Felicia told me that Lily's preschool class had embarked upon their own *tzedakah* project this year. After collecting coins, the class discussed where the charity should go. Lily's teacher called to say that Lily raised her hand and expressed her wish. She described going to the doctor and finding children in the office who had just a few toys and crayons to play with as they waited. Some toys were broken and old.

"Can we give the charity to my doctor's office?" she asked.

The decision was unanimous.

If this child, amid her pain, can think of others and see their needs, what about us? Can we not sensitize ourselves despite the stress and burdens that we shoulder, to open our eyes and bring a kindness each day into this world of ours?

Parents, especially, need to remember that the greatest kindness begins at home. There are times that we have patience for the world but our own children and spouses remain longing for a compassionate word or a sympathetic ear. The next time your daughter asks for a bedtime story or your son for a game of catch, just say yes. And say it with a smile, as if you really do want to spend time together. Take a moment to call your spouse during the day, even send a text. Don't get into your daily aggravations or which bills need to be paid. Instead, simply say "I love you." "I can't wait to see you,"

Jennifer, a mother who is an old college friend of Felicia's, wanted to "do something" for Lily, but what?

Recognizing the power of doing mitzvahs in the merit of another, Jennifer started a campaign called "Lights for Lily." Each week she sends out hundreds of emails that are then forwarded to hundreds more, asking women to light their Shabbos candles and add a special prayer for Lily. Some of these women have never lit Shabbos candles before. Some have never even really prayed. But we are a family and we are responsible for each other.

So this week, and each week to come, as you kindle your Shabbos lights, please close your eyes and pierce the heavens above. Take a moment and say a prayer for Leah Chana bas Frayda Rochel. Choose a new mitzvah, do an act of kindness, give charity, and think of this little girl who has taught me how to handle life's challenges while thinking of others. And when you are done reading this article, pass it on. Let us join together as one people.

Lily is surely painting a most incredible banner. Now it is our turn.

Epilogue: Lily's Magic

Three months ago I wrote a column for Aish.com called *Better or Bitter*. I described spending a day with five-year-old Lily, whose mother, Felicia, attends my parenting classes. Lily received a diagnosis of a brain tumor and I went to visit with her as she was facing the battle of her life.

I was moved beyond words. This little girl taught me a lesson that inspired me and touched the innermost crevices of my soul.

We were sitting at Lily's little play table as she was coloring a tzedakah box that I had brought over. Lily carefully peeled off the little Hebrew stickers that spelled her name and decorated her box. She chose the most vibrant colors that she could find and eagerly colored despite her pain. It was obviously hard for her, but she giggled her sweet little giggle with each colorful stroke. Then she asked her mother if she could fill her charity box. But only the shiniest and most beautiful pennies would do. Carefully, Lily counted each coin as they clinked inside.

"One ... two ... three ...." Her face filled with delight as she dropped each bright penny inside.

Living With Joy

I was awed by this little child. I returned home and I was inspired to write. *How could this be,* I thought to myself, *that this child who must be so frightened and pained can rise above it all and feel the pain of another?* So often, we adults are stressed or feeling hurt and we cannot see beyond our own reflection. We cannot feel beyond the throbbing aches that beat within ourselves. Whether emotional or physical, it doesn't really matter. The test of life is this: when I go through my challenge, will I grow better or bitter? This beautiful child taught me the way to go.

Despite her constant challenges and difficult tests, she grew kinder and sweeter with each day. She wrapped herself in pink ribbons, purple dress-up feathers, shiny jeweled necklaces, and happily insisted on getting to school on time despite her difficult chemotherapy treatments. She called her father "my cheerleader" and swallowed her awful medications just to see her daddy smile.

Each week Lily embraced the mitzvah of Shabbos with heart and soul. She'd count the days till it was time for the whole family to sit together and bask in the comfort of the Shabbos candles. As the candles danced she'd proudly sing her Shabbos songs and dance beside them. She'd love the feeling of being blessed by her mother at the Shabbos table. Lily's fifth birthday was celebrated in school as the special "Shabbos girl." What a great day, Shabbos and a birthday combined!

Every sunrise would bring Lily another day, another opportunity to love life and teach us adults how to live with joy despite it all.

From One Heart to Another

Last week, I traveled to Silver Spring, Maryland to speak about parenting. As I stood at the podium, a woman approached me.

"I saw your article about Lily on Aish.com," she said. "My children and I were so inspired. This child has real courage and my girls want to be a part of her *tzedakah*."

She handed me an envelope that had been decorated with bright red magic markers. I could feel the coins and dollars inside. There were hearts colored all around and in middle of the envelope in huge letters was written, "LILY'S TZEDAKAH." And at the bottom in children's scrawl: "Samantha and Hannah, Silver Spring, Maryland," along with more red hearts.

Here I was about to make a speech and I found myself speechless

What special children we have! Two children inspired to bring goodness into this world through a little girl that they only read about but never met! Isn't this all that we pray for and try to bequeath to our children? Feel for others, think about others, do well for others, and rise above yourselves.

Touched by an Angel

Thursday morning, I returned home. I must have just walked through the door when I received the painful news. Lily. Our sweet, beautiful Leah Chana returned her soul to the heavens above. I gave out a gasp and realized that I was crying.

This past summer, I was touched by an angel…

So began my words about Lily at her funeral. I described Lily's *tzedakah* project and her ability to rise above her challenges by growing better instead of bitter. I then held up the envelope with "LILY'S TZEDAKAH" written boldly across the center and told the story behind the bright red hearts.

I wanted to share this message with Lily's parents and family. I wanted to convey this thought to the hundreds and hundreds of people who filled the room that morning. And I want to impart my words from that day to you, my dear readers:

As Lily was taking her last breaths we could not imagine that this child was still accomplishing in this world. Though it was her final day here on earth she was still inspiring others. Unbelievably, she was bringing mitzvot and good deeds into this universe. And this is the magic of our sweet Lily.

For the past 16 months hundreds of women have kindled their Shabbos candles with a prayer for Lily on their lips. We have taken this mitzvah upon ourselves as Felicia's friend, Jennifer, sent out hundreds of emails each Friday that were then forwarded to countless more women. Some of these women never lit Shabbos candles before. Many never knew Lily but were praying for her and kindling their "lights for Lily" with great love.

I can tell you this: When Lily's soul returned to Shamayim, to the heavens above, she was surrounded by thousands of magnificent lights that had been kindled in her honor. Lily was lifted upon the wings of thousands of prayers. We will continue to light our Shabbos candles and through our mitzvahs, honor our Leah Chana.

Felicia and Greg, it is written that in the heavens, God has a treasure house of souls. The purest of souls are kept beneath the throne of God. These are the holiest of souls. These are God's diamonds. They must only come into this world for a short amount of time before they complete their mission. They then return to the heavens above.

To whom should God entrust His precious jewels?

Only to the kindest and most trustworthy parents. Only to those parents who safeguard this diamond, watch over it, and guard it well. Parents like you who have been chosen to watch over God's jewel and though it is incredibly painful, to return the diamond when it is time.

I know that I speak for countless people when I tell you that it has been our privilege to be a part of this beautiful child's life. In her five years she has accomplished and taught us more life lessons than some adults do with their long years. She is our pure soul, our treasured jewel and her radiant light will live on in our hearts.

After hearing about Lily's glorious life on that very painful day, many people who have never studied Torah before asked how they can begin to learn about Jewish wisdom. In my heart I know that Lily is still working her magic.

Meatloaf for Mourners

I learned lots of things when Leslie's father died.

Robin Greenman

When I heard that Leslie's father had died, I thought, *what should I do?* I honestly had no idea. Leslie and I belonged to the same congregation, but I didn't know her well. All I knew was that she was more religious than I was. Then again, who wasn't?

We had recently moved from Los Angeles to Portland, Oregon and had been hunting around for temples. Back in L.A. we had taken an Introduction to Judaism class because we realized that we had to pass down *something* to our new baby.

The class required regular attendance at a temple of your choice, so we went to a Reform one, where we felt comfortable. Due to events that I won't bore you with, we spent a year in Vancouver, BC where Reform is more like Conservative. In this Reform "shul," as they called it, you wrapped tefillin. To me, that was the height of piety — strapping those black boxes on your forehead.

When we moved to Portland, we were suddenly too religious for

---

Robin Greenman lives with her husband, Adam, and daughter, Eleanor, in Portland, Oregon, where they attend Congregation Kesser Israel.

the Reform temple; we, who knew practically nothing. I thought of my father intoning the ultimate Yiddish put-down to all pretentiousness: *"Ka-nocker."* Look who thinks she's such a big shot.

The next weekend we went to the Conservative shul. Too big. We tried Reconstructionist. Instead of a rabbi, services were led by people like us, only wearing Birkenstocks. Jewish Revival? Too much music; I wanted to grab one of those infernal tambourines and break it over my knee. There had to be someplace for people like us.

"Oh no, not me! If you want to go there, you go alone!" That was my loving reaction when my husband suggested going to the Orthodox shul. He had taken a class given by the new rabbi there.

"He's really a nice guy. Let's try it," pleaded Adam.

"But it's got one of those ... " my hand made a frantic chopping sign. "Those things down the middle that separate the men from the women."

Long story short, I went and I HATED IT. I went again, and I cried through the whole service. "I miss L.A.!" I sobbed into my prayer book turned to the wrong page. I went again, and asked the woman standing next to me, "How do you know all these songs?"

She answered, "You just come." Oh, so easy. I heard my father's voice — *"Ka-nocker."* Nothing's ever that easy for me. I can't whistle, I can't knit, and I sure can't learn to sing songs in Hebrew.

But we kept coming back, and not just because we'd run out of choices. I had never seen people pray with such sincerity. I knew I'd never be that woman in long sleeves rocking back and forth, but I envied her intensity, her belief that God was actually listening.

We had been going to Kesser Israel for about six months when Leslie's father died. Not knowing what to do for her, I called and asked. "Do you guys need anything? Dinner or ...."

Her husband saved me, "No, thanks, we're fine."

I was off the hook, that is, until I heard that people were visiting Leslie while she sat *shivah*, the seven days of Jewish mourning. Cold as it may sound, I was not in the habit of doing things for people I wasn't close to. I was a good friend to my friends, and I did volunteer work for strangers, but this in-between status threw me. I forced myself to visit her, unsure of what I should do or say.

As I approached Leslie's door, I saw Sarah, another congregant coming up the walk. She was carrying a large tin-foil container.

"What did you bring?" I asked, ashamed of my empty-handedness.

Sarah smiled. "I made lasagna."

"Oh, I would have brought dinner, but Michael said they didn't need anything."

"I know, people never tell you."

"You just come," the singing woman had said. "You just do," Sarah didn't need to say.

Sarah walked in without knocking, like Snow White, and put her lasagna unannounced in the refrigerator. She had trouble finding room among all the other dinners that had been brought without being requested. I followed her into the living room where Leslie was sitting on a low stool. Sarah quietly hugged her and sat down. To compensate for this curiously mute moment, I told Leslie how very sorry I was for her loss. She smiled and thanked me.

Several months later I lost my own father. It was then that I learned about the custom of entering a *shivah* home without knocking — to spare the mourner from having to get up to greet you. I also learned the reason for Sarah's initial silence; visitors let the mourner set the tone. She can speak or not speak. Or she can just cry. She's not a hostess at a party.

I deeply appreciated not having to hang up people's coats and offer them something to drink. My father was dead, I was sad, and they were there to support me in my grief. "They" were all the people in my congregation, people I loved, liked, or barely knew. It didn't matter. They came because "You just come, you just do."

My refrigerator was full. If I hadn't been so depressed I would have enjoyed peeling back silver foil to reveal dinners I hadn't had to make.

Grateful and humbled, I realized what I needed: my own moment's-notice *shivah* recipe. The answer appeared on page 117 of the kosher cookbook my best friend, Meredith, had given me: Meatloaf. It was quick, easy, and best of all, comforting. I vowed to always have ground beef and aluminum tins on hand, and over the years, unfortunately, I've had many occasions to make it. Incredibly, I've also learned a few Hebrew songs along the way.

Time of Death

You never know when can be the last time.

Yael Mauer

Mrs. B had been my patient for 10 days while I was doing a medicine clerkship as a third-year medical student. She had come to the hospital because of difficulty breathing, complicated by a history of chronic pulmonary disease, lung cancer, breast cancer, and other things. She was 75. I liked her immediately, she was intelligent and funny. Seeing her was my favorite part of the day. We connected from the beginning.

She had a daughter whom she did not want to burden, a brother, and grandchildren. Her granddaughter's name was Amy; she had recently gotten married. During all the time we spent together, I never saw anyone visit her. I felt she was somewhat lonely, but I was humbled by her positive spirits and strong will.

Yesterday things were looking better. Her numbers were up, her wheezing was gone. We were planning to discharge her to a rehab center where she would complete her recovery and soon after go home. She was very anxious to go home because she had bills to pay and she also missed her neighbors.

Yael Mauer is originally from Buenos Aires, and currently lives with her husband, Yoel, in Passaic, New Jersey. She is finishing her fourth year of medical school and plans to become a hematologist/oncologist.

We stopped by her room for one last checkup and she looked ready to take off. A few minutes into our visit, another patient's heart stopped. Doctors were called to help and I ran to assist. When I came back to Mrs. B, her room was full of doctors and nurses; she was breathing very heavily and her heart was racing, so the staff was trying to control her pulse. I saw that she was scared. I held her hand and asked her about her plans for after discharge. I asked her about her daughter and grandkids. She could barely breathe but was eager to tell me. After a half hour, her heart went back to normal and things seemed under control.

"Are you okay?" I asked.

"I feel like dancing," she replied.

Before going home last night, I went to check on Mrs. B. one last time. She was doing well. She had heard that she was going to be transferred to the cardiac unit instead of going to the rehab center, so that we could watch out for more arrhythmias like the ones she had experienced earlier in the day.

"Doctor, I'm not going to come out of the hospital," she said to me. I told her about a study in which patients who thought they wouldn't come out of the hospital were more likely to die in the hospital than patients who thought they would. I made her tell me she'd come out of the hospital fine. Then I told her that I was going home, that I had only stopped to say goodbye.

"Don't go home," she implored.

"What should I do?"

"Sleep here!"

"Why do you want me to sleep here?" I asked.

"Because I trust you."

"And you don't trust anyone else?" I asked, laughing.

"I don't," she replied.

We laughed again. I told her I'd see her first thing in the morning. As I was walking out the door she said to me, smiling, "Bright and early tomorrow, Doc. I'll be here." I smiled back at her and went home.

This morning I came to the hospital to find out that she was intubated. She had gone into respiratory failure and had to be transferred to the critical care unit. I went to see her immediately. She was heavily sedated, intubated, and wearing cushioned gloves to prevent her from hurting herself or anyone else. The nurse told me she had been aggressive.

The woman lying in the bed looked nothing like Mrs. B; she didn't even look like a person. The monitors were beeping and flashing, doctors and nurses were coming in and out of her room, pushing me away. I told the attending physician I wanted to wake her up and say good morning to her, I wanted her to see a familiar face, she must had been so scared! He asked me not to wake her because she had been very combative. So I didn't.

A few hours later, I was walking to the cafeteria when I got a text from a classmate — Mrs. B's heart had stopped and she was dying. I ran to the critical care unit to find a sea of white coats and blue scrubs coming in and out of the unit. There was almost no space to move. I pushed my way through the crowd and into the room. The medical team had just finished one cycle of CPR. The attending physician asked, "Would she want more aggressive CPR or for us to let her go?"

The staff was frantically calling her family, but they were not getting through. I kept on thinking how they'd feel to find out later they had missed this call, a last call. Everyone was at a loss; there were no advanced directives, no instructions in her chart. From the back of the room I said, "From what I knew about Mrs. B, I think she'd like us to try it all, until the end." I suddenly understood that she was dying and I was the closest person to her who could be reached at that moment.

"Start another cycle of CPR!" said the doctor. They all rushed to their positions and began CPR.

"We need more people to help," the nurse said. "Who wants to help?" I ran to put on gloves and rushed to her side.

The doctor looked at me and said, "It's your turn, give it your best." I compressed her chest until I thought I'd pass out from the heat. Someone else took over, and we alternated every two minutes, for many long minutes. She was bleeding through her neck and unresponsive. She was dying. I prayed for her as I performed CPR.

With no response there was nothing left for us to do. "Anyone else has any ideas?" the doctor asked. Silence filled the crowd. No ideas. He asked us to let go. "1:06 is the time of death," he said. Suddenly the coats and scrubs were marching out of the room, the equipment was turned off, the tension was over.

I walked into the waiting room and grabbed a chair. My classmates were waiting for me, speechless. I started crying and a few nurses came to console me. "You did good ... you did your best ...." All I could think about was how sadly she died, surrounded by strangers. I wondered if she knew I came to visit her this morning, and gave her chest compressions until she was gone.

I know I did my best. I don't regret one antibiotic I suggested for her, or one x-ray. But I'll always regret not having told her last night how much I enjoyed getting to know her and how honored I felt that she trusted me so much.

Shocked Into Silence

Responding to the horrific murder of Leiby Kletzky ob'm

Rabbi Nechemia Coopersmith

I was in the unenviable position of having to inform my wife that they found the body of Leiby Kletzky. Her face turned white.

"What happened to him?"

I was silent. I could not bring myself to describe the horrific manner in which this innocent child was brutally murdered. By a Jew. The words, even if whispered in a hushed tone, could not leave my mouth.

"Worse than anything you can imagine ... I can't talk about it."

I wasn't the only one who was shocked into silence. The most prevailing response in the *2000 plus comments expressing readers' condolences* from around the world was "there are no words." It felt as if the Jewish nation was rendered speechless, reeling from a punch in the gut, unable to grasp such incomprehensible horror.

Rabbi Nechemia Coopersmith is the chief editor of Aish.com. He lives in Jerusalem with his wife and children. He is the author *of Shmooze: A Guide to Thought-Provoking Discussion on Essential Jewish Issues* — a must-have little book for anyone who loves a good question.

Our silence in the face of tragedy is reminiscent of Aaron's response to the sudden death of his two sons, budding leaders of the Jewish people, who were cut down in the prime of life. "And Aaron was silent" (*Leviticus* 10:3).

However, Aaron's silence was born from a total acceptance of Divine will, despite his enormous loss. Our silence, at least in part, stems from denial, the first instinctual response that provides a modicum of safety: the belief that our world can remain the same, kids can go to camp unharmed, our Jewish neighborhood is a haven of basically good people. If we don't talk about it, we can push away the weight of grief and horror.

But perhaps the universal reaction of silence hints to something else, something that goes to the core of what it means to be human.

When God creates man, fusing the dust of the earth with the breath of life — a soul — the Torah says "and man became a living soul." The translator Onkelos interprets "living soul" to mean a "speaking spirit." It is our unique ability to speak that makes us truly human. Speech is the bridge that joins the world of thought to the world of action, where heaven meets earth, where the spiritual and the physical — the body and the soul — come together to create the inherent tension point of free will.

Being exposed to unimaginable brutality, graphically described in the reports of Leiby Kletzky's murder, affects us. Evil that had previously not been a part of our world crashes through our psyche's door and penetrates our soul. It chips away at our humanity, leaving us numb to the core. How can any human being commit such crimes?

The result is that we are struck dumb. Speech, the defining characteristic of being human, "goes into exile" as the Kabbalists describe it, because our humanity is shaken. We are less human.

The last few days I've been walking around in a fog of sadness and grief, as if I have suffered a personal trauma. And I know so many others feel the same.

The Sages of the Talmud tell us the "silence is tantamount to admission." If you don't agree with a proposition or accusation leveled at you, say something. Otherwise your silence speaks volumes.

Witnessing such horror and debasement, we have been shocked

into silence, feeling that there are no words, only tears. However, we dare not remain silent. When our speech is in exile, when our humanity has been weakened, we need to do something to restore our humanity, to restore our speech. We need to strengthen and elevate our humanity by activating our souls.

The Talmud (*Sotah* 2a) instructs one who has witnessed a person accused of immorality to take an extra stringency upon himself in that area, to actively distance himself further from evil, even though he himself has not engaged in any sinful act. Since his reality has been expanded to include something so negative and destructive, he must work on increasing the positive forces in his life to restore the balance.

The word "mitzvah" (commandment) shares the Hebrew root "to connect" — mitzvot are the avenue to transcend the physical, remove ourselves from the churning storm of evil, and re-attach ourselves to God and to what is good and true in the world.

I can leave the fog that is encasing me when I reach out to give my children an extra hug, when I choose to be patient and caring, when I choose to get out of my own petty concerns and think about others. Instead of only reeling from this horrific tragedy, let's work to channel our pain and shock toward doing good, strengthening our souls individually and collectively. Taking on a specific mitzvah that speaks to you not only helps to elevate the soul of Leiby Kletzky, it elevates your soul as well.

A Drop of Humor

Deep Center

My kind of position. No pressure, no embarrassing errors, and no one gets hurt.

Adam Greenman

As a kid, I was a complete loser at baseball. I was pudgy. I was clumsy. I was scared of the ball. In fact, I was a complete loser at all sports. This not only proved personally embarrassing, but painful for the team forced to take me as their last pick. They'd need to find some position for me where I would do the least damage to their chances for success. In baseball that position is called "deep center."

Starting out from home plate toward second base, one arrives at the position by continuing past the second baseman, then past the *regular* center fielder. Eventually the cries of "keep going" fade away and you turn back to face the diamond. If you can see the curvature of the earth, you've arrived. Deep center. Sure, it sometimes got lonely out beyond the horizon line, and yes, there were times I was so far away I'd miss whole innings of the game. But in truth, I was happy out there. I'd think about life. I'd sing to myself. I'd wonder

---

Adam Greenman lives in Portland, Oregon with his wife and daughter whom he adores. He is a recovering screenwriter who just graduated law school at 50 years old. Visit his site at www.script-mentor.com.

how the other guys got their mitts to work so effortlessly while mine was so uselessly stiff. Best of all, there was no pressure, no embarrassing errors, and no one got hurt. My kind of position.

Many years later, now a grown man, I am staying over Shabbat with my mom while visiting Los Angeles on business. I've lost a fair amount of hair, I'm even "pudgier" than before, and I'm also starting to become "observant." How that happened is a long story, but suffice it to say that after a lifetime of complete assimilation, I've now got six months of traditional Judaism under my belt, I've got a *tallis* the size of a bedsheet, a shiny new pair of *tefillin*, and absolutely no idea what I'm doing with any of it. Still, the gear is impressive and as I explain it to my mom it sounds like I really know what I'm talking about.

"You know so *much*," she says in amazement.

"Thank God," I modestly reply.

She tells me about the handful of small Orthodox shuls in the area, but I already know where I'll be going. Adat Ari El. It's a huge place with stained glass windows and a bar mitzvah scheduled for this Shabbat. That's what I wanted. After all, you can't play "deep center" in a small shul. Everyone notices you. Everyone wants to know what position you play, what your lifetime stats are, which teams you've previously played for. But at Adat Ari El with a bar mitzvah scheduled, I am assured of not being called to the Torah for an *aliyah* and not having to worry about embarrassing myself. I can take a seat in back and enjoy a nice restful Shabbat in "deep center." Perfect.

✻✻✻

The temperature on Shabbat morning was already in the nineties as I left my mom's apartment and began the half-mile walk to Adat Ari El. I had my dark suit on, which was even warmer than normal thanks to the king-sized *tallis* bunched up under the jacket. But I knew I'd be there in ten minutes, and for sure they'd have air conditioning, so everything would be fine as soon as —

"— *vait*. Mister . . . are you *goink* to Ari El?"

Two blocks from my mom's apartment, I was standing in front of a retirement hotel where several old women sat in plastic chairs. One of them, dressed nicer than the others, was struggling to rise.

"Yes," I smiled modestly.

"Guuut. You take me *viss* you." She was now halfway between sitting and standing. Easily a thousand years old, bent over in a "C" shape, with one hand clutching one of those four-pronged walkers.

"Um ... well ... okay, I guess. But are you sure?" I watched her take another step. We were still a good half mile from —

"— don't listen to her," the other old ladies motioned for me to keep walking. "She's crazy. She'll never make it"

"Please ... you *vait*," she took another step. "They hate me," she said about the others on the balcony. "They're mean to me."

I stood motionless on the sidewalk. The sun beat down. I felt a trickle of sweat beneath my blue suit, pinpoint oxford shirt, king-sized *tallis*. "Miss, it's getting kinda hot and Adat Ari El's a good half mile —"

"Please!" Her bony fingers clamped into my forearm. "Don't leave me."

She peered into my eyes, and whether it was palsy or iron-willed determination I felt her body shaking as she gripped my arm. "You do it," she whispered with fierce determination. "You daven *viss* me right here."

Trapped, I stood like a deer in the headlights, my mind racing desperately —

"— *guut*," she decided, ending the discussion. "You come," she motioned to me as she turned and four-pronged toward the hotel.

I fought panic. In the 20 minutes it took for me to accompany Lillian Kimmel to her room, I reassured myself over and over, *"Be cool. She probably just wants you to keep her company for a few minutes, maybe mumble a couple prayers, and you're out of there. Ten minutes, tops."*

Her room smelled like Lysol and dust. The shades were drawn and the Fedders *QuietCool* was blowing hot air. "Uh ... I ah ... I'm not very good at —"

"— here. You do it." She plopped down in the only chair and handed me a worn blue siddur. "You sing. I *vill* follow."

Sing? I stared, frozen. Who does she think I am?

"My son is a rabbi, you know."

Oh swell, I thought. *That's just great.*

"Go ahead," she waved a bony hand at me. "You start."

By now I was sweating *through* the *tzitzit*, the pinpoint oxford shirt, and the bedspread *tallis* which was still bunched up inside my jacket. I opened the unfamiliar *siddur* and somehow found a page I recognized and cleared my throat. "*Shochen ad* —"

"*Dat's* where you're starting?!"

I stared at Mrs. Kimmel, the mother of the rabbi. "Where would you like me to start?"

"*Da* beginning!" The woman was getting annoyed. "You *do* it!"

I searched through the prayer book again. It wasn't like the ArtScroll siddur I had become accustomed to. Not that I *understood* the ArtScroll siddur or knew what I was saying, but it was orderly. You march along, one page to the next, either reading the English or mumbling the Hebrew and eventually you come to *Aleinu*. Not so with this prayer book. I'm finding poems, meditations, a recipe —

"Here. I'll show you." She snatched the book from my hand and flipped to a page. "*Dis* is *vere* you start."

"Okay," I took the book back. I could do this one. "*Ma tovu . . . o-ha-lecha Yakov . . .*"

But now the door s l o w l y opened, revealing another woman who had to be 100 years old. "*Vat's diss?!*" she hollered, cocking a hearing aid the size of a transistor radio.

"He's making Shabbos," the mother of the rabbi yelled back.

"*Vait!* I get my *sheitel*!" the centenarian began the process of turning and starting back down the hallway, which I saw was filled with even more oldsters shuffling toward me and gesticulating, "*Vait! . . . Vait! . . .* I'm coming too!"

The details of what follows are lost in a blur of heat apoplexy. The next thing I remember was staggering back to my mother's apartment looking like someone had dumped a bucket of water over my head. I had been there for hours, struggling to find the right page, to find the right words, to sing the right melody, and essentially doing a pretty rotten job. Plucked from deep center and repositioned at short-stop, I bobbled, dropped, and mangled every line drive of the morning *Shacharit* Service. And while the elderly Bonds, A-Rods, and Jeters all thanked me when it was over, the truth was it wasn't much of a game. Any one of them knew more than I did, and don't forget, Mrs. Kimmel's son "was a rabbi."

In the end I couldn't help wondering "why." Other than giving God a good laugh, what really could have been the point of this debacle?

✼✼✼

"Did you have a nice time, honey?" my mom asked as I collapsed on her couch.

"Uh huh."

"What was the Torah portion about?"

My eyes went blank. The Torah portion. I had forgotten all about it, as had my captors, or I'm sure I'd still be there. "I never got that far."

My mother gave me a confused look, but I was already back on my feet. "I think I'm going to lie down for a while," I said, collecting my *Chumash* and starting for the bedroom.

It was nice in there. Cool and air conditioned and relaxing. I read through the Torah portion in English. There was lots to get out of it, and lots surely went over my head, but the last line stayed with me. Apparently all the men must appear before God in the Temple, and not empty-handed. Each man must bring what he can individually give in order to receive a blessing from God.

Well, I figured I brought what I had today, and it's a long walk back to the outfield once you've found your way home from deep center.

The God of Large and Small

My day in traffic court

Rabbi Yaakov Salomon

I was driving northbound on Hamilton Ave. en route to the Brooklyn Battery Tunnel. I've taken the route hundreds of times. But instead of veering left into the lane for the tunnel, I decided to swerve right — into the lane headed for the Brooklyn Bridge. And there he was.

"Okay buddy, pull over here," he seemed to be saying with his dramatic hand movements. He was short for a cop; a bit stocky, and very animated.

"License, registration, and insurance card," he demanded.

I do not enjoy being pulled over by a law enforcement officer. It falls somewhere between toenail fungus and sea sickness on my "Must Experience" list. I'm not sure if I attempted some lame, incoherent muttering explaining why I crossed that dreaded SOLID WHITE LINE, but I am sure that it made no impact on Officer Stankowski.

"The instructions are on the back," he kindly informed me while handing me the yellow summons. "Have a nice day."

During the five minutes or so that he took to write the ticket, I

For a biographical note on the author, please see page 152.

got out of the car and took pictures of the pavement markings and signs posted in the crime scene area. It was something I had seen others do, but never done before myself. I had no idea why I was doing it, but it seemed like my only way to express my innocence to Stankowski. *"If I'm taking pictures, then I MUST NOT be guilty."* Don't worry. It made no sense to me either.

In the ensuing months I made the usual inquiries of friends, some of them attorneys, to help craft and strategize my approach to the infraction. One avenue was clearly consensual: "Push this off as long as you can. You never know what could happen."

- Police officers move out of town, get transferred, or run for District Attorney or other such positions all the time.
- Maybe the law will change.
- Nuclear war could beckon.

Dutifully, I cooperated. Nearly a full year went past, but, my luck, the World remained at relative peace. That meant that April 8th was D-Day.

My Secret Weapon

The sun shone brightly that Friday morning. I trimmed the beard and chose a dark tie. Stomach in flutters, I skipped breakfast. I drove (very carefully) to the courthouse and saw my name on the hearing ledger taped to the wall next to Room 5. The paint was peeling. There was no smell. I was early. I'm never early.

I guess a lot of people were early, as most of the seats were already occupied by my fellow defendants. They peered at me as I walked in. *They* knew I was innocent, as much as I knew the same about them. It's like a club, these hearing rooms, with new members joining every few hours. *"It's us against the cops. How dare they pronounce us guilty until proven innocent! It's anti-American. We will band together and we WILL defeat them!"*

Right.

In walked the enemy. A group of six or seven uniformed officers in full regalia — as if they were actually setting out to real combat. It seemed unfair. Stankowski, in knee-high boots, oversized revolver, gleaming badges and medals, and perfectly pressed slacks versus Salomon ... in the dark tie.

But unbeknownst to the prosecution, Salomon had brought a secret weapon — a manila envelope containing copies of Section 3A.01 of the MUTCD. Not familiar with the Manual on Uniform Traffic Control Devices? Neither was I, until my research uncovered that the "Bible" of Traffic Law indicated that (read carefully), *"A SOLID line usually indicates that crossing the line is discouraged."* It goes on to explain that there are actually different widths of solid lines that suggest different levels of restriction. And, according to the pictures that I (so brilliantly) took, that solid line that I crossed *could* have been construed as very crossable, thank you.

The first case involved a woman charged with driving while talking on her cell phone. She totally denied it — patently and emphatically. It was basically her word against the cop.

"Guilty as charged!" bellowed the judge. "One hundred and forty dollars plus two points on your license. No appeals allowed. See the clerk. Next!"

A pall fell over the gallery. The club members were distraught. How was that justified?

The next brother was called. *Unsafe lane change* was his alleged violation. The arguments were spirited on both sides, with my new comrade making a strong case for how the traffic pattern demanded that he switch lanes at that time.

"Guilty as charged!" bellowed the judge. "One hundred and forty dollars plus two points on your license. No appeals allowed. See the clerk. Next!"

At this point I was happy that I had skipped breakfast, as a dour sensation of sudden nausea invaded my digestive tract. I held on to my manila envelope extra tight, but began to question its potential influence.

Two more sisters followed — both with cell phone violations issued by different officers. The verdicts were of similar ilk. They shuffled out of the courtroom pale, with heads bowed and wallets opened. (One of the sisters also had a manila envelope.)

I started feeling a bit light-headed and a slight quiver emerged on my bottom lip.

Wow, I thought, *I am really nervous about this thing. How absurd is that?*

I found myself in touch with my deepening tension and anxiety and I began to feel . . . well . . . embarrassed.

What's the big deal? It's only a traffic ticket! And just because you already have two points on your license, that's a reason to panic? Nausea? Quiver? IT'S ONLY TRAFFIC COURT, FOR HEAVEN'S SAKE!

And then, instinctively, I actually began to pray — yes . . . pray. I said some psalms by heart and spoke to God — asking for His intervention. Stankowski — even in his boots — was no match for the Almighty, I reasoned.

The gallery was slowly starting to empty. The next victim . . . er . . . accused, was an older gentleman. He looked so sweet and yes, innocent. I couldn't hear too many of the details, but one part came through loud and clear.

"Guilty as charged! One hundred and forty dollars plus two points on your license. No appeals allowed. See the clerk. Next!"

That thud you heard was the lump that egressed in my larynx.

Now I was sweating and intensifying my prayers. It was clear to me that without some kind of supernal assistance I would be on line at the cashier in just a few minutes. But as my entreaties were compounding, so too was my shame.

This is what you pray for? This? Do you think God has time for such trivialities? World hunger, terrorism, apostasy, apathy, disease, abuse are all rampant. And you're worried about two points on your license and a few dollars? What has gotten into you??

What kind of self-respecting person would feel compelled by terror in Traffic Court to pray to God for salvation? But, on the other hand, just as there is no such thing as "too big" for God, there is no concept of "too small" either. It's not as if God is *too tied up* with the really important stuff, so He can't attend to the trifling details of our lives. That would imply human-like restriction to the All Powerful.

The same way we make a blessing on a 32-oz. filet mignon, we also recite a blessing before drinking a tiny cup of water. In fact, it is actually the very same blessing that we make on both. My praying to Him when facing serious illness in no way precludes my praying when Stankowski looms before me.

Armed with my new artillery, I clutched that manila envelope ever so snugly, closed my eyes, and freely asked God for help.

Seconds later we stood before the judge. A surprising calm descended. The nausea was gone. My voice trembled just a bit when I pleaded, "Not guilty," but I felt ready to accept His decision. I looked to my right. There stood Stankowski. He was ruffling through his papers.

The judge asked if he was ready to proceed. Stankowski continued to ruffle. Now his feet were shuffling too. I thought I detected a bead of sweat or perhaps a hair skid out of place.

"Officer Stankowski — are you ready to proceed?"

Silence. Now he was shaking his head. A couple of summonses fell to the floor. He bent down to retrieve them.

"Your Honor, I ... er ... I cannot seem to locate the ticket or my notes on this case."

I thought my legs were going to leave their sockets.

"If you cannot proceed, I will have no choice but to dismiss these charges."

Stankowski was done and he knew it. He pretended to continue his search for the missing documents, but it was to no avail.

"I'm sorry. I cannot find anything on this violation."

"All right then. Let the record state that I am entering a verdict of 'Not guilty.' No points or fine are assessed. You are free to go."

I thanked the judge and wobbled away.

On the way out, I did three things. First, I glanced over at the remaining fraternity members and smiled. They gave me lots of thumbs up and lots of smiles. One brother pointed to heaven ... really.

Second, I said a prayer of thanks. I apologized for my overreaction, but acknowledged that He is truly the God of large and small.

And finally, I tossed that manila envelope into the trash bin.

The Rabbi and the Cabinet Minister

An expired driver's license results in a magical Shabbat experience.

Rabbi Moshe Zionce

Last year I was planning a plane trip to the United States. Canadian law required a passport.

In preparation, my wife gathered our papers together. She went into my wallet, pulled out my license, and giggled. "Is my picture that bad?" I asked.

"Um, Moshe, I think your license has expired."

My heart skipped a beat as I inspected the license. It was true. Not only was it expired, but it was expired by three years and two weeks!

No big deal, I thought. I called the licensing office. The lady said, "No problem sir, you can always renew a license. How expired is it?"

Born and bred in Toronto, **Rabbi Moshe Zionce** at an early age always felt the deep desire to teach Jews of all backgrounds about their rich heritage. Moshe graduated from Ner Israel Yeshivah of Toronto in 1990 and went on to further his education in higher Judaic studies in New York. It is there that he was introduced to his wife, Penina. They settled in Toronto where Moshe received *semichah,* ordination. Seven kids and 25 pounds later, Rabbi Zionce is the director of Project Inspire Toronto. "Life is a constant balancing act between family, making ends meet, spirituality, and eating my wife's home-made challah."
Rabbi Moshe's inspirational and informative five-minute Torah classes can be found on his popular internet channel *The Chai Cafe.*

"It's about three year's worth," I responded.

The lady took a moment to confirm the dates. "I'm sorry sir, you're two weeks over. You will have to start from scratch."

"What do you mean from scratch?"

"You will be required to complete the mandatory Ontario graduated licensing system. That's the written permit test, the level one road test and the level two highway test. There is nothing I can do. It's the law."

The words "start from scratch" rang in my ears. I had flashbacks to my 16th birthday.

Then reality hit me. Carpools? Seeing clients? Getting to shul to teach? My life had suddenly spun out of control and I was stranded on the side of the road, helpless.

I called again. A different woman answered and I explained the situation to her. "But I received a new license just a few years ago."

She checked my records. "Yes, in fact, you were issued a new license four years ago; however, that was merely a change of address. The license was not renewed at that time."

In desperation I asked, "Is there anyone I can speak to about this?"

"No, I'm sorry. It's the law."

That night I lay in my bed, thinking hard. Our Rabbis teach us, "Even if the blade of the sword is at your throat, one must never give up hope." There had to be a solution .... Then it suddenly hit me.

I ran to my office. In moments, I found the Ontario Minister of Transportation's direct email! The Honorable Donna Cansfield.

I fired off an email, entitled "Desperate Driving Dilemma."

The Honorable Donna Cansfield, I have a problem I'm hoping you could help me with. I'm sure you have issues of much greater importance to concern yourself with, however this is of utmost importance to me ... I received my license at age 18 and I have a perfect driving record. I am 34 years old ...

I knew I had to lay it on thick.

Life at the best of times is overwhelming. We just had our sixth child a month ago. My wife needs my help. I work, teach, and the thought of not having my full license for over a year is devastating. I was wondering if there is anything that could be done . . .

First thing in the morning I received a phone call. I scrambled to pick it up. A voice on the other end said, "Hello, this is Donna Cansfield." I was shocked; it was really her! I explained the situation and we had a laugh or two. The Minister was down to earth and very understanding. "We're still trying to get over the fact that you are 34 and have six kids . . . I'm going to connect you to someone who can resolve the issue. Please call me back if there are any problems."

I thanked her profusely and we hung up. Just like that, I went right to the top in 12 hours. Not only did the Cabinet Minister respond personally, but she wanted to help! This was going to work!

The lady that I subsequently spoke to was again very sympathetic. She said she would look into the matter and get back to me. However, later that day she explained to me that in fact this was the law and there was nothing anyone could do to help. I experienced cold flashes as I had visions of my wife in the driver's seat and me as her passenger.

After accepting defeat I knew there was only one thing left to do: to thank the Minister in an email.

Desperate Driving Dilemma 2.

I really appreciate all your efforts! I'm so impressed that you took the time to follow up and to actually give me a personal call for my relatively minuscule matter.

Unfortunately, Mrs. B. said there is nothing that could be done.

I wanted to wish you much success in all your endeavors, happiness, health, and may your deepest dreams and wishes be answered.

I've attached some pics of my six little monsters. [The kids were wearing yarmulkes; it was obvious we were Jewish.] *If you would ever like to meet the family and have a cultural experience, it would be an honor to host you and your husband or friend for a traditional Friday-night meal at my house. My wife's homemade bread is to die for. Call any time at all.*

What possessed me to invite the Minister for a Shabbat meal I can't say. Friday night is magical even for the most secular person;

it is always a hit. I guess I felt it was an important bridge to build. It was a spur of the moment decision and I hadn't even told my wife.

Two weeks later, after coming back from passing the first road test, there was an email waiting for me.

"I have been reviewing Minister Cansfield's calendar to find a Friday evening when she could drop in to meet your family and taste your wife's homemade bread .... Minister Cansfield will not be able to stay for dinner but she would love to meet your family and sample some homemade bread. If this date doesn't work, we can always find other Friday nights. Thanks."

At this point I thought I should probably inform my wife.

In a Stranger's Home

The big day finally arrived. The Transportation Minister, the Honorable Donna Cansfield, would be a guest at our Shabbat table! I understood the Minister did not want to commit to stay for any length of time. But I knew that if she walked through the door, she would not be leaving so fast. The Friday-night Shabbat meal is always sheer enchantment; not an experience to be missed or rushed through.

I was committed not to change a thing in how we ran our Shabbat meal. By the standards of most observant people my singing before *kiddush* is unusually long. I have the custom to recite an extended version, "chassidic Bobov style." Even though it would take quite a while until we would finally eat, I felt it was important that my children see that nothing was altered. (Usually I explain to guests that this is the strategy to keep them in suspense, so they will really enjoy the challah once it finally comes). We did make one minor modification. There would be no clear, bulletproof plastic cover over the tablecloth. (I prayed my children wouldn't spill this week).

The doorbell rang and my family gathered at the front door. The Minister was alone, and I immediately felt her discomfort. She was standing in a stranger's home, confronted by a strange religion, with all eyes focused on her. And yet she was poised and collected. The Minister commented on how beautiful all the children were dressed.

She admitted that she had no idea what to expect and therefore mistakenly dressed down after work. I told her we were simply honored and delighted that she could make it.

We took our seats and went around the table with introductions. Obviously, the names were foreign to her. My wife and I aided the children by providing the English equivalent of their names, however she insisted on learning them in Hebrew. She was quite a natural. She even mastered our son Chesky's name. We all felt comfortable in no time. We laughed and joked.

I presented Minister Cansfield with a translated *bencher* and showed her the page. My children sang with me, most beautifully. The Minister seemed both amazed and delighted at the sight before her. A smile rested on her face as she glanced from one child to the next.

I explained everything. *Shalom aleichem* — the welcoming of the angels; *aishet chayil* — the praises of the woman; the blessing of the children; and I shared some inspirational anecdotes.

"We are going to wash our hands before partaking of the bread," I said. "Feel free to remain seated." She insisted on washing with the family. I made *hamotzie* and pointed out that my custom is to cut my wife a larger piece than my own, as a husband is obligated to honor his wife more than himself. My wife's challah, as always, was right on target. This was obvious from the Minister's reaction. Now I was certain that she wasn't leaving so fast.

We talked and laughed some more as I related my entire license episode. The Minister explained that the reason she really came was to meet the woman who has six kids and bakes her own bread.

My five-year-old son, Yossi, brought out his page of questions and answers on the weekly Torah portion in Yiddish, and we translated. Shuli, my eldest son, gave a *dvar Torah*.

The night seemed to fly by. After two hours, just before dessert was served, the Minister said, "I really should be going." We insisted on packing her up some homemade chocolate cake. She asked if we could spare a couple of extra pieces for her husband and son at home. By the end of the night, she knew the words "Shabbos" and "challah" and all the kids' names. Before she left, she hugged my wife and asked us to keep in touch.

The door closed and there were high fives for everyone. I don't think it could have gone any better. Thank God my children chose this night to be on their best behavior.

What an incredible country and what incredible representation we have. After a mere email and subsequent invitation from a stranger, a government minister came into a strange home and an even stranger religion without fear or the need for security.

The following week, we received a letter from the Ministry of Transportation. It was not my license, but a lovely, handwritten letter, on the Minister's personal letterhead. Amongst other beautiful comments she wrote, "It is an amazing memory I will carry with me always. Who knew an expired license could result in such an event."

After changing some bad driving habits (long enough to pass the road tests), I painlessly obtained my full license in just a few weeks. With each turn of the wheel I could not help but feel that God was "smiling" the entire way through.

Salami and Shiites

A first-hand report from the only Jewish chaplain in Iraq

Chaplain (CPT) Shlomo Shulman

It was just hours before the start of the Succot holiday, as the Blackhawk helicopter cut across the Iraqi desert, on a mission to transport important cargo. No, these were not top-secret military supplies, nor ammunition for the battle against Iraqi insurgents. Actually, it was an emergency supply of lulavs and etrogs.

As the only Jewish chaplain stationed in Iraq, life is, well, interesting. Iraq was once the pinnacle of the Jewish world — dating back 2,500 years ago when Jews were exiled from Israel after the destruction of the first Holy Temple. The Talmud was written here, and several prophets are buried here.

And now, I am leading services at the only synagogue in town. My "shul" is a prefabricated plywood building that serves as the chapel here at Camp Striker, adjacent to Baghdad International Airport, where I've been stationed since May.

After his tour of duty in Iraq, **Chaplain Shlomo Shulman**, an alumni of Aish HaTorah in Jerusalem, headed home to his wife and two daughters at Hunter Army Airfield in Savannah, Georgia, where he is stationed. Shulman grew up in Beverly Hills, graduated with a degree in journalism from San Diego State, and worked in the field of environmental education. Write to him at a.shulman@us.army.mil.

My main responsibility is to ensure every soldier's free exercise of his religion, as guaranteed by the U.S. Constitution. That means contacting Jewish soldiers and helping them with their needs — whether it be counseling, kosher food, or the question of whether it's permitted to wear regulation leather Army boots in light of the restriction against wearing leather shoes on Yom Kippur.

How many Jewish soldiers are stationed in Iraq? It's difficult to get an accurate count, because they often avoid designating their "faith group" in military databases, especially once they find out they'll be deployed to an Arab country. They may not want the word "Jewish" printed on their ID necklaces (dog tags). If they're captured in Iraq or Afghanistan, what kind of treatment could they expect?

Once a week or so, I'll ride in a Humvee up to Camp Victory, the massive military complex from which the generals run the war, using Saddam's lakefront Al-Faw Palace as their headquarters. Saddam's initials are everywhere, his egomaniacal way of making sure a conqueror would have to dismantle the whole building to erase his legacy. The place is quite ostentatious, with the second-largest chandelier in the world (after one that hangs in Buckingham Palace). Camp Victory also has an array of ornate stone and marble vacation cottages that had been reserved for Saddam's family and cronies. It's all arranged around an enormous man-made lake — the perfect location for my "congregants" and me to do the *Tashlich* service after Rosh Hashanah.

The High Holidays were really great. On Rosh Hashanah I served about 130 meals — using only a one-burner stove and without running water. We had apples dipped in honey, pomegranates, gefilte fish, and honey cakes that my wife sent from the U.S. About 40 people showed up on the first night. I had plastic flower centerpieces on the tables, and I managed to get kosher wine for *kiddush*, which was a big hit; since alcohol is strictly forbidden by the Army in Iraq, for many soldiers this was the first taste of alcohol they'd had in a long time.

How did I get here in the first place? After spending a few years learning at Aish HaTorah in Jerusalem, I'd been working in Boston on a Jewish community development project, and was looking for something different. I came across the U.S. Army Chaplaincy website late one night and sent an email for more information. From that point on, the Army recruiter handled all the details, putting me in touch with other observant Jewish chaplains. I signed up for a three-year hitch.

In January, I left my wife and two little girls in Boston and signed in at the three-month-long chaplain school at Ft. Jackson, SC. There were about 80 students, some from denominations I'd never even heard of. We learned how to interview a soldier applying to be a conscientious objector, dialogue with foreign religious leaders, request federal funds for religious programming, and other tasks of the trade. We spent weeks role-playing counseling situations, slept out in the field for several nights at a time, and had long philosophical discussions about good and evil.

Six weeks after I graduated I was on a plane to Iraq, joining the fabled Third Infantry Division's aviation brigade outside of Baghdad. My battalion consists of about 400 soldiers who maintain, fix, and fly Blackhawk helicopters, the U.S. Army's version of the minivan. Our pilots pick up and deliver everything: mail, food, medical supplies, and of course assault teams of camouflaged soldiers on missions to take out suspected terrorists or search for weapons.

At first my wife thought I was nuts. But she saw the excitement on my face and knew this is what I wanted to do. But more so, she realized the importance of helping Jews reconnect with their heritage, no matter where they're located.

I try to call home every day, but it's tough with the time difference. My joke is that Iraq is "eight hours ahead of the East Coast, but a thousand years behind." If I time my call right, I can catch my wife and kids in the car as they head to school in the morning. Then I try to call my wife again when she's by herself and have a longer conversation. We email all the time, and occasionally get to see each other on the webcam. I'll see them sitting in our home in Boston, and they're looking at an oasis of date palms behind me, while helicopters fly overhead. If someone's looking for a surreal moment, he'll find plenty here.

Jewish Networking

As the only Jewish chaplain in Iraq, I'm a bit of an oddity, to say the least. Wherever I go, I see soldiers squinting at the patch on my uniform, just above my name tag on my right chest. It's an embroidered depiction of the two tablets of the Ten Commandments, crowned by a small Star of David.

All types of Jews are in the military. Young enlisted guys barely out of their teens, women with master's degrees who fly helicopters, veterinarians (yes, the Army still has a Veterinary Corps), doctors, psychologists, lawyers, infantry foot soldiers, Arabic interpreters. We've got privates and colonels in Army, Navy, Air Force, and Marine uniforms, plus civilians working here for the U.S. State Department or private contractors. Guys with last names like O'Laughlin, McCann, and McCay, and others named Cohen, Sternberg, and Kaufman.

There's the reporter for the *Wall Street Journal*. The farm girl from Montana who is now a sergeant and eats only kosher food. And there's the Jewish grandmother from New York who is in Iraq, incongruously, to help interrogate high-value terrorist suspects.

The other day, as I stepped into the transient housing tent known as "The Stables," a young civilian standing there spotted the Ten Commandments patch and introduced himself. He said he was originally from Tennessee, but now lives in the Philippines, where he's an active congregant in one of the two synagogues there. He'd just arrived in Iraq beginning his second tour as a private "security consultant," headed to Fallujah for the next year or so. We exchanged email addresses, and I promised to put him in touch with another Jewish contractor I'd met who's working in Fallujah — a retired Denver cop teaching police tactics to Iraqi law enforcement officers. Jewish networking is alive and well here, too.

Chow Hall

"Camp" is an accurate word for our Army base. It's pretty spartan — really just a huge cluster of dusty tents, trailers, and a few plywood constructions housing about 13,000 Americans. Permanent structures are few, because U.S. policy is to give the impression that we're not in Iraq for the duration — only long enough to help the Iraqis run their own country.

A big lizard scurried in front of me today. It was the first live creature, other than humans, that I've seen in five months here. This place is so hot that nothing seems to live here. I never imagined heat like this. It's like sticking yourself into an oven set to 125 degrees. Our "tents" are actually rows and rows of CHUs ("containerized housing units"), the Army's way of describing a converted metal shipping container big enough for two people.

Have I become accustomed to life here? Well, spend enough time in 125-degree temperatures with choking sand and dust in every nook and cranny, listening to the unbelievably loud and terrifying booms of outgoing and incoming artillery rounds, as well as the round-the-clock deafening roar of helicopters flying through the sky; living in tents with a dozen other soldiers or converted metal shipping containers barely seven-feet wide; and in a bizarre way, you just get used to it.

There isn't much kosher food for me to eat in the chow hall, so I usually bring in a self-heating camping meal from a care package or a kosher MRE ("Meals, Ready to Eat") — long-life military rations. Our battalion food service officer dropped off 23 cases of them at my office not long ago, so I can never claim to go hungry.

I mainly go to the chow hall to grab a Dr Pepper and schmooze with my fellow soldiers. The chow hall is the unofficial hub of the camp, where people meet each other, seminars and promotion parties are held in the side rooms, and giant flat-panel TV sets line the walls broadcasting CNN, Fox News, and other shows taped earlier in the U.S.

More than once, a soldier has spotted my yarmulke and introduced himself as a fellow Jew. So I try to eat there at least once a day, for good visibility if nothing else.

War Routine

I am frequently reminded of the danger and tragedy of war. I've been called to assist in counseling a squad that lost three guys in one day, as well as an entire helicopter crew who witnessed a mortally wounded soldier die in the back of their aircraft.

In a counseling capacity, I often deal with guys who have reached "The Point." The Point is usually reached nine or 10 months into a deployment, when a soldier has been in some hot, dusty, nasty, inhospitable corner of the world so long he's forgotten why he's there to begin with. He takes on what the Army would define as a really bad attitude, often gets into trouble, and then I, the chaplain, am called in to help him "chill out," to use the medical term.

Above all, a chaplain needs to be a good listener. That's why I posted a translated verse from the Book of *Proverbs* on my office door: "A worry in a person's heart — he should discuss it with others."

As I write this, I'm still thinking of the soldier I spoke with yesterday, the youngest of nine children, whose father unexpectedly passed away two months ago. At age 22, he didn't have a lot of life experience and was having difficulty coping with his personal tragedy.

About 45 minutes into the conversation, I realized that he was at the verge of suicide. I asked him about it, and he said that he'd returned to his bunk just two nights before with the intention of shooting himself in the head with his Army-issued rifle. It turns out he'd forgotten to bring his ammunition with him, but if not for that detail, he'd have been dead that night.

I had him leave his weapon in the office, and we walked together down to the camp clinic where fortunately I found a psychologist friend of mine on duty. The three of us had a long conversation, and the soldier was sent to an extended group therapy retreat up north at Camp Liberty.

And then there's the time I got called to testify for a soldier stationed at a small patrol base in Baghdad, who claimed that Judaism forbade him from washing pots in which pork products had been cooked. I had to inform his superiors that, regrettably, this claim was not true. (He may have confused us with Muslims.) We later discovered the guy wasn't even Jewish — he was just looking for a creative way to get out of work. Unfortunately for him, he picked the wrong religion to pretend to belong to.

And so goes the day.

Light Unto Nations

Shabbat is the best part of the week. That's when I host services and a meal, either here at Camp Striker or at some dusty outpost my assistant and I have been flown to, joining with guys who perhaps haven't heard Hebrew or worn a *kippah* in months or even years.

I try to get everything ready on Thursdays, because no matter what time Shabbat comes in each week, no matter where you are in the world, there just doesn't seem to be enough time to get everything done. It's like a rule of life. You could be unemployed with absolutely nothing to do all day in Alaska in the summertime, and I guarantee you will be rushing to get everything ready before you have to light candles at 11 p.m.

I've received lots and lots of care packages from synagogues, Hebrew schools, and individual supporters in New York, California, and everywhere else in between — even Israel. People send prayer books, food, and all the other necessities a Jew would require while living in a plywood-lined tent without a kitchen or running water and less-than-reliable electrical power.

The Torah prophesizes that we Jews will be exiled from our land and scattered to the four corners of the earth, where our job is to find ways to spiritually elevate our surroundings and be a "light unto the nations." That's why Jews seem to be everywhere on the planet, and a U.S. Army camp in Iraq is no exception.

So while the news is filled with battles of Sunni vs. Shiite, and insurgents vs. surge, my slice of military life has more to do with scrounging for kosher salami and trying to convince non-Jewish guys from the Arkansas National Guard to help build me a *succah*.

Six Ways to Attain Misery

The sobering fact is that serenity and joy are natural states for us all. Fear not. Practiced regularly, these strategies vastly improve our odds of attaining despair.

Sol Herzig, Ph.D

Many people innocently believe that all they have to do is sit back, coast through life, and misery will come to them. Nothing could be further from the truth! The sobering fact is that serenity and joy are natural states for us all. Just observe a child at play, yourself on a favorite vacation, or anyone absorbed in creative activity. As our minds clear of clutter and negative thinking, a profound sense of peace and contentment often emerges. Does this mean there's no hope? Absolutely not! The strategies outlined below, practiced regularly, vastly improve our odds of achieving misery.

1. Cling To Entitlement

You are perfectly entitled to feelings of entitlement. It is your birthright to expect unfailing attention, loyalty, respect, and

---

Sol Herzig is a licensed psychologist with offices in Highland Park, New Jersey and Brooklyn, New York. This article was approved by his mother.

subservience from others. Contemplate the inherent, self-evident unfairness of anyone having something you want. Strive to see compromise, accommodation, patience, and responsibility as somehow relevant only to "the other guy." In general, be aware that life owes you and that you were put on this planet to collect.

2. It's All Personal

Malicious intent is always present if you just look carefully enough. This is particularly true regarding family members. Suppose your spouse overlooks one of your preferences. Seize the opportunity to view this as conclusive proof that you don't really matter to your spouse and probably never have. If your children dawdle at bedtime, see them as viciously spiteful and yourself as a sorry excuse for a parent. It's really very simple. Ignore nothing, and always assume evil intent. Remember, if you don't take things personally, no one will do it for you.

3. Focus on Problems

There is really very little sense in having problems if you don't focus on them. It's crucial therefore to keep careful track of all your problems and constantly review them. Nurture the attitude that you can't really move on to anything unless everything is resolved first. Remember also that there is no solution without a problem, if you look closely enough. Always resist the temptation to ponder where problems go when you don't think about them.

4. Magnify

Too often people cheat themselves out of misery by maintaining perspective. This is both needless as well as extremely counterproductive. Why would anyone ever want to think of themselves as "just human" when "fatally flawed" and "irredeemably warped" are available? Similarly, when recalling past mistakes, why stop at instructive regret when paralyzing guilt is within reach? Sure it requires a bit of effort, but the payoff can be enormous. Just imagine the benefits of eventually believing that your negative thinking actually reflects reality.

5. Expect Catastrophe

It is critical to remember that really terrible things can occur at any moment. Let's start with the body. Begin by paying close attention to changes in bodily sensation, no matter how trivial. Next, let your imagination run wild. Anything involving flesh-eating bacteria or intestinal parasites will usually do the trick. People sometimes protest that their bodies feel perfectly fine. Not to worry! Think "Silent Killers." Feeling perfectly fine places you squarely at risk for these. Of course, there is no reason to stop at personal health issues. The range of potential catastrophe is vast. For example, there are suitcase bombs, encroaching asteroids, global recession, pandemics, killer bees, and so on. Simply use your imagination to craft a realistic sense of impending doom. Savor the pride you'll feel on your death bed knowing that nothing ever caught you by surprise.

6. Just Say "No Thanks" to Gratitude

Gratitude is to misery what Kryptonite is to Superman. All the hard work you've invested in misery will go down the drain if you start fiddling around with gratitude. A zero-tolerance policy is very much in order. This is very challenging, however, as life runs rampant with opportunities for gratefulness. Begin, therefore, by thoroughly discounting all the good in your life as a "given." Next, focus your mind on the many ways in which life continues to disappoint you. At an advanced level, you can even learn to see the bad in the good. For instance, should you get a big raise you could immediately focus on the tax implications. Eliminate gratitude from your life and misery will be right around the corner.

A final word. The beauty of misery is that the more you share it with others, the more you wind up having. So share generously. After all, misery loves company.

A Button's Life

Everyone has a mission in life. What about me?

Rabbi Yaakov Salomon

It's not easy being a button.

For one thing, my home is a factory. It's noisy, hot, and crowded. Life for me and my fellow buttons is mostly dominated by waiting for the chance to connect to a suit.

I was born several months ago in New Delhi. They say New Delhi is nice, but I wouldn't know. I have spent 100% of my time in a huge crate, surrounded by friends of similar ilk. I simply wait . . . patiently or otherwise, to be put to use. So I don't get out much.

Some of my fellow buttons are much older than me. Many of them have already appeared on various jackets, or coats, or shirts and they guide us rookies who are still awaiting their initial foray into the *World of the Garment*. When the lights go dim in the factory each night and the button buzz begins, I listen to the veterans tell their "war stories" — getting lost after a painful separation, cracking, or sometimes just being summarily replaced. It's scary how one day you can be King of the Hill on a cashmere Burberry two-piece and the next day you could be kicked onto the tracks of a Brighton-bound D train.

For a biographical note on the author, please see page 152.

I try to stay positive. The factory is busy. Every morning the tailors and seamstresses file in and do their thing. I just sit and wait and watch and hope.

Will today be the day? When will I be chosen? How long must I wait, watching my friends being picked out, sewn on, and fulfilling their special purpose in life?

Wow! Look at that! My friend was just affixed to a gorgeous, beige, silk chiffon evening gown. She looks so proud. I am so happy for her. She'll go to the nicest places and mingle with the "upscale" crowd. That's what she always wanted.

Me? I'm just a dark navy, natural material, genuine horn suit button. Sometimes I wish I was a shiny brass snap or a zinc alloy or a pewter buckle or maybe one of those adorable, hip, pink toggles. But let's face it. I'm not. I'm just not. That doesn't mean I don't have an important role to play. Yes, one day my time *will* come. I'm sure of it.

One Month Later

It was late one Wednesday afternoon. I had spent the day like most others ... waiting. At least 30 buttons from my crate had been selected. That's a lot of goodbyes for one day. To say I didn't feel sad would be a lie. And then it happened. *Whoosh!* I felt myself lifted with a sudden burst of energy and cradled into the softest hand I could ever imagine.

"So this is what it's like," I mumbled to myself. I didn't know whether to laugh or cry. I think I did both. I knew I'd miss my friends and my home, but at last I'd be somebody. I would have purpose, a mission.

Raj, the tailor, was quick but precise. He had just finished what seemed like a wool blazer for a small boy and was preparing to adorn it with three front buttons. I waited my turn next to the sewing machine without making a sound. I watched Raj carefully place the first button on. If not for the cacophony of the machinery, the whole plant would have heard my pounding heartbeat.

Raj lifted the button beside me and gently secured it in the second position — about two inches below the top button. The anticipation was overwhelming. And then ... out of nowhere ... it hit me! I was going to be placed in position number three! After all my waiting, after all the dreams and hopes, I was suddenly designated for the useless, barren wasteland of bottom buttonhood.

In my excitement at finally being chosen, I had totally forgotten about "the curse." The bottom button is just there for show. It is never closed, never used, and usually never noticed. It lays dormant for the lifespan of the garment and gets tossed away when the jacket dies. What kind of life is that?

Raj ran the needle and thread through my broken heart and perfectly centered me to life imprisonment. Life had just begun and it was already over. I simply hung in place — useless. What choice did I have in the matter?

I endured several weeks of storage and transport and eventually made my way to a rack in a small boys' shop in Baltimore. The customers were nice enough, the prospects for finding a warm and loving home seemed reasonable. I made peace with my position in life, but understood that true fulfillment would, sadly, be unattainable.

One day a mother and son arrived and asked to see a blazer that totally fit my description. The lady wore fancy jewelry and expensive shoes, and the boy walked with a kind of swagger that made him look older than he probably was. I began picturing a life that might be comfortable, even lavish, albeit unrealized. I said a silent prayer, hoping that they would make me part of their family. Mom surveyed the aisle and actually took me off the hanger.

"Try this one on, David," she offered. My heart was pounding again. I liked the name David and I was desperate to find someplace I could call home. But alas, I was the wrong size. David must like burgers and pancakes. Even buttons one and two were in danger of popping. I, of course, was never even attempted. Sadly, I returned to my perch.

Later that afternoon I noticed another mother/son tandem enter the store. This woman looked rather plain. Her clothes were neat but haphazard, and I wasn't sure what to make of her son. His features were different than most kids. His eyes were slightly slanted upward and his nose seemed small, almost flat. His ears were small too. But his smile was beautiful. He didn't talk much, and when he did his words were sort of garbled.

Mr. Rabinowitz steered them in my direction. Again my hopes rose, but they were filled with conflict. I wasn't sure if this was the harbor I had always dreamed of docking my ship at.

Mom was checking the price tags on the jackets in the corner, but the boy seemed to be staring right at me.

"Stay close to Mommy, sweetheart. You'll get lost over there," she beckoned.

But Sweetheart paid no heed. He lumbered his way right in front of my section and with a mind very much his own, clutched me and my jacket and clumsily dropped us to the floor.

"You're making a mess," Mom quietly said, taking him by the hand and drawing him close.

I felt bad for Sweetheart. He wasn't trying to misbehave. He was just trying to be independent. Meanwhile I lay on the floor awaiting retrieval. Mr. Rabinowitz was nowhere in sight. I wondered how much time I'd have to stay on the cold floor, but not for long. Here was Sweetheart, breaking loose from his mother's grasp and running toward me again. This time he successfully nestled the jacket in his soft hands and began to put his arms through the sleeves.

Having completed his mission, a huge grin appeared on his face. He looked absolutely adorable. With the pride of a foreign ambassador, Sweetheart marched himself over to a nearby mirror. Mom noticed him from across the way and with familiar resignation strode toward him. She closed buttons one and two and seemed to give the possibility some serious consideration. As usual, I simply waited.

She turned to find Mr. Rabinowitz and left us alone for just an instant. It was all he needed. Sweetheart took a confident gaze into the mirror and reached down to my neighborhood. I thought I would shriek from exhilaration. Sweetheart fumbled me in his sweaty palms. I thought he might yank me across the room. It took a few seconds, but it really happened. *He closed me.* Me! Button number three — the useless one!

Mr. Rabinowitz came over and tried to teach Sweetheart proper style and etiquette. He undid me once ... twice ... but Sweetheart was having none of it. Mom made a few attempts too, but my new friend had his mind made up. I would not be left out. Ever.

We made our way to the checkout counter, but Sweetheart and I would not part. He insisted on wearing the jacket home — buttoned: one, two, *and* three.

Sweetheart loved that jacket and wore it whenever he could. And when he outgrew it . . . he just wore it anyway — as long as he could.

Yes, Sweetheart loved that jacket.

And I loved Sweetheart.

A Drop of Wisdom

The Greatness of Rabbi Noach Weinberg zt"l

Rav Noach took responsibility for the entire Jewish people.

Rabbi Eric Coopersmith

The day after my beloved rebbe, Rabbi Noach Weinberg, the founder and Rosh Yeshivah of Aish HaTorah, was diagnosed with a very aggressive, lethal form of lung cancer, we were meeting in his office. He stood up, and after pausing for a few moments, turned to me and said, "I am just not ready to quit fighting for *Klal Yisrael*. If the Almighty calls me home, I am personally ready to go, but I just don't see anyone else who is going to step into the fray and fight the fight that needs to be fought."

This conversation encapsulates what drove the Rosh Yeshivah zt"l. It was never about him — at all. Rav Noach's only desire was what was best for *Klal Yisrael*. With every fiber of his being, he wanted to fight, work, create and find ways to empower the Jewish

---

Rabbi Eric Coopersmith is CEO of Aish International. Originally from Toronto, Eric received rabbinic ordination from Aish HaTorah and the Chief Rabbi of Jerusalem. In 1996 he became CEO, working closely with Rabbi Noach Weinberg *zt"l* to develop strategy and manpower for Aish International and the Jerusalem Yeshiva. He was formerly the North American director of the Discovery Seminars, and compiled Aish's *kiruv* primer, *The Eye of a Needle*. In addition to administrative duties, he is also a lecturer at Yeshiva Aish HaTorah and the Executive Learning Center.

People to accomplish its purpose of being a Light unto the Nations.

During the 14 months that the Rosh Yeshivah was sick, he suffered from many painful, even debilitating, ailments that were brought on by the cancer and the various treatments he underwent. At times, he was in excruciating physical pain. For several months he was unable to lie down because of terrible back pain, and was forced to sleep sitting up in a chair. Although these pains were physically devastating, to him they were trivial compared to the pain of being unable to actively lead Aish HaTorah in its fight against assimilation and the physical threats facing *Klal Yisrael*.

According to the calendar, he died one week before his 79th birthday. But all who knew him know he died a very young and vigorous man. He had accomplished so much. His brother Rav Yaakov Weinberg *zt"l*, the Rosh Yeshivah of Ner Yisroel in Baltimore, once said that his brother Rav Noach had done more for the Jewish people than anyone else in this generation. He built an international organization that touches the lives of one million people a year. Tens of thousands of people are today Torah observant because of his groundbreaking efforts, but if you met him, you could make the mistake of thinking he was just starting out. He was so hungry, so passionate, so frustrated at not being able to do more. You never would have believed that this was a man who had so many accomplishments to his credit.

Many men half his age could not keep up with him. There were many times that I would tell him, "I have to leave the office now because I am so completely overwhelmed with the responsibilities and the plans that you want to implement."

His fire did not come from the desire to accomplish great things. If that were the case, he could have become complacent long ago. What drove him was the desire to fulfill the Almighty's will, which meant *Tikkun Olam*, repairing the world. Since the world was not yet perfected, we could not rest. There was still plenty of work that needed to be done to accomplish our goal.

Taking Responsibility

During the planning for Aish HaTorah's Partners Conference this past December, the Rosh Yeshivah insisted that the conference articulate two very basic but profound concepts. The first was, "If you take real responsibility to do the will of God, you will succeed." And the second was, "If you really care, then you will take responsibility." This was the engine that drove the Rosh Yeshivah, and this is why he wanted these concepts clearly expressed at the last conference. This was the Rosh Yeshivah; he took responsibility and did so because to him every Jew was family.

I believe the Rosh Yeshivah's role model was Sara Schneirer, the woman who founded the Bais Yaakov school system for girls. He loved to tell over the story about Rav Chatzkel Sarna, the former Rosh Yeshivah of Chevron, who while speaking at a *bris* attended by many *Roshei Yeshivahs* and leading rabbis, challenged them saying, "I know each one of you here thinks that it was either their father or their grandfather who did the most for *Klal Yisrael* in the last 100 years. But I am here to tell you that that all of you are wrong. Not only that, but the person who did the most for *Klal Yisrael* was an uneducated Jew who could not even learn a page of Talmud. And furthermore, when I tell you the person's name, you will all agree with me. That person is Sara Schneirer."

The Rosh Yeshivah would explain, what drove her? What enabled her to merit making such a far-reaching transformation in *Klal Yisrael* that even the leading rabbis of that time did not initiate? The Rosh Yeshivah would explain that in Sara Schneirer's diary, she told over her secret. She was a seamstress, and young Jewish girls from observant homes would come to her to have their clothing made. She would talk to them and see up close how far away they really were from Torah and mitzvot, and she would cry for them saying, "Although I clothe their bodies, what will be with them if they have no mitzvot to clothe their souls?"

The Rosh Yeshivah would then tell everyone and anyone who would listen that this is the ultimate key. If you want something bad enough, so badly that you are willing to cry for it, then you will undertake the responsibility, and the Almighty will give you the heavenly assistance to accomplish it.

The Rosh Yeshivah, more than anything else, stressed the importance of taking responsibility. I once showed him something from Rav Chaim Shmulevitz's zt"l *Sichos Mussar* that gave him an enormous amount of pleasure. In his essay on responsibility, Rav Shmulevitz says that responsibility is the measure of a person. Therefore a king has the highest standing among the Jewish people because he is taking the most responsibility for *Klal Yisrael*.

But this level of responsibility is not limited to those who are formally appointed king. Rav Shmulevitz asked, how is it possible for Esther to tell Mordechai, the leading rabbi of his generation, to organize a fast on Passover? If it was the right thing to do, then why didn't Mordechai initiate it himself? And if it was the wrong thing to do, why did he listen to her? Rav Shmulevitz explains that the sentence in the Book of *Esther* says that "Esther wore the raiment of a queen." This does not refer to just her clothing, but to her character as well. Since she was now taking complete responsibility for the well-being of the Jewish people, she attained the status of a queen, and therefore it was fitting for her to initiate the fast and instruct Mordechai to implement it.

The Rosh Yeshivah took responsibility for the entire Jewish people. This was his true greatness.

Torah Genius

In addition to the Rosh Yeshivah's concern for *Klal Yisrael* and sense of responsibility was his Torah genius. He had the unique gift of being able to take the timeless principles of Torah, distill them to their essence, and then develop unbelievably creative ways of explaining and illustrating these concepts to the most uninitiated Jews, in a way that would show them the profound depth and relevance of traditional Torah and Judaism. He wrote curriculums that accomplished this purpose. *The 48 Ways to Wisdom*, based on the *mishnah* in the sixth *perek* of *Pirkei Avos*; *The Five Levels of Pleasure*, based on the first paragraph of the *Shema*; *The Six Constant Mitzvot*;

his Foundations Materials that present a comprehensive overview of Jewish philosophy and thought — they were all incredibly original in their presentation, but completely anchored to the chain of tradition.

I believe his greatest accomplishment was his belief in the powers of an individual. He took at face value the *mishnah* in *Pirkei Avos* that said, "Cherished is man for he is created in the image of God." Who else could take a group of completely disenfranchised young Jewish men, most of whom could not read *aleph-beis*, many of them quite antagonistic to religion in general and Judaism in particular, and see within these young men the members of an organization he wanted to create? Many religious Jews would cross the street if they saw these fellows walking down their block. The Rosh Yeshivah was undaunted by their physical appearance. Not only did he see their souls and their thirsting for Torah Judaism, but he believed in them. He believed in their sense of idealism, and that they, together with him, could change the world.

To all of us who are involved with Aish HaTorah, that was his greatest gift — to give us the privilege of being able to join him in making a difference for our people.

This is his lasting legacy, and I am 100% convinced that the message he wants us to learn from his passing is that we all have a responsibility to fight for the Jewish people, and that all of us, with God's help, can make that difference.

His loss is devastating. Rav Noach was one-of-a-kind and is completely irreplaceable. The only way to translate this into something positive is if each of us hears this message. He told me many times that he hoped his passing would enable us to hear this message in a way that we were unable to while he was alive. If we do, this will be the greatest gift that we can give to him.

I Am a Wall

The magic formula to giving others the support they need.

Sara Yoheved Rigler

I sat in the car, parked at the end of the trail, nervously waiting for my children. We usually did family hikes, but the Yehudiya, Israel's most popular hike, is "for experienced hikers only," with several steep ascents. That disqualified me. Our 19-year-old daughter Pliyah and 13-year-old son Yisrael were anxious to do the hike, so my husband and I decided to let them go by themselves. My husband had dropped the kids off at the trailhead at 10 that morning. Now, at 4 p.m., allowing extra time for a hike that was supposed to take five hours, I started to worry.

I couldn't phone them because they had purposely not taken their cell phones. The trail cuts off at the top of an 8-meter waterfall. The hiker has to jump into the large, deep pool below, swim across, and resume the trail on the other side. Only water-friendly devices survive.

I recited *Psalms*, trying to remain calm, but after 40 minutes of waiting, I left the car by the locked roadblock and started to walk along the trail from the end. I had been walking less than five minutes

---

For a biographical note on the author, please see page 29.

when I spotted a figure coming toward me. It was my son Yisrael. He was alone.

My heart clutched in fear. *What had happened to Pliyah?* I ran toward Yisrael, frantically shouting, "Where's Pliyah? What happened to Pliyah!?"

Yisrael assured me that Pliyah was okay, then quickly amended his statement. "She's not injured. She's stuck on the trail. We were climbing the last, steep part of the trail, and we got to this place where you have to go straight up, even more than straight up, like the rock comes out toward you, and Pliyah was too scared to keep going. I tried to help her, I showed her exactly where to put her foot, I begged her to try, but she refused. We spent a long time on that narrow ledge. She finally told me to go ahead without her and get help."

I raced back to the car and found the National Park brochure. At the bottom, in large print, was the EMERGENCY TELEPHONE NUMBER. I dialed and tried to explain to the park ranger, who was obviously used to panicked calls from desperate mothers, that my daughter was marooned on the side of a cliff. He noted our location and told us he would send help right away.

I sat there nervously trying to figure out how they were going to get a 5'10" girl weighing 135 pounds up the side of a rather sheer cliff. Five minutes later two uniformed men in a pickup truck pulled up. In the back of the pickup were a stretcher, a huge coil of thick rope, and some metal hooks. Apparently they were going to put my daughter into the stretcher and somehow pull it up the cliff, an operation fraught with its own dangers.

As one of the rangers unlocked the roadblock, he asked me if my daughter was injured.

"No, just scared." I asked if I could go with them.

"No, you and your son stay here," the ranger replied. "We'll take care of your daughter. Don't worry." Then, looking at the Book of *Psalms* I was clutching, he added, "You just pray."

Having the rescue personnel tell me to pray was less than reassuring, but pray I did. An eternity later, the pickup returned, with my daughter smiling in the back.

Amid hugs, tears, and thanks to the rangers, I got my children into our car. On the way back to our Golan cabin, I asked Pliyah how they had managed to get her in the stretcher up the cliff.

"They didn't use the stretcher," she replied. "I climbed up myself."

"Y-y-you climbed up yourself?" I was stunned. "But I thought you were too scared?"

"I was," Pliyah explained. "But the two guys came to where I was, and the taller guy stood right behind me and said, *'Ani homa. Ta'ali.* I am a wall. Go up.' And I realized that if I fell back, I would fall on him. So I wasn't scared any more, and I just climbed up. No problem."

"I am a wall. Go up." What was this magic formula that had turned my daughter's fear into confidence and propelled her upward?

Times of Paralysis

Life is a trail. When a person has undergone a devastating divorce, or given birth to a special-needs child, or received a dreaded diagnosis, or gone bankrupt, or suffered a death in the family, that person may be too paralyzed to move forward.

We, the friends or relatives, want to be helpful. But the person's predicament is so complicated or the loss so severe, that pulling the person up the cliff would require far more rope and much more strength than we possess. So, despairing of our own ability to rescue him or her, we slither away.

I have a friend whose 21-year-old daughter was killed in a terror attack. In the wake of the murder, our community responded with an outpouring of love and support. Three months later, however, my friend mentioned to me that one of her oldest, dearest friends was avoiding her. This friend, who lives far away, visited every year on the holiday of Succot, but the past Succot she had neither come nor called. I was sure this bereaved mother was misreading the situation. Then she told me that as she walked through the narrow lanes of our Old City neighborhood, she often saw neighbors in the distance coming toward her, and then she'd see them abruptly duck into an intersecting lane in order to avoid meeting her.

This phenomenon is, in fact, widespread, and is discussed in the psychological literature. People are at a loss for what to say, or are so afraid of saying the wrong thing and making matters worse, that they avoid the victim of tragedy exactly when their support is most needed. They labor under the fallacy that their job is to pull the person up the cliff, and since this is humanly impossible, their sense of helplessness drives them to cruel avoidance.

From the Israeli park ranger I learned a different way: To stand firmly behind the person and say, in words or even with silence, "I am a wall. I'm here for you. You are capable of going up." That may give them the courage to take the next step whenever they are ready.

This means relinquishing the role of the Great Rescuer. It means not philosophizing, not offering unsolicited advice, and not questioning the choices they have made. ("Why did you choose chemo without even trying alternative therapy?" "I wish you had seen Dr. Miracle the Marriage Counselor before going for a divorce.") It means not patronizing with pity. ("I'm so sorry your baby is impaired." "I'm so sorry your financial reverses mean you can't send your son to the same school this year.")

For those afraid of saying the wrong thing, here's a four-word formula that never goes wrong: "I'm here for you." And mean it.

My friend Shoshana Leibman is an exemplar of the I Am a Wall approach. When everyone in our community was reeling because a mother of many children had been diagnosed with a serious illness, Shoshana walked into their house and announced. "I'm here. Give me laundry to fold."

Of course, to be a wall for another person, you yourself have to be strong, not in muscles but in faith. You must absolutely believe the foundations of Judaism:

- That everything (including what is painful and challenging) comes from God.
- That everything (including what is painful and challenging) is for our ultimate benefit.
- That everything (especially what is painful or challenging) is an opportunity for spiritual growth.

In addition to faith in God, you must also have faith in the other person's ability to go up. Tamar was 51 years old when her husband walked out on her and their four children. Suddenly, she had to support the family, but she had not worked in her field for the last 20 years that she was raising children. Recently she called her friend Cookie and told her, "You were the only one who had faith in me that I could go back to school and catch up with the changes in my profession. Now I'm almost ready to rejoin the workforce. I couldn't have done it without your faith in me."

Barbara and her husband Josh are baseball enthusiasts. After six years of waiting, they gave birth to a baby with Down syndrome. Barbara was shattered with disappointment and, yes, embarrassment. The next day, her sister Hannah arrived at the hospital bearing a large bouquet with a note reading: "I thought you two were good Little League players, but apparently God thinks you're ready for the Major Leagues." Then Hannah sat next to Barbara's bed for four hours. The first two hours, Barbara cried, while Hannah held the newborn and said nothing at all. Slowly, gradually, Barbara and Josh started to move forward, searching for websites of organizations that deal with babies with Down's and talking about the *bris*.

When Hannah left, Josh said, "Thanks for coming. You helped us a lot."

Hannah protested, "I barely said anything."

Walls specialize in silent support ....

In an Instant

That's how long it can take for our lives to be dramatically changed.

Emuna Braverman

A number of years ago, I read Lee and Bob Woodruff's book, *In An Instant,* the moving and revealing story of how their lives were affected when an IED went off near the tank Bob was riding in while embedded with the US military in Iraq. The book contains many tales of perseverance, of kindness, and of what marriage, family, and friends really mean.

What I want to focus on now is the title, *In An Instant*. The book has taken up semi-permanent residence in our home and I find myself frequently confronted by the title, *In An Instant*. And it makes me reflect. Our lives can be changed — dramatically so — in an instant. It focuses me on how precious and important even a

---

Emuna Braverman has a law degree from the University of Toronto and a Master's in Clinical Psychology with an emphasis on Marriage and Family Therapy from Pepperdine University. She lives with her husband and nine children in Los Angeles where they both work for Aish HaTorah. When she isn't writing for the Internet or taking care of her family, Emuna teaches classes on Judaism, organizes gourmet kosher cooking groups, and hosts many Shabbos guests. She is the cofounder of www.gourmetkoshercooking.com and the author of *A Diamond for Your Daughter — A Parent's Guide to Navigating Shidduchim Effectively*, available through Judaica Press

nanosecond can be. And how we need to maintain our alertness and consciousness even for the briefest of instants.

Someone I know described how she briefly turned around to hand her child a drink in the car and hit a pedestrian crossing the street. An engineer turned away momentarily to text some friends and, in an instant, caused a massive train wreck. In a drunken instant a broker may move millions of dollars to the wrong investment and bankrupt himself and his company. In an instant, some fanatic can put their finger on the trigger of a nuclear warhead and destroy the lives of thousands of civilians.

Instants matter. And it's not just in other people's lives, in other people's stories. In an instant we may utter hurtful words that ruin friendships, careers, marriages — words that can't be taken back. In an instant we can say something demeaning to our children, a harsh line of criticism that may cause serious damage to their sense of self. In an instant, we can give the wrong advice to a friend and grave harm may result. In an instant, we may turn our head away and not see that child run into the street.

Lives are shaped by those instants. And it's hard to be constantly vigilant. But the *yetzer hara* — that part of us that tries to trip us up and lower ourselves — lies in wait for those lax moments and we need to be ever battle-ready. In fact, we need to be proactive — on guard, on hyper-alert — and take initiative in a *positive* direction.

After all, it's not just negative situations or behaviors that occur in an instant. Positive differences can be made in an instant as well.

In an instant, our smile can brighten someone's day. In an instant, our "Good morning" can make another person feel noticed. In an instant, our "How are you?" can show a fellow human being we care. In an instant, we can pick up papers that someone else dropped. In an instant, we can put change in someone's meter so they don't get a ticket. In (slightly more than) an instant, we can help carry someone's groceries to their car. In an instant, we can hold open a door or give up a seat or let someone with two items in front of us in line. In an instant, we can invite a new acquaintance to join us for an evening out. In an instant, we can make a lifelong commitment to marriage. In an instant, we can say "I love you" — and mean it.

In an instant, we can say thank you to the Almighty for all the blessings He has given us.

Instants are powerful. We shouldn't dismiss them or treat them cavalierly. Lives — ours and those around us — can be changed — in an instant.

Oblivious to the Music

Would you notice one of the world's greatest violinists playing in the midst of rush hour?

Bassi Gruen

What would happen if one of the greatest violinists alive, playing on a Stradivarius worth several million dollars, was plunked into the sterile environment of a Washington D.C. metro station at the height of morning rush hour? Would anyone stop to listen? Would anyone recognize the genius, the soaring beauty of the playing?

Gene Weingarten, a *Washington Post* staff writer, was determined to find out.

The idea was born two years ago, when Weingarten left a crowded metro station and noticed a ragged-looking man playing the keyboard. The musician was quite good, but he was receiving virtually no notice. Looking at the amorphous mass of humanity rushing by, Weingarten felt a surge of anger. The thought crossed his mind that even the greatest of musicians wouldn't be able to touch

---

Bassi Gruen is a licensed social worker and a professional writer. She's published hundreds of articles in numerous Jewish publications. Bassi is the author of *A Mother's Musings* (ArtScroll/Mesorah) a collection of stories about the challenges and joys, the fears and the hopes of motherhood. She lives with her husband, her children, and her dreams in Beitar Illit.

these rushing creatures. But he decided to test his hypothesis before indicting the public.

The result was an intriguing social experiment. Weingarten approached Joshua Bell, one of the finest classical musicians in the world. Bell, 39, is a consummate violinist who plays before awestruck crowds across the globe. His instrument is a violin crafted by Antonio Stradivari in 1713, at the end of the Italian master's career. Bell purchased the violin at an auction several years ago, for 3.5 million dollars. Bell and his violin are musical mastery at its absolute height.

Bell acquiesced to the request with surprising ease. Finding a venue proved more difficult, as metro laws forbid busking, but Weingarten overcame this obstacle when he discovered a station with an indoor arcade owned by a private company. The owner graciously agreed to allow the experiment to take place. The stage was set.

On Jan. 12, 2007, at 7:51 on a Friday morning, Bell, dressed in jeans, a long-sleeved T-shirt, and a Washington Nationals baseball cap, opened his violin case, threw a few dollars in as seed money, and began to play. The pieces he performed were not popular, well-known ditties. They were complex, breathtaking masterpieces that have endured for centuries. Bell put his heart and soul into his music, coaxing pristine, resonant notes from his instrument. He played six pieces in 43 minutes.

During that time, 1,097 people walked by the virtuoso.

Seven stopped to hear the music for more than a minute.

Twenty-seven tossed in some money while hurrying on.

The rest rushed by, oblivious.

Weingarten wrote up the results of his experiment early April in the *Washington Post*, two days before Joshua Bell accepted the Avery Fisher Prize, the greatest honor a classical musician in America can receive.

And the reactions poured in. "This story got the largest and most global response of anything I have ever written, for any publication," remarked Weingarten. Over 1,000 comments came from around the globe. More than ten percent of the readers wrote that the article made them cry. Cry for the deadened souls that couldn't stop to appreciate the beauty that surrounded them. Cry for the lost moments, the opportunities that slip through our hands never to return. Cry for the rush of life which sucks up the essence of life itself.

Like the vast majority of readers, I found myself contemplating how I would have reacted had I been at the L'Enfant Plaza station in D.C. that Friday morning. *Surely*, I thought, *I would have noticed the brilliant music, even if I was rushing past on my way to work. How could I not have been one of the select few who grasped that this musician, this music, was different?*

I didn't have long to ponder. A pressing doctor's appointment pulled me away from my computer screen. I gathered up my jacket and purse, and raced half a block to catch the next bus. Rushing down the familiar street, I was surrounded by the tantalizing beauty of spring. To my left, an apple tree was just beginning to bud, the small sapling crowned with a shower of delicate white blossoms. Further along, a garden boasted irises in full bloom, their deep purple heads nodding in the soft breeze. Above, fluffy clouds raced each other on a blindingly blue sky.

But, in my haste that morning, I saw none of it. I was deaf to the music surrounding me on all sides.

Hacked

I contacted the scammer in Nigeria who stole my email account and he actually replied.

Rabbi Benjamin Blech

Last week I was viciously assaulted.

No, this wasn't a physical attack. And I've since discovered I wasn't the only one to suffer the horrific consequences of a new kind of criminality made possible by modern technology.

What was stolen from me was not my money but my identity. I have no idea how it was done. As part of the generation who still remembers using the old Remington Royal typewriter, computer language is geek to me and Google is a miracle that totally transcends my understanding. But I've come to treasure my email and wonder how I ever got along with the snail mail of stamps and postal service. I love how I can reach out to all of my contacts with just a touch of the keyboard — or at least I did until I discovered that someone could somehow steal my password, reach out to all the people I know, and tell them whatever suits his nefarious purpose.

I first began to suspect something was wrong when I could no longer access my account. Next thing I knew, people called my home to commiserate and ask for more details. From them we learned the text of the e-mail sent out in my name.

For a biographical note on the author, please see page 77.

It was a brilliant scam. With a header that had but one word, *trouble*, it briefly laid out the following scenario, a pastiche of lies that might readily pass as true:

"Hi, apologies for having to reach out to you like this, but I made a quick trip two days ago, to London, United Kingdom and had my bag stolen from me with my passport and credit cards in it. The embassy is willing to help by authorizing me to fly without my passport, I just have to pay for a ticket and settle hotel bills. Unfortunately, I can't have access to funds without my credit card, I've made contact with my bank but they need more time to come up with a new one. I was thinking of asking you to lend me some quick funds that I can give back as soon as I get in. I really need to be on the next available flight. I can forward you details on how you can get money to me. You can reach me via email *(and here the thief inserted an email address very similar to mine but with an added letter which would go directly to him, enabling him to "verify" his request)* or hotel's desk phone, *(and here the thief had an actual number in England which went either to an accomplice of his or was rerouted to Nigeria, his home base, which I subsequently discovered by a careful analysis of his email)*. Waiting for response. Thanks."

The man who stole my identity was hoping for about $2000 from at least a few of the hundreds of people on my contact list, which he assumed included friends who care enough about my well-being to help me in a time of desperate need.

This time he got nothing. Many of my friends were aware of the scam. Others called my home to make certain it was not a fraud and had their suspicions confirmed.

But the most amazing part of the story is something that followed. Perhaps foolishly, I decided to try to take on the mastermind of this international scheme. My friends advised me to drop the matter but I wouldn't listen.

I realized I had a way of directly "speaking" to the thief. My slightly altered email address was the one that obviously went directly to him. So I wrote him a note.

I told him that he had crossed a very serious line in his criminal activities and that he must be aware that there are consequences to his evil deeds. I said that in my lifetime I very often felt things intuitively and now there is one thing I know beyond any measure of doubt — he would be stricken both financially and physically in the near future as a consequence of his actions. For whatever good it might do, I felt my words might at the very least be a goad to his conscience, if not implant a small measure of fear for the results of his misdeeds.

A few hours later, incredibly enough, I received a response. The hacker, the Nigerian con man, actually answered me!

Yes, he was sorry that he caused me pain, he said. And yes, he too agreed that there is a God Who is aware of what he did. But he assured me that God is a God of love Who will continue to love him no matter what he does. He has no reason to be afraid since he will be forgiven for all sins, no matter their severity.

It was a stunning example of the danger implicit in a theology that proclaims divine love as the sole and supreme rule of the universe. If evildoers need never fear heavenly retribution they can merrily go on their way content in their knowledge that they have carte blanche from God for their wicked behavior. A God Who loves us no matter what we do in the end becomes more than a friend; in fact, for the truly evil, he is an accomplice.

Judaism is far more demanding. Jews are judged on the scale of deeds, weighing good actions against the bad and carefully keeping count of all of our activities. Forgiveness is not an undeserved gift from God; Jews are required to do *teshuvah*, a threefold process of repentance that necessitates recognition of guilt, remorse for the past, and a firm commitment never to repeat the sin in the future. And if one's actions caused harm to another, the fourth step requires seeking forgiveness from the wronged party. According to Judaism, forgiveness is not given, it is earned.

I won't be corresponding with my hacker anymore. I've said my piece. I know why he is not concerned. But I'm truly grateful that he hasn't really stolen my identity. He hasn't begun to grasp what I know from my Jewish heritage, that precisely because God loves me so much He holds me accountable for my actions. In that way He permits me to realize my greatest potential — not simply to *get* but to *earn* His love.

The Lights on the Tree

A Jewish family comes home to discover their house festooned with holiday lights.

Jonathan Rosenblum

Rabbi Berel Wein was once invited to a meeting with the editor of the *Detroit Free Press*. After introductions had been made, the editor told him the following story.

His mother, Mary, had immigrated to America from Ireland as an uneducated, 18-year-old peasant girl. She was hired as a domestic maid by an observant Jewish family. The head of the house was the president of the neighboring Orthodox shul.

Mary knew nothing about Judaism and had probably never met a Jew before arriving in America. The family went on vacation during Mary's first December in America, leaving Mary alone in the house. They were scheduled to return on the night of December 24, and Mary realized that there would be no tree to greet them when they did. This bothered her greatly, and using the money the family had left her, she went out and purchased not only a fine fir tree but all kinds of festive decorations to hang on the front of the house.

Jonathan Rosenblum is the author of eight biographies of modern Jewish leaders, and a regular columnist with *The Jerusalem Post* and a host of Anglo-Jewish magazines and weeklies around the world. He is a graduate of the University of Chicago and Yale Law School. He lives in Jerusalem.

When the family returned from vacation, they saw the tree through the living room window and the rest of the house festooned with holiday lights. They assumed that they had somehow pulled into the wrong driveway and drove around the block. But alas, it was their address.

The head of the family entered the house contemplating how to explain the tree and lights to the members of the shul, most of whom walked right past his house on their way to services. Meanwhile, Mary was eagerly anticipating the family's excitement when they realized that they would not be without their holiday tree.

After entering the house, the head of the family called Mary into his study. He told her, "In my whole life no one has ever done such a beautiful thing for me as you did." Then he took out a $100 bill — a very large sum in the middle of the Depression — and gave it to her. Only after that did he explain that Jews do not observe this day.

When he had finished telling the story, the editor told Rabbi Wein, "And that is why there has never been an editorial critical of Israel in the *Detroit Free Press* since I became editor, and never will be as long as I am the editor."

The shul president's reaction to Mary's mistake — sympathy instead of anger — was not because he dreamed that one day her son would the editor of a major metropolitan paper, and thus in a position to aid Israel. (Israel was not yet born.) He acted as he did because it was the right thing to do.

That's what it means to be a *Kiddush Hashem*, to sanctify God's Name. It is a goal to which we can all strive.

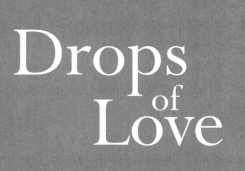

Drops of Love

Father of the Bride

We were marrying off our eldest daughter. Why was I feeling so much pain?

Rabbi Ephraim Shore

I don't cry.
 Or rather: I never used to cry. Until my daughter got engaged.
 When Yael announced that she was getting married, that she'd found the man with whom she wanted to spend her life and build a family, my wife and I were naturally thrilled.

But no sooner had I absorbed the wonderful joy of this news than something else crept up from behind, circled in front, and slammed me in the stomach.

Was this pain I was feeling? Or love? Could it be sadness? For some reason, there was a tinge of mourning. Where was this coming from? I didn't know, but it sure packed a mean punch.

Now generally speaking, I'm not an emotional guy. I pride myself in taking the level-headed approach to life.

Yet for three days straight, I could hardly sleep. I found myself crying myself to an uneasy sleep, then waking in the middle of the night and wandering the house with nothing to comfort me until I opened up Yael's photo album and sobbed over her pictures until they got soggy.

For a biographical note on the author, please see page 108.

I couldn't quite place this unexpected and seemingly irrational reaction but it felt sad and sweet all at the same time. And really deep.

I felt that in some way I was losing my daughter. I was losing my gorgeous little baby (overnight, she reverted to being about one year old again). Memories I hadn't remembered in years flooded through me in Technicolor detail, with heart-wrenching violin accompaniment: Yael smiling in her crib after her nap, Yael in the puddles after a rain overshadowed by a huge umbrella, Yael holding our hands on a path in a forest, Yael riding in her stroller, Yael stuffing her face with popcorn, Yael lighting Chanukah candles, and thousands of nights saying the *Shema* together and kissing her to sleep while singing her personalized Yael-songs.

It was all so over-the-top mushy it was approaching the ridiculous. But what did that matter? My mind was no longer in control — my emotions had taken over the reins and were dancing gleefully through me at breakneck speed and intensity.

And I felt it wasn't just my daughter I was losing. The whole fabric of my family was about to change. My beautiful, precious family, all with their own beds under one cozy roof, was going to be shattered, ended, never to return — EVER.

And thrown into the mix was the feeling of my own life moving on. This wonderful stage that had lasted for 20 years was now radically altering. *But I don't want it to end!!*

Then I got better. For a while. The excitement and energy of wedding arrangements took over and I was chugging away in my usual action-mode, coping in the traditional manner with this happy time of our lives.

Then suddenly the day of the wedding was around the corner and the waves of emotion returned in full force, swells that surged and ebbed without warning. I began to fear the wedding — the *chuppah* was liable to become an embarrassing tsunami if I didn't get a grip on myself.

(Don't get me wrong. My son-in-law is a wonderful young man and none of this had anything to do with him.)

I spoke to friends who had married off their daughters and I discovered a secret phenomenon. I was not alone. I had uncovered the father-marrying-off-his-first-kid-and-she's-a-girl syndrome. Why had no one warned me of this before?

This seems unique to fathers. On some subterranean level we sense the tectonic movements taking place in the relationship; my daughter's orbit is shifting to another man.

My case was not all that extreme. One friend confided that from the night before his daughter's wedding until the end of the week of *Sheva Berachot* celebrations, he didn't stop crying. Another said he could hardly speak to his son-in-law for a month. Another described bawling his eyes out uncontrollably at the *bedekin* (veiling) ceremony.

But they also consoled me with some reassuring news. They discovered that they didn't really lose their daughter and eventually things got wonderful again, albeit in a whole new way: a new son in the family, grandchildren (with God's help) in the future, and a whole new phase of life and pleasures.

On the day of Yael's wedding, obsessed by images of me collapsing under the *chuppah* and spoiling her joy, I barged into my rabbi's office to seek wise counsel. His response was sharp.

"Ephraim, what are children for?" he asked me, moving right past my sentimentality and getting straight to the point.

"Um, mmm, umm …," I babbled, my brain a soggy puddle. Reaching, I vaguely recalled some distant reason for having children.

"Children aren't entrusted to us by God to enjoy their cuteness," he sliced through me. "They are to teach us about our relationship with our Creator. Our love for our children is the easiest lesson we have to teach us how much the Almighty loves us. That's why He designed these relationships: To educate us how to get close to Him. And just like His greatest pleasure is to see us reach our potential, to reach personal greatness and to become independent, similarly we as parents guide our children to their own independent happiness and fulfillment."

My blurry, bloodshot eyes began to re-focus.

"Our greatest pleasure as parents is to see our kids reach their potential. We *want* them to have their own families and they need to do so in order to reach their own personal destiny. Her independence is your pleasure. That's why you brought her into this world."

His wisdom strengthened me. I made it through the day in one piece. But just before the *chuppah*, when I started to give Yael the traditional blessing, I lost it. There was simply far too much emotion to fit into the words and it flowed over the two of us.

As she circled her husband-to-be seven times, the past 20 years of joy and warmth and love all merged together into one overwhelming sensation. It felt like we'd been rocketed into the heavens where we basked in the presence of the Almighty Himself as He showered the young couple with His love and affectionately tied their souls together for eternity.

And I wasn't too bad under the *chuppah*. I did have a very good cry. It was sweet and sad, and full of love and hope and memories and dreams. And most of all, happiness in seeing my darling Yael take this leap into her future and knowing my wife and I had done something very right.

My Enemy, My Friend

My new neighbor wanted nothing to do with religious Jews.

Rochel Feld

Today I lost a friend, someone who was initially my adversary. Chava Leah bas Feivel returned her soul to her maker. I miss her already.

Our unlikely friendship began five years ago. We were preparing to move into a new home. Right away there was tension and I had not yet even met my new neighbor. She kept calling the police and the building inspector to say our grass wasn't cut short enough or often enough. Or maybe a soda can was left by the painters in the driveway. Every day was a new summons and a new nightmare. Was this how everyone was welcomed to the neighborhood?

Come moving day, my new next-door neighbor, a woman in her mid-70s, introduced herself. "Hi I'm your neighbor, we are not happy with the Orthodox taking over the block. We are Reform Jews. Don't even think of trying to influence us!"

She left me with my jaw still on the floor. "Hi ... I guess."

That was just the beginning. The police were called regularly if a ball rolled into her yard. So the kids had to play on the street. Well, wouldn't you know it, there is a long lost, rarely enforced ordinance that ball playing on the street is not allowed in my New Jersey town. Guess who made sure it was enforced now?

We lived in constant fear of this woman, never knowing what tomorrow would bring.

My husband, who is a lot nicer and more level-headed than I am, came up with a strategy for defense: let's overwhelm her with kindness!

You're kidding, I thought.

"Send her Shabbos flowers," my husband suggested, "but have them delivered because if she catches you on her property ...."

Anyhow, we sent her Purim *shalach manos,* invited her to our daughter's wedding and our son's bar mitzvah celebration. She had never attended Orthodox celebrations before and she had so many questions, needed so many answers. She was so taken by the meaning of it all, how everything had significance. She was moved by how Judaism was a way of life for us, in our celebrations, our mourning, even our rituals upon waking up.

Shortly after, she fell ill. She left a message on our answering machine, "I'm sick in the hospital, don't really know who else to call, thought you may want to come visit."

Really? You want me ... to visit you?

And so I did. I went to visit her a few times until she returned home.

While in the hospital, the Jewish chaplain left several books on my neighbor's bedside on various topics on Judaism. Some were complex and she asked me to explain these concepts to her.

Once she returned home I would try to go over each day to bring some meals and provide some good cheer, but she wanted me to explain to her the concepts in these books.

It came to the point that if I was not able to make it one day, there was a message on my answering machine, "Where are you? I need my fix of Torah."

We learned the weekly Torah portion and the wonderful lessons gleaned within it, we talked about the purpose of life, the soul after death, the reasons for certain mitzvot, we studied the meanings of various prayers, we spoke about the holidays, and we discussed any questions that came to her mind.

As she recovered we had her and her husband over for Shabbos meals. "Your children sit with you at the table for three hours every week?" she asked in astonishment. "They sing and laugh together every week? Your 6-year-old knows the *parashah* each week?"

I explained that the secret is the Shabbos itself.

My neighbor became a regular at our home every Friday night, on time to light the Shabbos candles with me and to study the weekly Torah portion.

I would take her to various Torah classes in the neighborhood that I thought would be of interest to her.

She would often come to sit in my kitchen on a Thursday to smell and taste the food being prepared for Shabbos as we discussed all kinds of philosophical concepts.

My new friend left no stone unturned, never had a question she didn't ask.

The police stopped being called and my children became her "adopted grandchildren."

"So, what is your daughter wearing for Shabbos this week? Isn't your son graduating high school this month? Isn't the older one ready for a *shidduch* soon?"

This is the story of my friend who spoke with God each day. My friend who sought to help others. To cheer up everyone she met, to enlighten them by urging them to consider the higher purpose for which they were created.

My friend who got sick and told me she sees the hand of God is with her every moment.

My friend who got sick and could not hold on any longer.

We said the *Shema* together when she could barely speak anymore.

My friend, I will miss your messages on my machine and joining us on Friday nights.

You studied so hard to make up for all the years you did not know. And now you know. Now it's all clear to you.

I will cherish all the times you challenged me to become a better version of myself. To study harder, to prepare more, to do more research to quench your thirst for *Yiddishkeit*.

When we started you didn't understand that the end of this life is the beginning of something on an even higher realm. Now you know.

My dear reader, perhaps you have a neighbor, a co-worker, or a relative who seems antagonistic toward Judaism and observant Jews. They may actually be calling out to you. They may see the beauty in the life you lead and yearn for it too.

See past their anger and sarcasm. Reach out to them.

May this be a merit for the *neshamah* of Chava Leah bas Feivel My friend.

True Romance

I knew exactly how I was supposed to feel about the man I'd marry. Until the day I met him.

Yehudit Channen

I spent a lot of my childhood reading my grandmother's large collection of *True Romance* magazines. My grandmother immigrated to America from Hungary when she was a teenager, and that's the highest literary level she ever achieved. Either that or she really enjoyed the glamour and escape those periodicals provided after a long day in the grocery store she owned with my grandfather.

At any rate, I found the melodramatic stories terribly intriguing, with all the complications and anxiety that romance can provide. There was always some sort of love triangle going on or an awful misunderstanding, with break-ups and make-ups that continued on into sequels. I was fascinated by the obsessions and heartache the characters endured, and I assumed I was learning all about love relationships. True Romance 101.

Yehudit Channen is a writer/editor for different publications and a *madrichah* at Melabev, a day care center for memory-impaired elderly. She lives in Ramat Beit Shemesh with her husband and children and is blessed to have many grandchildren living close by.

That was the beginning of an education that I should never have acquired. I got the rest of my romantic expectations from pop music and Hollywood films. Some of the major messages seemed to be:
- Love involves emotions such as jealousy, possessiveness, and the constant fear of losing your beloved to someone else.
- You shouldn't care what anyone else, even close family members and good friends, think about your beloved.
- Unrequited love is a noble thing, and it's understandable to want to die if you're rejected by someone with whom you are infatuated.

By the time I was ready for marriage in the 1970s, I knew exactly how I was supposed to feel about the man I would marry. Until the day I met him.

The man who wanted to marry me aroused feelings much less intense and exciting than I was primed for. On some of our dates I was even slightly bored and happy to return to the chatter and chaos of my all-girl apartment. This man was open, reliable, ambitious, and interested in me. He was not moody, never unpredictable, lacked mystery, and had absolutely no criminal tendencies. He was straightforward and to my mind, dull beyond description. He seemed like a good person to have for a neighbor, not my golden opportunity for passion and glory. Where were the fireworks, the thumping heart, the tears of torment, the moments of rapture? I was miserable that I wasn't sick with longing. I hadn't lost my appetite and I slept just fine. How could this be love?

Thankfully, at that stage in my life, I was attending Torah classes and learning new lessons about love and marriage. I was supposed to look for good character traits, like humility and compassion. My friends and I dreamed of marriage to a Judaic scholar, a role model for the children, an asset to the community. That didn't sound like the musicians or artistic types I had always dreamed of.

The man who wanted to marry me was so normal. And my father actually liked him, which was something brand new. I just couldn't reconcile myself to him being "the one."

Yet after awhile, his sweetness grew on me. So I took the plunge (I wasn't getting any younger) and we finally got married. Slowly and tenderly, we began to build our relationship, although I sometimes still fretted that our relationship would never be the inspiration for a story in *True Romance*.

A few months later I was thrilled to discover that I was expecting a baby. One afternoon as we were walking through town, I decided we must have ice cream cones. In my state, I chose the black walnut raisin and brandy flavor. My husband opted for vanilla. "Oh c'mon!" I teased him. "Try something exciting!"

"No, I like vanilla." he insisted, "that's always good."

We paid for our ice creams and sat down to eat them in a nearby park. I took a big lick of my quickly melting cone and it was absolutely revolting! I couldn't believe this had been my choice and I had ordered a triple scoop! I watched my husband settle down to enjoy his plain white ice cream and began to covet it intensely.

"What's wrong?" he asked me. "Everything okay?"

"This tastes terrible!" I admitted. "I can't eat this!" I felt especially bad because in those days we had so little money and an ice cream cone, believe it or not, was a luxury item.

He looked at me with a straight face and said' "You probably want me to trade with you, right?"

"Well," I said to my new husband, "I don't want to be rude."

"No, no, it's all right. Here, take mine."

He held out his cone and I gave him mine. He tried it. "Oh yum," he said loudly. "This is great, really delicious."

I looked at him gratefully and tried his vanilla. It was wonderful. And then I realized: so was he.

"Exotic" may look good, but that's only from the outside. When you're building a home, in it for the long run, and you're hot and tired (and expecting a baby), you want something — not "boring" — but steady, reliable, and dependable.

What I now call *True Romance*.

Stepmother

Like a thief, resentment crept in. I didn't like sharing my husband, his attention, his time, or his money.

Rea Bochner

I was 24 when I met my husband. A unique series of events landed me (literally) at his door, and we knew almost instantly that we were meant to be together.

One night he sat me down and told me there was something I should know. "I'm divorced," he said.

Okay, I thought. *Not a deal breaker.*

"And I have children."

Oy.

It's not that I didn't like children; at the time, I made my living as an elementary school teacher. But according to the timeline I'd mapped out in my mind, I wouldn't be having my own children for a long while yet. Marrying a man with kids would throw a heavy-duty monkey wrench into my best-laid plans.

"Do you have a picture of them?" I asked.

He produced a wallet-sized snapshot of two little girls in matching dresses, one three and one four, smiling brightly at the camera.

For a biographical note on the author, please see page 48.

The older one had dark hair and a sweet-cheeked Eskimo face. The younger one was lighter and still round with baby fat, but she shared her sister's smile.

They were lovely.

My limited experience had shown that to be with someone you love, sometimes you have to make compromises. You learn to let go of the little things — the gossipy best friend, the obsession with fly-fishing — and accept the bigger ones. This was how my own parents had lived in tandem together, mostly happily, for three decades. If I wanted to marry this man, it would mean chucking my timeline and diving into parenthood right off the bat.

I looked from the little faces in the picture back up to his and knew I'd already made my decision. We were married a few months later.

Not What I Bargained For

According to Jewish tradition, the first year of marriage is a rich time for couples, allowing them to iron out the details of making a home together while growing in intimacy and connection and enjoying their special time alone. With Naomi and Arielle as part of the equation, our first year of marriage did not quite fit the mold. When the girls came to stay with us we were in full parent mode, devoting most of our energy and attention to them. Any free time we had was spent caring for them, getting them dressed, putting them to sleep, and shuttling them from their house to ours and back again. Our social life was cramped, our plans compromised, and our time alone piecemeal. The reality of stepparenthood quickly blew the romantic haze away with the force of a hurricane.

Even when the girls were not with us, we had to make decisions with them in mind. Moving to Israel after our wedding was out of the question. We had to find a place to live within a certain distance of New York where the girls lived. Exploring Jewish communities on the West Coast or down South was simply not an option for us. Accustomed to picking up and going wherever the wind took me in my single-gal days, being forcibly rooted felt like a jail sentence.

Then there was the money. Like it or not, a good chunk of whatever my husband earned went to the girls. Intellectually, I knew it was rightfully theirs, but I couldn't help but think of how much easier it would be for us if child support was not part of the picture.

A few months into our marriage, I found myself on hands and knees in the middle of the night, scrubbing the bathroom after one of the girls had a physics-defying bathroom episode. While my husband facilitated a quick pajama-change in the next room, I looked down at the sponge in my hand and thought, *This is so not what I signed up for.*

I never had to consider others in my decision-making process before I got married, nor make serious sacrifices for anyone, let alone children who were not even mine. Like a thief, resentment crept in. I didn't like sharing my husband, his attention, his time, or his money. I didn't like having to compromise my own plans and desires. Being a stepmother was a nice idea in theory, but in practice, it was a drag.

I became irritable and snappish whenever the girls came to stay with us, and in my heart, I distanced myself from the children.

But what amazed me is that the girls didn't seem to notice. From the beginning, they opened their hearts to me with abandon, with no trace of jealousy that I was taking so much of their father's attention; I was just someone else to love them. They would curl into me like kittens when we read together, and bring me projects and pictures that they made for me in school. Even when I lost my patience and stormed around the house, they would quietly give me my space until I was calm; then they would ask if they could help me make dinner. Once in a while I was able to soften, but mostly I stewed, deliberately ignoring that when it came to handling our blended family, I was more a child than they were.

Then I got the news; I was going to have a baby.

Like most expectant mothers, I was both fearful and excited about bringing a new little person into the world. As for the girls, they were thrilled. They came up with lists of possible names (my suggestion of "Cookie Monster" was unanimously ruled out), and grew more and more excited as their soon-to-be-sibling's arrival drew closer.

The day after my son was born the girls came to the hospital to see him. They stared down at him with awe and wonder, touching him lightly and smiling into his little face. They held him with unbelievable care and giggled at his sleeping noises. Instantly, they were in love.

How could they give their hearts away so easily? How could they just accept this baby into their lives? Didn't they see him as a threat, a competition for attention? How could they not see what they were losing?

I, meanwhile, felt the urge the build up the walls around "my" family. In my eyes, the girls' presence cast a shadow over what should have been a special bonding time for my husband, our new son, and me.

My Mother's Love

A few months later, my mother passed away. I was devastated, and felt as if there was suddenly a gaping hole in my spirit. Aside from my siblings, who else could have understood, really, what it meant to lose such unabashed, unconditional love? It broke my heart to think that my babies would never know her or the amazing things she did for her family.

The girls felt the loss intensely. From the time they came into my life, they considered my mother as much a flesh-and-blood grandmother as the real thing. My mother, in turn, loved them completely, and took every opportunity to make life an adventure for them. She would tape some wrapping paper to the table, shake up a bottle of Bisquick and transform her kitchen into a "Dora the Explorer Pancake Party." She took the girls to the Big Apple Circus and on their first subway ride. Mom even made a visit to the American Girl Store so exciting that we all forgot the biting cold as we walked the streets of Manhattan. She made sure the girls knew how much she loved them, telling them constantly and showering them with affection. As I watched her love my stepdaughters, I could see her weaving magic into their memories, the same magic I recalled from my own childhood.

The following spring my second son was born. Between planning his *bris* and the wild, exhausting transition of having a new baby in the house, I barely registered that Mother's Day was coming up. I would have forgotten about it completely if Naomi had not approached me with a card.

"I know you're not my real mother," the card said, "but I love you like a real mother."

I was amazed.

They had known so much confusion, so much loss, these girls, and yet they still had the strength to keep their hearts open. I had acted, in my worst moments, like a real-life Evil Stepmother, in my best like a petulant kindergartener, but my stepdaughters loved me anyway.

Suddenly, I remembered a conversation I had with my mother that last year, when she and my father had taken the girls on a late-night run to Toys R Us. Mom was undergoing chemo and was almost bedridden, but wanted to get the girls Chanukah presents.

"Thank you," I said to her one time after she had arrived home.

"What for?" Mom shrugged. "These are my *grandchildren*."

It was as simple as that. She loved the girls because they were given to her to love. She didn't see them as an inconvenience or a drain on her bank account; she saw them as an *opportunity*.

I had been so blind. After becoming a stepmother, I was too busy focusing on what I was losing to realize how much I'd gained. My stepdaughters were a gift, straight from God to me. I realized I was lucky to have them; not only were they sweet, good girls, but they had given me the finest education in what it meant to love.

The same opportunity my mother recognized could still be mine, if I took it before it was too late.

Since then, my resentment has been replaced with joy, gratitude, and even humor. The girls are not my real daughters, but I love them as if they were. And they know it. All of my children adore each other and the house is filled with laughter when everyone is together. Finally, we are truly a family.

More than that, I no longer have to worry that my babies will never know the wonderful things my mother did; they have two big sisters who are more than happy to tell them all about it.

Confessions of an American Jewish Teenager

Parents don't want to hear about our struggles because they're hiding from the truth themselves.

Rachel Levy

While I am Jewish, American, and a teenager, I don't think words can ever define me. Every teenager has a different story, a different background — a different dream. I was raised with care, love, and a strong Jewish upbringing. *Shema* was sung to me every night and my Torah projects were proudly attached to the fridge. My parents invested love into me and as a child I felt safe, secure. When a bully pushed me down in kindergarten I realized for the first time that not everyone loved me. I rushed home crying and my mother soothed me. Not everyone is as fortunate as I am.

Braving the cold Brooklyn streets I saw people of all shapes, sizes, races, and religions, but I assuredly knew that I had my own people. I was not a part of these swearing, angry ones. I was the little girl in shul searching for my father's *tallis,* the child playing merrily in the autumn leaves, oblivious to the kids doing drugs behind the innocent red benches.

In fifth grade a teenager smacked my Bais Yaakov school bus and screamed "Dirty Jews!" We ten-year-old girls were not shocked, just morbidly fascinated.

When my family moved to the south everyone was friendly; the cashiers knew your name and smiled, and the lines got blurry. Gentile neighbors walking their dogs would say "Good Morning" and sometimes even "Good Sabbath." Where did we belong if they also seemed right?

I think the reason why teenagers are branded with the "scarlet letter" of being emotional, rebellious, and filled with angst is that we are sniffing for the truth. When we feel like we cannot speak, like we cannot express our longing, when we are packaged into a mold that does not fit, we want to escape. I am blessed. Many of my friends cannot talk to their parents.

I know I can always talk to my mother. And not just talk — really talk. If adults were more honest with us, then we would talk. Really talk. But most of them are deluding themselves. Most of them have the same *yetzer haras*, the same passions and desires that we do. How can a girl struggling to seek past externals ask her mother for help when her mother is suffering with the same problem? Even more so when her mother doesn't even admit or know about the issue?

Jealousy, anger, insincerity, stealing, gossiping — these struggles plague everyone, age one and up. It may be easier to blame these traits on "those teenagers" but wake up, America — the problems affect everyone. I am not saying that in order for a parent to communicate with his child he must be a perfect angel. But a parent has to be honest that he has flaws. Flaws are okay, flaws are imperative for human growth — embrace them! How can you expect your teen to be perfect when you are human too?

I have a lot of friends. One friend goes to a really religious school and tells me that if her principal knew she had an email address she would be kicked out. Another friend goes to public school and tells me how hard it is to be in the cafeteria and not buy the spicy fries. These girls would probably feel a lot better if they could tell their parents their struggles. But struggles sometimes are not permitted. Parents really don't want to hear it. Because they are hiding from the truth themselves.

We are searching, searching, searching. It does not help when the adults who we assume have already found the truth shame us, undermine us, misunderstand us. It is even worse when the adults we trust are hypocrites. When we find that out, we don't know what to believe in anymore.

Some of my friends are deep. We talk about, as we sometimes put it, "the meaning of life." We talk about dating and marriage. We talk about real issues. We learn, we drink it in. We are seeking the truth, seeking to be good people.

And believe in us. We are, after all, the future.

My New Dad

*Real change is possible after 50.
I know because I saw it happen.*

Debbie Fisch

The male midlife crisis is famous for the trade-in of cars, jobs, and wives for updated models. Standing eye to eye with mortality, after all, can give you a good bone chill.

But my father must have seen something else when he peered down the shortening corridor of his life.

Growing up with my father was not easy. From the beginning of his medical training, my brothers and I were often left bereft of our father's presence, as the hospital ever so neatly seemed to need him whenever we did. Long nights away from home were de rigueur, and all of the bedtime rituals and middle of the night cuddles were left in the domain of our mom. As his career expanded and he became an eminent cardiologist, the life-saving advice that others sought from him always seemed to cast our childish needs in a trivial pallor.

His variegated hobbies also vied for his attention. My father was proficient in just about everything from ancient history to modern

---

The author is using a pseudonym.

technology. Lauded as a Renaissance man by the world at large, the small world around him keenly felt his absence.

When he was around, things weren't all that pleasant either. Exhausted from his long days at the office and the hospital, his fuse was short and his temper often flared over small infractions. Groomed to be a family man, he insisted on Sunday afternoon family trips, perhaps as a way to assuage his own guilt at not being around more. How we dreaded those trips! We all piled into the car, headed towards some boring educational destination, and if something went awry — watch out!

To be fair, my childhood was basically happy nonetheless. My parents were happy with each other, my mother was super-mom, my brothers were fiercely protective of their only sister, and we all got used to my dad's absence. And we had many memorable times together as a family that were not peppered by my father's outbursts.

But my father's aloofness, volatility, and critical nature imperceptibly clouded the felicitous nature of our family.

I think he sensed the need for change somewhere around his 40th birthday. I started seeing self-help manuals on his nightstand (they sure didn't seem to be helping). Already a know-it-all teenager myself, I scoffed at the thought that one could change their nature at such a late stage.

But I was wrong.

Inexplicably, my father viewed his midlife crisis as the time to expose the rawness of his character to the harsh elements of introspection to allow the sunlight to slowly heal him. It didn't happen overnight, but ever so slowly we all began to notice a change which eventually morphed into an utter transformation.

My father had never been a member of a synagogue before, so we were astounded when he opted to move to a new community in a new city for the sole purpose of being in close proximity to an Orthodox synagogue. He was 50 years old.

Leaving behind friends and all that is familiar after 30 years in a community is not easy for anyone, let alone my father, who is a real creature of habit. But he did it. He started attending Torah classes, and met regularly with the Rabbi, for whom he cultivated a great respect.

And his character was changing right along with him. His ire, which had once so defined him, slowed and then stopped completely, as if a dam had been built to curb his flare-ups. At first you could see him going through the motions of holding back, but after a number of years it became second nature to him, and you could tell that the struggle was behind him. My father cut back his hours at work, spending more time at home with his children and grandchildren. And we chose to live nearby to enjoy the pleasure of his company.

Instead of moping at the Shabbos table, my father was giving over Torah thoughts. He began working for the community, arranging benefits and utilizing his varied talents to help to build the Jewish community.

Instead of criticism there was praise, pouring forth from his mouth like a surplus of diamonds. He complimented my abilities as a wife, a mother, and best of all, as a daughter.

At the recent bar-mitzvah of my son, my normally laid back personality caved in under the stress of the experience. I had not ordered enough cups, and I was concerned that the guests milling about were thirsty. I was extremely agitated, frantically trying to figure out what to do. My father approached me and put his arms on my shoulders.

"Debbie," he said softly. "Perspective. It's going to be okay. I'll get the cups. This will pass. I want you to enjoy yourself. Let's not sweat the small stuff." I had to marvel at the role reversal in a man who used to fly off the handle if someone forgot to shut the light when they left the room.

And when a malpractice lawsuit threatened all of his assets, my father maintained his equilibrium throughout the long litigation process. We never saw him sweat anymore, even over the big stuff.

Maybe I shouldn't have been so shocked by my father's metamorphosis. As Judaism became more of a substantive part of his life, as it did in my own life, I supposed he realized the Torah's belief in the power of change. Maimonides says that every human being has the power to be as great as Moses himself, should he choose to do so. And every year we are afforded the opportunity during the Days of Repentance to clean the slate and start anew. It's no easy feat, but if my father could do it at 50, it certainly isn't impossible.

My brother and I recently called our father together. "I love you," he said at the end of the conversation.

My brother looked at me. "Do you remember when the pussycat used to be a tiger?"

"No," I responded. "I don't remember."

"Neither do I," he said, and we both laughed.

In the Blink of an Eye

My little daughter is growing up way too fast.

Ross Hirschmann

It happens every time I hear that song, "Theme from *A Summer's Place*." That beautiful, melodic instrumental takes me right back there, back to five years ago when our first daughter, Aleeza, was only 6 months old. It was the first song she ever responded to. I would play the CD and she would smile at me, motioning that she wanted me to hold her. I'd pick her up, she'd press her little cheek against mine, and then we'd dance around the den like two ballroom dancers from some Fred Astaire movie.

How I relished that time, the smell of her cheek, that toothless smile. That was our routine about every other night, and I thought it would last forever. Only it didn't; it couldn't. One day I played the song and she just sat there. She no longer cared. Her now toothy smile no longer showed.

Somewhere along the way of those eight months of our routine,

---

Ross Hirschmann is a former civil litigator who saw the light and got out of law. He then got into pharmaceutical sales where he has been for the past 14 years. He earned his JD from the University of California Hastings College of the Law and his BA in history from UCLA. He lives in Los Angeles with his incredible wife and two very cute daughters.

an era came and went. My daughter started growing up. And it all seemed to happen in the blink of an eye.

I still remember bringing Aleeza home from the hospital. That tiny six-and-a-half-pound baby doll. My wife Debbie and I marveled at how incredible it was that fingers could be so small and have tiny fingernails to match. We used to literally count the number of days since her birth. "She's only been in God's world seven days ... eight days ... nine days ..." and so on. She would lie there on the couch and smile at us, that beautiful, toothless smile. And it seemed like she'd always be that toothless, silent doll.

Then one day we went to get her from the crib and she was standing, waiting for us. Still smiling, still silent. Only now, we could see a tooth coming through. Then two, and before we knew it, she had a full set of teeth and was talking.

One night I said to my wife, "Do you remember when Aleeza couldn't talk at all?"

Debbie thought about it and said, "No, I can't anymore. Can you?"

"Me neither. It seems like she's always been talking." I tried to conjure up the image of that tiny, silent baby lying on our couch, unable to sit up, but I couldn't. I just sat there feeling somewhat sad.

I blinked and an era came and went.

I remember when Aleeza started nursery school at one of the Jewish day schools. She didn't want us to leave after we took her into her classroom. She had to always have long good-byes complete with hugs, kisses — both given and blown — and of course waving until we couldn't see each other anymore in the hall. That was our routine, even when I was running late for a business appointment. I didn't care. I lived for these moments, knowing they wouldn't last.

Fast forward to the present. Aleeza is in her third year of school and I am driving her to school. This year is special since it is her first year of wearing uniforms. She looks so cute in her uniform — that little three-quarters-sized girl — that I could just eat her up with a big wooden spoon! I drive her to school and pull into the carpool lane. I get out as I always have and unlock her door. Our "Good-Bye Routine" at car pool is the same as the hallway routine of the previous two years. She gets out, hugs and kisses me good-bye, makes a heart on her chest, and points to me. I then make one back and point at her and raise two fingers. It means, "I love you too." And then we wave until we can't see each other any more.

This morning, however, as I took Aleeza out of the car I turned to answer a quick question from one of the teachers. When I turned around Aleeza was gone. I looked and saw her walking up the stairs into school. I became desperate and panicked. "Aleeza!" I cried out, "Aleeza!"

She turned to me on the steps and smiled. "Have a good day, little girl!" I said.

She just waved and turned to go. I realized that there would be no more kisses at carpool. No more hearts drawn. No more waving until we couldn't see each other any more.

But then, at the last minute, Aleeza stopped and did a double take. She must have seen how crestfallen my face was. She turned, waved and mouthed, "I love you, Daddy!" Then she turned and was gone. And so were the days of our good-bye routine.

I blinked and yet another era came and was gone.

Sometimes life moves too fast, and if we're not careful, we can miss it passing us by. I can't stop my daughter from growing up — nor would I want to. But I can make sure that I'm there with her, loving her, enjoying her, marveling over her, before I blink and say good-bye to another era which has come and gone.

A Stone's Throw

A small revolution began with a broken window.

Riva Pomerantz

In a rundown, rough-'n-tumble neighborhood in East Cleveland, a group of Orthodox Jews sporting beards and kippahs stand out like sore thumbs. But every morning, they make their way downtown to their warehouse buildings, seemingly oblivious to the forlorn surroundings.

Shimon Weiner is one of these men. From his office on East 131 Street, he often sees people, mainly African-Americans, wandering aimlessly down deserted streets. Sometimes he catches a glimpse of the occasional fight, and every day without fail he sees swarms of children running to and from the public school around the corner.

It was at the end of a school day when the first window was broken. Shimon heard a loud crack as a perfectly aimed stoned found its mark. Hoots of laughter accompanied the shower of broken glass. When the window-breaking spiraled from a one-time incident to a favored leisure activity, Shimon decided he was not going to sit still.

Riva (Henig) Pomerantz lives with her husband and four children in Ramat Beit Shemesh. Her stories and articles appear on aish.com, in *Mishpacha Magazine*, and in several other publications. Her latest book, *Green Fences*, was published by Targum Press. You can visit Riva's website and read her blog at www.rivapomerantz.com.

When the next stone hit his window, Shimon hit the roof.

He raced down the stairs and collared the first kid he could. After exchanging a few choice words with the group of terrified youngsters, he finally let them off the hook with threats should there be a reoccurrence.

He was surprised when the next day began with a satisfying *crrrack*.

Shimon Weiner is not a small man. When he barreled down the street that morning, the kids began to quake. After expressing his rage, Shimon released his captives with the threat that if they ever threw another stone, they'd wish they had never been born.

Oy! Shimon said to himself, as he made his way back to the office, calming himself down. *What in the world have I done?* Messing with inner city kids is not the wisest thing to do, and he felt the ramifications of his reaction sinking in fast. He dialed the school and asked to speak to the principal.

"A group of your kids are on their way to school and they're probably a little shaken up," he admitted sheepishly. "They've been breaking my windows and I really lost my cool." Then he added, "I want to think of a constructive way to stop their behavior."

The principal took the initiative to give Shimon's number to the parents of the offending students. It was not long before he received a call.

"Is this Mr. Weiner?"

"Yes," said Shimon, preparing to get lambasted for intimidating the children.

"I wanted to apologize for my son breaking your windows. I'm so sorry," said the voice on the other line.

Shimon was flabbergasted.

"Well," he said. "Why don't you and some of the other parents come down to my office? I have an idea how we might be able to stop these boys from damaging more windows."

A few hours later a group of parents joined Shimon in his downtown office for some cake and juice. Shimon explained his idea.

"I figure that if the kids and I could get to know each other a bit, they won't want to break my windows," he said simply.

Later that day, a small group of elementary school students walked into the offices of DryCast Inc. Shimon greeted them warmly, offered them some snacks, then paid them to do some light work in his warehouse. The meeting was a huge success. As they were leaving, Shimon told the kids, "You're always welcome to come to my office. Whether you need a bathroom, a drink, or help, the door is always open. "

The next morning, Shimon had a bunch of kids knocking on his door eager to say good morning to "Simon."

Now they come often. Before school and after school they stop in to say hello and chat with Shimon and his partner, Avraham. He asks them about their aspirations in life, about who their heroes are. Some of these children live in homes without father figures; many of them wake up each morning to face a difficult, uncertain world. With his gentle guidance and warmth, Shimon has become a source of hope to dozens of kids.

He is brainstorming on how to expand this kernel of success to help more inner-city kids realize their full potential.

This story speaks volumes to any of us — all of us — who deal with our imperfections and failures. Torah wasn't given to angels; it was given to imperfect human beings who are striving to bring spirituality into their day-to-day life. Shimon realized his mistake of acting in anger and wanted to repair the damage. He picked up the pieces of that broken glass and made it whole again.

Shimon's tiny revolution started with a broken window. Your next beautiful experience may be only a stone's throw away.

Forgiving My Father

After 10 years, I wanted to heal.

Anonymous

Every year on July 22, I celebrate my birthday. I might get together with friends, or perhaps go away on vacation. There's only one thing I know for sure. On July 22, I plan to call my father so he can wish me a happy birthday. My dad knows it's my birthday, and I know he wants to talk to me, but he is unable to call.

Growing up, I went to a private school on scholarship. Most of the other kids' parents were successful in business, and could afford the tuition. My mom was a housewife, and my dad a carpenter — when he went to work. There were many times my father was out of work, putting an even bigger financial strain on the family. Not only did we not have money, but we were also trying to "keep up with the Schwartzes." It was hard to understand what was going on in my father's life, and why he was unable to provide the life we wanted. The life I felt I deserved. I was angry and upset with my father for not properly providing for us. I blamed him personally.

As a child, I didn't know why my dad was in and out of the house, and at times he was out of work and just "not around." I know my family was trying to protect my innocence by not explaining things to me, but by not being told what was happening, I could not understand the situation. In the absence of any information, I just thought the man didn't care.

By the time I was old enough to comprehend the truth of the situation, I had convinced myself that my father was a terrible man who didn't love me, didn't care about me, didn't want to be a part of my life. And I thought to myself, perhaps this was because I was unlovable? I thought, maybe I am unworthy of being loved or cared for?

I looked at the man who "made me feel this way" and blamed him for everything.

My mom and dad divorced, and as a pre-teen I moved in with my grandmother and cut all ties with my father.

As I grew up, I began taking classes and reading books about self-improvement and self-empowerment. A recurring theme seemed to emerge: Fix the relationship with your father.

I was stuck in the "daddy doesn't love me" syndrome, which affected my everyday life, and all of my relationships. I knew the answer was to get over the past, and go see my father.

One of the hardest things in life is change. To be where I am is a lot easier than to implement a big change. It's just easier to go on with the hurt and pain with which I am already familiar and accustomed. To change means hard work. It means getting past the past. It may be over, but in my mind it still is very much there. To go see my father and let go of the anger and hurt was a big step. Perhaps I could just go on and forget about it.

After a slew of failed relationships, I realized I was unable to have a healthy relationship without it, and I decided to make that big step.

It wasn't easy to even find my father after all those years. I almost gave up, as the search proved to be an additional difficulty in this already painful process. It would have been so easy to just stop and go back to life as it was. But I knew I would never be able to truly go forward and let go of the past without healing this wound.

After almost 10 years of no contact whatsoever, I went to see my father. On the way there, I envisioned the fight we would have. Perhaps I would put the blame in words, to finally express how I felt all those years. Maybe he'd have things to say to me as well. I might leave in a huff and never go back. In my mind, the possibilities were endless. And none of them were pleasant.

As I entered the house where my dad lives, I got the answer to a lot of my questions. My father lives in a nursing home for the mentally ill.

He shuffled toward me and gave me a weak hug. Then we sat and talked. It was a simple conversation, no more than the level of a small child. But my healing was in that meeting.

There was no fight, no blame, no hurt. Just two people who have love to give and desperately would like to have it reciprocated, both open to the possibility of having a new relationship.

All those years of blame, hurt, and pain! They were all for nothing. I had brought upon myself feelings of resentment toward my father, and feelings of insecurity within myself. If I had only been willing to open my eyes and see what was really happening, I could have spared myself years of hurt and pain. There is no deeper wound than the abandonment by a parent. But I was not abandoned. If anyone did the abandoning, it was me.

I now saw my dad in a whole new light. A man who gave me life, and then tried to cope as best as he could. And maybe life would have been better if I had been able to support him through his illness.

My dad was sick. And though it would be egotistical of me to think I had the right to be angry in the first place, I forgave him. I let go of the past, and recognized that it was what it was, and there is no way I can change that now. All I can do is make a new start for myself in this moment, with a pure forgiveness, from the heart, for any old "hurts."

I knew I had made mistakes as well. Perhaps all these years would have been different, if I had seen the whole picture long ago. If I had accepted my father for who he was, and who he wasn't. If I was able to look past my selfishness and realize that in a family, it's not just the parents who provide for the children, it's a team effort. I apologized to my father, and he forgave me with pleasure.

And I realized that there was something I had to do that might even be harder than forgiving him: I began the road to forgiving myself. Realizing that the only way to make up for all those lost years is to do what's right in this moment, and avail myself of the relationship I never let us have.

In the Bedtime *Shema* prayers, there is a beautiful passage about forgiveness: "Master of the universe, I hereby forgive anyone who angered or antagonized me … whether he did so accidentally, willfully, carelessly, or purposely."

There is an incredible power in forgiveness. I discovered that my forgiveness toward my father was an amazing opportunity for me to open myself to the possibility of meaningful relationships in my life. Without this, I was stuck on a merry-go-round of blame and anger.

But with the power of forgiveness, anything is possible.

Shortly after I re-opened my relationship with my father, my life dramatically improved. My relationships were on a deeper level, and they took on more meaning. I was able to relate to people with a basis of trust and openness.

The commandment to "honor your father and mother" always had seemed to me like a one-sided deal. But now I am able to experience the benefits of this crucial part of my life. By deciding to accept my father for who he is, and who he isn't, I am able to accept others, including myself.

Now, I call my father on a regular basis, and visit him quite often. I take him on walks and sometimes we go out for dinner. I check on him to make sure he is getting along with his roommate, and that the nurses at his home are taking good care of him. God has given me a special challenge, and I am up for it. I choose my life exactly as it is. I choose my dad exactly as he is. And every day is a new opportunity to make choices in life. Today, I choose to utilize the power of forgiveness.

As I walked away from writing this article, I wondered how to end it. I flipped on the radio, and this song was playing my barest thoughts:

"I don't wanna be angry no more. It's just another heartache on my list. I don't wanna be lonely anymore."

Stairway to Heaven

*One long, dark, memorable night
I discovered my mother.*

Rabbi Yaakov Salomon

"Why are you coming to the wedding?"
"What kind of question is that?" Mom answered. "I'm going because I was invited."

If you knew my mom, you'd understand why the conversation ended right there. My brother-in-law's daughter was getting married (no relation to her), in a wedding hall that was a good hour from her home (she didn't drive), on the hottest day of the summer (she was 93 at the time).

But her attendance was never in doubt. It was a joyous occasion, she loved life, and... well, you heard her — she was invited.

She looked beautiful that sweltering August night in 2003 and the guests were, as usual, drawn to her. People lined up to speak to Mrs. Lea Salomon. It was worth the wait.

It was a few minutes after the soup. The news filtered into the ballroom lobby in incremental waves. Much of the East Coast had been blanketed with a major blackout. Millions were plunged into sudden and crippling darkness. News outlets were reporting that

---

For a biographical note on the author, please see page 152.

repairs did not seem imminent. A state of emergency was declared in eight states and parts of Canada.

But inside the hall, the trumpets blared, the chandeliers shone brightly and the dance floor laughed. Inexplicably, in the midst of a vast sea of supreme darkness, this one wedding hall was a festive oasis of unremitting delight.

The buzz among the guests was uni-focused.

"Did you hear about the blackout?"

"Can you believe we have power here?"

"Do you think there will be looting?"

"Where are you going to sleep tonight?"

It was that last question that troubled most of us. Many of my friends (myself included), were on their way to summer bungalows in the mountains which, while without power, at least afforded us a bearable sleeping climate. And it was there that I proposed to take Mom after the wedding. Going back to her Manhattan apartment was not an option. Without lights, an elevator (she lived on the 7th floor), or air conditioning, Mom basically was left with two choices — our cramped, but cooler bungalow, or a night in nearby Monsey with one of my wife's brothers.

Her response, as always, was clear and definitive: "I want to go home."

I could tell you I was surprised, but I'd be lying. Mom reveled in the impossible, but now she was crossing the line.

"You know I'd be glad to drive you home, Mom, but tonight is just not going to work. The bungalow is really not so crowded. You'll be fine."

My logic was quite powerful — just not quite as powerful as this 70-pound giant.

"I'm not a young woman. I need to sleep in my own bed. Take me home. Now."

What would you have done? Think about it. You know that home was clearly not feasible, yet here was my totally autonomous 93-year-old Champion Mom insisting that she would not take "No" for an answer. Predictably, minutes later I caved.

"Whatever you say, Mom. It's a wasted trip to the city because we'll just have to come back, but you need to see that for yourself. I understand."

We strode to the car, sans flashlight. I knew we'd be returning soon.

Into the Darkness

The trip to Manhattan was eerily uneventful and uncharacteristically traffic-free. Apparently people feared driving on unlit highways or chose to remain near loved ones. It was, after all, a legitimate crisis. We rode mostly in silence. My thoughts centered on what time we would get back — it was already close to 1 a.m. Who knows what Mom was thinking ... but thinking she was. Thinking was her greatest life passion. I would soon find out.

We exited the Hudson Parkway at 96th street and were abruptly engulfed in full-scale darkness. The highway had been partially lit by the headlights of other cars, but the side streets were pitch-black. I swallowed hard and flashed my brights on, while proceeding at about 10 mph. I stole a glance to the passenger seat — no reaction ... at all.

A few minutes later we arrived. The clock read 1:16 a.m. I squeezed into a surprising parking space and shut off the engine (and the car lights), accentuating my point. We were now submerged in total darkness. Eerie is not the word. The seven-floor apartment building stood proudly to our left, I suppose. I couldn't even see it. I turned to Mom with a triumphant expression, as if to say, "I told you so." She was no more than four feet away from me, but I couldn't see her face.

But my ears were operating quite well. I heard her shuffling and then I heard a click. She was unlocking her seat belt.

"Where do you think you are going!?" I asked with a tinge of irreverence and incredulousness.

"To my apartment," she answered matter-of-factly.

"Mom, don't be ridiculous. We can't even see the building!"

There was no response.

Next thing I knew the passenger door swung open, the car dome light went on, and she was bolting her way, cane in hand, on to her destination. I flew out myself and grasped her forearm as she crossed the abandoned, darkened street. I was hoping to re-direct her back into the car, but she would have none of that.

"Be reasonable, Mom," I pleaded. "You live on the seventh floor. There are no lights in the whole building and no elevator! It's just not safe!"

My words swiftly drifted into the moonless night. She bounded forward, walking with a resolve and a determination that was alien to me. In seconds, we were touching the building's exterior glass door. It was heavy. I usually opened it for her. Not tonight. Tonight was reserved for powers I had never before witnessed.

Mom thrust the big door open while simultaneously shoving me aside — just in case I continued my intrusive efforts. The dark somehow got darker. The vestibule covered about 16 feet until we reached the next roadblock — the interior ... LOCKED ... glass door. I heard her fumble in her pocket for her keys. This was getting very crazy. Valiantly, I made one final attempt.

"PLEASE, MOMMY! YOU CAN'T GO IN THERE! IT'S DANGEROUS! THERE ARE NO LIGHTS ANYWHERE AND NO ELEVATOR AND NO AIR CONDITIONING! PLEASE RECONSIDER!"

The only answer I got was the sound of the key entering the lock. We were now in the lobby. I couldn't see an inch in front me. I shuddered thinking this is what blindness must be like.

It was time for me to surrender. I worried terribly how this saga would end. What possible plan could she have? But a strange semi-calm was on its way. It comes with a resignation and an awareness that something very sublime was now in control.

Knock ... knock ... knock ....

"What are you doing?" I called out.

"I'm trying to find the Super," she said.

She banged again, a little harder. She knew that the building superintendent lived in the first apartment on the left. Somehow she had found her way to what must have been his door. Seconds later, we heard a frightened voice, with a Spanish accent.

"Who's there?"

"It's Mrs. Salomon, from 7D," she answered.

Still seeing nothing, I heard the door squeak open. The Super knew Mom. Everyone knew Mom. With the door now open, I could see Mr. Lopez in the shadow of a kitchen candle that flickered in the background. He was wearing pajamas and a befuddled, but half-grinning expression. As I said ... he knew Mom. Still, even he was surprised.

"Mrs. Salomon! What can you be doing here??"

His English was less than polished, but his amazement was more than clear.

I peered over at Mom. Due to the faint flicker from inside the apartment, I could finally see her. There she stood at the threshold; a hunched 4 foot 10 figure, thin as a rail but tall as a monument. The scene was beyond incongruous. There was Mom, bedecked in perfectly coiffed and stylish brunette wig, adorned by a stunning gold wedding gown with beige trim and fabulous shoes, facing (at 1:30 in the morning), in total darkness, Mr. Lopez.

"I need a candle," she declared. Mom never minced words. No further explanation was forthcoming.

"But Mrs. Salomon," argued Lopez, "you cannot go upstairs. We have no electricity ... no elevator!"

"Just give me a candle," she insisted.

Lopez knew enough not to mess further. He returned in a minute with a large and lit candle.

"Thank you," she said and turned toward the elevator, candle in hand.

But she didn't stop at the elevator. She kept on walking. I found myself a couple of steps behind. The heat was unbearable, but only I seemed to be sweating. I watched her advancement, but hardly believed what I saw. She was headed for the sweltering stairwell.

"You're not walking up seven flights of stairs, Mom. No way."

She was.

One proud step at a time she climbed; this giant mountain of pride and determination. The flame danced before her. Holding her bony arm and walking beside on her right, I breathed heavily and sweated some more. I wasn't quite sure who was helping whom. The stairwell shone brightly that magical August night and I held back a torrent of tears that were generated from a mixture of awe and unmitigated respect.

The pace slowed around floor number four and I began to fear for her health. This was serious stuff and I considered my very few options. No matter — she just kept going, throwing caution to the wind. But by the time the fifth floor appeared, I noticed the wobbling. She IS human, I remember thinking.

She gently placed her petite frame on the landing … smiled … and spoke to me.

"I don't think I can continue," she admitted.

I sat down beside her and draped my sweaty arm around her suddenly broad shoulders. Like two wounded soldiers on a historic battlefield, we embraced. It was a moment that would be forever etched in a loving canvas.

But defeat was not in this heroine's lexicon. She could smell the finish line and would not be denied. She fumbled for her keys again. She always loved those keys. They were personal symbols of her prized independence. She handed them to me.

"Take the keys," she said. Her voice was faint, but her resolve was unyielding.

"You go upstairs. Go into my apartment and bring me a glass of water — room temperature. I'll wait here. I'll be fine."

"But Mom, I need the candle to go up. I can't leave you here in total darkness."

"I'm fine. I'm fine," she reassured. "Just go."

I bumbled up the last two flights, entered the pitch-black apartment and filled a glass with water — room temperature. When I returned to the fifth floor, she was waiting patiently. Sip by sip she downed the water and smiled at me.

"I'm ready," she declared.

The final two flights were no match for this champion. She had climbed her Everest and planted her flag.

She was home.

***

We didn't get much sleep that night, but the dream had already occurred before we went to bed. Power was restored the next morning.

We never again spoke about the events of the night of August 14, 2003. In the rare time that I broached the topic, she shunned the discussion. I wasn't sure if she was embarrassed or just too modest ... or maybe both. No matter. To me it was a defining declaration of the power of the human spirit.

It was that remarkable strength that allowed her to survive two world wars and a lifetime of incessant hardships and challenges. No wonder that when she finally succumbed nearly five years later, no one could believe that she died.

If there are weddings in Heaven, you can bet Lea Salomon is there.

And why not?

She was invited.